CHINA LAW

ADMINISTRATIVE LAW PROCEDURES AND REMEDIES IN CHINA

Recommended Stockists

Australia and New Zealand
The Law Book Company
Brisbane, Sydney, Melbourne, Perth

Canada and USA
Carswell
Ottawa, Toronto, Calgary, Montreal, Vancouver

Hong Kong
Bloomsbury Books Ltd

India
N.M. Tripathi (Private) Ltd
Bombay

Eastern Law House (Private) Ltd
Calcutta

M.P.P. House
Bangalore

Universal Book Traders
Delhi

Aditya Books
Delhi

Japan
Kinokuniya Co. Ltd
Tokyo

Kokusai Shobo Ltd
Tokyo

Maruzen Co. Ltd
Tokyo

Yushodo Co. Ltd
Tokyo

Pakistan
Pakistan Law House
Karachi, Lahore

Singapore & Malaysia
Thomson Information (S.E. Asia)

South Korea
Information & Culture Korea
Seoul

Thailand
DK Book House Co. Ltd
Bangkok

Nibondh & Company Ltd
Bangkok

Pasit Limited Partnership
Bangkok

ADMINISTRATIVE LAW PROCEDURES AND REMEDIES IN CHINA

by

Lin Feng, LL.B, LL.M

*Assistant Professor, Departmant of Law
City University of Hong Kong*

HONG KONG ● LONDON
SWEET & MAXWELL
1996

Published in 1996 by
Sweet & Maxwell Limited of
17/F Lyndhurst Tower, 1 Lyndhurst Terrace
Central, Hong Kong
and
100 Avenue Road, Swiss Cottage,
London NW3, England

Typeset by Best-set Typesetter Ltd.,
Hong Kong

Printed in China

A CIP catalogue record for this book is
available from the British Library

ISBN 0 421 56020 7

All rights reserved

No part of this publication may be reproduced or transmitted in any form
or by any means, or stored in any retrieval system of any nature without
prior written permission, except for permitted fair dealing under the
Copyright, Designs and Patents Act 1988, or in accordance with the terms
of a licence issued by the Copyright Licensing Agency in respect of
photocopying and/or reprographic reproduction.
Application for permission for other use of copyright material including
permission to reproduce extracts in other published works
shall be made to the publishers.
Full acknowledgment of the author, publisher and source must be given.

© Lin Feng 1996

This book is dedicated to my mother and father,
Xu Xifeng and Lin Rongkui

PREFACE

Chinese administrative law, including both substantive and procedural laws, has developed very quickly over the last two decades. It is important to the protection of the legitimate rights and interests of natural and legal persons. As far as foreign investors are concerned, they need to deal with administrative organs at every stage of their investment in China; and they need to know what they can do if they are not satisfied with the decisions of any administrative organ. It is therefore essential for them, and their legal and business advisors, to understand Chinese administrative law.

As the first book written in English on the subject, this book introduces Chinese administrative law and the relevant judicial remedies to those who are interested in, but not familiar with, this area of the law. Apart from a brief introduction of the theory of administrative law in China, the emphasis of this book is on the discussion of available legal procedures through which people can address their grievance against administrative organs. Legal practitioners and foreign investors can use this book as a guide in helping them decide whether or not they may bring legal actions against the decisions of relevant administrative organs, and if they do, what the relevant remedies available to them will be.

The staff of my publisher, Sweet & Maxwell, have been extremely supportive from the very beginning in producing this book. I would like to express my sincere thanks to all of them, especially Mr Rory Manchee, Ms Paula Harris, Ms Kate Wyllie and Ms Liza Robbins, for their patience and efficiency. I am also indebted to my friends at the Legislative Affairs Commission of the Standing Committee of the National People's Congress, and the Legislative Affairs Bureau of the State Council. I have learned a lot from my interviews with them, and this has contributed to the completion of this book. I would also like to thank my two student helpers, Enzo and Jason, who I only hope will not complain about the pressure I imposed upon them. I would not have had their assistance without the kind financial support from the University Grant Committee whom I would also like to thank. I would

PREFACE

also like to record my thanks to our secretaries at the Law Department of City University of Hong Kong who worked very hard towards the completion of the manuscript of this book.

Lin Feng
Department of Law, City University of Hong Kong
Hong Kong, October 1996

CONTENTS

Preface vii
Table of Cases xiii
Table of Legislation xvii

PART 1 — INTRODUCTION

Chapter One
The Structure of Administrative Law 3
The Concept of Administrative Law 3
Historical Development of Administrative Law 7
Contents of Administrative Law 10
Function and Status of Administrative Law in China's Legal
   System 12
Structure of Administrative Law 13

Chapter Two
Administrative Law Theory 17
Administrative Relationship and Administrative Legal
   Relationship 17
General Principles of Administrative Law 23
Administrative Acts 27

PART 2 — ADMINISTRATIVE RECONSIDERATION

Chapter Three
The Structure of Administrative Reconsideration 51
Introduction 51
Sources and Development of Administrative
   Reconsideration 52
Nature and Function of Administrative Reconsideration 54
Conditions for Administrative Reconsideration 56
Administrative Reconsideration Organs 58
Principles of Administrative Reconsideration 61
Grounds for Administrative Reconsideration 65

Chapter Four
Scope of Administrative Reconsideration 71
Acts Affecting Personal or Proprietary Rights or Interests 72
Acts Affecting Other Kinds of Rights or Interests 82

Chapter Five
Jurisdiction 84
Governmental Structure 84
Jurisdiction by Administrative Organ at the Next Higher Level 85
Jurisdiction Transfer 91
Designation of Jurisdiction 91
Priority of Jurisdiction 92
Complaint to the Correspondence and Reception Department
   and Administrative Reconsideration 92
Other Jurisdiction 93

Chapter Six
Hearing of Reconsideration Cases and the Related Issues 95
The Format of Reconsideration 95
The Effect of the Concrete Administrative Act under
   Reconsideration 96
Withdrawal of Reconsideration Application 98
Applicable Legislation (Law) 98
Participants of Reconsideration 103
Remedies 104
Relationship between Administrative Reconsideration and
   Judicial Review 108
Conclusion 108

PART 3 — ADMINISTRATIVE LITIGATION (JUDICIAL REVIEW) IN CHINA

Chapter Seven
The Structure of Administrative Litigation 113
Introduction 113
Development of Judicial Review in China 114
Objectives of the ALL 117
Reasons for the Late Adoption of Judicial Review in China 119
Sources of Judicial Review 122
Conditions for Judicial Review 123

Chapter Eight
Scope of Jurisdiction in Judicial Review 128
Categories of Administrative Acts Subject to Judicial Review 130
Acts Not Subject to Judicial Review 139

Chapter Nine
Jurisdiction of the People's Courts 151
Vertical Jurisdiction 151
Horizontal (Geographical) Jurisdiction 154
Common Jurisdiction 155
Jurisdiction over Reconsidered Cases 156
Horizontal Transfer of Jurisdiction 157

Chapter Ten
Grounds for Judicial Review 160
The Principle of Legality 160
Insufficiency of Essential Evidence 163
Inaccuracy in the Application of Legislation 178
Violation of Legal Procedure 188
Excess of Legal Authority (Ultra Vires) 194

Chapter Eleven
Judicial Control of Discretionary Power 206
Background 206
Discretionary Power and its Development 207
Substantive Discretion 209
Procedural Discretion and the Necessity of Judicial Control of
    Discretionary Power 210
The Principles Governing the Control of Discretionary Power 211
Grounds for Judicial Control of Discretionary Power 213

Chapter Twelve
Applicable Legislation in Judicial Review 253
Introduction 253
Reasons for the Variety of Applicable Legislation 253
Variety of Applicable Legislation 255
Legal Effect of Various Applicable Legislation 259
Conflict between Legislation 261
The Implication of Section 53(2) 261

PART 4 — STATE COMPENSATION LAW

Chapter Thirteen
State Compensation Law 269
Introduction 269
Analysis of the SCL 270
Conclusion 302

APPENDICES

Regulations on Administrative Reconsideration of the People's Republic of China 311

Administrative Litigation Law of the Peoples Republic of China	321
Opinions of the Supreme People's Court on Some Issues Relating to the Implementation of the Administrative Litigation Law (for Trial Implementation)	332
Administrative Penalty Law of the People's Republic of China	346
Regulation on Administrative Supervision of the People's Republic of China	356
State Compensation Law of the People's Republic of China	364
Index	373

TABLE OF CASES

Anisminic Ltd v. Foreign Compensation Commission [1969] 1 ALL E.R. 208,
  [1060] 2 A.C. 147 (HL(E)) .... 8.24 n. 59
Associated Provincial Picture Houses Ltd v. Wednesbury Corp [1948] 1 K.B.
  223 (CA) .... 11.09 n. 22

Bao Huiqing v. Labour Bureau in Yangpu District in Shanghai 10.32

Che Fengying v. Rural Planning Administration Bureau in
  Xuzhou City 10.52
Chen Cunmei v. Tobacco Bureau in Zhen Yang County 10.25, 10.49
Chen (first plaintiff) and Economic and Technology Corporation in X County
  in ZheJiang Province (second plaintiff) v. Price Control Bureau in X
  District 11.16
Chen Jianfang v. Shanghai Municipal Public Security Bureau 11.42
Chen Jiayou v. The Real Property Administration Bureau in the Liuzhou
  City 10.11
Chi v. Public Security Bureau in X City of Zhejiang Province 11.32
Clothing Factory in X City v. Red Cotton Trading Company
  in X City 13.30
Council of Civil Service Unions v. Minister for the Civil Service [1985] A.C.
  374 .... 10.04 n. 14

Di v. Standard Measurement Bureau in X County 11.17
Ding v. Land Administration Bureau in X County 13.19
Dong Tai Sea Product Rearing Company v. Public Security Bureau in
  Xieyang 10.46

East Wind Leather Factory v. Xiang Yiang Trading Company 13.29

Feng v. Township People's Government 4.12
Fujian Provincial Electronic Products Supervision and Testing Institute v.
  Fujian Provincial Bureau of Standard Measurement 10.34

Guang Ming Electrical Appliances Plaza in X City v. Administration Bureau of
  Industry and Commerce in X City 13.28
Guo Debing v. Public Security Bureau of Jinghe County in Xinjian Uygur
  Autonomous Region 11.18

He Xiguang v. Administration Bureau of Industry and Commerce in Shanwei
  City 10.07
He Zheng County Grain and Cooking oil Trade Corporation v. The
  Administration Bureau of Industry and Commerce in Ning xia Hui
  Autonomous Region 11.31
Huang v. Forest Bureau in X District 13.35
Huaxia Animal Medicine Co v. Agricultural and Fishery Bureau 11.39

Ji v. Public Security Bureau in X City 11.30

TABLE OF CASES

Jiang v. People's Procuratorate at X City	13.23
Jiang v. Public Security Bureau in X County	13.37
Jiayuguan Branch of Xiliu Engineering and Construction Corporation v. Jiayuguan Municipal Taxation Bureau	3.14, 10.10, 10.23
Jin v. Procuratorate in X City	13.27
Jinghua Research Institute of Machinery and Technology in Shanghai v. The Administration Bureau of Industry and Commerce in Chang Ning District in Shanghai	10.44
Lao Ai Village v. The County People's Government	4.15
Lei and Qin v. Public Security Bureau	13.25
Li v. Bureau of Urban Construction in X County	11.22
Li v. Jie and Jin	13.22
Li v. Office in Charge of the Street Affairs in X City in Guizhou Province	11.23
Li v. Public Security Bureau at X Administrative Prefecture	3.22
Li v. Public Security Bureau of X District	13.08
Li v. the Management Committee of Rehabilitation through Labour in X City	9.08, 9.09
Li v. Public Security Bureau in X County	13.34
Li and others v. Phoenix Township People's Government	10.50
Li Guangru and Others v. The People's Goverment in Phoenix Town	11.13
Li Guoguang v. Huolong Township People's Government	10.23
Li Yunxiang and Others v. Shanghai Municipal Real Property Administration Bureau	10.18
Liang v. The People's Government in X Town Zhejiang Province	11.21
Lin v. Highway Management Division (HMD) of X City	13.10, 13.12
Lin v. Public Security Bureau in X County in Zhejiang	11.38
Lin v. X Branch of Shanghai Municipal Public Security Bureau	11.34
Liu v. Administration Bureau of Industry and Commerce in X City	10.26
Liu v. Public Security Bureau of X District	13.07
Liu v. Shanghai Municipal Construction Commission	4.04
Liu Chen Lian Hua Electronic Company in Ping Nan County v. Fishery Administration Station in Ping Nan County	10.16, 10.41
Liu Xuping v. The Urban and Rural Construction Committee in YiWu City	11.36
Lu v. Administration Bureau for Industry and Commerce	13.18
Lu Yunyang v. Administration Bureau in Lin Gui County	10.29, 10.42, 11.24
Luo v. Food Hygiene Inspection Bureau in X County	10.19
Luo v. Public Security Bureau in X City in Zhejiang Province	11.37
Luo Shufeng v. Public Security Bureau of Tianjing City	11.28
Ma v. Public Security Station on X Harbour	6.14
Mao Yunbing v. Gangdong Township People's Government	10.19, 10.24, 10.38
Min v. The Hygiene and Epidemic Prevention Station in X City	10.33
Mr. Li v. Nan Ming Branch of Public Security Bureau in X City	10.51
Nanjing Zhuangyuanlou Restaurant v. Nanjing Branch of National Bureau of Foreign Exchange Control	10.08, 10.23
Nie v. Shang Xin Township People's Government in X County	10.35
One Branch of the Construction Company in Po On County v. Guangming Branch of Shenzhen Municipal Public Security Bureau	10.48
Paper Mill in County A v. EPB in Count A, and EPB in County B	9.10
Peasants in Da Lin Bei Xin and Old Villages v. Township People's Government	4.03
Peasants in Li Village v. The County People's Government	4.14
Plastic Company in X City of Shanxi Province v. Siping Plastic Shoes Company in Siping Town of X County	13.31
Procuratorate in X County of Henan Province v. Jiang	13.24

TABLE OF CASES

Qing Hua Garment Factory in HuHeHaoTe City (appellent) v. Administration Bureau for Industry and Commerce in XinCheng District of HuHeHaoTe City (respondent) 13.16

Sha v. Public Security Bureau in X City of Jiangsu Province 11.33
Shanghai Alcohol Factory v. The People's Government of Changning District in Shanghai 11.43
Shanghai Huxi Liang You Transaction Department v. The Administration Bureau of Industry and Commerce in Bao Shan District in Shanghai 10.28
Si Keiwei v. Hongkou Branch of Shanghai Municipal Public Security Bureau 11.35
Sun v. Wu Xin Township People's Government in the Suburb of Beijing 10.53
Supply and Sales Department in X City v. Price Inspection Bureau in X City 10.42

Tang v. Public Security Bureau in X County 11.44

Wang v. Tax Bureau in X County 13.08
Wang v. Rural Branch of Public Security Bureau in X County 13.26
Wang Shijiang and Wang Shihai v. the People's Government of Huang Fa Town 10.12
Wang Wenping v. One Branch of Zhi Cheng Municipal Public Security Bureau 10.39
Wholesale Department Store of Electronic Goods v. Measurement Bureau in X City 6.07
Wong v. Land Administration Bureau and Urban Construction Bureau in Shi Zu Shan City of Ningxia Autonomous Region 11.40
Wu v. Tianhe Township People's Government 3.20

X Steel Company v. Environmental Protection Bureau and the People's Government in X City 13.33
Xiao Lianjie v. The Hygiene and Epidemic Prevention Station 11.21
Xie Junzhong v. People's Government in Tinzi Township in the Suburb of Nan Ning City 10.17, 10.30
Xu Deliao v. Patent Administration Bureau in Hu Bei Province 10.15

Yang Feng and 504 Other Residents v. Urban Planning Bureau in Ping Ding Shan City 11.45
Yang Xinlan v. Urban Branch of Yingchuan Municipal Administration Bureau of Industry and Commerce 10.46
Yang Xiulan v. The Administration Bureau of Industry and Commerce in Ying Chuan City 11.25
Yang Zhongsheng v. Public Security Bureau in Jian Yang County 11.20
Yie Ronghua (first plaintiff) and Ning Hong Hotel (second plaintiff) v. The Tax Bureau of Xiu Shui County 10.13

Zhang v. Administration Bureau for Industry and Commerce in X County 13.15
Zhang v. Education Bureau and Public Security Bureau in X City 6.08
Zhang v. The County Hygiene and Epidemic Prevention Station 13.05
Zhang and Chen v. Public Security Bureau in X City in Jiangsu Province 11.15
Zhang and Liu v. X Branch of Public Security Bureau in X District of X City of Guizhou Province 11.46
Zhang and Sha v. Shi, Director of Public Security Bureau of X County 13.21
Zhang Peirong v. Public Security Bureau in Akesu District 10.40
Zhang Sheyou v. Wangzai Township People's Government 10.45
Zhang Xizheng v. Land Administration Bureau 12.03
Zhang Xizheng and Medicine Purchase Station in Lin Tai County v. Land Administration Bureau in Lin Tai County 10.09
Zhang Xueju v. Administration Bureau of Industry and Commerce in X District of Xizhang (Tibet) Autonomous Region 11.14

TABLE OF CASES

Zhang Zhongnian v. Land Administration Bureau in HeLan County 11.47
Zhao v. Tax Bureau in X County 13.17
Zhao Yongping v. Tianshan Branch of Uygur Munipal Public Security Bureau
.... 11.29
Zhen v. X Forest Public Security Bureau 10.47
Zhou v. Public Security of X City in Jiang Xi Province 13.14
Zhu v. Land Administration Bureau in X County in Jiangxi Province 11.19
Zhu Jinru v. State Land Administration Bureau in Huizhou City 10.14, 10.42

TABLE OF LEGISLATION

Administrative Litigation Law (1989)
(ALL) 1.01, 13.32
s.1 .... 3.03, 7.06, 13.03
s.2 .... 7.15, 8.01, 10.02 n. 6
s.4(2)(d) 11.24
s.5 .... 10.02, 11.07, 11.27
s.9(2) 13.33
s.11 ...... 8.01, 8.03, 8.16, 8.19, 8.23,
9.08, 13.03
s.11(1) 11.26
s.11(2) 8.09, 13.18, 13.20
s.11(5) 8.12
s.12 .... 8.15, 12.08, 13.20
s.12(1) 8.19, 13.12
s.12(2) ... 8.21, 8.22, 8.23, 12.09, 12.10
s.12(3) 8.23
s.12(4) 8.24
s.13 .... 9.02
s.14 .... 9.03 n.5
s.14(2) 9.03 n.6
s.14(3) .... 9.03 n. 8
s.15 .... 9.04
s.17 .... 9.07 n. 16, 9.09 n. 22
s.18 .... 9.08 n. 17
s.19 .... 9.07
s.21 .... 9.07 n. 12
s.22 .... 9.07 n. 13, 9.10 n. 26
s.23 .... 9.06
s.31 .... 10.05 n. 18
s.32 .... 10.05
s.37 .... 5.03
s.41 .... 8.01
s.43 .... 10.06
s.44 .... 6.03
s.52 .... 12.02, 12.09, 12.11
s.52(2)(b) 10.20
s.52(2)(c) 10.20
s.53 ...... 12.02, 12.05, 12.09, 12.10
s.53(2) 12.11, 12.12
s.54 .... 11.10
s.54(1) 7.06, 10.04, 13.07
s.54(2) 10.04
s.54(2)(a) 10.04
s.54(2)(b) 10.04, 10.20
s.54(2)(c) ... 10.04, 10.20, 10.37, 10.43
s.54(2)(d) 10.04, 10.43
s.54(2)(e) .... 10.04 , 10.50

s.54(3) 10.04, 11.41, 11.42. 11.47
s.54(4) 10.04, 10.25, 11.26, 11.29, 11.35
s.54(5) 11.18
s.61 .... 13.16
s.61(1) 11.29
s.63(1) 10.08
s.67 .... 13.10, 13.36
s.68 .... 13.03, 13.10
s.69 .... 13.03
Administrative Penalty Law (APL)
.... 6.11
s.2 .... 2.26 n. 118
s.3 .... 2.25 n. 119
s.8 .... 2.26
s.9 .... 8.05, 8.07
s.10 .... 8.05, 8.07
s.11 .... 8.07
s.11(1) 8.08
s.12(3) 8.08
s.24 .... 2.26 n. 120
s.33–43 .... 2.26 n. 121
Air Pollution Law
s.31 .... 13.33
s.33 .... 13.33
s.34 .... 13.33
s.36 .... 13.33
British Foreign Compensation Act
(1950) 8.24
Civil Procedural Law (for Trial
Implementation CPL) (1982)
.... 1.06 n. 29, 7.06, 7.14, 13.12
s.3(2) .... 7.03, 7.06 n. 18, 8.17
s.51 .... 13.09 n. 31
s.85 .... 13.09 n. 31
Common Political Principles of
Democratic Governments in Each
Province and City in Northeast
China (1946) ...... 1.04 n. 17, 7.13
n. 36
Constitution 10.09, 12.07
s.4 .... 13.12
s.5 .... 10.36
s.27 .... 10.36
s.57 .... 7.08 n. 25
s.62 .... 7.13 n. 334
s.62(2) 7.13
s.62(3) 7.13

TABLE OF LEGISLATION

s.67 ..... 2.14 n. 66, 2.18, 7.13 n. 37, 8.22
s.67(2) 7.13
s.67(3) 7.13
s.67(4) 7.13
s.67(6) .... 7.08 n. 25
s.67(7) 2.14
s.67(8) 2.14
s.85 .... 7.08 n. 26, 12.04
s.89 .... 5.02, 8.22
s.89(1) 12.04
s.90 .... 12.07, 12.09
s.92 .... 7.08 n. 25
s.116 .... 12.06 n. 15
s.126 .... 7.08 n. 26
Constitution (1954)
s.97 ....
    7.02, 7.13 n. 36, 13.02
Constitution (1982)
s.4 .... 13.12 n. 52
s.41 .... 3.02, 7.13
s.92 .... 12.04
Constitutional Principles in Shan Gan
    Ning Districts (1939).... 1.04 n. 17
Criminal Law
s.139 .... 13.26
s.155 .... 13.27
Criminal Procedural Law .... 3.12, 8.09 n. 14
Customs Law (1987) 4.06
s.41 .... 7.15
s.46 .... 3.18
s.53 .... 3.11
s.54 .... 13.09 n. 32
Decision of the Standing Committee of
    the National People's Congress on
    Authorizing the People's Congress of
    Shenzhen City and Its Standing
    Committee and the People's
    Government of Shenzhen City to
    Formulate Regulations and Rules
    Respectively for Implementation in
    The Shenzhen Special Economic
    Zone (1992) .... 12.07 n. 16
Detailed Rules for the Implementation of
    the Statistics Law 5.09
Economic Contract Law (1981)
s.33 .... 13.02
Election Law of the National People's
    Congress and Local People's
    Congresses, 1979, s.25 ...... 7.03
Family Law 6.09
Fishery Law 2.23
s.13(2) .... 13.08 n. 29
Food and Hygiene Law 11.04, 13.06
Forest law 2.23
General Principles of Civil Law
    (GPCL)
s.2 .... 13.04 n. 15
s.12 .... 6.09
s.13 .... 6.09
s.15 .... 6.09
s.16 .... 6.09
s.59 .... 11.40
s.63(1) 10.08
s.117 .... 13.09
s.121 ..... 13.02, 13.03, 13.04, 13.09, 13.12
s.123 .... 13.12
s.124 .... 13.12
s.125 .... 13.12
s.126 .... 13.10, 13.12
s.127 .... 13.12
General Principles of the People's
    Political Consultative Committee
s.19 .... 7.02
Grassland Law 2.23
s.7(2) .... 13.08 n. 29
Hu Bei Province Land Administration
    Regulation
s.16 .... 4.04
s.17 .... 4.04
Implementation Procedure on the
    Land Administration Law in
    Guangzhou Province 10.14
Implementation Rules for the
    Metrology Law
s.36 .... 10.34
s.55 .... 10.34
Income Tax Law (1980)
s.15 .... 7.03
Interim Methods of the National
    Administration of Invoices... 10.23
Interim Provision on the
    Management of Harbours
Art. 20 .... 13.02 n. 1
Interim Regulation on Civil
    servants of the State 1.06
Interim Regulation on
    Management of Individual
    Business Owner in Urban and
    Rural Areas 13.08
Interim Regulation on Privately
    Owned Enterprises ..... 8.10 n. 15
Interim Regulation on the Investigation
    and Penalty for Fake and Low
    Quality Commodities
s 3(2) 6.07, 6.08
s.57 .... 6.07, 6.08
Interim Regulation on the Management
    of Urban and Township Sole
    Proprietors .... 8.10 n. 15
Interim Regulations on the
    Administration of All Urban and
    Rural Industrial and Commercial
    Entities
s.5 .... 10.51
s.6 .... 10.51
s.17 .... 10.51
s.22 .... 10.51
Interpretation of the ALL 8.19
Land Administration Law (1986).. 3.03,

xviii

	10.19, 11.47
s.13	4.14, 10.38
s.13(1)	11.43
s.38	10.24
s.41	4.04, 10.53
s.44(2)	3.20
s.45	3.20, 10.17, 10.23, 10.30, 10.35, 10.53, 13.19
s.47	10.14
s.48	4.04, 10.53
Land Administration Law and Mineral Resources Law	8.15
Land Management Law	2.23
Land Reform Law (1950)	7.02 n. 9
Law on Assemblies, Processions and Demonstrations (1989)	4.16
s.13	3.11, 5.03
Law on Control of Aliens (1985)	
s.21	8.25
s.22	8.25
s.29	8.25
Law on Control of the Entry and Exit of Citizens (the Law) (1985)	
s.5	11.41
s.15	8.25
Law on Ethnic Regional Autonomy	12.06
Law on the Prevention and Treatment of Infectious Diseases	
s.36	5.03
Law on the Protection of Consumers' Rights	13.11 n. 41
Law on Tobacco Administration	
s.17	10.25
Local Organization Law	6.05
Martial Law	2.09, 8.19
Military Law	13.12 n. 49
Notice Strictly Restricting the Use of Shelter for Examination	11.18
Opinions of the Supreme People's Court on the Interpretation of the Administrative Litigation Law *see* Opinions on the ALL	
Opinions on the ALL	3.08
s.2	7.15, 11.18
s.3	8.24
s.4	8.15
s.6	8.15
s.5	8.15
s.7	8.15
s.10	9.09 n. 24
s.11	9.02
s.11(8)	8.15
s.41	7.16
s.70	12.10 n. 29
Order No. 12 (1990) of the People's Government of the Guangxi Autonomous Region	11.24
Organic Law	5.05
Organic Law for People's Congresses at Different Levels	12.02
Organic Law of Local Congresses and Local People's Governments (1979)	5.02, 3.03, 12.07 n. 16
s.7	2.14 n. 66
s.7(11)	2.14
s.7(12)	2.14
s.35(1)	6.05 n. 11
s.48	5.02 n. 3
s.51	5.02 n. 3
s.55	5.02 n. 5
s.59	5.02 n. 6, 5.07
Organic Law of Local People's Congress and People's Governments (1986)	
s.51	12.07
Organic Law of the People's Courts (1979)	9.01 n.1
Organic Law of the State Council (1979)	
s.48	5.02
Organic Law of the State Council (1982)	3.03
Organic Law on Local People's Congresses and Local People's Governments	2.14, 2.19, 6.05
Outlines of People's Government Organs in North China (1948)	1.04 n. 17
Patent Law (1992)	
s.43	8.25
s.49	8.25
Procedural Law	2.26
Procedural Regulations on the Handling of Crimininal cases	10.39
Provisional Procedure Concerning the Registration of Title Over the premises in City and town	10.18
Provisional Procedures for the Control Over Nation-wide Commercial Invoices	
s.37(3)	10.10
Provisional Regulation of the Real Property Administration of Liuzhou City	10.11
Provisional Regulation on Administrative Penalty for Speculation	
s.3(1)	11.31
Provisional Regulation on Administration of Taxation and Levies	10.10
Provisional Regulation regarding the Job Waiting Insurance Policy	10.32
Regulation of the Business of Enterprises	11.14
Regulation on Administrative Penalty for Public Security	

TABLE OF LEGISLATION

(1986) 6.14, 7.04, 8.05, 10.37
          n. 73, 10.39, 11.25
s.5 .... 11.44
s.7 .... 11.20
s.19 .... 13.34
s.22 .... 3.22, 11.35, 11.38
s.22(1) 11.28, 11.29
s.22(3) 11.28
s.23 .... 11.38
s.33(2) 5.08
s.37 .... 11.20
s.39 .... 3.11
s.40 .... 6.03
s.42 .... 13.02
Regulation on Administrative
   Reconsideration (1990) (RAR)
   .... 3.02, 3.07, 8.03, 13.38
s.1 .... 3.03, 3.04, 6.03 n. 3
s.2 .... 3.08, 4.01
s.2(8) 4.12
s.2(9) 4.12
s.5 .... 3.18
s.8 .... 3.17 n. 48
s.9 .... 4.02
s.9(1) 4.04
s.9(8) 4.04, 4.11
s.9(9) 4.02, 4.11, 4.14, 4.16
s.10(3) 4.13
s.11 .... 5.03 n. 10
s.13 .... 5.06
s.17 .... 5.10 n. 17, 5.11 n. 19
s.20 .... 5.13 n. 21
s.21 .... 5.14
s.22 .... 5.15
s.25 .... 3.11 n. 32
s.26 .... 3.08
s.31 .... 3.09
s.31(1) 3.08
s.32 .... 4.12
s.35 .... 3.09
s.39 .... 3.08 n. 24, 3.11, 6.03 n. 4
s.40 .... 6.04 n. 6
s.41 .... 6.05
s.42 .... 4.04
s.42(2) 4.03
s.42(4) .... 3.23 n. 58
s.43 .... 6.07 n. 16
s.44 .... 4.04
Regulation on Administrative
   Supervision (1990) 1.06, 13.38
Regulation on Civil Service.. 8.23 n. 53
Regulation on Costs Borne by the
   Peasants and Labour
   Managagement 11.13
Regulation on Economic Contract
   Arbitration (1983) 2.23
Regulation on Environmental
   Administration (Trial) 11.23
Regulation on Exclusive Right to
   Sell Tobacco
   s. 17 .... 10.25

Regulation on Labour Dispute
   Resolution 2.23
Regulation on Metrology and
   Authentication of Products
   Quality Testing Institute 10.34
Regulation on Penalties against
   Public Securities 11.04
Regulation on Registration and
   Management of Social
   Organizations 4.16
Regulation on Requisition of Land
   for State Construction 10.09
Regulation on Road Administration
   in Guangxi 10.17
Regulation on Rural Collectively
   Owned Enterprises ..... 8.10 n. 15
Regulation on the Administration
   of Grassland in the
   Autonomous Region of Inner
   Mongolia 10.31
Regulation on the Control of
   Animal Medicine
   s.29(10) 11.39
   s.41 .... 11.39
Regulation on the Exemption of
   Customs Duty for Imported
   Goods by Joint Venture
   s.6 .... 7.15
Regulation on the Farmers' Burden
   in Sichuan Province
   s.22 .... 11.13
   s.25 .... 11.13
Regulation on the Implementation
   of the Fishery Law in Guanxi
   Autonomous Region 10.16
Regulation on the Organization of
   Representative Councils at
   Each Level in Shan Gan Ning
   District (1942) .... 1.04 n. 17
Regulation on the Protection of
   Juveniles 6.08
Regulation on the Structure of
   Office for Street Affairs 11.23
Regulation on the Supervision and
   Exemption of Customs Duty
   on Goods Imported and Exported
   by the Sino-Foreign Cooperative
   Enterprises
   s.9 .... 8.06
Regulation on the Transition of
   Business Management of
   State-owned Industrial
   Enterprises .... 8.10 n. 15
Regulation on the Use of Weapon
   and Caution by the People's
   Police 11.23
Regulation on Urban and
   Township Colletively Owned
   Enterprises .... 8.10 n. 15
Regulations on Governmental
   Organs in Shan Gan Ning

Districts (1939) .... 1.04 n. 17
Regulations on the Organization
 of Representative Councils at
 Each Level in Shan Gan Ning
 Districts (1942) .... 1.04 n. 17
Standard Law, Regulation on
 Industrial Products Quality
 Responsibility 6.07
State Compensation Law (SCL) .. 13.01,
                                 13.13
s.3 .... 13.09, 13.32, 13.13 n. 57
s.3(1) 13.14
s.3(2) 13.20
s.3(3) 13.20
s.4 .... 13.14, 13.20, 13.32
s.4(1) 13.15, 13.18
s.4(2) 13.17
s.9 .... 13.32 n. 86, 13.34
s.9(2) 13.20
s.10 .... 13.32 n. 86
s.12 .... 13.32 n. 86
s.14 .... 13.36, 13.37

s.14(1) 13.04
s.14(2) 13.04
s.15 .... 13.09, 13.24, 13.26
s.15(3) 13.22
s.20(1) 13.37
s.24 .... 13.37
s.26 .... 13.09
s.27 .... 13.09
s.31 .... 13.27, 13.31
State-owned Industrial Enterprise
 Law .... 8.10 n. 15
Trademark Law and Patent (1993)
 .... 3.11, 10.26
s.21 .... 8.25
s.22 .... 8.25
Trademark Review and
 Adjudication Board
s.28 .... 8.25
Urban Planning Law
s.32 .... 11.36, 11.45
Water Law 2.23, 11.45
s.24(3) 11.45

PART 1

INTRODUCTION

CHAPTER ONE
THE STRUCTURE OF ADMINISTRATIVE LAW

The Concept of Administrative Law

Administrative law has been widely accepted as a fully fledged law subject in China in the last two decades. The adoption of the Administrative Litigation Law of the People's Republic of China (hereinafter as ALL) has firmly established the status of administrative law.[1] The subject is still a relatively new area compared with other traditional subjects such as civil law and criminal law.[2] It has been realized that its importance is no less than those traditional ones. The systematic study of administrative law started in the early 1980s and has been heavily influenced by Western countries, both continental and common law jurisdictions.[3] The state government has promulgated relevant administrative legislation for the establishment of an administrative law framework.[4] Meanwhile, more in-depth academic research has also been undertaken to study various important issues of Chinese administrative law.[5] It is generally accepted that administrative law is a branch of law relating to public administration. As to the exact meaning and contents of administrative law, there is no authoritative definition that is unanimously accepted by scholars in the People's Republic of China (hereinafter as China). Some scholars have adopted the common law approach in the United States and the United Kingdom. They hold that administrative law aims at controlling the exercise of power by the executive branch of the government. There are also scholars influenced by the theories developed in the former Soviet Union. They maintain that the essence of administrative law is to meet the needs of public administration.[6] There are also those who adopt a hybrid approach, *i.e.* administrative law has both functions to play.[7]

Due to the different understanding of the focus of administrative law, scholars have tried to define the concept of administrative law from varying perspectives. There is the view that various factors, such as the sources, objects to be regulated, its legal status, and targets,

1.01

THE STRUCTURE OF ADMINISTRATIVE LAW

should be taken into account in the definition of administrative law. Others maintain that it is better to define the concept by revealing the most essential characteristics such as the objective or the contents of administrative law.[8] The main approaches can be summarized as follows.[9]

1.02   The first approach defines administrative law according to its external characteristics and its own status in the legal system. This holds that administrative law serves the needs of public administration. This is the very traditional approach. It believes that administrative law is, similar to other branches of law such as civil and criminal law, an important and independent area in the Chinese legal system. Its status should be the same as any other branches of law. According to this definition, administrative law covers all kinds of legislation on which a modern government relies to conduct public administration.

The second approach defines administrative law according to the objects to be regulated by administrative law. This emphasizes the administrative relationship, which refers to such social relationships that are the objects of administrative law. It describes administrative law as the law regulating administrative relationship.[10] Under this definition, the sources of administrative law cover all legal rules regulating administrative relationship. In other words, administrative law can be said to be an aggregation of laws and regulations governing the social relationship arising from the process through which the governmental administrative organs perform their functions.[11]

The third approach defines administrative law according to the contents of and the objects to be regulated by administrative law. It maintains that administrative law regulates the relationships between the administrative organs themselves, and between administrative organs and other organizations or individuals. Under this definition, the sources of administrative law consist of two kinds of legislation. The first kind includes those stipulating the structure of governmental administrative organs, their powers, working principles, administrative system and working procedures. The second kind covers those legislation regulating the relationship among the administrative organs as well as the legal relationship between such organs and other state organs, enterprises, social bodies and individuals. Whether or not organic law of administrative organs should be treated as part of administrative law is debatable as it is commonly discussed as part of constitutional law.[12]

The fourth approach defines administrative law according to the objects to be regulated by and functions of administrative law. It believes that administrative law is comprised of a set of legal rules which regulate the administrative relationship, *i.e.* various kinds of social relationship arising from the performance of their functions by governmental administrative organs. Their functions include implementation and enforcement acts, issue of orders and supervisory acts, and so on.[13]

The fifth approach defines administrative law according to its external structure, legal status and legal aims. It suggests that administrative law is an important branch of law regulating the exercise of executive power. This definition also holds that the sources of administrative law consist of all legislation relating to public administration. It emphasizes the legal status of administrative law and maintains that its status is only lower than the Constitution. Its objectives are to ensure the exercise of executive power to be scientific, democratic and lawful.

The sixth approach defines administrative law according to its structure and maintains that administrative law is comprised of all legal norms concerning governmental administrative organizations and their activities, and the supervision over those organizations and their activities. As any activities of administration have to be conducted through the functionaries of various administrative organs, they shall involve three elements. Firstly, the persons conducting administrative activities, *i.e.* the country's administrative organs and their functionaries who will be the subjects of the administrative relationship; secondly, the actual undertaking of those activities; and thirdly, the necessary supervision of the activities by both internal and external organs.[14] All activities relating to the three components must be provided and regulated by legislation, which will be treated as sources of administrative law. Under this approach, administrative law should therefore be described to include organic law of administrative organs, law relating to functionaries (or personnel) of administrative organs and administrative activities, and administrative supervision law.

The seventh approach defines administrative law according to the objectives (aims), tasks, functions, as well as the external characteristics of administrative law. It holds that administrative law consists of all legislation for the governmental administrative organs to execute their administrative functions, such as implementation and enforcement, issue of orders, and supervision for achieving governmental objectives and tasks. This definition emphasizes the execution of administrative functions and therefore reveals the unequal nature of administrative legal relationship. One party to such relationship represents the state and undertakes activities for the purpose of fulfilling governmental tasks and the achievement of national objectives. It plays a positive role and is in the position to issue orders, organize activities, implement and enforce rules and orders, and supervise activities of the other parties. Whereas the other parties are in a passive and obedient position.

THE STRUCTURE OF ADMINISTRATIVE LAW

The eighth approach defines administrative law according to the objects to be regulated by and contents of administrative law. It holds that administrative law regulates the relationship among governmental administrative organs themselves and their relationship formed with other state organs, enterprises, organizations and individuals in executing their administrative functions. The sources of administrative law should cover legislation on the country's administrative structure, principles of administrative activities, administrative power, and organic laws, working rules and all disciplinary rules.

The ninth approach defines administrative law according to its external characteristics and the objects to be regulated. It maintains that the sources of administrative law include all legislation made by the people's congresses at both central and local levels, the local people's governments at various levels, and all their departments to facilitate the administration of social activities by governmental organs. The purpose of those legislation is to regulate the social relationship between governmental administrative organs and all other aspects of the society under their administration.

The tenth approach defines administrative law according to its external characteristics, legal status and the objects to be regulated by administrative law. It holds that administrative law includes all legislation governing administrative relationship and supervisory administrative relationship. One special feature of this definition is that it classifies the objects to be regulated by administrative law into two categories: administrative relationship and supervisory relationship.[15]

1.03 Several elements of administrative law have been mentioned in one or another of the 10 definitions. They are the external characteristics, legal status, the objects to be regulated, the contents, the functions, the structure and the objectives. Scholars have chosen and used different combination of those elements to define administrative law. Each of those elements describes or represents one feature of administrative law. The first four definitions seem to emphasize a particular feature of administrative law, while the rest tends to cover several essential elements of administrative law. As each of those elements reveals one of the characteristics of administrative law, they are therefore all correct in the sense that each emphasizes different characteristics of administrative law. One has to study each of those elements in order to get a comprehensive understanding of administrative law in China. While acknowledging that it is impossible to bring all those elements into one definition, a definition of a subject should, nevertheless cover the main characteristics of the legal subject and does not give any misleading impression. Based on this reasoning, it is more appropriate to have a relatively comprehensive definition.

Historical Development of Administrative Law

1.04 Administrative law has been through, like other legal subjects in China, similar stages of development as a result of political uncertainty ever since the founding of the People's Republic of China.[16]

Although many administrative regulations and rules had been enacted by Chinese Communist Party well before it came into power,[17] the promulgation of the "General Principles of the People's Political Consultative Committee of the People's Republic of China", which functioned as interim Constitution and basis of administrative regulations, marked the beginning of development of administrative law of China. Soon after its enactment, various administrative regulations were promulgated, including organic laws of governments at both national and local levels, legislation on the actual operation of public administration, civil servants legislation, and legislation on the regulation of economy.[18] By the end of the first five-year national economic development plan (1953–57), more than 870 pieces of administrative legislation had been promulgated.[19] On the other hand, research on administrative law was conducted during the same period. It is mainly about the introduction of the theories on administrative law in the former Soviet Union. Some Russian scholarly works on administrative law were translated into Chinese and introduced to Chinese scholars and students. The approach that administrative law was the law to support public administration dominated during that period.[20]

The adoption of the 1954 Constitution brought the research on administrative law in China into a new period. Theories introduced from the Soviet Union were gradually combined with China's practice and scholars started to examine systematically China's own system of administrative law. Various scholarly writings were published. They were mainly on the general principles of public administration, its legal protection, organization system of administrative organs, and the administrative supervisory system. It was commented that China's research on administrative law got on the proper track and was ready to be fully developed.[21]

However, the anti-rightist movement in 1957 started to affect all kinds of legal research, including administrative law. Occasionally, you can see some articles published during the early period of the political movements. Scholars still published articles examining the objects and the system of administrative law in China.[22] After the cultural revolution was over research gradually resumed on administrative law. However, no treatises had been published on Chinese administrative law by the end of 1970s.

The Third Plenary of the 11th Central Committee of the Communist Party held in 1978 started economic reform and emphasized the importance of strengthening the democratic dictatorship and socialist democracy, and the establishment of a legal system.[23] Many legislation concerning public administration were promulgated to facilitate economic reform. The development of administrative law and its research benefited from the legislative practice of administrative legislation required by the economic reform.[24] Many works, including the legal volume of *China Encyclopaedia* and first law dictionary were published. Textbooks were written and courses on administrative law were formulated. All those revealed that China's research on administrative law had recovered and were ready to be further developed and improved.[25]

1.05   In 1982, the fourth Constitution was promulgated, which was, as fundamental law of a state, the main source of administrative legislation in China because the status of administrative regulation has been formally recognized in the 1982 Constitution. Its promulgation has facilitated the development and research of administrative law in China. As a result, a vast number of administrative regulations have been promulgated and more systematic research on administrative law has been undertaken. A series of discussions were conducted on the system of administrative responsibility and the relationship between the establishment of administrative law and the implementation of Constitution. New issues such as administrative procedural legislation were raised. It should be noted that it is obvious that administrative law was regarded as a tool to support economic reform since the Decision on the Reform of Economic System, adopted in 1984 by the Third Plenary of the 12th Central Committee, put forward the issue of separation of governmental administration from normal activities of enterprises. Administrative legislation was supposed to facilitate such a change.[26] This shows that the basic legal theory behind Chinese administrative legislation continues to be legal instrumentalism which reflects the Marxist jurisprudential theory. This theory also influenced research on administrative law in that period.

Since then, scholars started to examine the issue of how to establish an administrative litigation system with China's own characteristics. The academic research on administrative law before 1987 focused on the general principles of administrative organizations and administrative activities, including the meaning, nature and classification of administrative organizations, and the constitution, function, structure and working principles and the administration of civil servants, and so on. Major attention was on the function of administrative law as an instrument to safeguard public administration by administrative organs, while little attention was paid to the function of administrative law to supervise and control administrative power. The Thirteenth Central Committee of the Communist Party held in 1987 put forward the task clearly that administration should be conducted according to law, administrative organic law should be improved, and various kinds of administrative legislation should be enacted.[27] Scholarly works came out in late 1980s to discuss fundamental theoretical issues of administrative law, such as the concept, fundamental principles, legal relationships, administrative activities and supervision of administrative activities. The focus of research was on administrative litigation system, while other issues such as administrative compensation, administrative organic law and civil servants system were also discussed.

Academic research on administrative law and practice had contributed to the establishment of the subject of administrative law in the Chinese legal system. In practice, research on administrative organic law and civil servant legislation had laid down the theoretical grounds for the relevant legislation in China in the late 1980s. The shift in definition from the orthodox Russian approach of law in support of public administration, to the acceptance of the Western approach of the application of the rule of law in public administration has enlivened the discussion on the necessity of legal control of administrative power, which has laid down the preliminary theoretical ground for the establishment of administrative reconsideration and judicial review systems in China at a later stage.[28]

1.06 The promulgation of the ALL in 1989 was the crystallization of theoretical research on administrative law for many years. It marked the beginning of a new period. The ALL has made it possible for individuals to bring a case against the administration and also laid down the relevant criteria and procedures for administrative litigation. The corollary is that administration has to be undertaken according to law. Otherwise it will be very likely that concrete administrative decisions may be challenged before the people's courts. Although judicial review system is formally established by the ALL,[29] the concept of challenging the decisions of administrative organs or their personnel is quite new to Chinese traditional culture. The ALL is ahead of the development of the society.[30] Ordinary people were still somewhat puzzled by the endowment of such a right. Meanwhile, the civil servants were not used to it as well. The task facing the administration is therefore very urgent. That was possibly why the Interim Regulation on Civil Servants of the State was suggested for amendment. Soon after the adoption of the ALL, two more regulations were promulgated in 1990: the Regulation on Administrative Supervision in the People's Republic of China and the Regulation on Administrative Reconsideration. Academic research has also moved a step forward and issues such as the theory on supervision of administration, administrative legal responsibility and administrative remedies have been discussed. The issue of inter-relationship between different means to challenge administrative decisions has been examined.

Moreover, research was also conducted on the liability for administrative torts, which eventually led to the enactment of the State Compensation Law. By the time the State Compensation Law was promulgated in 1994, it was fair to say that a comprehensive system of administrative law was established in China. In March 1996, the Administrative Penalty Law was also enacted. An outstanding theme of all these administrative legislation is the supervision and control of the exercise of administrative power by the administration. In less than 20 years, China has established the legal framework of administrative law through the adoption of a series of legislation. That is in itself quite an achievement, although latter part of the book shall reveal that many aspects of the administrative law could still be further improved.[31]

Contents of Administrative Law

1.07 The contents of administrative law refer to the scope of administrative regulations. The contents depend on the adopted definition of administrative law and have been described from different perspectives and according to different criteria or standards.[32] The difference in the description is mainly caused by scholars' different understanding of the functions played by administrative law.[33] It is generally agreed that the contents should cover regulations relating to administrative organization and administrative activities. Difference exists as to whether or not regulation concerning the parties under administration (the governed) should be included. One commonly adopted description of the contents of administrative law is that administrative law covers both substantive and procedural administrative law.[34] This description limits the contents of administrative law to legislation.

A review of academic works will show that there is another element, *i.e.* administrative law theory, which should be treated as an essential component of administrative law. Books by Chinese scholars on administrative law can be classified into two categories. One is about administrative law theory, covering the concept of administrative law, fundamental principles of administrative law, administrative relationship, administrative organs, administrative activities (including administrative legislation, administrative licence, administrative supervision, administrative punishment, administrative compulsory enforcement, administrative judicial activities), administrative procedure and administrative responsibilities. These will usually have one chapter on administrative litigation (judicial review) which is an essential part of Chinese administrative law, although strictly speaking it is part of procedural law. The other category of books is on legal procedures challenging administrative decisions, mainly including administrative litigation and reconsideration. These will usually follow the structure of the ALL. They discuss the evolution and development of administrative litigation, legal relationship in administrative litigation, fundamental principles of administrative litigation, the scope of administrative litigation, the jurisdiction, parties to administrative litigation, evidence, compulsory measures in administrative litigation, conditions for administrative litigation, trial at first instance and second instance, adjudication supervisory procedure, administrative litigation in combination with civil litigation, administrative compensation litigation, enforcement procedures and administrative litigation concerning foreigners.[35] Certain books have adopted the Western approach by focusing exclusively on judicial review.[36] Administrative reconsideration is rarely discussed in any books on administrative law or administrative litigation law. It is usually discussed separately in books, dealing exclusively with administrative reconsideration.[37] Apart from administrative reconsideration and litigation, there are two more means currently available, under which the relevant parties may bring an action against administrative organs.[38] These are part of procedural administrative law, laying down the legal procedures for those under administration to bring legal actions to challenge the activities of administrative organs. Another part of procedural administrative law includes legislation with which administrative organs must comply in undertaking administrative activities.

Substantive administrative legislation, such as those relating to the administration of customs, public security, industry and commerce, labour, etc, are not usually discussed in books on administrative law, instead, it is discussed in legal books on those specific topics. Administrative law theory will discuss the common feature relating to various different kinds of administrative activities. With regard to the classification of the contents of administrative law, there exists two approaches.

The broad one holds that administrative law covers both substantive law and procedural law[39] and has been adopted and widely accepted recently. The narrow approach maintains that administrative law should be restricted to procedural administrative law.

Both broad and narrow definitions have touched certain aspects of administrative law. None can be said to be wrong as each simply approach the subject from a different angle. Unlike what is generally accepted in common law jurisdiction, where administrative law is almost equivalent to judicial review,[40] the concept of administrative law in China seems more adequate if the broad approach is adopted. It covers administrative law theory, and substantive and procedural administrative law.

Function and Status of Administrative Law in China's Legal System

1.08 The status and function of any branch of law are related to each other. The status of a branch of law is determined by the functions the law performs. In order to determine the status of administrative law in China's legal system, it is necessary to examine the functions it performs. However, different views have been expressed with regard to the exact functions performed by administrative law. Some scholars have tried to reveal this through the contents of administrative law; others have relied on the role played by administrative law in the present reform. The main focus of the debate among Chinese scholars is on whether administrative law is used to protect or restrain the administrative organs in their exercise of administrative power.[41]

One school argues that the origin of modern administrative law is from Western countries and is based on the constitutional principles of the rule of law and separation of powers. The application of the rule of law principle requires all administrative acts to be undertaken according to the law. The separation of powers doctrine enables the judiciary to exercise control of the undertaking of administrative acts. With growing interference of social activities by administrative organs, executive power is increasing and its improper or illegal exercise may infringe upon the rights of those under administration. In order to protect the legitimate interests of citizens and organizations, judicial review has been developed to control the exercise of administrative power. It holds that the function of administrative law is to control the unlawful exercise of executive power. The second school of thought relies on traditional Marxist legal theory, maintaining that China's socialist administrative law and Western bourgeois administrative law are fundamentally different in nature. Their purpose and function are different as the former protects the interests of the people, whereas the latter protects the interests of the ruling class.[42] The more commonly accepted approach asserts that administrative law in China has both functions to perform. On the one hand, administrative law has to ensure the effective exercise of administrative authority in order to achieve administrative efficiency, while on the other hand, administrative law has to protect the legitimate interest of people through controlling the exercise of executive power. This approach is supported and incorporated into the ALL.[43]

Having had an understanding of the functions of administrative law, it may be much easier to define its status in the Chinese legal system. Some have urged that the status of administrative law is only lower than the Constitution.[44] The issue is not so simple. Status is related to the contents of administrative law. If the broad approach is adopted, then the contents of administrative law shall cover legislation at different levels in the legal hierarchy. It is then very difficult to say what is the status of administrative law. A better approach would be to treat administrative law as a branch of law, the same as any other. Within the branch of administrative law, there is legislation at different levels. It is at least as equally important as any other branches of law.

Structure of Administrative Law

As mentioned at the beginning of this chapter and revealed through the above analysis, the concept of administrative law is much wider in China than its counterpart in common law jurisdiction. The definition, the contents, functions and status of administrative law are all related to and influence the structure of administrative law. From a legislative point of view, administrative law may be classified into two areas. One is substantive administrative legislation which grants power to administrative organs to make decisions on the rights and obligations of those under administration. The second is procedural administrative legislation which can be further divided into two: procedural legislation for administrative organs to follow in making decisions; and procedural legislation for the affected parties to challenge decisions of an administrative organ. From a theoretical point of view, administrative law includes three parts:

— general theory of administrative law, administrative authorities and activities;
— substantive administrative law; and
— procedural administrative law.

1.09

Most textbooks and monographs on administrative law only deal with the general theory and administrative authorities and activities. Some textbooks may also cover part of substantive administrative law, such as laws on military administration, external administration, civil affairs administration, public security administration, education and cultural administration, land administration, national economic administration, judicial administration, and so on. There are some monographs published on certain substantive administrative law. Procedural administrative law will deal mainly with the legal procedures by which administrative acts may be challenged. It will cover administrative reconsideration, administrative litigation and state compensation.

This book will follow the structure of academic classification. After this introductory chapter, the second chapter discusses the administrative law theory, which provides a theoretical analysis of essential components of administrative law and some bearing on the understanding of administrative procedural law. This book does not devote a separate section to substantive administrative law, but various kinds of substantive administrative legislation is mentioned as examples to explain how the second kind of procedural administrative law has been applied in practice to deal with issues arising from the implementation and enforcement of substantive administrative legislation. The book goes on to discuss in detail China's procedural administrative law for the handling of grievance against public administration and the mechanisms available in China for those under administration to challenge administrative decisions of various administrative organs and possible remedies. The reasons to adopt this methodology are quite simple. Firstly, the book is written for an audience with little knowledge of Chinese law, but with certain knowledge or background of the Western concept of judicial review, either in common law or continental law jurisdictions. Secondly, this book intends to provide a detailed description and analysis, through examples (cases), of the structure of the remedial measures available in China and their operation in procedure.

Notes

[1] See Yang Kaijun, *Wo Guo Xing Zhen Fa Xue Yan Jiu De Jue Qi* ("The Emerging of Administrative Law Research in China"), in *Collection of Legal Essays (Administrative Law)* 1990, pp. 9–14, at p. 9; see, also Xu Chongde and Pi Chunxie, *Comment on Administrative Law Study in Modern China*, Legal Science Press, pp. 1–7 (hereinafter as Xu and Pi).
[2] Civil and criminal law have historical tradition in China, though their recent development has also been influenced by Western legal systems, including both continental and common law systems. Administrative law is rather a new concept to China without much history. For detailed discussion, please refer to the section on historical development of administrative law in China.
[3] See Zhang Shangzhu, *Administrative Law*, Peking University Press, pp. 7–9.
[4] Well before the founding of the People's Republic of China, the state government started to promulgate legislation relating to public administration. Please refer to the section on historical development of administrative law in China for details.
[5] See the collection of literature and also the request for articles by China legal science.
[6] See Zhang Shangzu, p. 7.
[7] See Luo Haocai and Ying Songnian, *Administrative Law*, China University of Political Science and Law Press, Beijing, 1989, pp. 21–24.
[8] See Zhou Weiping et al., *Wo Guo Xing Zhen Fa Xue Ruo Gang Li Lun Wen Ti Yan Jiu Zong Shu* ("General Comments on Several Theoretical Issues of Administrative Law Research in China"), in *Collection of Legal Essays (Administrative Law)* 1990, Vol. 1, pp. 1–13, at p. 1.
[9] For details, see Xu and Pi, pp. 32–36.
[10] See also Luo Haocai and Ying Songnian, Administrative Law, pp. 2–5.
[11] It is debatable whether or not administrative law only regulates administrative relationship.

12. Most constitutional law will spend at least one chapter discussing the structure of administrative organs. See Wu Jialing, *Constitutional Law*, People's Press, Peking, 1983.
13. It actually talks about various administrative activities. For detailed discussion, refer to the section on administrative acts.
14. See Xu and Pi, p. 34. It is true that supervision of administration is very important to the protection of legitimate rights and interests of those under administration and prevention of unlawful or inappropriate exercise of administrative power. But whether or not it is an essential element of every administrative relationship is highly debatable.
15. Xu Chongde and Pi Chunxie believe that the tenth approach is more accurate and the study of the definition of administrative law should focus on three questions, *i.e.* the social relationship to be regulated by the administrative law; secondly, the necessity of supervision of governmental administrative activities; thirdly, the external characteristics which can distinguish this branch of law from other branches of law. See Xu and Pi, p. 36.
16. The PRC was founded in 1949 after the Communist Party overthrew the National Party in mainland China.
17. The legislation promulgated by the Communist Party during the period of 1939 to 1949 was mainly on constitutional structure, administrative organization and structure and governmental discipline, including 1939 Constitutional Principles in Shan Gan Ning Districts, 1939 Regulations on Governmental Organs in Shan Gan Ning Districts, 1942 Regulation on the Organization of Representative Councils at Each Level in Shan Gan Ning Districts, 1946 Common Political Principles of Democratice Governments in Each Province and City in Northeast China, and 1948 Outlines of People's Government Organs in North China. For details, refer to Lai, Qiuxian, *Zhong Guo Xing Zhen Fa Fa Zhan De Li Shi Kao Ca* ("A Historical Review of the Development of Administrative Law in the People's Republic of China"), in *Collection of Legal Essays 1990*, Vol. 1, pp. 1–8.
18. See Lai Qiuxian, pp. 3–4.
19. See Lai Qiuxian, p. 4.
20. See Xu and Pi, p. 1.
21. *Ibid*, pp. 2 and 3.
22. *Ibid*, p. 3. In fact, policies were often issued by the organs of Communist Party at various levels rather than by the government, and they were used in place of legislation. For details, refer to Lai Qiuxian, pp. 4–6.
23. It has been suggested that the Third Plenary marked the start of a new era in the development of administrative law in China. It is fair to say that there was administrative legislation before that. But the situation is quite different because 1. the importance of administration according to law has been widely appreciated; 2. more administrative legislation has been enacted; and 3. the ALL was under drafting. For more details, refer to Lai.
24. See Professor Luo Haocai, "The Current Situation and Trend of Development of Administrative Law Research" in Zhong Guo Fa Xue (*Chinese Legal Science*), Vol. 1, 1996, pp. 41–45, at p. 41.
25. *Ibid*, pp. 3 and 4.
26. *Ibid*, p. 5; see also Yang Haikun, above n. 1.
27. See Xu and Pi, p. 6.
28. See Luo Haocai et al., above n. 24.
29. In fact, people were already able to challenge the concrete decisions of administrative organs under the 1982 Civil Procedure Law. For discussion, refer to the relevant section on judicial review in this book.
30. See Chen Youxi, *Collection of Legal Essays (Administrative Litigation Law)* 1993, pp. 26–31, at p. 28.
31. One major problem facing administrative law in China is the implementation and enforcement. That is an issue not only for substarstive but also procedural administrative legislation.
32. Professor Zhi Fusheng, in his book entitled, *Textbook on Administrative Law*, discussed six different kinds of classifications. Xu and Pi mentioned four in their book.
33. See Zhou Weiping, p. 2.
34. See Luo and Ying, p. 27; see also p. 32 of Zhi. See also Zhang Shangzhu, pp. 16–17.

Procedural law may be further divided into those to be complied with by administrative organs in undertaking concrete administrative acts and those to be complied with by the affected parties to challenge administrative acts.

[35] The leading scholarly books on administrative law theory include:

    Xu Chongde and Pi Chunxie, *Xin Zhong Guo Xin Zheng Fa Xue Yan Jiu Zong Shu* (A Comprehensive Comment and Evaluation of Chiese Administrative Law Research), Legal Science Press, Beijing, 1991;

    Luo Haocai and Ying Songnian, *Administrative Law*, China University of Political Science and Law, Beijing, 1989;

    Wang Mingchan and Zhang Shangzhu, *Introduction to Administrative Law*, Legal Science Press, Beijing, 1983;

    Zhang Shangzhu and Yang Haikun, *Administrative Law*, Peking University Press, Beijing, 1990;

    Zhi Fusheng, *Textbook on Administrative Law*, Wuhan University Press, Wuhan, 1991;

    Zhang Shuyi and Lu Yao, *New Approach to Administrative Law*, Current Affairs Press, Beijing, 1990;

The books on administrative procedural law include:

    Luo Haocai and Ying Songnian, *Administrative Litigation Law*, China University of Political Science and Law, Beijing, 1990;

    Pi Chunxie and Hu Jingguang, *Textbook on Administrative Litigation Law*, People's University Press, 1993;

    Luo Haocai, *Examination of Issues Relating to Administrative Adjudication*, Peking University Press, Beijing, 1990;

    Luo Haocai, *Judicial Review System in China*, Peking University Press, Beijing, 1990;

    Ying Songnian, Yang Xiaojun and Fang Shirong, *Administrative Litigation Law*, China University of Political Science and Law, Beijing, 1994.

[36] See the two books edited by Professor Luo Haocai. Luo Haocai, *Examination of Issues Relating to Administrative Adjudication*, Peking University Press, Beijing, 1990 (hereinafter as Luo Haocai 1990); Luo Haocai, *Judicial Review System in China*, Peking University Press, Beijing, 1993 (hereinafter as Luo Haocai 1993).

[37] Some scholars also included the discussion of administrative reconsideration in their books on administrative law. For example, there is a chapter on administrative reconsideration in Yang Haikun's book entitled, *Administrative Law and Administrative Litigation Law*; there is also a part on administrative reconsideration in Zhang Shangzhu and Zhang Shuyi's book entitled *Chinese Administrative Law Coming out of Valley — a Comprehensive Comment and Evaluation of Chinese Administrative Law*.

[38] They refer to the possiblity under the Regulation on Administrative Supervision and the State Compensation Law.

[39] Refer to previous discussion on the scope of procedural law.

[40] The judicial has been held to be the main component of administrative law in common law jurisdiction, though the Ombudsman system is usually discussed in books on administrative law.

[41] Professor Xu has summarized different opinions of Chinese scholars in his book. For details, see Xu and Pi, pp. 71–77, See also Luo Haocai and Ying Songnian, *Administrative Law*, pp. 20–25.

[42] This is really an outdated approach and not many modern scholars still hold that approach.

[43] See Luo and Ying, *Administrative Law*, China University of Political Science and Law, Beijing, 1989. pp. 21–27 (hereinafter as Luo and Ying 1989).

[44] See Luo and Ying 1989, pp. 18–20.

CHAPTER TWO
ADMINISTRATIVE LAW THEORY

Administrative Relationship and Administrative Legal Relationship

Administrative legal relationship is what is formed through the regulation of administrative relationship by administrative legislation. In order to understand the concept of administrative legal relationship, the concept of administrative relationship should be examined. Administrative relationship is developed between the relevant administrative organs and other parties through the execution of administrative functions by relevant administrative organs. There are three kinds of administrative relationship. First is the relationship between the administrative organs themselves and those organs and civil servants, which is called internal administrative relationship. Second is the relationship between administrative organs and other organizations and individuals, which is called external administrative relationship. Third is the relationship between administrative organs and other state organs which are usually supervisory relationship.[1] Such administrative relationship, after being acknowledged and regulated by administrative legislation, including both substantive and procedural administrative legislation, will become an administrative legal relationship. It is a kind of relationship of rights and obligations as protected by the state.[2] Attempts have been made by Chinese scholars to define the exact contents and scope of administrative legal relationship. Some try to define according to the administrative legislation used to regulate administrative relationship; some define it according to the progress of the formation of administrative legal relationship; and others according to the contents of administrative legal relationship.[3] Some definitions may not be so comprehensive, but they are nevertheless all correct because they have revealed different aspects of administrative legal relationship.[4]

A relatively comprehensive and authoritative expression is provided by Professor Xu, which is as follows:[5]

2.01

Administrative legal relationship refers to those rights and obligations relationship formed between those governmental administrative organs, which are acknowledged and regulated by administrative legislation and undertake administration according to their authority, and other administrative organs under their authorization or instrument in the process of public administration on the one hand, and other state organs, enterprises and other economic organizations, institutions, social communities and organizations, citizens, foreigners who are residents in China and within China's jurisdiction and stateless persons on the other hand, and those legal relationship formed within administrative organs themselves.

It has been pointed out that administrative legal relationship has two different relationships at different levels: one is between the people as a whole and the state government which is abstract administrative act, and the other is between the state government and individuals which is a concrete administrative act.[6]

Elements of Administrative Legal Relationship[7]

2.02 There are three essential elements in administrative legal relationship, *i.e.* its subjects, objects and contents. Subjects of administrative legal relationship refer to the parties participating in administrative legal relationship, enjoying respective rights and bearing respective obligations. The discussion of any legal relationship should start with the subjects because they are the bearers of respective rights and obligations.

One issue concerning the subjects of administrative legal relationship is whether all parties to administrative legal relationship should be regarded as subjects, *i.e.* whether or not both administrative organs (including their personnel) and those under administration should be regarded as subjects, or only the administrative organs as subjects while those under administration should be treated as objects. It is generally accepted that state administrative organs should be subjects of administrative legal relationship. The dispute is mainly regarding suitability of individuals and legal persons as subjects of administrative legal relationship. The reason for some scholars to hold that those under administration should not be treated as objects is the passive nature of those under administration in administrative legal relationship. Whereas the administrative organs are always positive.[8] However, most scholars hold the view that those under administration are also subjects of administrative legal relationship.[9] Their approach is also consistent with the definition of subjects as they not only enjoy rights, but also bear obligations. According to this reasoning, those bearing obligation should also be regarded as subjects. This kind of argument also seems to be artificial as the classification of a specific party to administrative legal relationship as subject or object does not affect the respective legal rights and obligations it enjoys. It is therefore sensible to avoid such a debate by holding a different view, *i.e.* to treat both administrative organs and those under administration as parties to administrative legal relationship. Under substantive administrative legislation, such as legislation on taxation, public security or industry and commerce administration, both parties enjoy rights and need bear responsibilities. The only difference is that the rights enjoyed and the responsibilities borne by them are different. It is rarely the case that the administrative organs always enjoy rights, whereas those under administration only bear responsibilities.

When a governmental administrative organ deals with the other parties, it can play different roles. It may participate as an administrative organ by either giving orders or providing services. It may establish relationship on equal status with other parties through administrative contracts. It may also act as an arbitrator to handle disputes between other parties. These are just a few examples. There are many other ways it may get involved. Either way, its involvement may give rise to two kinds of legal relationship. If it exercises its administrative authority and implements relevant legislation, its authority must be granted under certain legislation. These kinds of relationship formed through the execution of administrative power granted by legislation are administrative legal relationship and are therefore regulated by administrative law.[10] If it forms relationship with other parties on an equal footing, without exercise of administrative power, then the legal relationship formed (*e.g.* through conclusion of ordinary contracts) will be ordinary civil legal relationship.

When natural or legal persons participate in administrative legal relationship, they mainly play a passive role as the other party to administrative legal relationship. They will be the party affected by the administrative acts. Nevertheless, they also enjoy certain rights and bear relevant responsibilities. Sometimes they are also authorized or entrusted by administrative organs to exercise certain administrative functions. If that is the case, they would play an active role as representative of the authorizing administrative organs. Under both circumstances, they should be treated as subjects to administrative legal relationship.

Objects refer to the target of the relevant rights and obligations of the parties to the administrative legal relationship. They include tangible goods, intangible property, action and inaction.[11]

Contents of administrative legal relationship comprise all the rights enjoyed and obligations borne by the parties to the administrative legal relationship.[12] They are recognized and protected by relevant administrative legislation. The main rights enjoyed by the administrative

2.03

organs include the rights to issue orders, impose sanctions, implement and enforce administrative regulations and orders, conduct supervision, and so on.[13] The main obligations borne by administrative organs include the obligations to act within the law, to protect the interests of the people, to accept supervision and so on. The rights enjoyed by individuals and social organizations include freedom (such as personal freedom, freedom of expression, religion, assembly and gathering, communication and publication), the right of equality, the right to participate in administration, the right to request protection, the right to benefit, and the right to sue. The obligations borne by them may include the obligations to comply with administrative legislation, to obey the lawful administrative decisions of administrative organs, and so on.[14] Such rights and obligations are dependent upon the administrative functions performed by the relevant administrative organs. Different administrative organs will have quite different rights and obligations, depending upon the provisions of relevant legislation.

All the three elements are essential components of administrative legal relationship. If one is missing, then there will not be any administrative legal relationship. For example, in the routine administration of administrative organs, they often make suggestions or recommendations. However, if they are not provided for by any administrative legislation, then those suggestions or recommendations will not give rise to any rights and obligations. Under such circumstances, no administrative legal relationship is formed because of lack of contents.

Characteristics of Administrative Legal Relationship

2.04 Due to the uniqueness of administrative relationship, the relevant administrative legal relationship is also quite different from other kinds of legal relationships such as civil or criminal. Administrative legal relationship has several characteristics which distinguish it from others.

Firstly, one party should be governmental administrative organs or their authorized organs, institutions, communities or individuals and have the legal authority to undertake administrative acts. The other party could be anything, such as state organs, institutions, enterprises and individuals. There must be one party in the administrative legal relationship which represents the state government.

Secondly, unlike in civil legal relationship, the status of the parties in the same administrative legal relationship is unequal in administrative legal relationship. An administrative organ participates in the name of the state and its exercise of authority is backed up with state force. Enforcement measures can be invoked if the other party fails to fulfil its obligations. Moreover, unilateral activity taken by an administrative organ can create new or change existing administrative legal relationship without the consent of the other parties[15]. However, it does not mean that the parties are unequal before law. Both parties have to act according to the law. The administrative organ has to bear respective responsibility for the action it takes and be under the supervision of legislature, judiciary and the public. One point which has been argued by Chinese scholars and also adopted in judicial practice is that this inequality reflects the principle that individuals should be subordinate to the state and this inequality is the necessary guarantee for the interest of the majority.[16] This argument is certainly debatable as the administrative organ in a democratic country may argue that it actually represents the interests of the majority. Even then, it is not the case that a representative organ can say that it is always right. Furthermore, whether or not an individual's interests should always give way to the interests of the majority is also questionable.

Thirdly, the relevant rights and obligations should be provided for in advance by relevant legal regulations. Whereas in civil legal relationship, parties can create by themselves relevant rights and obligations.

Fourthly, the rights and obligations under the same administrative legal relationship should correspond to each other and are unified. For example, the administrative function such as the grant of licence, is, on the one hand, the right of the relevant administrative organ, but on the other hand, it is also an obligation because it cannot be ignored by the administrative organ and has to be performed. If an applicant for licence satisfies all the requirement, then the relevant administrative organ has the obligation to issue him a licence accordingly. Likewise failure to impose appropriate penalty may also be regarded as failure to perform its obligation.

Fifthly, all controversies caused by administrative legal relationship are normally dealt with first by administrative organs according to administrative procedure or by administrative adjudicative organs according to quasi-judicial procedure. Only under clear legal provisions can ordinary courts handle disputes according to judicial procedure. These are the main, but not the only, characteristics of administrative legal relationship. Some scholars have also mentioned some other characteristics, such as compulsoriness, procedural legality, and so on.[17]

Classification of Administrative Legal Relationship[18]

Classification of administrative legal relationships can be made according to different standards. Most scholars would classify according

2.05

to the nature of the connection between the parties,. *i.e.* the classification of administrative relationship formed between the parties. They include the legal relationships between the administrative organs; between administrative organs and their internal administrative personnel; between administrative organs and other state organs; between administrative organs and enterprises, institutions and social organizations; between administrative organs and citizens; and between administrative organs and foreign organizations and foreigners.[19]

More simply, administrative legal relationship can be categorized into two groups. One is external administrative legal relationship, where the relevant administrative organ is one party which forms legal relationship with the other party, that is not within state administrative system, by the execution of its administrative function that reflects administration of the society by the state. The other is internal administrative legal relationship, where both parties are state organs or their personnel, which reflects internal administration of the state.[20] Both kinds of relationships are subject to the regulation of administrative legislation. In this sense the concept of administrative law in China is much broader than its counterpart in common law countries such as the United Kingdom.

Another classification which has been proposed is based on the legislation involved in the formation of administrative legal relationship, *i.e.* whether or not the legislation is a substantive or procedural legislation. In this way, administrative legal relationship may be classified into substantive administrative legal relationship and procedural administrative legal relationship. The latter may be further divided into procedural legal relationship formed by application of procedural legislation by administrative organs to undertake an ordinary administrative act and procedural legal relationship formed by the application of special procedural legislation for the resolution of administrative disputes.[21]

Alternatively, administrative legal relationship may also be classified according to the objectives into positive and passive ones, or according to the contents into property-related and non-property-related ones, or according to the frequency into frequent and occasional ones.[22]

2.06 All kinds of administrative legal relationship are the result of regulation of certain administrative relationship by administrative legislation. They are all subject to supervision in one way or another, including administrative, legislative and judicial supervision. But only certain kinds of administrative legal relationship will be subject to judicial control in China.[23] The concept of administrative legal relationship is a very important one in Chinese administrative law. Firstly, it is the object which is subject to supervision of substantive administrative legislation. Secondly, the scope of administrative legal relationship is directly related to the scope of judicial review. Thirdly, it is also related to the question who are qualified as the parties to such relationship.

A striking contrast, which should be noticed by common law lawyers, is the nature of contractual relationship between the administrative organ and another party. It is submitted that those administrative contracts, *i.e.* contracts entered in order to fulfil certain targets of state administration, will be regulated by administrative law. Though Chinese scholars generally agree that administrative contracts should be regulated by administrative law. However, there is no relevant legislation. Arguments still exist as to which division of the court should have jurisdiction over disputes arising from administrative contracts,[24] division of economic law, or division of administrative law. Whereas in common law countries, at least the United Kingdom and Hong Kong, the judicial approach is to treat all contractual relationship as private law issue and to be regulated by the law of contract.

General Principles of Administrative Law

General principles of administrative law refer to the principles to be followed in the enactment and implementation of all administrative legislation. They are reflected in all administrative legislation.[25] Chinese scholars have now reached the consensus that administrative law should have its own independent principles which are not only the grounds to distinguish administrative law from other branches of law, but also the basis for the existence of administrative law.[26] Different understandings still exist with regard to what are the fundamental principles of administrative law.

2.07

According to one source, Chinese scholars have raised 30 principles, including four basic principles (under the Constitution); separation of the communist party from the government and separation of communist party from enterprises; participation by people in state administration; democratic dictatorship; the principle of simplicity and convenience; equality of all nationalities; compliance with objective principles and effective administration; administration according to law; the emergency principle; administrative effectiveness (harmony between democracy and efficiency); the combination of unified leadership and hierarchical administration; the executive responsibility system; regional convenience; state planning administration; compliance with the communist party's guidelines and policies; democratic administration; efficiency; administrative uniformity; an administrative time limit; administrative openness, service; administrative responsibility; legality of administration; fairness of administration;

reasonableness of administration; sovereignty of the National People's Congress; check and balance between powers; and *ultra vires* principles.[27]

These are the principles which have been put forward by Chinese scholars. Whether or not they are all general principles of administrative law and how to classify these principles are issues over which different scholarly opinions exist. As summarized by Professors Xu and Pi in their book, the first principle is a constitutional principle. The second to the eighth are fundamental principles of public administration, not of administrative law. The ninth is the rule for administrative organs alone, not consistent with the understanding that fundamental principles must be general throughout administrative law. The other principles should be regarded as general principles of administrative law though different opinions exist still as to the exact contents of each of those principles.[28]

Another approach is to classify all these principles into two or three categories, one is those social and political principles formulated through the restriction or impact of external social relationship and environment on the contents of administrative law. It can be further divided into two, *i.e.* constitutional and political principles.[29] The other is those basic principles unique to administrative law.[30] They can also be further divided into those fundamental principles and more specific principles. Fundamental principles shall have guiding effect and play leading roles in administrative law and are related to the grant and control of power. More specific principles only touch upon certain aspects of administrative law.[31] Some other scholars are more modest by only raising several principles such as the four general principles, principle of legality, principle of democracy and principle of reasonableness.[32]

If one accepts that administrative law evolves from the constitutional law and is based on the constitutional principles of rule of law and allocation of powers among the three main organs of the state, the general principles of administrative law should be closely related to the principles of constitutional law. First of all, they must be legal, not political principles. Secondly, they should be unique and special to administrative law. Those constitutional principles are the sources of principles of administrative law, but should not be regarded as principles of administrative law themselves. Thirdly, the general principles must be applicable and incorporated into both substantive and procedural administrative legislation. Those exclusively to procedural administrative legislation[33] should not be treated as general principles. If these guidelines are followed, then most scholars generally agree that there are two principles which are unique and absolutely essential to the administrative law. They are the principle of legality and the principle of reasonableness.[34]

Principle of Legality

The principle of legality requires that the existence and exercise of any administrative power should be in accordance with legislation.[35] In other words, all administrative activities should be conducted according to laws and regulations and no administrative organs or individuals should enjoy any special power beyond legal provisions.[36]

The principle of legality in administrative law is the evolution of the constitutional principle of rule of law and its specific application in administrative law. Most Chinese scholars accept that the principle of legality is one originated from Western capitalist countries. They believe that it is an important principle of administrative law and generally applicable to and should also be regarded as a fundamental principle of Chinese administrative law.[37]

The principle of legality requires the compliance with both substantive and procedural law. Here the concept of law should be interpreted broadly and it may be more appropriate to replace the word "law" with the word "legislation". In common law jurisdiction such as the United Kingdom and Hong Kong, law includes primary legislation by the Parliament (in the case of United Kingdom) and Legislative Council together with the Governor (in the case of Hong Kong), subsidiary legislation by various executive branches of the government, and also case laws.[38] In China, law should include laws enacted by the National People's Congress and its Standing Committee, administrative regulations from the State Council, departmental regulations issued by various ministries and governmental organs, local legislation by local people's congresses and normative documents issued by various governmental departments, but not case laws.[39]

As to the exact meaning or contents of the principle of legality, different descriptions have been provided. One source suggests that the principle of legality has three requirements:

— the existence of any administrative authority must be based on legislation;
— the exercise of any administrative authority must be in accordance with legislation; and
— the entrustment and its exercise of any administrative power must be in accordance with legislation and consistent with the objectives of the relevant legislation.[40]

The last requirement here has in fact implied the requirement of reasonableness. Another source provides a more detailed prescription including five elements. Firstly, the establishment and existence of any administrative power must have legal grounds; secondly, the allocation and exercise of administrative power must be made by laws; thirdly, the contents of administrative acts must comply with legal provisions; fourthly, the exercise of administrative power must be in accordance with legal procedures; and fifthly, any violation of legislation must be dealt with according to law.[41] The argument as to whether or not the principle of legality has three or five elements is not essential. The essence of the principle is that all administration has to be done in accordance with legislation. Bearing in mind this point, the specific requirements may be put forward according to the variety of administrative activities. A more simple way to look at the contents of principle of legality is to examine the elements of administrative relationship. The principle of legality requires each element to be lawful.

It has been argued that any administrative acts undertaken in violation of any of those requirements shall be regarded as outside the jurisdiction of the administrative organ and therefore invalid.[42] However, if the acts were subsequently approved by law, they may also be regarded as valid or within the jurisdiction. Under special circumstances, the principle of emergency (*force majeure*) may be argued to justify an administrative act in violation of one of the requirements. Public interest, war or natural disaster are examples of *force majeure*.[43]

In fact, a monograph has been published on the law relating to emergency.[44] The monograph has discussed various issues such as the definition of emergency, legislation to handle emergency in both China and abroad, the variety of emergency and the relevant remedies, and so on. Emergency is an exception to the ordinary circumstance and may be regarded as an exceptional case. The main legal sources in China dealing with emergency include section 89 of the Constitution, and the Martial Law under which the state may exercise exceptional authority which they do not enjoy under ordinary circumstances. However, the exercise of such authority under relevant legislation relating to emergency should follow the principles of legality (reasonableness) due procedures and a responsibility system.[45] Failure to follow these requirements may lead to state compensation.

The Principle of Reasonableness

2.10   The principle of reasonableness is another important principle of administrative law and an important component of the principle of administration according to law. It means that the contents of any administrative decisions must be objective, appropriate and reasonable.[46] The development of this principle is mainly due to the existence and expansion of administrative discretionary power.[47] Due to the complexity of administration, it is unavoidable to grant discretionary power to administrative organs concerning the methods and manners, kinds and scope of administrative activities. The principle of reasonableness requires the contents of administrative actions to be reasonable and appropriate. It is regarded as the development and extension of the principle of legality. In formality, unreasonable administrative acts meet the requirements of relevant legislation. However, an examination of the objective and the final results of the relevant administrative acts shall reveal that the undertaking of those acts is not consistent with the objective of the relevant legislation. As to the relationship between illegality and unreasonableness, it all depends on the relevant legislation. With the development of legislation, it is very likely that certain kinds of unreasonable administrative activities may be prescribed by legislation as unlawful activities. Then the issue of reasonableness shall be changed into an issue of legality.[48]

The specific requirements of the principle of reasonableness includes the intention for the undertaking of the administrative act must be consistent with legislative objective(s); the administrative act must be undertaken by taking into account relevant (not irrelevant) considerations; the contents of the administrative act must be reasonable.[49] Some scholars also suggest that the principle of reasonableness should also require the exercise of discretionary power be consistent with the fundamental interests of the state and its people, and in accordance with the requirement of justice.[50] More detailed discussion of this principle shall be made in latter chapters on procedural administrative law, especially the chapter on judicial control of discretionary power.

Administrative Acts[51]

It is one of the main issues in administrative law theory because all other issues in administrative law are related to administrative acts in one way or another.[52] For example, the formation of administrative legal relationship will be through the undertaking of administrative acts. Any administrative disputes will only be caused by the undertaking of administrative acts. What judicial review and administrative reconsideration examine are the impact of administrative acts on the rights and interests of citizens, legal persons and other organizations. The standardization and legalization of the undertaking of various administrative acts are the primary issues to be discussed. Only when those issues are solved can the issue of liability be discussed. They are the basis of an administrative responsibility system. Administrative acts, in essence, refer to those undertaken by the administrative organs through the exercise of administrative power according to law in the process of public administration. They are the acts of administrative organs or those under their authorization.[53] Those acts shall have direct or indirect administrative legal effects upon the other parties to admin-

2.11

istrative legal relationship.[54] It means the activities must affect the rights and interests of the other parties to the administrative relationship.[55] Though administrative organs are usually the ones which are granted the authority to exercise administrative power, they are not the only ones. Sometimes institutions, enterprises or individuals may, upon proper authorization, exercise administrative power and undertake administrative acts.

Different definitions have been proposed by Chinese scholars on administrative act. There are the broadest, broad and narrow definitions.[56] It all depends on the criteria adopted by the scholars for the definition.[57] An examination of the definition of administrative act in other jurisdictions will reveal that the difference in definition seems to be caused by the different scopes of judicial review adopted in different countries.[58] The subjects of administrative acts can only be administrative organs or their authorized or entrusted bodies or persons. The nature of such acts is the execution of administrative functions or the performance of public affairs.[59] In this sense, it should be distinguished from the acts regulated by civil law. Those activities undertaken by administrative organs in civil legal relationship on equal basis are only civil acts rather than administrative acts.[60]

Characteristics of Administrative Acts[61]

2.12   The Characteristics of administrative acts may be summarized into two categories: one are the substantive characteristics and the other are those in formality. Professors Xu and Pi have listed five substantive characteristics. The first is that administrative acts represent the will of the state as they are undertaken by administrative organs in the name of the state. The second is that the undertaking and enforcement of administrative acts are according to legislation and will have legal effects on the other side to the administrative relationship. The third is their compulsory feature, which is the corollary of the first characteristics because the will of the state is backed by state force which can always be enforced. The fourth is the unilateral feature where the administrative organs may unilaterally undertake administrative acts without consulting the others. Once they are undertaken they will have legal effects. The other parties have to comply with them. The fifth is the positive feature as the relevant administrative organ initiates the administrative acts. Administrative organs may undertake an administrative act positively without any application from the other side. Whereas the judiciary will not take any action unless somebody applies for its interference. That distinguishes the administrative act from judicial acts.

There are three characteristics in formality. Firstly, administrative acts may only be undertaken by administrative organs or their personnel. Secondly, the grounds on which administrative organs undertake administrative acts must be relevant provisions in legislation. Thirdly, administrative organs must follow administrative procedure in undertaking administrative acts.[62]

The understanding of substantive characteristics of administrative acts help us to understand the nature of administrative acts. The comprehension of the characteristics of administrative acts in formality contribute to the understanding of the procedural requirements for the undertaking of administrative acts and the means to supervise the undertaking of administrative acts.

Classification of Administrative Acts

Administrative acts can be classified in different ways according to different standards or criteria. They may be classified according to their purpose, intention, relationship with other administrative activities, legal restrictions, characteristics, scope of validity, scope of applicability, format, and so on. Altogether, 22 kinds of categorization have been proposed,[63] but not all of them are commonly referred to. Here, only three classifications which are often used and also closely related to the discussion of procedural administrative law for administrative dispute resolution, will be discussed.

2.13

Concrete and Abstract Administrative Acts[64]

Concrete and abstract administrative acts are a pair of concepts. This classification is made according to the scope of application of administrative acts. Concrete administrative acts are those decisions or activities undertaken by relevant administrative organs which directly affect the rights or interests of the other parties.[65] Abstract administrative acts refer to the acts of administrative organs to make administrative regulations, rules or decisions and orders which have general binding effect, either on a group of people or in a certain area. Compared with concrete administrative acts, the targets and the scope to which the abstract administrative acts are applicable are quite different as they are aimed at citizens, legal persons or organizations instead of a specific one. This classification is based on the allocation of supervisory functions exercised by the legislature, executive and judiciary over administration, including the undertaking of both abstract and concrete administrative acts. Before the enactment of the ALL and the Regulation on Administrative Reconsideration (RAR), abstract administrative acts were already subject to legislative and administrative supervision. Means have been provided by laws to deal with the issues of their illegality and inappropriateness. The Constitution and the

2.14

Organic Law of the Local People's Congresses and Local People's Governments provide that the legislature at national and local levels will have the authority to annual relevant inconsistent legislation, rules and orders.[66] This is one of the reasons why the ALL and the RAR are restricted to concrete administrative acts only, *i.e.* to avoid the duplication of supervision and also potential conflicts between different state organs.

Internal and External Administrative Acts[67]

2.15 This classification is made according to the objects under administration. Internal administrative acts refer to various measures or decisions taken by administrative organs against other administrative organs or their own staff. Those against other administrative organs include administration, supervision, audit, approval decisions of other administrative organs. Acts against their personnel include warning, recording a demerit, removal from position, stay on probation, dismissal and any other disciplinary actions. Disputes with regard to these internal acts are expected to be resolved within the original administrative organ, by the organ at the next level above, or supervision department because of the necessity of administrative efficiency. External administrative acts refer to actions taken by administrative organs towards citizens, legal persons or other organizations not within the same administrative organ. They may be subject to administrative reconsideration and judicial review. It has been argued that internal and external administrative acts are quite different and therefore should not be dealt with through the same procedure.[68] Whether or not internal administrative acts should be subject to administrative reconsideration or judicial review is certainly debatable. In theory, there does not exist much justification why they are excluded from those remedial measures, provided that the rights or interests of those under administration are affected.[69]

Administrative Legislation, Implementation and Adjudication Acts

2.16 This classification is made according to the nature of the acts undertaken by administrative organs. The three main functions performed by the executive branch of the government are administrative legislation, implementation and enforcement, and adjudication. As detailed discussions of each of them will be conducted in the next section of this chapter, it suffices to say here that this classification has been generally accepted by Chinese scholars and provides a reasonably clear picture of administrative acts.[70] Generally speaking, these three kinds of administrative acts are distinguishable from each other. But occasionally, there are some acts which may be on the border-line, especially between administrative implementation and adjudication.[71]

Apart from these three kinds of classification, there are several other kinds of classification which are also commonly used. Administrative acts may be classified as Restricted and Discretionary Administrative Activities, Unilateral, Bilateral and Multilateral Administrative Activities, Administrative Activities with and without legally Required Formalities, Administrative Action and In-action, Independent and Supplementary Activities, and Substantive and Procedural Administrative Activities.[72]

Analysis of Administrative Acts

As mentioned above, there are variety of administrative acts. The important administrative acts undertaken by governmental organs include administrative legislation, implementation and enforcement of legislation, administrative judicial activities, administrative supervision, conclusion of administrative contracts, and so on. It is impossible to discuss all of them here as a comprehensive discussion of even the major ones deserves a book.[73] What this section does is to discuss briefly several important administrative acts and the relevant legal requirements for their undertaking.

2.17

Administrative Legislation[74]

Different views exist between scholars specializing in legislation and those specializing in administrative law about the exact meaning of administrative legislation. Their difference in opinions is mainly about whether or not administrative organs enjoy inherent legislative power.[75] However, they all agree that as a kind of administrative act, administrative legislation does exist. It refers to the enactment of administrative regulations and rules with legal effect by properly authorized governmental administrative organs at different levels.[76] They include both central administrative organs, such as State Council, various Ministries and Commissions, and local administrative organs, such as local people's government. The administrative regulations and rules thus enacted are generally applicable within the jurisdiction of the administrative organs which enact them. Apart from substantive requirements, administrative legislation has to follow proper procedures.[77]

2.18

Such administrative legislative activities have the characteristics of both legislation and administration. It has the common features of legislation such as generality, normality and compulsoriness.[78]

Meanwhile, administrative legislative activities are also one kind of abstract administrative act. They also have the common features of administration. But they are different from concrete administrative acts in the sense that only those organs properly authorized by laws have the authority to undertake administrative legislative acts, which is also a characteristic distinguishing administrative legislative activities from other abstract administrative acts. Apart from that, administrative legislative activities have also the following features which belong to all abstract administrative acts. The targets of the administrative legislative activities are general public or a category of people or matters, not any specific person or matter. The validity of administrative legislative activities is longer than concrete administrative activities. The procedures of administrative legislative activities are more formal and stricter than their counterparts for the undertaking of any concrete administrative acts.[79]

The sources of administrative legislation may be delegation by the legislature through legislation or due to the functions performed by the administrative organs concerned.[80] For example, section 67 of the Constitution defines the functions and authorities of the Standing Committee of the National People's Congress (NPC); Section 89 defines the functions and authorities of the State Council; Sections 99 and 100 define the functions and authorities of local people's congresses and people's governments.[81] In this sense, it is quite different from subsidiary legislation in Western countries, which should always be based on primary legislation.

Administrative legislative activities may also be classified in other different ways such as central and local administrative legislative activities, or implementing administrative legislation and creative administrative legislation.[82]

2.19 One issue which needs to be discussed is what shall amount to administrative legislation. In other words, what is the scope of administrative legislation, especially whether or not rules or decisions with generally binding effect should be regarded as administrative legislative activities. According to existing legislative structure, as laid down in the Constitution and Organic Law on Local People's Congresses and Local People's Governments, local administrative organs other than the people's government do not enjoy legislative power.[83] Following these lines, those normative documents or orders with general binding effect should not be regarded as legislation.

The second important issue is whether or not the administrative organs may promulgate regulations to create new rights and obligations which have not been provided for by any laws enacted by the NPC or its Standing Committee. Different views exist. Some hold that administrative legislation should be implementary in nature and not create any new rights or obligations. While most scholars maintain that new rights and obligations may be created by regulations, but special authorization is needed from the representative organ, *i.e.* the legislature.[84] The latter approach is also consistent with China's situation.

The third important issue concerning administrative legislation is the status of different kinds of administrative legislation. Different views exist in this aspect and that is why applicable law is an important issue in judicial review in China. The main reason for the existence of different views is that the status of different kinds of administrative legislation is not defined in any legislation, especially the Constitution and different organic laws.[85]

The fourth issue is the legal control of administrative legislative activities.[86] There are different kinds of legal control over administrative activities. The most important one is the control exercised by the legislature at both national and local levels. The legislature has been granted the power to annul those inconsistent legislation including administrative regulations, regulations, rules and orders, and other normative documents.[87]

The second kind of legal control is the recording system. Under relevant legislation, all administrative regulations enacted by the State Council should be submitted to the Standing Committee of the National People's Congress for record. All regulations enacted by various Ministries and Commissioners and local people's government should be submitted to the State Council for its examination and record. This is in theory a kind of prior supervision to ensure the consistency among laws, administrative regulations and regulations. In practice, the supervisory function of both the Standing Committee of the NPC and the State Council have hardly been invoked.[88]

The third kind of legal control is exercised by the judiciary which is a rather limited type of control compared with the previous two and will be discussed in the Chapter on judicial review. It should be noted that judicial control is only an indirect control because only those whose rights or interests have been affected by concrete administrative acts basing on administrative legislation are qualified to resort to judicial control. The affected party may bring an action to challenge the concrete administrative acts. In doing so, he can indirectly challenge the administrative legislation concerned.[89]

Administrative Implementation and Enforcement[90]

In order to implement laws, administrative regulations, regulations, and other decisions and orders with general binding effect, administrative organs will take certain measures against specific persons or matters in order to affect their rights and obligations and to perform administrative functions. Such administrative acts are referred to as administrative implementation and enforcement acts. Most adminis-

2.20

trative organs are involved nowadays in the implementation and enforcement of legislation in one way or another. It is the manifestation of the exercise of executive power.[91]

Different views exist as to whether or not administrative implementation and enforcement are executed by all administrative organs or only specific organs as mentioned in legislation. The difference is held to be the power to impose administrative penalties.[92] In Chinese, the term is "*zhi fa*" of which the literal translation is implementation of legislation. An examination of the contents covered by *zhi fa* shows that it also includes enforcement of legislation. It is therefore more appropriate to divide the concept of *zhi fa* into administrative implementation of legislation and administrative enforcement of legislation. The former function may be exercised by all kinds of administrative organs in the undertaking of administrative acts. The latter function is only granted to limited organs. Administrative implementation and enforcement is different from judicial enforcement in the sense that the former is a kind of positive implementation and enforcement. The administrative organ will take positive action whereas judicial enforcement only functions when one of the parties in a dispute applies for judicial enforcement. The courts will never initiate any enforcement action.

For an administrative implementation and enforcement act to be effective, several requirements need to be satisfied. Firstly, the subject matter must be lawful, meaning that the administrative organ must be lawfully constituted and has the proper authority to execute administration, and the authority is exercised within its legal limits. Secondly, the activity of the administrative organ must be the true expression of its will. Thirdly, the exercise of the authority must follow the proper legal procedure. Fourthly, the individuals must have legal capacity, satisfying minimum legal requirements.[93]

Administrative implementation and enforcement acts are, in essence, administrative acts and therefore have the common features of administrative acts, *i.e.* defined by legislation, specific, compulsory, and active. The main problem facing administrative implementation and enforcement is that many administrative laws and regulations have been enacted, such as laws relating to the administration of land, medicine, forest, environment, mineral resources and compulsory education, etc. However, it has been reported that only 30 per cent of legislation has been properly implemented by administrative organs, and even worse, it has been very difficult for both the administrative organs and judiciary to enforce the administrative legislation.[94]

There are different kinds of administrative implementation and enforcement activities, *e.g.* administrative decisions (including administrative approval, refusal, licensing and exemption), administrative supervision, administrative compulsory enforcement measures. Unlawful or inappropriate undertaking of administrative and enforcement activities may be subject to challenge under one of the remedial measures.

Administrative Licensing Acts[95]

Administrative licensing refers to such activities by which the administrative organ, upon the application of the applicants and after examination, grant the applicants the right or capacity to undertake certain activities which ordinary people are usually prohibited from undertaking.[96] The grant of business licence by the Administration Bureau of Industry and Commerce is one example of numerous administrative licensing acts.

2.21

It is one means through which administrative organs conduct administration. Its purpose is to put under administration some special areas concerning important interests of the state, society and citizens.[97] A licensing system has been widely used in the administration of industry and commerce, especially relating to business licences, pollutant emission permits and production licences for food and medicine. Whether or not to adopt licensing administration in a specific area depends on the balance of the necessity of state control and normal freedom which should be enjoyed by the people.[98]

In the case of China, the administration used to be conducted according to direct instructions or orders from administrative organs under the previous planned economy. Economic reform has gradually changed the direct leadership of enterprises by administrative organs. A licensing system has been widely used to maintain the proper order of various administrative activities.

Whether or not to grant a licence is the consequence or result of administrative licensing acts. Whether or not to grant a permit or licence is an authority enjoyed by the relevant administrative organs.[99] Their decisions may affect the interests of the applicants by refusing to grant a licence, detaining a licence or revoking a licence. Because of the potential seriousness of the consequences of administrative licensing activities, its exercise has to be in accordance with proper legal procedure and under legal control. The grant, termination and revocation of any licence have to follow proper legal procedures and are with legal grounds. Remedial measures are normally provided for the applicants to challenge the refusal by administrative organs to grant licences. It is because the consequence of refusal is very serious and the applicant will lose the right to engage in certain activities. Two important remedial procedures are administrative reconsideration, which is an administrative remedial measure, and judicial review, which is a judicial procedure and will be discussed in the later part of the book. Apart from them, there also exist other administrative remedial measures such as the supervision by administrative supervisory organs and auditing organs, and legislative control of licensing systems, which may be exercised by incorporating into legislation detailed requirements for the application and grant of licences.[100]

Once a licence is granted, it will have legal effect. The holder of the licence shall have the right to undertake certain activities and the licence is the evidence of that capacity. It is binding to both the holder and the issuing administrative organ. It cannot be arbitrarily changed, either by the licence holder or the administrative organ. Any change or amendment must follow proper examination and approval procedure. It can be revoked if the licence holder fails to perform its legal obligations, which is an administrative penalty and can be judicially reviewed.

The procedures for the undertaking of administrative licensing acts should follow two general principles. One is openness. That is to say all qualified persons should be allowed to apply on an equal footing. The other is reasonableness. As a licensing authority, in essence, is still a discretionary power enjoyed by the administrative organ concerned and therefore the principle of reasonableness should be followed.[101]

Administrative Adjudicating Acts[102]

2.22   Administrative adjudication refers to the resolution of certain kinds of disputes, as defined in legislation, by administrative organs according to quasi-judicial procedure. Administrative adjudicating organs will only function as third party for dispute resolution. They do not have any administrative relationship with the parties to the disputes. There are several reasons for the involvement of administrative organs in the dispute resolution. Firstly, those cases may be relating to public administration or require special expertise or knowledge for their resolution. Secondly, the parties to the disputes are not on an equal footing and such disputes relate to administrative regulations and rules, policies and standards. It may be more appropriate to subject them to internal supervision first. The main justification here seems to be the necessity to provide an opportunity to the administrative organ to rectify its own wrongs. Thirdly, certain activities which were previously subject to ordinary administrative procedure are changed to be subject to quasi-judicial procedure, as required and practised under a modern democratic system.[103]

Administrative adjudication is a very new concept and practice in China. It is quite different from the practice of Western countries, mainly because China had a long historical tradition of solving disputes through administrative orders. However, the traditional system is currently under reform. A new adjudicating system has been developed in China.[104]

There are two kinds of administrative adjudication. One is used to resolve disputes relating to administrative activities (administrative disputes). Administrative disputes refer to disputes arising through the exercise of administrative authority between the administrative organ concerned and other administrative organs, or its civil servants, or organizations or individuals. Only certain kinds of administrative disputes will be subject to an administrative adjudicating system, that is, administrative reconsideration.[105] More legislation has provided for administrative reconsideration as the first dispute resolution mechanism for administrative disputes. The enactment of the RAR has standardized the procedure for administrative reconsideration and made the resolution of administrative disputes by administration more similar to judicial procedure.[106]

The other is relating to administrative adjudication of civil disputes, including economic and technological contracts disputes, labour disputes, intellectual property disputes, and so on, of which there are several. For this category of administrative adjudication, the adjudicating organs are normally established according to law. They only hear those cases upon the application of relevant parties.[107]

Apart from directly dealing with the parties concerned in the process of exercising its executive authority, administrative organs often become involved as third parties in civil disputes to conduct arbitration, mediation or other rulings. Administrative arbitration is concerned with arbitration of civil disputes conducted by administrative organs.

The 1983 Regulation on Economic Contract Arbitration in the PRC has brought administrative adjudicating procedure into the handling of economic disputes by administrative organs. Regulation on Labour Dispute Resolution within Enterprises has brought administrative adjudicating procedure into the handling of labour disputes. Trade Mark Law and Patent Law also provide for the establishment of special administrative tribunals to handle respective disputes which require special expertise. Some special tribunals have been established under those legislation for the handling of special kinds of disputes which often require expertise in the respective areas. Administrative arbitration has certain features. The institute conducting arbitration must be a special institute within administrative organ, the institute's authority to conduct arbitration is provided by law, not upon the agreement of the parties concerned. The dispute is a civil one, and there is no administrative relationship between the administrative organ and the parties concerned. No application for administrative reconsideration can be lodged if the parties are not satisfied with the verdict of arbitration. Instead, they can only file a case with the people's courts as provided by law. 2.23

Administrative mediation is the mediation of civil disputes by administrative organs. Usually, the administrative organs conduct mediation on those matters within their administrative jurisdiction and according to law.

Special administrative rulings are about the handling of civil disputes by administrative organs according to provisions in specific legislation. Legislation such as the Forest Law, Land Management Law, Water Law, Grassland Law and Fishery Law have all provided for the handling of disputes by relevant administrative organs. These are just a few examples. There are many other legislation which has also provided for the dispute resolution method by special administrative organs concerned.

An administrative adjudicating system is one that ensures justice, democracy and openness in public administration. On the one hand, it is a system which can protect the rights and interests of individuals and organizations against infringement of arbitrary administration. On the other hand, it also provides the administrative organs and their personnel a kind of supervision and balance, which will contribute to the prevention of unlawful, ultra vibes and power-abusing activities.

Administrative Compulsory Enforcement

2.24 If an individual or organization fails to perform the prescribed legal obligations, the relevant administrative organ may compulsorily force him/it to perform his/its obligations.[108] Such an activity undertaken by the administrative organ is called compulsory enforcement. The condition for administrative compulsory enforcement is that the individual or organization fails to perform his/its legal obligations. There are two possibilities: one is the undertaking of prohibited activities; the other is failure to perform the prescribed obligations. To build a private dwelling house without a proper permit and failure to pay tax are two examples.[109] Administrative compulsory enforcement must have proper legal grounds. In other words, there must be clear legal provisions to stipulate the use of administrative compulsory enforcement. In China, there does not exist a uniform legislation prescribing the conditions, procedures for administrative compulsory measures. They are scattered in different legislation. The following issue is what kind of legislation can provide for administrative compulsory measures. It is generally agreed that laws and administrative regulations can stipulate administrative compulsory measures. The only dispute is about departmental and local regulations.[110] Taking into account China's practical situation, the answer should be positive.[111]

The enforcement organ is usually an administrative organ, which will, as part of its own authority and duty, enforce the relevant administrative decisions according to the authorization of legislation. However, whether or not administrative organs should be the only ones for administrative compulsory enforcement is debatable. Unlike in Western countries where enforcement is normally a task of the courts, it is treated in China as an issue of allocation of power. The popular view is that certain serious compulsory measures relating to personal or important proprietary rights should be enforced by the courts, while others by administrative organs.[112] In the former case, the relevant administrative organ will apply to the people's courts for compulsory enforcement of administrative decisions. It will arise when the enforcement administrative organ does not have the authority to undertake certain kinds of activities which are essential for the completion of its public duty, *e.g.* compulsory transfer of money from bank account, demolition, refund, and so on.[113] It should be noted that whether the judiciary or administrative organ or both of them should be enforcement organs is closely related to the legal culture of the country concerned. In the case of China where administrative organs used to enjoy enormous power, it is not surprising that the executive organs still enjoy certain power to take enforcement actions.

A related concept are compulsory measures. Administrative compulsory enforcement is an abstract concept and can only be shown through the implementation of compulsory measures. Various compulsory measures have been provided for by legislation in China. Different classification may be made. Here one popular classification shall be introduced. It classifies compulsory measures into three categories. The first is against personal freedom such as compulsory custody, summons or deportation, and so on. The second is against an act such as compulsory demolition, inspection, removal, cancellation of licence, destruction, and so on. The third is against property such as compulsory deduction, transfer, collection (of money), and so on.

In order for a compulsory enforcement to be effective, four requirements must be satisfied: (i) the individual or organization must have an obligation either under legal provision or due to some administrative decisions; (ii) the individual or organization fails to perform its obligation intentionally; (iii) there is clear legal provisions stating that administrative compulsory measures may be taken when failure to perform occurs; and (iv) the organ which issues the order must have the authority to make such a decision.[114]

Apart from those substantive requirements mentioned above, administrative compulsory enforcement should also follow proper procedural requirements. A notice should be issued by the administrative organ to the relative party to inform it to perform its obligations. Otherwise compulsory enforcement will come into play. The actual enforcement should also follow proper procedures as stipulated in legislation.

Administrative Penalty[115]

Administrative penalty is a kind of administrative sanction by which the administrative organs shall punish those individuals or organiza- 2.25

tions which violate laws, administrative regulations, regulations or rules. The existence of unlawful acts is the condition for the imposition of administrative penalty. Administrative penalties have to be undertaken by specific administrative organs. It must be provided by legislation which states what kind of violation of legislation will be sanctioned by which administrative organs.[160] Administrative Penalty Law of the PRC (APL) was enacted on March 17, 1996. It will come into force on October 1, 1996. From then onwards, the establishment and imposition of administrative penalty shall follow the legal requirements in that law. It has formalized the establishment, imposition, enforcement organs, jurisdiction, applicability and the procedures for the imposition of administrative punishment.[117]

The creation of any administrative penalty must be provided for by legislation and follow proper legal procedure. Otherwise the administrative penalty will be invalid. Penalty restricting personal freedom can only be established by laws adopted by the National People's Congress or its Standing Committee.[118] Administrative regulations may establish any other kinds of administrative penalty. Local regulation may establish administrative penalty other than those restricting personal freedom or revocation of enterprise business licence.[119]

2.26 The main variety of administrative penalties have been provided for by section 8 of the APL, including warning, fine, confiscation of illegal income and unlawful property, the order to stop production or business, temporary detention or revocation of permit or licence, administrative detention. They are by no means the only ones. The same section also states that other administrative penalties may be provided for by other laws and administrative regulations.

Administrative penalty must follow the principle of fairness and openness. That means the creation and imposition of administrative penalty must be based on facts and be compatible with the facts, nature and circumstances of the violation and the degree of danger to the society. The provisions imposing administrative penalty must be publicised. Otherwise they cannot be used as grounds for the imposition of administrative punishment.

Administrative penalty can only be imposed by those legally authorized organs within their defined scope of authority. The penalty restricting personal freedom may only be imposed by public security bureaus. Under certain circumstances, administrative organs may entrust other organs to impose administrative penalty on their behalf. Such delegation of authority must be in accordance with provisions in laws, administrative regulations and rules. The entrusting organ will bear the legal responsibilities.

For the same unlawful act, administrative penalty can only be imposed once,[120] even if the original penalty imposed was obviously too light. There are several consideration behind this principle. Moreover, the imposition of administrative penalty must follow certain procedural requirements. Three kinds of procedures have been stipulated in the 1996 Administrative Penalty Law. They are the summary procedure, ordinary procedure and hearing procedure.[121]

Administrative Supervision

Administration is subject to different kinds of supervision. One is the supervision within the administration by the superior administrative organ over an inferior administrative organ, which is the ordinary internal supervision of administration. There could also be specially established organs within the administration to undertake the task of supervision of administration, which is called special administrative supervision.[122] There are two kinds of special supervision of administration. One is administrative supervision which is carried out by the Ministry of Supervision and its local branches. The other is audit supervision carried out by auditing departments of the state government. National auditing system was confirmed in the 1982 Constitution and has been re-established since then. The Ministry of Supervision and its local branches were established at the end of 1986.[123]

2.27

Ordinary administrative supervision is mainly based on the functions exercised by the superior administrative organs. Their supervisory roles are normally provided for in relevant legislation. For example, section 89 of the Constitution states that the State Council has the authority to alter or annul inappropriate orders, directives and regulations issued by the ministries or commissions and to alter or annul inappropriate decisions and orders issued by local organs of state administration at various levels. Section 108 of the Constitution provides that local people's governments at and above the county level, direct the work of their subordinate departments and of people's governments at lower levels, and have the power to alter or annul inappropriate decisions of their subordinate departments and of the people's governments at lower levels.

It is also possible for lower people's governments to play a supervisory role of superior people's governments by submitting comments and criticism to the latter which is required to deal with them seriously and reply accordingly.[124] In theory it is possible. In practice, it hardly works. Furthermore, supervision may also be carried out among different governmental departments or organs horizontally. Various governmental departments will, within its authority, exercise supervision over other governmental departments. For example, the Ministry of Finance shall supervise the finance budget and balance in other ministries or local people's governments.

Administrative supervision[125] conducted by the Ministry of Supervision and its local branches with regard to whether or not governmental organs and their personnel properly perform their functions, comply with legislation and governmental discipline is another important special supervision. It is a type of external supervision by the Ministry of Supervision over the other governmental organs of the executive branch. The target of such supervision is administrative organs and their personnel (civil servants). The main contents of their supervision include the implementation of laws, administrative regulations, policies and governmental disciplines; the activities of administrative organs or its personnel in violation of laws, administrative regulations, policies, and governmental disciplines, complaints against administrative organs or their personnel in those aspects, and appeals by civil servants against administrative decisions.

Act of State

2.28 Acts of state are those taken in the name of the state and are sovereign actions. It is a unique category of administrative acts. For the purpose of protecting national interests, every state grants special status to state acts. China is not an exception. Acts of state are not subject to administrative reconsideration. There are mainly two common categories. One relates to national defence, such as war and military practice. The other relates to diplomatic relationship, such as relationship with other countries or international organizations, establishment, severance of diplomatic relationship with foreign countries, and conclusion of treaties. Besides, acts of state also include other important acts relating to state interests, such as imposition of curfew by the State Council in certain areas or regions. Any complaints against acts of state should not be resolved according to the ALL or RAR. Instead they can only be duly addressed through other means.[126]

Notes

1. See Luo and Ying 1989, pp. 3–4.
2. See Zhang Shangzhu, *Administrative Law*, p. 18.
3. See Xu and Pi, pp. 54–55.
4. See Xu and Pi, pp. 54–56; Luo and Ying 1989, pp. 11–12.
5. See Xu and Pi, pp. 55–56.
6. See Ma Changshan, *Lun Xing Zhen Fa Lu Guan Xi De Er Yuan Ji Gou* ("Comment on the Two Levels of Structure in Administrative Legal Relationship"), in *Collection of Legal Essays (Administrative Law) 1990*, Vol. 1, pp. 19–21.
7. See Luo and Ying 1989, pp. 12–17; Xu and Pi, pp. 62–69; Zheng Shangzhu, Pi and Hu, pp. 35–39.
8. See Zhang Shangzhu, Administrative Law, pp. 18–20.
9. See Luo and Ying 1989, pp. 12–13.
10. See Xu and Pi, p. 66.
11. See Luo and Ying 1989, p. 13.
12. Some scholars suggests that the contents of administrative legal relationship should

also include, apart from rights and obligations, the causes and facts inducing the change of legal relationship. See Luo and Ying 1989, p. 14.
[13] This is only one kind of classification. Other kinds of classification may also be made. See Luo and Ying 1989, p. 14.
[14] See Zhang Shangzhu, Administrative Law, pp. 20–22. See also Luo and Ying 1989, pp. 14–15.
[15] In the Western legal system, normally public consultation or prior notice are necessary for administrative organs, either to create new or change existing obligations unless national security or other justification may be provided as in GCHQ case.
[16] See Xu and Pi, p. 57.
[17] For the detailed description of the characteristics, refer to Xu and Pi, pp. 56–59.
[18] Compulsoriness is another expression of unequality whereas procedural legality may not be exclusive to administrative legal relationship. However, it is indeed very important in administrative law as failure to comply with legal procedures may cause the administrative acts undertaken to be challenged. See Xu and Pi, pp. 60–62.
[19] See Xu and Pi, pp. 60–62.
[20] See Xu and Pi, p. 60.
[21] See Zhao Jian Hua, *Wo Guo Xing Zhen Ji Guan Zai Xing Zhen Fa Lu Guan Xi Zhong De Quan Li Yi Wu* ("Rights and Obligations of Administrative Organs in Administrative Legal Relationship in China") in *Collection of Legal Essays (Administrative Law)* 1993, Vol. 2, pp. 28–29; see also Xu and Pi, p. 62.
[22] The classification of administrative legal relationship corresponds to the classification of administrative acts and relationships. Refer to the section on administrative acts.
[23] For detailed discussion of the kinds of administrative legal relationship subject to judicial review, refer to the section on the scope of judiciary in the latter chapter on judicial review.
[24] For detailed discussion of administrative contracts, refer to Ying Songnian, *Law on Administrative Acts*, chapter 16, People's Press, 1991, Beijing.
[25] There used to exist different views as to whether or not there exist separate fundamental principles for administrative law. For detailed discussion, refer to Xu and Pi, pp. 98–99. See also Zhang Shangzhu, Administrative Law, pp. 29–39.
[26] *Ibid*, p. 99.
[27] See Xu and Pi, pp. 106–08.
[28] See Xu and Pi, pp. 106–08.
[29] Zhou Weiping, in his article, made this further division. See Zhou Weiping, pp. 2–3.
[30] See Yang Haikun, *Lun Wo Guo Xing Zhen Fa De Ji Ben Yuan Ze* ("Analysis of the Basic Principles of Administrative Law in China"), in the *Collection of Legal Essays (Administrative Law)* 1990, Vol. 1, pp. 22–29.
[31] See Zhou Weiping, pp. 2–3. However, Professor Luo Haocai does not support this view. Instead, he holds that principles of administrative law should not be further divided. See Luo Haocai, *Administrative Law*, p. 26.
[32] See Zhang Zhen, *Shi Lun Wo Guo She Hui Zhu Yi Xing Zhen Fa De Ji Ben Yuan Ze* ("Discussion of the General Principles of Socialist Administrative Law in China"), in the *Collection of Legal Essays (Administrative Law) 1990*, Vol. 1, pp. 30–34.
[33] See the discussion on the principles of administrative reconsideration and judicial review.
[34] See Zhang Shangzhu, pp. 29–39.
[35] See Luo and Ying 1989, p. 37; also, Xu and Pi, p. 116; Zhang Shangzhu, p. 33. For the classification of legislation, refer to the chapter on applicable legislation.
[36] See Xu and Pi, p. 116.
[37] See Xu and Pi, pp. 116–18; Zhang, pp. 33–36; Luo and Ying 1989, pp. 37–39.
[38] As far as administrative law is concerned, most rules are developed by the judiciary.
[39] It should be noted that different views exist on whether or not departmental regulations and normative documents should be regarded as legislation. As to typical cases, they have legal effect in practice, though not in theory. Their effect seems to be limited to judiciary.
[40] See Luo and Ying 1989, p. 39. The principle will be further elaborated in the chapter on judicial review.

41 See Luo Haocai 1993, pp. 32–33.
42 It may be more appropriate to say that they are avoidable.
43 *Ibid.*
44 Mo Jihong and Xu Gao, *Jin Ji Zhuang Tai Fa Xue* (Law relating to Emergency), China People's Public Security University Press, 1992, Beijing.
45 See Mo Jihong and Xu Gao, pp. 22–27.
46 See Luo and Ying 1989, p. 41.
47 For detailed discussion of discretionary power, refer to the chapter on judicial control of the exercise of discretionary power.
48 The relationship between illegality and unreasonableness will be further discussed in the relevant section under administrative reconsideration and litigation.
49 See Luo and Ying 1989, p. 43.
50 See Xu and Pi, pp. 122–23. See also Zhang Shangzhu, pp. 36–39; Luo Haocai 1989, pp. 41–45.
51 Discussion of administrative acts is a popular topic of administrative law in China. Many academic works have been published. The most representative one is Professor Ying Songnian's book entitled *Law on Administrative Acts*.
52 See Ying Songnian, *Law on Administrative Acts*, the preface.
53 See Xu and Pi, p. 178.
54 *Ibid*, p. 179.
55 See Zhang Shangzhu, p. 169.
56 See Zhou Weiping, pp. 3–4.
57 For detailed discussion of the definition of administrative activities, see Xu and Pi, pp. 176–82; also Zhang Shangzhu, pp. 165–69.
58 See Zhou Weiping, pp. 3–4.
59 See Ying Songnian, pp. 1–2.
60 See Xu and Pi, p. 178; also Zhang Shangzhu, p. 169.
61 See Xu and Pi, pp. 182–84. These characteristics correspond with the characteristics of administrative legal relationship.
62 See Ying Songnian, pp. 1–2.
63 For detailed description of those 22 kinds of classification; see Xu and Pi, pp. 190–97. Professor Pi Chun Xie and Wu Dexing suggested 18 kinds of classification in their article entitled *Xing Zhen Xing Wei Feng Lei De Yan Jiu* ("Study of the Classification of Administrative Acts") in *Collection of Legal Essays (Administrative Law) 1991*, Vol. 1, pp. 39–42.
64 Ying Songnian, pp. 4–5.
65 A judicial definition is provided by the Supreme People's Court is s. 1 of the Opinions of the Supreme People's Court on Some Issues relating to the Implementation of the ALL.
66 Section 67 of the Constitution provides that:
  The Standing Committtee of the National People's Congress exercises the following functions and powers:
    (7) to annul those administrative rules and regulations, decisions or orders of the State Council that contravene the Constitution or the law;
    (8) to annul those local regulations or decisions of the organs of state power of provinces, autonomous regions, and municipalities directly under the Central Government that contravene the Constitution, the law or the administrative rules and regulations;
  Section 7 of the Organic Law of the Local People's Congresses and Local People's Governments of the People's Republic of China provides that:
  local people's congresses at and above the county level shall exercise the following functions and powers:
    (11) to alter or annul inappropriate resolutions and orders of the people's governments at the corresponding levels;
    (12) to alter or annul inappropriate resolutions of the people's congresses and inappropriate resolutions and orders of the people's governments at the next lower level.
67 See Ying Songnian, pp. 5–6.
68 See Liu, below n. 90, p. 16 and Sheyi, p. 38.
69 More detailed discussion will be provided in the latter part of the book when the

issues of scope of jurisdiction are discussed under administrative reconsideration and judicial review.

70 This classification has also its own problems. The main one is whether or not this classification has included all administrative acts. If so, in which category shall the act to issue normative documents fall. See Ying Songnian, p. 4.
71 See Ying Songnian, p. 4.
72 Refer to Xu and Pi for detailed discussion of those classification, pp. 190–97.
73 Professor Ying Songnian's treatise of *Law on Administrative Acts* is an example.
74 Professor Ying Songnian spends six chapters on the discussion of administrative legislation.
75 Scholars on legislation as represented by Professor Zhou Wangshang do not agree that administrative organs have inherent legislative power.
76 See Ying Songnian, p. 40.
77 See Ying Songnian, chapter 5, s. 4; discusses the procedure for administrative legislation in detail. The State Council enacted an interim regulation on the procedures for the enactment of administrative regulation in 1987.
78 See Ying Songnian, p. 43.
79 See Luo and Ying 1989, pp. 91–93; see also Ying Songnian, pp. 41–44.
80 This argument is supported by Zhou Weiping who maintains in his article that administrative legislation is an authority inherent in the administrative organ due to China's constitutional arrangement of the combination of the legislative and the executive powers in the National People's Congress and people's congresses at local levels. See Zhou Weiping, pp. 6–8. However, Professor Zhou Wangsheng does not agree to this opinion. He holds that the combination of legislative and executive powers only refer to people's congresses. The State Council and people's government at local levels are the executive organs of the people's congress at the corresponding level. The people's congresses at different levels enjoy legislative which does not mean that its executive organ also enjoys inherent legislative power.
81 See Luo and Ying 1989, pp. 94–100.
82 *Ibid*.
83 See Ying Songnian, pp. 93–168; also Zhou Wangsheng, Treatise on Legislation, pp. 426–427.
84 See Ying Songnian, p. 47; see also Zhou Wangshang, pp. 443–458.
85 See Ying Songnian, pp. 169–226.
86 Very few Chinese scholars discuss legal control of administrative legislative activities in great detail, they only mention the issue briefly, though most of them have realized the existence of the problem.
87 See ss. 62, 67, 89 and 108 of the Constitution.
88 See The Notice on the Recording of Regulation from Local Government and Various Department under the State Council, promulgated by the General Office of State Council on March 1, 1987, and The Notice on the Recording of Local Regulation, on May 25, 1987.
89 Refer to the discussion in the chapter on applicable legislation.
90 Many articles have been published discussing administrative implementaiton and enforcement of legislation. Liu Xue zheng, *Shi Lun Xing Zhen Zhi Fa* ("Analysis of Administrative Implementation of Legislation") in the *Collection of Legal Essays (Administrative Law) 1990*, Vol. 2, pp. 54–58; Zhou Guochao, *Xing Zhen Ji Guan Zhi Fa Zhou Yi* ("Analysis of Implementation of Legislation by Administrative Organs"), in *Collection of Legal Essays (Administrative Law) 1990*, Vol. 2, pp. 59–62; Cui Zhuolan, *Xing Zhen Zhi Fa Xing Wei Cheng Xu Zhou Yi* ("Discussion of the Procedures for Administrative Implementation Acts") in the *Collective of Legal Essays (Administrative Law) 1990*, Vol. 2, pp. 63–65; Zhou Wei, and Zhang Jie, *Guan Yu Xing Zhen Zhi Fa Wen Ti De Yan Jiu* ("Examination of Issues relating to Administrative Implementation and Enforcement") in the *Collection of Legal Essays (Administrative Law) 1990*, Vol. 2, pp. 761–73; Li Pei Chuan, *Gia Qiang Zhen Fu Fa Zhi Jian She Ji Ji Jian Li He Wan Shan Xing Zheng Zhi Fa Jian Du Ji Zhi* ("Strengthening the Establishment of Legal System of Government and Actively Establishing and Improving the Supervisory Mechanism of Administrative Implementation and Enforcement of Legislation") in the *Collection of Legal Essays (Administrative Law) 1991*, Vol. 2, pp. 1–6.

[91] See Luo and Ying 1989, pp. 133–135, p. 174.
[92] See Zhou Wei and Zhang Jie, pp. 71–78.
[93] See Ying Songnian pp. 328–31. See also Luo and Ying 1989, pp. 135–36.
[94] See Jiang Mingli, *Jia Qiang He Gai Jing Xing Zheng Zhi Fa De Si Kao* ("Thoughts on Strengthening and Improving Administrative Implementation of Legislation") in *Collection of Legal Essays (Administrative Law)*, 1993, Vol. 3, pp. 11–14.
[95] Professor Ying has discussed administrative licensing action in detail in chapter 11 of his book, pp. 418–59; see also Yang Haikun, *Xing Zhen Xu Ke Jian Lun* (An Overview of Administrative Licensing) at pp. 162–69; Wang Pingping, *Gui Fan Xing Zhen Xu Ke Zou Yi* (The Regulation of Administrative Licence), at pp. 70–71 in the *Collection of Legal Essays (Administrative Law)* 1992, Vol. 2; see also He Sanzhen, *Shi Lun Te Xu Zhi Du* (Examination of Licensing System) at pp. 89–92, and Shi Xiaojie, *Lun Xing Zhen Xu Ke De Xing Ze* ("Analysis of the Characteristics of Administrative Licensing") in *Collection of Legal Essays (Administrative Law) 1993* at pp. 93–96, Vol. 3.
[96] See Ying Songnian, p. 418.
[97] See Ying Songnian, p. 427.
[98] See Ying Songnian, pp. 437–38.
[99] Different opinions exist with regard to the nature of licensing actions. But it is agreed that the applicants will obtain certain rights once licences are granted. See Ying Songnian, pp. 421–22.
[100] See Ying Songnian, pp. 448–52.
[101] See Ying Songnian, p. 444.
[102] Wang Yan, *Xing Zhen Si Fa Fan Wei Tan Xi* ("Analysis of the Scope of Administrative Adjudication"), at pp. 1–5 in the *Collection of Legal Essays (Administrative Law) 1992*, Vol. 3.
[103] See Luo and Ying, pp. 178–179.
[104] In Chinese history, executive and judiciary were combined in one. It was common practice for an administrative organ at a higher level to deal with disputes relating to those at lower level. That was adopted by communist party to a certain extent in its early years. But its theoretical basis was different. See Ying Songnian, pp. 665–68.
[105] Detailed discussion of the administrative reconsideration system shall be dealt with in the next chapter of this book.
[106] Detailed discussion of administrative reconsideration system will be discussed in the next chapter.
[107] Some scholars have treated this category as a special kind of administrative reconsideration.
[108] There exist four different views on administrative compulsory enforcement. The reasons causing such differences are relating to a different understanding of the subjects, objects and grounds for administrative compulsory enforcement. For details, see Ying Songnian, pp. 520–23.
[109] See Ying Songnian, pp. 539–41.
[110] See Ying Songnian, pp. 537–38.
[111] Refer to previous section on administrative legislation.
[112] See Ying Songnian, pp. 543–47.
[113] See Luo and Ying 1989, p. 149.
[114] See Luo and Ying 1989, p. 150.
[115] See Chen Yanging and Zhang Shicheng, *Xing Zheng Chu Fa Fa Di Yi Yi Jie Qi Ji Ban Yuan Ze* ("The Meaning of Administrative Penalty Law and Its Basic Principles") *Zhong Guo Fa Xue*, 1995, pp. 40–46.
[116] See Luo and Ying, pp. 155–56.
[117] Each of these topics has a separate chapter on the Administrative Penalty Law.
[118] See s. 2 of the Administrative Penalty Law.
[119] For details, see chapter 3 of the Administrative Penalty Law of the People's Republic of China.
[120] See s. 24 of the Administrative Penalty Law 1996.
[121] See ss. 33–43 of the Administrative Penalty Law 1996.
[122] See Luo and Ying 1989, p. 209.
[123] See Luo and Ying 1989, pp. 212–13.
[124] See Luo and Ying 1989, p. 214.
[125] For detailed discussion of administrative supervision, see Fang Sheng and He

Weihong, *Study of the Regulation on Administrative Supervision*, Hunan Press, 1992.
[126] For more detailed discussion of the acts of state, refer to the relevant section in Part 3 of this book.

PART 2

ADMINISTRATIVE RECONSIDERATION

CHAPTER THREE

THE STRUCTURE OF ADMINISTRATIVE RECONSIDERATION[1]

Introduction

Administrative reconsideration is, in nature, an administrative activity undertaken by the executive branch of the government. It is a kind of concrete administrative act taken by the administrative organ at the higher level above or any other organs provided by law or regulation after reconsidering, upon the application of the relative parties, the original concrete administrative act with which citizens, legal persons or any other organizations, are not satisfied and appeal against.[2] It could either be described as an administrative-judicial activity by the administrative bodies to handle disputes caused by administrative activities in accordance with law, or a legal mechanism established by law for aggrieved parties to bring an action for reconsideration of the original decision. The main intention is, as mentioned above, to establish an internal supervisory system within the administration to ensure that all public administrative activities will be carried out according to law and the legitimate interests of those under administration will be protected.[3]

Administrative reconsideration has been described as an important remedial measure to resolve administrative disputes, *i.e.* disputes relating to the exercise of executive power. This part of the book will examine the system of administrative reconsideration in China and the way it functions to resolve disputes.

3.01

Sources and Development of Administrative Reconsideration

Constitutional Source and the Development of Administrative Reconsideration[4]

It is a relatively new concept in China to keep the public administration under proper legal control. Section 41 of the 1982 Constitution recognizes such necessity for the first time. It provides that:

> Citizens of the People's Republic of China have the right to criticize and make suggestions regarding any state organ or functionary. Citizens have the right to make to relevant state organs complaints or charges against, or exposures of, any state organ or functionary for violation of the law or dereliction of duty; but fabrication or distortion of facts for purposes of libel or false incrimination is prohibited.
>
> The state organ concerned must deal with complaints, charges or exposures made by citizens in a responsible manner after ascertaining the facts. No one may suppress such complaints, charges and exposures or retaliate against the citizens making them.
>
> Citizens who have suffered losses as a result of infringement of their civic rights by any state organ or functionary have the right to compensation in accordance with the law.

3.02 After the promulgation of the 1982 Constitution and before the adoption of the 1990 Regulation on Administrative Reconsideration (RAR), the system of administrative reconsideration had already been provided in more than 100 laws and regulations. They have touched upon many areas of public administration, including entry and exit (China) administration, public security, election of (both national and local) people's congresses, public gathering, patent application and registration, telecommunication, domestic and foreign trade, transportation, labour administration, and so on. Every province, autonomous region and municipality under direct administration of the State Council have enacted some local regulations which have incorporated administrative reconsideration as a method of administrative dispute resolution.[5] It has been submitted that those provisions had contributed to the effective resolution of administrative disputes and strengthening of supervision by administrative organs.[6] With the adoption of the Administrative Litigation Law, the importance of administrative reconsideration has become even more obvious and the requirement of administrative reconsideration has been enhanced. It is because the ALL has provided that the aggrieved party may apply for administrative reconsideration before bringing a case for judicial review. Moreover, one source has revealed that about 90 per cent of administrative litigation cases and 85 per cent of public security cases have been through the stage of administrative reconsideration.[7]

However, many important issues regarding administrative reconsideration, such as the conditions for application, jurisdiction, scope of reconsideration and procedures for handling reconsideration cases were not stipulated in any legislation prior to the promulgation of the RAR. All these justify the prompt adoption of a relevant legislation. The Legislative Affairs Bureau of the State Council took the initiative to draft the regulation in July 1989 and consulted the Legislative Affairs Commission of the National People's Congress, Supreme People's Court, Supreme People's Procuratorate, various ministries, provincial governments, legal scholars and experts, and so on. The regulation was adopted by the State Council in 1990, with effect from January 1, 1991.

Other Legal Sources of the Regulation on Administrative Reconsideration

As the RAR is a piece of secondary legislation enacted by the State Council, its legal status is lower than primary legislation adopted by the National People's Congress or its Standing Committee. It must also rely on certain primary legislation. It is clearly mentioned in section 1 of the RAR that the Constitution and other pertinent laws are the legal source. However, it is not clear what these pertinent laws are.

3.03

One interpretation is that the term of pertinent laws include the Administrative Litigation Law 1989, the Organic Law of the State Council of the People's Republic of China 1982, the Organic Law of the Local People's Congresses and the Local People's Governments of the People's Republic of China 1979 and other laws which have incorporated provisions on administrative reconsideration (*e.g.* Land Administration Law of the People's Republic of China 1986). It virtually covers all primary legislation which provides for administration reconsideration.[8]

It is a feasible argument in the sense that all those primary legislation usually provides that administrative reconsideration is available. But they do not have any detailed provisions as to which administrative organ will have jurisdiction, what procedure is supposed to be followed, and some other procedural issues. The RAR has therefore clarified, and given foundation to those provisions in primary legislation. Moreover, the RAR has provided for the scope of administrative reconsideration. That has made it no longer necessary to stipulate the availability of administrative reconsideration in every primary or subsidiary legislation, apart from those not falling within the listed categories of the regulation.[9]

Nature and Function of Administrative Reconsideration[10]

3.04 The main purpose of enacting the RAR is, as provided by section 1 of the RAR, to safeguard and supervise administrative organs by exercising their functions and powers, prevent and correct any malfeasant or improper concrete administrative acts, and protect the lawful rights and interests of citizens, legal persons and other organizations. This legislative purpose reveals that the activity of administrative reconsideration has several impacts upon the administrative organs which have exercised their authorities and made the relevant decisions, and with the intention of achieving several results.

As to the exact nature of administrative reconsideration, scholars hold different views. One approach is that administrative reconsideration as a means to resolve administrative disputes is a grant of dispute resolution authority from the judiciary to the administration, though such a grant is at lower level and is limited. It should be distinguished from ordinary administrative supervision for two reasons: administrative reconsideration is brought by third parties external to the administrative organ; and the direct objective of administrative reconsideration is to protect the legitimate interests of the third parties.[11] Moreover, administrative reconsideration plays the function of dispute resolution which is similar to the function played by the judiciary. Because of these reasons, administrative reconsideration should be regarded as an administrative judicial activity or quasi-judicial activity.

Some other scholars hold a different view. They maintain that administrative reconsideration lacks the fundamental feature of judicial activity, *i.e.* impartiality as an independent third party to the dispute for its resolution. It is, in nature, only an internal administrative supervision by administrative organs at higher levels over those at lower levels. Moreover, most reconsideration decisions are still subject to judicial review. Therefore, it should only be treated as an administrative supervisory activity instead of quasi-judicial act.[12]

These two approaches have emphasized different aspects of administrative reconsideration. The first approach emphasizes its function of dispute resolution. The second one emphasizes its nature, *i.e.* it remains part of administration. These are the two main characteristics of administrative reconsideration. As to the exact objective or legislative purpose of the RAR, it has been generally accepted that they are the following.[13]

Protection of Legitimate Interests of the Those under Administration

The first objective of the RAR is to protect the legitimate interests of the citizens, legal persons and other organizations. Chinese Constitution assures that citizens' rights and freedom enjoy practical and effective protection.[14] To serve the people is also the purpose of state governmental organs. In modern society, public administration is getting more and more complicated and diversified. Government has been involved in all sorts of activities. Whenever a decision is made by a governmental organ, it is bound to affect the citizens, legal persons and other organizations in one way or another. In every country, especially a developing country like China, it is quite natural that certain administrative tortious activities are committed. Furthermore, it should not be surprising, as reality shows in China, that some state administrative organs or their functionaries may, while exercising their authorities, misuse or even abuse their powers. As a result of that, the interests of the relevant parties will be affected. Administrative disputes will arise.

Therefore, the state should provide remedial measures for the aggrieved parties to redress their grievance and get compensation wherever it is appropriate. Administrative reconsideration is one of such remedial measures. It is of administrative nature as it is an administrative organ at the same level or the higher level will, through reconsidering the original decision, maintain, rescind or change an illegal or inappropriate concrete administrative act so as to effectively protect the legitimate interests of the aggrieved parties.

3.05

Supervision of Those under Administration

Another function of administrative reconsideration is to supervise the administrative organs in exercising their functions and powers. Through administrative reconsideration, the administrative organ at a higher level may examine the concrete decisions made by the organ at a lower level in order to see whether it is illegal or inappropriate. If it is, then a respective decision will be made to rectify the wrong committed by the original administrative organ. In so doing, the illegal or inappropriate concrete administrative act can be rectified within the system of administration without resorting to judicial system, *i.e.* administrative litigation. There are obvious advantages. Firstly, it is to reduce the workload of the people's courts, which are already overburdened. Secondly, it may speed up the grievance addressing process and

3.06

the efficiency of administration. However, as the whole process is within the administration, it is quite natural for the aggrieved parties to have suspicion that the administrative reconsideration organ may be biased and therefore its decision will not be impartial.[15] That has, in fact, been proved in many cases.[16]

Protection of Administrative Efficiency

3.07 The above two functions serve mainly to guarantee that administrative power is exercised properly and according to law so that the relevant parties' interests can be protected. However, administrative reconsideration has another equally important role to play, *i.e.* to protect and maintain administrative decisions taken properly according to law. Administrative reconsideration is provided by legislation and has to be conducted according to the conditions and procedures as laid down in the RAR. The aggrieved party has to follow strictly those conditions and procedures. Moreover, it is provided that administrative reconsideration shall apply a single-level system of reconsideration[17] apart from very few legislation providing double or multiple reconsideration. This provision can prevent the aggrieved party from bothering the administrative organ indefinitely and the legality of a concrete administrative act can be recognized in time and the efficiency of administration can be guaranteed. If the aggrieved party is still not satisfied with the decision of the administrative reconsideration organ, it may, under most circumstances, bring an action for administrative litigation to the people's court.

These three objectives may well conflict with each other in reality when the system of administrative reconsideration is in operation. Therefore a balance needs to be achieved between different objectives.

Conditions for Administrative Reconsideration[18]

3.08 In order to bring a case for administrative reconsideration, the aggrieved party must prove that the following conditions are satisfied. Firstly, the party to be appealed against must be administrative organs, and legal persons or other organizations which are authorized by laws or regulations to exercise executive powers. It covers two situations. One is that administrative organs are directly involved in disputes with the aggrieved party through exercising their administrative powers. The other is that the party complained against is non-governmental organs or other organizations which are nevertheless authorized by laws or regulations to exercise administrative power. For example,

CONDITIONS FOR ADMINISTRATIVE RECONSIDERATION

professional banks are authorized to exercise certain management authorities. If an aggrieved party is not satisfied with their decisions, it can appeal to the people's bank at the same level.[19]

The second condition is that an aggrieved party can only apply for administrative reconsideration when he believes that his own lawful rights or interests have been infringed upon by the concrete act of an administrative organ or its functionary. It should be noted that it suffices that the aggrieved party genuinely believes he has a case and there does not have to be real infringement. It is a subjective test. This is only one of the conditions for the applicant to bring a case for reconsideration. This right does not imply that the administrative organ involved has committed tortious action and the applicant is therefore entitled to compensation. That is not the case as it may well be that what the administrative organ did is perfectly lawful but still constitutes restriction or limit upon the lawful rights or interests of the aggrieved party. Only infringement caused by unlawful or inappropriate administrative act may lead to compensation.[20]

One related issue is whether the applicant should be a person under the administration of the relevant administrative organ. A literal interpretation of section 2, combined with section 26 and section 31(1), will lead to the conclusion that anybody will do, as long as he believes that his interests have been affected by the concrete administrative acts of the relevant administrative organ. It is not a right exclusive to the person under administration. Practically speaking, the interests of those not under administration may well be affected by the decisions of the latter.[21]

The third condition is that only a concrete administrative act can be reconsidered. A concrete administrative act refers to an administrative act, taken in the process of administration, which affects the rights and obligations of specific citizens, legal persons or other organizations.[22] For example, the refusal by the land administration bureau to grant land-use rights illegally or unreasonably. Excluded are abstract administrative acts and other acts. Other acts include administrative organs' acts to handle civil affairs or civil affairs conducted by the administrative organs themselves.[23]

Sometimes relevant laws or regulations may also provide that the aggrieved party must fulfill the obligations imposed by the concrete administrative act before bringing a case against that decision. Taxation law provides a typical example. If a person is not satisfied with a decision of a taxation bureau, he has to pay the tax first before he can bring a case for reconsideration. The exact legislative intention behind such legislation is not clearly defined. It may well be to ensure that revenue can be properly collected and the efficiency of administration can be guaranteed, and to discourage certain parties from abusing the right to administrative reconsideration.[24]

Once an application for administrative reconsideration is lodged, it **3.09**

THE STRUCTURE OF ADMINISTRATIVE RECONSIDERATION

has to be reviewed by the administrative reconsideration organ first. Only if certain legal conditions are satisfied can the application be accepted. Those conditions are provided by section 31 of the RAR as follows:

i. the applicant shall be a citizen, a legal person, or any other organization that holds that a concrete administrative act has directly infringed upon his/her or its lawful rights and interests;
ii. there must be a specific defending party or parties of an applications;
iii. there must be a specific claim for reconsideration and a corresponding factual basis;
iv. the case must fall within the scope for application for reconsideration;
v. the case must fall under the jurisdiction of the administrative organ that accepts the said case;
vi. other requirements stipulated by the laws and regulations.

Once all the above-mentioned conditions have been satisfied, the applicant will have the standing. If an application for reconsideration has been filed, the administrative reconsideration organ shall not refuse to accept or fail to respond to the application without any proper justification. Sometimes the administrative reconsideration organ may simply refuse to accept, or not make a decision on whether or not to accept the application after the expiration of the time limit for application, or intentionally lay down obstacles to delay the application which will soon exceed the time limit. Late application for reconsideration may also be caused by the fault or negligence of the staff in the administrative reconsideration organ, or any unforeseeable situations caused by the administrative organ which caused the excess of the time limit.[25]

If the administrative reconsideration organ refuses to accept an application for any of the reasons mentioned above, it shall be classified as refusal without proper reasons. And the administrative organ at the next higher level or the administrative organ prescribed by the laws or regulations, shall instruct the said administrative reconsideration organ to accept the said application or to respond to the application.[26] Only under grounds provided by laws or regulations can the administrative reconsideration organ refuse to accept an application.

Administrative Reconsideration Organs[27]

3.10 The administrative reconsideration organs refer to those administrative organs which accept applications for reconsideration, and shall, according to laws and regulations conduct review of concrete administrative acts, and make decisions accordingly. Not all administrative organs will undertake the task of administrative reconsideration. State Council is, as the highest administrative organ, logically speaking, supposed to undertake responsibility of administrative reconsideration. However, the RAR provides the contrary. The reason is to relieve the State Council of getting too involved in specific affairs. Therefore, any complaints against provincial, autonomous regional and autonomous municipal people's governments will be handled by them respectively. Similarly any complaints against any ministries will be dealt with by them. Secondly, any departments under county people's government, which do not have any further established institutions under their control, will not have the responsibility of administrative reconsideration. For those departments which have further established institutions under their control, they will not have the responsibility if the further established institutions do not perform the concrete administrative acts in their own names. The responsibility remains in the hands of county people's government. Thirdly, township people's governments do not have the responsibility because they are at the grassroots level and do not have any working departments under their control.[28]

It is not those administrative organs that actually reconsider the original concrete administrative acts. Instead, there are reconsideration offices which are set up within the administrative organs for reconsideration and are responsible for the affairs relating to the reconsideration. Such offices are internal components of administrative organs and do not have the status of independent legal persons as administrative organs. They can not therefore make any decisions in their own names. They just review the legality and appropriateness of concrete administrative acts. All decisions have to be finally made in the name of the administrative organs to which they belong.[29]

Structure (or Organization) of Administrative Reconsideration

The structure (or organization) of administrative reconsideration and its personnel are essential to the effectiveness of administrative reconsideration system. Without well-qualified personnel to actually conduct administrative reconsideration and a proper structure of reconsideration office, it will be extremely difficult to achieve the legislative objectives. The RAR does not have any detailed provisions as to what structure should be adopted for administrative reconsideration offices and what the qualification of their personnel should be. The reconsideration office is an office established within an administrative reconsideration organ to handle specifically reconsideration

3.11

THE STRUCTURE OF ADMINISTRATIVE RECONSIDERATION

cases. It is different from administrative organs in that it does not have independent legal personality and only acts in the name of the administrative reconsideration organ. It is not compulsory to set up a reconsideration office for all administrative organs. It depends wholly on the necessity and the number of cases. As administrative reconsideration deals with various kinds of cases, many of which require special expertise, it would make sense to appoint either some full-time personnel or set up a special office to handle reconsideration cases to develop the necessary expertise. That may also contribute to the reduction of potential judicial review cases if the administrative reconsideration office or personnel can work effectively to discover and rectify immediately those illegal or inappropriate action.[30]

There exist different kinds of administrative reconsideration offices. There are three main types. One is the administrative organ at the next higher level. There are two possibilities for this: firstly, the people's government which is at the same level of the administrative organ undertaking the concrete administrative act; section 13 of the 1989 Law on Assemblies, Processions and Demonstrations states, "If the person(s) responsible for an assembly, a procession or a demonstration does not accept the competent authorities' decision not to grant permission, he may apply to the people's government at the same level for reconsideration within three days of receiving the notice on the decision, and the people's government shall make a decision within three days of receiving the application for reconsideration." Secondly, the administrative organ at the next level above. For example section 39 of the 1986 Regulation of the PRC on Administrative Penalties for Public Security states:

> If an offender or victim protests the ruling of the public security organ or the people's governments of townships or towns, he may petition the public security organs at the next higher level within five days after receiving the notice, and the public security organs at the next higher level shall make a new ruling within five days after receiving the petition. Whoever protests the ruling of the public security organ at the next higher level may file suit with the local people's court within five days after the notice.[31]

The second is the original body which undertakes the concrete administrative act. For example, section 53 of the 1987 Customs Law of the PRC provides:

> If the party concerned objects to the Customs decision of punishment, he may hand in an application for reconsideration of the case, either to the Customs establishment making the decision or to one at the next higher level within 30 days of the receipt of the notification on punishment or, in case notification is impossible, within 30 days of the public announcement of

punishment. If the party concerned finds the decision reached after reconsideration still unacceptable, he may file a suit in a people's court within 30 days of the receipt of the decision. The party concerned may also file a suit directly in a people's court within 30 days of the receipt of the notification on punishment or within 30 days of the public announcement of the punishment. If the party concerned refuses to carry out the Customs decision and fails to apply for a reconsideration of the case or file a suit in a people's court within the prescribed time limit, the Customs establishment making the decision of punishment may confiscate the deposit of the party concerned or sell off the goods, articles or means of transport it has detained to substitute for the penalty, or ask the people's court for mandatory execution of the decision.

The third type is a specially established reconsideration office such as those established under the Trademark Law and Patent Law. Such organs are similar to administrative tribunals available in Western countries. Their procedures and working rules are similar to their counterparts in the judiciary. It should be pointed out that such special committees are not responsible solely for administrative reconsideration cases. They usually also deal with other cases within the same category.

Under the leadership of the administrative reconsideration organ, the reconsideration office or personnel has the following functions or duties to carry out, *i.e.* to review whether reconsideration applications are in conformity with the statutory requirements; to conduct investigations among, and collect evidence from, both parties to a dispute and relevant units and personnel, and to consult relevant documents and materials; to organize the handling of reconsideration cases; to draft reconsideration decisions; to respond to prosecution in court, as entrusted by the legal representative of the administrative reconsideration organ; and to carry out other functions and duties stipulated by the laws and regulations.[32]

Principles of Administrative Reconsideration[33]

Principles of administrative reconsideration refer to those principles underlying the whole process of administrative reconsideration. They should be defined through legislation, particularly the RAR. They include no unlawful interference, legality, timeliness, accuracy, convenience for the people, one level jurisdiction, no conciliation, written jurisdiction, and so on. Some Chinese scholars have argued that these principles are unique to administrative reconsideration.[34] That approach is debatable. An examination of other procedural legislation in

3.12

China, such as civil procedural law, criminal procedural law and administrative procedural law, shall reveal that some of those principles mentioned above, such as legality, timeless, accuracy and convenience, are also included in the other three procedural legislation. Therefore it seems that those principles can be argued to be the general principles essential to judicial resolution of disputes. Some other principles may be argued to be exclusive to administrative reconsideration.[35]

Legality

3.13 Legality is by far the most important principle which any administrative reconsideration has to comply with. It has several requirements. Firstly, the organ exercising the authority of administrative reconsideration should be lawful. That means the organ should be duly established according to law and be granted the authority of administrative reconsideration under law or regulation. All the applications do fall within its jurisdiction. Secondly, administrative reconsideration is not only an authority of respective administrative organs, but also their legal obligations. They should not therefore refuse to accept any applications which have complied with the legal conditions.[36] Thirdly, administrative organs for reconsideration should exercise its authority strictly according to legal authorization and legal procedure laid down in the RAR.[37] Fourthly, the legal basis for reviewing reconsideration cases should be lawful. That is to say that all the legislation relied on by the administrative organ for reconsideration should be valid at the moment. Legislation may include the Constitution, the laws, administrative regulations, local regulations and other normative documents adopted by administrative organs at the higher levels.[38] There are several situations under which the legislation cannot not be used as a basis, *i.e.* the legislation was not promulgated, or had lost its legal validity, or contradictory to legislation at the level above and therefore be annulled when the concrete administrative act to be complained against was made.[39] Finally, administrative reconsideration should be independent and not be illegally interfered with by any other organs, public organizations and individuals.

It has been argued that the organ at the higher level in charge of administrative reconsideration has the administrative authority to interfere if it so wishes. However, it should only interfere if there is any element illegal found in the process of reconsideration process. It is correct to say that administrative organs at higher level have a supervisory role to play over those at lower level. However, administrative reconsideration is a system established by legislation. Everything relating to reconsideration has to be done according to the RAR. It is therefore debatable whether or not all administrative organs at higher level shall have supervision over administrative reconsideration conducted by those at lower level. Moreover, the interference should be conducted according to law. Any illegal interference should be turned down by the administrative reconsideration organ.

Timeliness[40]

3.14 Timeliness is another principle that needs to be followed in administrative reconsideration. Administrative reconsideration is a means of internal supervision by the administrative organ at the next higher level within the administration.[41] Under most circumstances, it is not final and still subject to judicial supervision, *i.e.* judicial review. Administrative reconsideration has, therefore, the nature of both administration and judiciary. A balance between administrative efficiency and justice has to be achieved somewhere along the line. The principle of timeliness must be followed throughout the process of administrative reconsideration. Firstly, the acceptance of application must be timely.[42] After receiving the application, the administrative organ for reconsideration should review the application in time to see whether all legal conditions are satisfied and then make the decision as to whether or not to accept the case. Secondly, the reviewing process must be timely. That means the organ should, after receiving the case, conduct investigation, collection of evidence and material, and so on, as soon as possible and without any undue delay. Thirdly, to reach a decision on the legality or appropriateness of the original concrete administrative act timely. Fourthly, to handle the failure to comply with the decision of administrative reconsideration organ timely. If necessary, application can be made by the party concerned to the people's court for enforcement. If the failure to comply with the reconsideration decision is due to the fault of administrative organ concerned, the relevant person in charge may be held responsible and face administrative punishment.[43]

In the case of *Jiayuguan Branch of Xilin Engineering & Construction Corporation v. Jiayuguan Municipal Taxation Bureau*, the plaintiff applied to the administrative reconsideration organ for reconsideration of a decision made by the defendant, the reconsideration organ failed to make a decision in two months. The plaintiff then brought the case for judicial review. The people's court accepted the case. Judicial review can be an alternative to administrative reconsideration.

Accuracy

3.15 Accuracy is the third principle to be followed in administrative reconsideration. It mainly refers to accuracy in the process of reviewing cases by administrative reconsideration organs. It has two aspects. Firstly, it is the accuracy in the identification organ of the facts and any other matters relating to administrative reconsideration cases. It is because the accuracy in identifying the facts is the pre-condition to a fair result. Secondly, the accuracy in the application of legislation. The staff in charge of actual administrative reconsideration should properly understand the meaning of relevant legal provisions and rely on them to determine whether or not the concrete administrative act is legal or appropriate.[44]

Convenience to the People

3.16 Convenience to the people is the fourth principle laid down by the RAR. This requires the administrative reconsideration organ to always keep in mind the necessity to provide convenience to the parties concerned and do whatever they can to make sure that they can fully exercise their right to apply for administrative reconsideration. For example, the administrative reconsideration organ is expected to take oral statement from the applicant who is unable to write and then ask him to sign the statement to form a written application for reconsideration. Moreover, no other means of review should be taken whenever written review is appropriate and capable of resolving the problem. In so doing, the applicant can avoid unnecessary waste of time, expenses and energy.[45] After the amendment to the RAR, certain kinds of reconsideration cases will be considered by the people's government at the same level of the administrative organ undertaking the concrete administrative act. It is because they normally situate in the same city where the applicant is located, which will be convenient to the applicant.[46]

No Conciliation

3.17 The fifth principle is that conciliation is not allowed in handling reconsideration cases. Conciliation or mediation is an important means of dispute resolution and is often given priority and encouraged by Chinese legislation.[47] However, it cannot be applied to administrative reconsideration due to the nature of administrative reconsideration. Administrative disputes arise when the aggrieved party is not satisfied with the concrete administrative act taken in the process of administrative organs' exercise of executive power. The administrative organ is, as one party to the dispute, exercising its executive power, which is a right and also a legal obligation. The administrative organ concerned has to execute faithfully its obligation according to law. It

Others

Apart from the principles mentioned above, there are a couple of other principles which have been advocated by Chinese scholars. One is one level jurisdiction. It means that, unless otherwise provided by legislation, administrative reconsideration will only be conducted once. If the aggrieved party is not satisfied with the administrative reconsideration decision, it cannot bring the case to a higher administrative organ for second reconsideration.[49] The main consideration behind is that administrative reconsideration decisions are usually not final. Even if two or three levels of reconsideration are provided for, the aggrieved party may still bring a case for judicial review. In this sense, more levels of reconsideration will not necessarily contribute to successful resolution of the dispute. It may even slow down the whole process of dispute resolution. That is not consistent with the requirement of administrative efficiency. However, there are exceptions to this principle. For certain highly technical or professional concrete administrative acts, several levels of reconsideration are stipulated to enable the expertise of those administrative organs be better used. One example is section 46 of the Customs Law which provides:

3.18

> Where the obligatory Customs duty payer is involved in a dispute over duty payment with the Customs, he shall first pay the duties and may, within 30 days of the issuance of the duty memorandum, apply to the Customs in writing for a reconsideration of the case. The Customs shall reach a decision within 15 days of the receipt of the application. If the obligatory customs duty payer refuses to accept the decision, he may apply to the General Customs Administration for a reconsideration of the case within 15 days of the receipt of the decision. If the decision of the General Customs Administration is still considered unacceptable by the obligatory customs duty payer, he may file a suit in a people's court within 15 days of the receipt of the decision.

Another principle is a vertical jurisdiction, mainly based on the consideration of familiarity with work within the same administrative system. This needs to be balanced with the principle of convenience.

Grounds for Administrative Reconsideration

There are two main grounds for administrative reconsideration. One is illegality and the other is inappropriateness. That means the adminis-

3.19

trative reconsideration organ can review whether or not the concrete administrative act is legal or appropriate. Legality covers three different aspects. The first one is whether or not the administrative organ taking the concrete administrative act has exceeded its lawful authority; the second is whether the concrete administrative act complies with the provisions of laws and regulations; and the third is whether the administrative organ taking the concrete administrative act has followed the legal procedure.⁵⁰ Moreover, a concrete administrative act taken without sufficient evidence, through abuse of power, or *ultra vires* is also regarded as illegal. It is therefore not difficult to see that the concept of illegality in China's administrative reconsideration is much wider than its counterpart in common law.⁵¹ The following is a case where illegality has been argued.

Wu v. Tianhe Township People's Government[52]

3.20 Wu (the plaintiff) applied to the Tianhe Township People's Government (the defendant) for the construction of a three-bedroom house of 148.2 square metres in 1987. This was subsequently approved by the defendant. In September 1989, a dispute arose between Wu and his neighbour about the size of the land used for construction. The defendant carried out inspection and found out that the land Wu had occupied was 15 square metres more than what had been approved. On October 7, 1989, according to the Notice on Land Administration in Tianhe Township, issued by the Township People's Government, the defendant imposed a fine of RMB1,000 upon the plaintiff and requested the plaintiff to go to the defendant to re-register the occupied land and get another land-use certificate. Dissatisfied with the decision, Wu filed an action to the people's court on October 13. During the process of litigation, the defendant revoked its sanction against the plaintiff. The plaintiff applied for the withdrawal of his case from the people's court which was approved.

This is a case concerning land administration which should be governed by the 1986 Land Administrative Law of the PRC. Section 44(2) of the law states that "if the amount of land occupied exceeds the approved amount, the excessive portion shall be handled as in the case of unlawful encroachment of land." Section 45 of the law provides that "Rural residents who unlawfully encroach upon land to build residences without approval or with fraudulently obtained approval shall be ordered to return such land and demolish within a definite period of time, the houses newly built on such land, or such newly built houses shall be confiscated." The law does not grant the township people's government the authority to impose a fine upon those who encroach upon the land. But the local normative document issued by the township people's government provides that a fine of RMB100 to RMB2,000 may be imposed. Such provision is obviously in conflict with the Land

Administration Law and therefore should be void. According to the hierarchy of legislation, the Tianhe Township People's Government should apply the Land Administration Law instead of the local Township People's Government's Notice.

Inappropriateness[53]

3.21 The other ground is inappropriateness of concrete administrative acts. This ground is concerned mainly with the exercise of discretionary power. It is impossible for laws and regulations to make detailed provisions in every aspect. There are bound to be discretion left of the executive, *i.e.* administrative organs. If an administrative organ exercises its discretionary power within its limits, the concrete act undertaken will be lawful. But it may not be appropriate or reasonable. That is how the issue of inappropriateness arises. The RAR grants the administrative reconsideration organ the power to review the appropriateness of a concrete act. If a concrete act is inappropriate or unreasonable,[54] then the administrative reconsideration organ may alter or change the concrete act partially or completely, depending on the necessity. As an inappropriate act is a lawful one, review of inappropriateness will only take place after the review of the legality of the concrete act. It is therefore at the second level. It should be noted that the exercise of discretionary power may also be unlawful. One scholar has argued that abuse of discretionary should be treated as unlawful concrete administrative act.[55]

A concrete administrative act may become inappropriate due to various reasons. A decision may be inappropriate if the decision maker takes into account irrelevant consideration or fails to take into account relevant consideration. It may be inappropriate if the decision is unfair because of unproportionality, or unequal treatment or unusual deviation from generally accepted customs. A decision may be inappropriate if the decision maker adopts improper method. A decision may also be inappropriate if there is undue delay in the undertaking of a concrete administrative act.[56] These are just some examples of possible inappropriate administrative acts. The fundamental criterion to determine whether or not an administrative act is appropriate seems to be the principle of reasonableness. The following is a case where the ground of inappropriateness is invoked.

Li v. Public Security Bureau at X Administrative Prefecture[57]

3.22 On their way to X county on March 3, 1989 Li, together with her mother and two sisters, met Zhang at the bus station where they quarrelled because of an event that happened in the past. In the afternoon of the next day, Li went to work by bicycle. When she got close to the bus station, Zhang ran towards her and dragged her down from her bicycle. Together with her younger sister, Zhang struck Li on the floor and pulled her clothes off causing Li's upper part of her body to be naked. Medical reports showed that Li suffered injury to her chest, neck, right leg and the left knee. The incident was reported to the Public Security Bureau in X County which carried out an investigation and imposed penalties upon Zhang and her sister. The decision was that Zhang and her sister to be put into custody for 15 and seven days respectively, according to section 22 of the Regulation on Administrative Penalty for Public Security. Zhang and her sister applied for administrative reconsideration to the Public Security Bureau in X Administrative Prefecture (the defendant). The defendant changed the original decision and decided to impose a fine of RMB100 upon Zhang and a fine of RMB70 upon her sister. Li filed an action to the people's court, requesting the court to restore the original penalties imposed by the Public Security Bureau of X County. The court held that the Public Security Bureau in X Administrative Prefecture acted in violation of legal procedures and applied the wrong legislation. There is no legal ground for the Public Security Bureau in X Administrative Region to revoke the penalties imposed by the Public Security Bureau in X County. The people's court restored the original penalties.

In this case, it seems that the administrative penalties imposed by the Public Security Bureau in X Administrative Prefecture are not proportional to the offence committed by Zhang and her sister. That makes the decision of the defendant unfair to Li. The decision is therefore an inappropriate one and can be changed through judicial review.

More Specific Grounds

3.23   Illegality and inappropriateness are two general grounds for administrative reconsiderations. From them more detailed grounds for reconsideration have evolved and been recognized by the RAR. There are altogether six of them, including unclear essential facts, wrongful application of legislation and normative rules, violation of legal procedure, excess or abuse of power, and obvious inappropriateness.[58] They are more or less the same as the grounds for judicial review.[59] The only one missing here is delay or failure in the performance of statutory duty, which is a ground for judicial review. It is not clear why it is so. Arguably cases brought under this ground may be challenged either under wrongful application of legislation or obvious inappropriateness.

The grounds for administrative reconsideration is much wider than the grounds for judicial review in China.[60] Illegality is the ground for both administrative reconsideration and judicial review. The difference exists with regard to inappropriateness. For administrative reconsideration, all inappropriate concrete acts are reviewable by the administrative reconsideration organ. However, when judicial review is concerned, only obviously unfair concrete act can be judicially reviewed. It is therefore much more restricted. That is one of the main differences between administrative reconsideration and judicial review. The other differences will be discussed in later sections.

Notes

[1] The main legal source of administrative reconsideration is the 1990 Regulation on Administrative Reconsideration. It is very likely, according to information from the State Council, that Administrative Reconsideration Law will be enacted later in 1996.
[2] See Xu and Pi, p. 404.
[3] Refer to the section on administrative adjudicating acts in part two (administrative law theory).
[4] See He Jiangui, *Textbook on Administrative Reconsideration*, Legal Science Press, Beijing, 1991, at pp. 25–29.
[5] See Liu Zhengqi, *Xing Zhen Fu Yi yu Xing Zhen Ying Shu Gong Zu Zi Dao* ("Guide on Administrative Reconsideration and Respondence"), China Democratic and Legal Press pp. 169–682. In this book, the editors have listed 139 laws and administrative regulations which have provisions for administrative reconsideration. All those were enacted before the adoption of the Regulation on Administrative Reconsideration in 1990.
[6] See Legislative Bureau of State Council (editor), *Xin Zhen Fu Yi Tiao Li She Yi* ("Interpretation and Explanation of the Regulation on the Administrative Reconsideration") (hereinafter as Sheyi), China Legal Science Press, Beijing, 1990, at p. 159.
[7] See Sheyi, p. 159.
[8] See Chang Hongliang, *Xin Zheng Fu Yi* ("Administrative Reconsideration"), Ching University of Political Science and Law Press, Beijing, 1993, at pp. 27–28.
[9] See later section on the scope of jurisdiction.
[10] Different views have been expressed by Chinese scholars, for detailed discussion, see Cui Zuolan, *Xing Zhen Fu Yi Xing Wei Bian Xi* (Analysis of Administrative Reconsideration Acts) at pp. 6–9, and Li Chunming and Wei Xing, *Xing Zhen Fu Yi Ruo Gan Wen Ti Zhi Wo Jian* (Comments on Several Issues relating to Administrative Reconsideration) at pp. 9–10.
[11] See Cui Zhuolan, pp. 6–7.
[12] See Li Chunming and Wei Xing, p. 9.
[13] See He Jiangui, pp. 22–25.
[14] There is one chapter in the Constitution on the basic rights and freedom enjoyed by the citizens and other provisions for their protection.
[15] See, Yang Haiku, who thinks that it should not be the case.
[16] An examination of those cases discussed in this book will reveal how frequently the original administrative decisions are sustained by the administrative reconsideration organs.
[17] See section J of the RAR.
[18] See Fang Xi, chapter 8, pp. 115–26.
[19] See Sheyi, p. 7.
[20] Compensation will be discussed in the chapter on state compensation in this book.
[21] See Zhao Xiangsheng and Fu Gang, *Fu Yi Sheng Qin Ren Zi Ge Ren Ding Guang Miu* ("Rectification of Mistake Relating to the Identification of the Qualification of the

[22] Applicant for Reconsideration") in the *Collection of Legal Essays 1993*, Vol. 4, at pp. 58–59.
[22] The definition of concrete administrative act is provided in the opinions on the ALL.
[23] *Ibid*, p. 8.
[24] It can also be argued as the application of the general principle as stated in s. 39 of the RAR.
[25] See Chang Hong-liang, *Administrative Reconsideration*, Cap. 9, China University of Political Science and Law Press, 1993, Beijing.
[26] See s. 35 of the RAR.
[27] See Chang Hong-liang, pp. 164–72.
[28] See Shi Qingben, *The Theory and Practice of Administrative Reconsideration*, at pp. 98–107, Police Education Press, 1992, Beijing.
[29] See Shi Qingben, pp. 105–07.
[30] See Ren Gaoming, *Guan Yu Guan Ce ShiShi Shi Zhen Fu Yi Tiao Li Ji Ge Wen Ti De Si Kao* ("Analysis of Several Issues Relating to the Implementation of the Regulation on Administrative Reconsideration"), in the *Collection of Legal Essays 1991*, Vol. 2, pp. 108–11, at pp. 109–10.
[31] See Chang Hong-liang, p. 109.
[32] See section 25 of the RAR; also Sheyi, pp. 68–71; Chang Hongliang, pp. 164–172.
[33] See Chang Hong-liang, pp. 73–106; Shi Qingben, pp. 27–52.
[34] See Liu Zhenqi, p. 7.
[35] In fact, it is debatable whether or not they are principles as they seem to be a specific arrangement of the system, *i.e.* how the reconsideration shall be conducted.
[36] See Sheyi, pp. 9–10; and *Administrative Reconsideration*, China University of Political Science and Law Press, pp. 76–77.
[37] See Sheyi, p. 15.
[38] For discussion on this, refer to latter section on applicable legislation.
[39] See Sheyi, pp. 14–15.
[40] See Chang Hong-liang, pp. 77–79.
[41] There are some exceptions.
[42] It varies from one kind of cases to another.
[43] See Chang Hongliang, pp. 78–79.
[44] *Ibid*, pp. 79–80.
[45] Written consideration has been argued by some scholars to be a separate principle for administrative reconsideration.
[46] This is the major change brought by the 1994 amendment. The consideration behind it is also the principle of convenience both for the people and the reconsideration itself.
[47] It is because conciliation or mediation is a traditional means for dispute resolution practised in China for thousands of years. Even during court hearing process for civil cases, mediation is encouraged.
[48] See section 8 of the RAR; also Chang Hongliang, pp. 45–47; Sheyi, pp. 19–21.
[49] See s. 5 of the RAR; Shi Qingben, pp. 49–50; Sheyi, pp. 12–13.
[50] See Xu and Pi, p. 9; and Sheyi, pp. 18–19.
[51] See s. 42(4) of the RAR.
[52] See Li Peichuan, p. 338.
[53] Also refer to the discussion of this in Part Three on judicial review.
[54] In administrative reconsideration, inappropriateness and unreasonableness have the same meaning and will be used interchangeably.
[55] See Li Peichuan, p. 125.
[56] See Li Peichuan, pp. 126–28.
[57] See Li Peichuan, pp. 355–56.
[58] See s. 42(4) of the RAR.
[59] Refer to discussion in Part Three of the book.
[60] Refer to the chapter on judicial review is Part Three of this book.

CHAPTER FOUR
SCOPE OF ADMINISTRATIVE RECONSIDERATION[1]

4.01 The scope of administrative reconsideration deals with the issue of what kinds of concrete administrative acts are reviewable by the administrative reconsideration organ. It determines the breadth and depth of administrative supervision and remedies available. In British administrative law, there exists a test for determining whether an administrative action is subject to judicial review, *i.e.* the source of its power or the nature of the power.[2] That test has been formulated through the decisions of the courts, *i.e.* common law.

In China, which is a country adopting mainly continental legal system, principles or tests are usually written in legislation. Section 2 of the RAR provides that "citizens, legal persons and other organizations may apply to the competent administrative organ for administrative reconsideration, when they believe that their legitimate rights and interests are infringed by the concrete administrative act of an administrative organ." Relying on this section alone, it seems that any concrete administrative act falling within this category is subject to administrative reconsideration. In practice, that is not the case and the interpretation of section 2 is restricted by Chapter 2 of the RAR.

Chapter 2 has, without laying down any general principles in determining the scope of administrative reconsideration, listed the categories of concrete administrative acts which are subject to administrative reconsideration and what are not subject to administrative reconsideration. This chapter will examine in details the scope of administrative reconsideration and then try to summarize certain rules which can be used as guidelines for determining the scope of administrative reconsideration.

Cases subject to administrative reconsideration may be classified into two: one are those affecting the personal or proprietary rights or interests of those under administration; and the other are those affecting other kinds of rights or interests of the parties concerned.

Acts Affecting Personal or Proprietary Rights or Interests

4.02 Section 9 of the RAR lists seven categories of administrative acts to be subject to administrative reconsideration, including administrative penalties, administrative compulsory measures, infringement of decision-making autonomy, refusal or failure to issue license, failure to perform statutory function, failure to pay pension, unlawful request for the performance of duty, and the infringement of other personal or propriatory rights. These seven categories do not constitute an exclusive list of all concrete administrative acts which are subject to administrative reconsideration. Section 9(9) leaves the list open-ended. Later on, if necessary, other legislation may add extra category of concrete administrative acts to those under administrative reconsideration. The following is a case where the propriatory interests of the applicants is in dispute.

Peasants in Da Lin Bei Xin and Old Villages v. X Township People's Government[3]

4.03 There was a dispute over the payment of land requisition fee on August 31, 1990. The Da Cen Bei Xin Wu, Lao Wu Village Committee claimed that the disputed land had always been jointly managed by the two applicants and a third party, and thus the payment received should be divided up equally among them. It was held, by the Township People's Government, that the disputed land was under the control of Mei Wei Village since 1969; no complaints were received from the other parties since then; the payment should be solely made to the Mei Wei Village.

A mine requisited land from Xi Bian Village, for three times in the years of 1969, 1979 and 1983 respectively. Mei Wei Village was the only one involved with the mine. Later on it was found that the area of land actually utilized by the mine owner exceeded what was originally intended. Another supplementary agreement was signed on August 31, 1990, between the mine and representatives from Xi Bian Village, Da Cen Bei Xin Wu Village, Lao Wu Village and Mei Wei Village, with the support from the County Land Administration Bureau for the requisition of the exceeded land. The agreement specified the exact boundary of the land to be requisited and the additional payment, amounting to a total of RMB16,000, to be made by the mine. Only one-tenth of the land requisited belonged to the Mei Wei Village. The ownership of the rest was not stated in the agreement. The land had been managed jointly by Da Cen Bei Xin Wu, Lao Wu and Mei Wei villages since 1965, and all incomes had been divided up equally among the three villages. The Da Cen Bei Xin Wu and Lao Wu villages were not satisfied with the decision made by the village government. Da Cen went for administrative reconsideration on February 6, 1991.

The County People's Government held that the land was jointly managed by the three villages and so all income should be divided equally among them; the decision made by the village government, which left all income to Mei Wei, was clearly wrong. According to section 42(2) of the RAR, the County People's Government held that the decision of the Township People's Government shall be revoked; and that the other villages should be compensated. Out of the RMB5,120 Da Cen Bei Xin Wu Village should receive RMB1,410, Da Cen Bei Lao Wu Village RMB1,410, Mei Wei Village RMB2,300. Mei Wei Village brought the case to the county people's court. Then the County People's Government decided to make some changes to the proportions out of the RMB16,000. Da Cen Bei Xin Wu Village should receive RMB4,800, Da Cen Bei Lao Wu Village RMB4,800, and Mei Wei Village RMB6,400. Mei Wei was happy with the changes and thus withdrew the action from the court.

Administrative Penalties

The first category is administrative penalties, including detention, fine, rescission of a permit or licence, or order to suspend production or business operations or confiscation of property and articles, which a citizen, legal person or other organization refuses to accept.[4] Administrative penalty is a punishing sanction imposed by an administrative organ or other organizations authorized by law or regulation against any citizens, legal persons or other organizations for violation of law, regulation or rules. It should be noted that what has been listed in section 9(1) is just a few main forms of administrative penalties. They are by no means the only ones subject to administrative reconsideration. In fact, there are many other kinds of administrative penalties, such as circulation of a notice of criticism, warning, and destruction of food products which are prohibited to be produced, confiscation of illegal income, fake medicine, and so on. Section 9(8) provides that cases where administrative organ is regarded to have infringed upon other personal rights or proprietary rights are also subject to administrative reconsideration. Therefore, the effect of section 9(1) and (8) is that any kinds of administrative penalties are subject to administrative reconsideration provided that they have infringed upon either personal or proprietary rights or interests of those under administration.

4.04

Liu v. Shanghai Municipal Construction Commission[5]

Here is a case concerned with the rescission of licence. Liu, in the name of his mother, applied for land for building purposes in May

1985. This was approved. A land-use certificate, concerning 140 square metres of land was issued in July 1987. The Municipal People's Government wanted to requisite land to build office premises, which requires Sun a third party, to "move" his house so as to give way to the office premises. Sun was originally assigned 100 square metres of land situated to the north of what was granted to Liu. This piece of land turned out to be less than 100 square metres. Sun requested to cancel out part of the pathway that was supposed to exist between the two houses so as to "make up" for what he should have owned. Liu agreed provided that Sun should build a house in no less than four metres away from his. Instead, only two metres were left in between and thus a dispute arose between the parties. Not willing to tolerate any more arguments, over the obstruction of light and ventilation with Sun, Liu proposed to sell his house and re-applied for land to build another one. In order to settle the dispute, another piece of land, with an area of 100 square metres was granted to Liu by the Mumicipal People's Government in the same area in July 1988. However, it was later found out that Sun's house did not cause any obstruction of light and ventilation to Liu's house and Liu's house was not sold. Liu started the construction of the second house in April 1989 which occupied an area of 106.99 square metres. Despite of prohibition from the government, the construction work continued until July 9, when the major parts of the house were completed. The estimated total cost of construction was about RMB28,000. Liu had already spent RMB20,055 on the house. The matter was dealt with by the Land Administration Bureau.

It held that the land-use certificate granted in July 1988 shall be repudiated; the house built on the land occupied unlawfully should be confiscated by the State's Finance Administration Bureau and the land-use right should be forfeited. Dissatisfied with the outcome, Liu applied for administrative reconsideration to the Municipal Land Administrative Bureau, on the grounds that the construction of the house was with approval. If there was any problem with the validity of the approval of the land-use right, the approving authority should be responsible. If the authority wanted to withdraw the land-use right due to any mistake concerning its granting, he should be compensated for all lawful investments made during the time when he was allowed to use the land. The Land Administration Bureau argued that there was no actual obstruction of light or ventilation caused by Sun's house, and Liu did not sell the first house. What Liu did amounted to fraud upon application.

After an investigation made by the reconsideration organ, it held that according to section 41 of the PRC Land Administration Law and sections 16 and 17 of the Hu Bei Province Land Administration Regulation, the grant of land-use right of 100 square metres by the approving authority was unlawful, the authority should be primarily liable for the loss suffered by Liu, since Liu's unlawful use was caused by the unlawful approval of the authority. Liu was also liable for the loss suffered because he intentionally violated the relevant legislation by applying for another piece of land without selling the first piece of land. Liu was solely liable for the extended area of 6.9 square metres and responsible for the continuous construction, despite of governmental prohibition.

Relying on sections 42 and 44 of RAR and section 48 of the PRC Land Administrative Law, the reconsideration organ upheld the original decision on the imposition of administrative sanctions. It decided that the approving authority should bear three-quarters of the loss suffered by Liu as administrative compensation.

Administrative Compulsory Measures[6]

The second category is administrative compulsory measures which can be further divided into two groups. One are those measures restricting personal freedom, such as shelter for examination, compulsory medical treatment, compulsory expatriation and administrative detention. The other are those measures restricting the flow of property, such as the sealing up, distraint or freezing of property, which one refuses to accept.

4.05

Measures Restricting Personal Freedom

The first group includes the following main measures. Shelter for investigation is the first, which is an effective measure adopted by the Public Security Bureau, in practice, to combat crimes, though the State Council once made the decision to unify shelter for investigation into reform through labour.[7] It is mainly targeted against those suspects or those with criminal records who failed to tell their true names and addresses. It must be determined by the public security bureau at the county level or above, and cannot exceed three months.

4.06

Education through labour is a compulsory educational reform measure. Two conditions should be met. Firstly, the person fails to change after penalty for infringing public security administration or commits minor crimes which are not yet punishable under criminal law. Secondly, the person still has the capacity to labour. The decision of education through labour should be approved by the management committee of education through labour of which the Public Security Bureau is one member. The duration is between one to three years and can be extended for another year if necessary. Education through labour has duel functions, *i.e.* both educational and punishing. It is a kind of administrative penalty and should be distinguished from reform through labour which is targeted at criminals and executed by prisons or labour reform teams.

Compulsory repatriation of wanderers is a compulsory measure to send those wanderers back to their homeland. It used to be taken by the civil affairs department as remedial measures towards wanderers with the intention to facilitate them to return home. However, there are certain people who become wanderers voluntarily, which has disturbed social order. It is therefore necessary to send those persons back compulsorily. Whether compulsory repatriation will solve the problem at the end is doubtful as they can always go out again if they so wish.

Administrative detention is an administrative compulsory measure to restrict personal freedom for a short while. Under Customs Law for example, suspected smugglers can, after approval by the head of customs office, be detained for 24 hours, which can be extended to 48 hours under special circumstances with the intention to transfer to the judicial organs. There are also other kinds of compulsory administrative measures, such as segregation, compulsory restraint of drinkers against which a person can also bring an action to an administrative reconsideration organ.

Measures Restricting the Moving of Property[8]

4.07   The second group is regarding the restriction on property, including the sealing up, distraint and freezing of property. The sealing up is a measure to seal up movable or immovable property so as to prevent its owner from disposing of it. The property concerned will be sealed up where it locates and will not be transferred to the administrative organ. However, the seal cannot be removed by the property owner without the permission of the administrative organ. Restraint is a measure to take movable property under the control of the administrative organ, either for the purpose of collecting evidence or preventing the party concerned from moving the property away. Freezing is a measure to freeze the bank account of the party concerned by the bank upon the request of the administrative organ to prevent the party to dispose of the money in its account.

The above-mentioned compulsory administrative measures should be distinguished from compulsory administrative enforcement measures. The latter refer to those concrete administrative acts where the administrative organs with the enforcement authority take necessary enforcement measures according to law when citizens, legal persons or other organizations fail to fulfill their administrative obligations. Its precondition is that citizens, legal persons or other organizations have failed to fulfill the obligations imposed by the concrete administrative acts taken by the administrative organs according to law. It could be that the party concerned fails either to apply for administrative reconsideration during the period allowed or to fulfill its obligations, or the party fails to take certain concrete administrative acts which are the prerequisite for administrative reconsideration, or the administrative reconsideration as provided by law is final.[9]

Compulsory enforcement measures may take either direct or indirect forms. The former refers to the situation where the administrative organs take direct actions such as compulsory confiscation and demolition of building. The latter refers to the situation under which the administrative organ may fulfill the obligation on behalf of the party concerned and then claim the cost from him. The main reason to distinguish administrative compulsory measures and compulsory administrative enforcement measures is that the former is reviewable by administrative organ for reconsideration, but the latter is not.

Infringement upon Managerial Decision-Making Power

4.08 The third one is about infringement upon one's managerial decision-making as stipulated by the laws and regulations, which is held to have been perpetrated by an administrative organ. It has been argued that the provision really aims to protect the managerial decision-making authority of state-owned enterprises because it used to be the case that it was not distinguished between administration and enterprises, between property ownership and managerial authority in the enterprises.[10] Various legislation has been passed to separate the ownership from managerial authority. However, the reality reveals that it has not been that successful. This provision is therefore still useful in the sense that it protects managerial autonomy, including the right to possess, to use and to dispose of the property.

The development of market economy has brought with it many other kinds of business entities, such as privately owned enterprises, joint ventures and wholly foreign-owned enterprises. They have been granted various kinds of autonomy under legislation. Those autonomous rights are essential for the establishment of a market economy and the confidence of investors, and are entitled to legal protection. Specifically speaking, those autonomous rights include the ownership of property, the right to use its property, the right to distribute its benefits, the right to appropriate its assets, and so on.

Acts Concerning Licences or Permits

4.09 The fourth one is related to the application and grant of licences or permits. There may be two possibilities. One is that an administrative

SCOPE OF ADMINISTRATIVE RECONSIDERATION

organ refuses to issue a permit or licence, which the applicant holds himself legally qualified to apply for. The other is that an administrative organ fails to respond to the application. Whether or not a kind of activity needs licence or permit is governed by legislation and the administrative organ concerned does not have the discretion to determine. Currently, a licence or permit system has been widely used in many areas, such as the protection and maintenance of important resources and ecological environment, the protection of public safety and health, the maintenance of normal economic order, the management of cultural activities, and so on.

There are several conditions which have to be satisfied by the applicant in order to obtain a licence. Firstly, the administrative organ must have the authority to grant the licence. Secondly, the applicant must apply within the lawful scope (not forbidden activities). That is to say the contents of the licence must be lawful and not prohibited by the state government. Thirdly, the applicant has the capacity. Fourthly, application must follow proper legal procedures and conditions.[11]

Citizens, legal persons or other organizations may bring a case for administrative reconsideration if they believe that they have met all the conditions, but the administrative organ concerned either refuses to respond, or fails to issue a licence to them. Once a licence or permit is issued according to law, it will have legal effect. Its change and cancellation can only be done according to law.

Failure to Perform Statutory Duty

4.10 The fifth is about refusal by an administrative organ to perform its statutory duty. For example, the duties to protect one's personal rights and propriatory rights, as one has applied for, or its failure to respond to the application. It should be noted that only those organs which have the legal responsibility to protect personal and property rights can be complained against under this specific provision. A good example is the Public Security Bureau whose primary function is to protect the security of citizens. If a person is insulted by a hooligan and a police officer on duty refuses to interfere, then the case can be brought for administrative reconsideration. The protection will only be provided upon the application, either oral or written. The second condition is that the administrative organ must have failed to perform its statutory duty. It may directly refuse the application or fails to reply within the time limit or a reasonable time period. The third condition is that the protection must be about either personal or proprietary rights or interests. If any other rights or interests are involved, administrative reconsideration is only possible if it is clearly provided by any other legislation as required by section 9(9) of the Regulation on Administration Reconsideration.[12]

Failure to Pay Subsidies or Pensions

The sixth is about cases where an administrative organ is held to have failed to pay the pensions for the disabled or the family of the deceased soldiers according to law. The main kind of pension is that paid to disabled soldiers or the children and other relatives of deceased soldiers. Two conditions must be satisfied here. Firstly, the pension must be provided for by the law. Secondly, the administrative organ is provided for by law to pay the pension. If relevant law provides that the enterprise or institution concerned will pay the pension, then the dispute over the payment of pension will be labour dispute, not administrative dispute. Administrative reconsideration may not then be applied for. The dispute shall be handled according to relevant labour legislation.

4.10

Unlawful Request for Performance of Obligations

What has been discussed above are about one aspect of the power enjoyed by administrative organs, *i.e.* the power to grant to or deprive the party concerned its rights. The seventh category is about the other aspect, *i.e.* the power to impose upon or relieve from someone the obligation. It is about cases where an administrative organ is held to have illegally demanded the performance of duties. All duties imposed should have clear legal basis. However, in theory it seems a far cry from what happens in practice. Reports are often heard with regard to the collection of fees and other unlawful imposition of duties. The parties concerned can not only refuse to pay, but also apply for administrative reconsideration. However, it is argued that no application for administrative reconsideration is allowed if the administrative organ concerned request the citizens, legal persons or other organizations to pay in the name of donation, provided that no administrative authority is used.[13] This does not seem logical. When an administrative organ is involved, it is quite natural that people will be afraid that administrative power will be invoked if they do not pay the so-called donation. The best way seems to stop administrative organs from requesting donation completely.

4.11

Categories one to seven have listed some examples of concrete administrative acts which are subject to administrative reconsideration. But they are just examples and by no means exhaustive. In fact, section 9(8) provides that all kinds of concrete administrative acts are

SCOPE OF ADMINISTRATIVE RECONSIDERATION

subject to administrative reconsideration if they have infringed upon either other personal rights and/or other property rights not covered in categories one to seven. Furthermore, section 9(9) further broadens the scope of reconsideration by allowing other legislation to add more acts into the scope of reconsideration. The following are some examples in the categories of sections 9(8) and (9).

Feng v. Township People's Government[14]

4.12 No exact boundaries were ever defined between the Jiang Jin County and the He Jiang County. There was a dispute as to the jurisdiction and ownership of a certain piece of land situated near the border in 1988 and 1989. Negotiations were made but no agreements were reached. The Si Chuan Provincial People's Government thus issued a normative document entitled the "decision", laying down the rules for the determination of the boundary and requested representatives from the two counties to conduct an investigation to decide the boundary according to the "decision".

Before any work was done, an application for reconsideration was made by the He Jiang County requesting the Provincial People's Government to include the area within the county's jurisdiction. Their ground of application was that the decision being made amounted to an infringement of the county's legal rights and interests. They alleged that the decision should not be made based on the dispute that arose between the two counties. The county also had evidence showing that the disputed area was long under their control and management since it was abandoned. The action was taken in accordance with sections 2(9)(8) and 32 of the RAR.

4.13 After reconsideration, the Provincial People's Government held that the "decision" made was not one of concrete administrative act. It was made to solve jurisdiction problems that arose between the two counties, not affecting a specified or particular individual, legal person or other organization.

Secondly, the determination of a boundary is a kind of act of state, which is outside the scope of administrative reconsideration. Even if it were a concrete administrative act, the "decision", as claimed by the applicant to be relating to forest rights, it would be a civil dispute in nature and, according to section 10(3) of the RAR, it is still outside the scope of jurisdiction. Therefore the Provincial People's Government decided not to accept the case.

Peasants in Li Village v. The County People's Government[15]

4.14 A house was rebuilt by Feng with the approval of a proper governmental organ in November 1981. Nevertheless, certain designs were secretly altered and the house ended up with an area of 240 square metres instead of the approved 150 square metres. In January 1989, a review of rural land for private dwelling was conducted according to the instructions from the County People's Government for the issue of the land-use certificate. When Feng's house was inspected, it was found that there was an unlawful enlargement of the house causing an obstruction to a nearby pathway. The Township People's Government decided that a certain part of the house occupied by Feng would be designated to make way for the path. Dissatisfied with the decision, Feng applied for administrative reconsideration to the County People's Government. His grounds of application were that a certificate was already previously issued and thus the decision was *ultra vires* and amounted to an infringement of Feng's lawful land-use right.

According to section 13 of the Land Administration Law, negotiations should be made, should any dispute arise between the two parties. If such negotiations break down, then an individual may seek help from the People's Government. It was also stated that the Township People's Government or the County People's Government shall be responsible to deal with such disputes. In this case, the unlawful expansion did amount to an obstruction of a public pathway and complaints made by Feng's neighbours concerning land use were received. The Township People's Government had the jurisdiction to handle such cases.

Feng's expansion of 90 square metres more-than-approved area was also unlawful. Nevertheless, since this was made before the implementation of Regulation on Land Administration in Rural Areas concerning the Construction of Dwelling Houses. It is therefore a historical issue. No fine should be imposed. However, if the expansion was inconsistent with the planning. The decision made by the Township People's Government was really due to the necessity of town planning. It was therefore adequate and lawful that Feng's action was dismissed.

Lao Ai Village v. The County People's Government[16]

A piece of land, namely beach land, was granted by the County People's Government to the Lao Ai Village for development purposes. A certificate of authorization was issued in May 1983 accordingly. But little development was carried out since then. In order to make the most of the beach land, with the permission of the Lao Ai, part of the beach land was used by two other villages for culturing shrimps. Another part was used by the Lao Ai Village for the same purposes, leaving the rest intact. The income was low. The situation was better in 1989. The place became famous for its shrimps and the beach land became popular. Dispute arose as to the use of the beach land for further development. Serious destruction to the beach land and destructive catching of shrimps often occurred. In order to solve these problems, the Township People's Government, on February 15, 1991,

4.15

applied to the county government for advice. On February 26, when there was no reply from the County People's Government, the Township People's Government issued a notice to strengthen the management of beach land and granted part of Lao Ai's beach land to two other villages. Dissatisfied with the decision, Lao Ai filed an action to the People's Government. At the same time, the County People's Government, after several unsuccessful mediation, confirmed the notice issued by the Township People's Government, revoked the certificate originally issued to Lao Ai Village in May 1983, and further granted two-thirds of the beach land to the two other villages. Having received the decision, the Lao Ai Village applied for administrative reconsideration to the Municipal People's Government.

The Municipal People's Government decided, after reconsideration, to uphold the decision made by the County People's Government, and requested the County People's Government to rearrange the proportions of beach land use among the parties. Still dissatisfied with the decision, Lao Ai Village filed an action to the County People's Court. The court held that the effect of the decision made by the County People's Government was concerned with the administration of the beach land and the decision is generally applicable to all three villages concerned and therefore was an abstract administrative act which is outside the scope of administrative reconsideration. The action was dismissed.

This seems to be a wrong decision. The main issue is whether or not the decision made by the County People's Government is an abstract or concrete administrative act. To be an abstract administrative act, it must be of general applicability and can be applied to any persons within the category. Here the decision is targeted at the specific beach land. Once it is made, the dispute concerning the land-use right over the beach land will be solved and the decision can not be applied repeatedly later. It seems to be a concrete rather than an abstract administrative act.

Acts Affecting Other Kinds of Rights or Interests

4.16 Section 9(9) has further broadened the scope of administrative reconsideration by providing that application for administrative reconsideration can be lodged against any other concrete administrative acts against which, according to the laws and regulations, an administrative lawsuit or an application for reconsideration may be instituted. That could cover other kinds of rights and interests other than personal and proprietary rights or interests.

One kind of application which could be lodged under section 9(9) are complaints against infringement upon rights other than personal or proprietary rights, such as civil and political rights. Election right is one example.¹⁷ Another point which should be noted is that the RAR is enacted after the promulgation of the ALL, the intention of the State Council to bring the RAR in line with the ALL is only too obvious. This sub-section provides that all concrete administrative acts which are judicially reviewable shall be subject to administrative reconsideration. Moreover, it is possible that certain concrete administrative acts which are not judicially reviewable due to various reasons may be subject to administrative reconsideration, as long as the specific laws or regulations so provide. It is reasonable as one or another remedial measures should be provided as long as rights or interests of the party concerned are infringed upon. The 1989 Law of the People's Republic of China on Assemblies, Processions and Demonstrations is one such example where judicial review is not allowed, but administrative reconsideration is nevertheless allowed. The Regulation on Registration and Management of Social Organizations is another one. In this sense administrative reconsideration can be said to be supplementary to judicial review.[18]

Notes

[1] Before the promulgation of the Regulation on Administrative Reconsideration, scholars had argued that the scope of administrative reconsideration should cover not only concrete administrative acts but also abstract administrative acts. For detailed discussion, see Yu Zhongming, *Jian Lun Xing Zhen Fu Yi De Shou An Fan Wei* ("A Brief Discussion of the Scope of Administrative Reconsideration"), in the *Collection of Legal Essays (Administrative Law) 1990*, Vol. 2, at pp. 177–180.
[2] The test has developed over the years from the source of power to the nature of power.
[3] See Li Peichuan, pp. 332–34.
[4] See s. 9(1) of the RAR.
[5] See Li Peichuan, pp. 364–67.
[6] See Chang Hongliang, pp. 119–120.
[7] *Ibid*.
[8] See Chang Hongliang, p. 120.
[9] See Sheyi, p. 26.
[10] See Sheyi, pp. 27–29.
[11] See Sheyi, pp. 29–32; Chang Hongliang, pp. 122–123.
[12] See Sheyi, pp. 33–34.
[13] Sheyi, p. 34.
[14] See Li Peichuan, p. 300.
[15] See Chang Hongliang, p. 303.
[16] *Ibid*, p. 314.
[17] See Sheyi, p. 35.
[18] See Sheyi, p. 36.

CHAPTER FIVE

JURISDICTION[1]

5.01 Jurisdiction is concerned mainly with the issue of allocation and authority to accept cases for administrative reconsideration. It is inherently related to the structure of administration. A good understanding of the structure and the interrelationship between various governmental organs is essential to the comprehension of which administrative organ shall have jurisdiction over a particular administrative complaint.

Governmental Structure

5.02 It should be noted that China's administration system has been in a process of constant change in order to adapt to the changing needs of the society. On the one hand, it has its own uniqueness; on the other, it also has a lot of unreasonable elements. The main structure of administration is, however, laid down in the two organic laws, *i.e.* 1982 Organic Law of the State Council and 1979 Organic Law of the Local People's Congresses and Local People's Governments. A detailed discussion of administrative structure in China is beyond the scope of this chapter.[2] It suffices to mention the main features here. The State Council shall exercise the functions and powers prescribed in section 89 of the Constitution. It will set up various ministries and if necessary a certain number of direct subordinate agencies to be in charge of various specialized work and a certain number of administrative offices to assist the Premier in handling specialized affairs. Currently, there are 16 special commissions in this category. The local people's governments at various levels throughout the country shall be state administrative organs under the unified leadership of the State Council and shall be subordinate to it.[3] A local people's government at or above the county level shall, among other things, direct the work of its subordinate departments and of the people's governments at lower levels.[4] It shall establish necessary working offices in accordance with work requirements and the principle of compact and efficient organization.[5] When necessary and with the approval of the people's government at the higher level, a local people's government may establish certain agencies.[6]

Different views exist with regard to the jurisdiction of administrative reconsideration and the establishment of reconsideration organs. Jurisdiction is normally directly related to administrative authority of relevant administrative organ.[7] The general principle for the determination of jurisdiction of administrative reconsideration is the principle of professional jurisdiction. It implies vertical jurisdiction, *i.e.* the administrative organ at the next higher level shall have jurisdiction of reconsideration cases against the organ at the lower level.[8] This will contribute to administrative efficiency. There also exists exception to this principle. Sometimes because of the requirement of special expertise, special tribunals will be established to deal with specific kinds of cases. On other occasions, it may be more convenient for the people's government at the same level to handle reconsideration cases against relevant administrative organs.[9] Relying on the general principle and those exceptions, there are currently three kinds of jurisdictions:

— jurisdiction by the administrative organ in charge at the next higher level;
— jurisdiction by local people's government at the same level; and
— jurisdiction by the same administrative organ undertaking the administrative act.

Jurisdiction by Administrative Organ at the Next Higher Level

Jurisdiction over the Working Department of a Local People's Government at or above County Level

There are several rules provided by laws and regulations with regard to application for administrative reconsideration against concrete administrative acts taken by the working department of a local people's government at or above the county level. The first rule is to bring the case to the competent department at a higher level.[10] Some other legislation have similar provisions. For example, section 36 of the Law of the People's Republic of China on the Prevention and Treatment of Infectious Diseases provides that "any party who refuses to accept a decision on fine may, within 15 days of receiving the notice on the punishment decision, apply to the health administration department at the next higher level for reconsideration. . . ."

5.03

The second rule is that the case will be under the jurisdiction of the people's government at the same level. The main consideration for this rule is the convenience to the aggrieved party as well as reconsideration organ. This rule is only applicable under two situations. One is that there is no corresponding competent department at a higher level. It only happens due to requirements of new development which is unique to some localities. The establishment of an administrative bureau for express motorways or underground railways is typical example. These local organs do not have corresponding competent department at the level above. The second is about the cases that shall be under the jurisdiction of the people's governments as stipulated by the provisions of the laws and regulations. There are not so many of such provisions. One example is provided by section 13 of 1989 Law of the People's Republic of China on Assemblies, Processions and Demonstrations, which provides that "if the persons(s) responsible for an assembly, a procession or a demonstration does not accept the competent authorities' decision not to grant permission, he may apply to the people's government at the same level for reconsideration within three days of receiving the notice on the decision, and the people's government shall make a decision within three days of receiving the application for reconsideration."[11]

The third rule is not as specific as the previous two and just provides for the jurisdiction of the administrative organ at the next higher level. This means it could be the competent department or the people's government at the next higher level. The aggrieved party shall have the right to choose. Section 37 of the ALL is an example, which provides that "a citizen, a legal person or any other organization may, within the scope of cases acceptable to the people's courts, apply to an administrative organ at the next higher level or to an administrative organ as prescribed by the law or regulations for reconsideration. . . ."

5.04 If this is the case, a related issue is which of the two is then primarily responsible for jurisdiction. One scholarly interpretation is that it should be the competent department at the next higher level.[12] Several reasons have been suggested. Firstly, each working department of a local government represents that government in that specific area. Administrative reconsideration is an important mechanism for each working department to represent its government at the same level to exercise its administrative authority. It is also a means for the working department to represent its government to supervise the working departments at the lower level. Secondly, local people's governments should be decision-making organs. They should not get bogged down in routine work which may be undertaken by its working departments. It will provide opportunity for the working department to give full play to its role. Thirdly, many administrative actions are technical and have their professional characteristics. It is therefore better for the competent working department to have the jurisdiction. Fourthly, the competent working department is more distanced than local government from the original decision-making body. It will not give outsiders too much of an impression of the existence of bias.[13]

With regard to the supervision of concrete administrative acts undertaken by any ministries or commissions under the State Council, the general rule indicates that the State Council should have jurisdiction. However, it has been argued that the State Council is the highest administrative authority within administration. Its main task is to make important policy decisions and should not become involved in too detailed administrative work. Based on this reasoning, the RAR provides that the specific ministry or commission concerned shall have the jurisdiction to take the case for reconsideration. This is highly problematic because the same organ making the administrative decisions shall also conduct the reconsideration. There is great possibility of bias.

Jurisdiction over Concrete Administrative Act of Local Governments

The concrete administrative acts of local governments mainly involve administrative activities in the area of land, mineral resources, forest, and so on. If an applicant does not accept a specific decision, he can then file an application for administrative reconsideration to the people's government at the next higher level, but not to the competent department at the next higher level. It is because the competent department at the next higher level does not have, under the Organic Law, the power to supervise or give order to the people's government at the lower level. Nor does it have the power to annul a concrete administrative act undertaken by the lower people's government. 5.05

With regard to concrete administrative acts of people's governments at provincial level, including provinces, autonomous regions and municipalities directly under the central government, the cases shall be under the jurisdiction of the people's government which has undertaken the aforesaid concrete administrative acts. The reason is exactly the same as those discussed above for ministerial organs to handle administrative reconsideration cases.

Jurisdiction over Acts Taken in the Name of Two or More Administrative Organs

In practice, a concrete administrative act may be undertaken in the name of two or more administrative organs. It will then be called a joint administrative act. Sometimes, an act is adopted by one administrative organ after discussion with several others. There are also cases 5.06

JURISDICTION

where an act is adopted in the name of two or more organs, without any discussion among them. The first issue is to identify whether or not an act is a joint one. It has been suggested that the final criterion is to look at the names appearing in the decision.[14] Section 13 of the RAR provides that the case shall be under the jurisdiction of an administrative organ at the next higher level over the aforesaid two or more administrative organs. There may be three possibilities: one is that two or more working department of the same local governments jointly undertake a concrete administrative act. The act will be subject to the jurisdiction of the local government concerned. The second one is that two or more working departments at different levels of local governments, *e.g.* one is at municipal level, while the other is at district level, jointly undertake an act, it is then subject to the jurisdiction of the municipal people's government. The third situation is that two different local governments, *e.g.* two district people's governments, jointly undertake an action. Then the municipal people's government will have the jurisdiction over the act.

Jurisdiction over Acts Made by Agencies of Local Governments

5.07 As provided by section 59 of 1979 Organic Law of Local Congresses and Local People's Governments of the People's Republic of China, local people's governments at or above county level have the authority to establish agencies. Those agencies are under direct leadership and supervision of the relevant local people's governments. It is therefore natural to grant jurisdiction of administrative reconsideration to them over any cases brought against their agencies.

Some laws and regulations provide certain agencies with the authority to undertake concrete administrative act in their own names, *e.g.* the public security bureau, administration bureau of industry and commerce, and local tax bureau. If that is the case, the RAR stipulates that the case shall be under the jurisdiction of the department which has established the agency. Therefore whether or not the decision is made in the name of the said agency is the criterion to determine which administrative organ shall have jurisdiction for administrative reconsideration.

Jurisdiction over Acts by Authorized or Entrusted Organizations

5.08 A legally authorized organization is different from an entrusted organization. The former can, through the authorization of laws, regulations or rules, have administrative capacity in certain aspects and therefore exercise its authority and undertake corresponding legal responsibility arising therefrom in its own name. Such an organization is originally a non-administrative organ. Only after its authorization shall it enjoy administrative power. A case filed against an authorized organization shall be under the jurisdiction of the competent administrative organ immediately above the said organization.

It has been argued that only laws, administrative regulations, local legislations and rules can grant authorization. Authority granted through other normative documents with a status lower than rules can only be regarded as an entrusted authority, which refers to the situation where an administrative organ entrusts certain matters to another organ, working staff or other individual or organization to handle. The entrusted person or body does not have the capacity to act as an administrative subject. Instead, it can only act in the name of the entrusting organ. The legal responsibility caused thereby will be borne by the entrustor. One example is in section 33(2) of 1986 Regulation on Administrative Penalty for Public Security, which provides that "warnings and fines of a maximum of fifty yuan can be ruled on by local police stations; in rural areas where there is no local police station, the people's government of a town can be entrusted with the ruling." Here the people's government of a town will make a ruling in the name of local police station, which will be responsible if something is wrong with the ruling. In a word, the act of the entrusted organ is deemed to be one of the entrusting organ. The main purpose of entrustment is to facilitate efficient administration and the frequency of such ruling[15]. However, it should also be noted that there does not exist any detailed rules on whether and when one administrative organ can entrust another one. As a result, it often happens that administrative organs abuse entrusted authorities, or the entrusted body or person does not meet the imposed requirements. All these factors have influenced the effectiveness of an entrusting system. The requirements of entrusted bodies or persons are often not provided in any legislation. What they should be is a question for further discussion and research. There should be some legal requirements as to whether or not, when and how one administrative organ may entrust another one.

Jurisdiction over Acts Which Need Approval of An Administrative Organ at the Next Higher Level

The acts which need approval refer to those concrete administrative acts which will not have any legal effect until the approval is granted by the relevant administrative organ. Different views have been expressed with regard to the effect of approval. One opinion is that the approval is supplementary or procedural and will not affect or change the nature of the approved concrete administrative act. The other

5.09

JURISDICTION

opinion is that the approval determines the existence and the legal effect of the approved concrete act.¹⁶ The approval and the act which needs approval can not exist independently. Without approval, the latter will not have any legal effect. Logically speaking, the second approach seems to be consistent with practice. One example can be used to illustrate. The Detailed Rules for the Implementation of the Statistics Law of the People's Republic of China is enacted by the National Statistics Bureau with the approval of the State Council and have the same legal effect as any other regulations or rules adopted by the State Council. At present there are some kinds of concrete administrative acts which need approval of relevant governmental organs, such as the use of state-owned land needs the approval of people's governments at or above county level.

In fact most of the acts which need approval often have policy nature and only the approving organ has the authority to make that kind of decisions. The approval itself is a type of supervision. It has been argued that to grant the jurisdiction to the approving authority will enable it to better exercise its approval authority. That is why it is provided that an application for administrative reconsideration against a concrete act which is subject to approval, shall be under the jurisdiction of the administrative organ which makes the final decision, unless otherwise provided for by the laws and regulations. Whether or not the argument raised above can stand is certainly arguable. It can also be counterclaimed that the approving authority will be, once knowing it will have the authority of administrative reconsideration, likely to abuse its approving authority as it will have another say about the case. Alternatively, they may be biased when they conduct administrative reconsideration.

Jurisdiction over Acts Made by an Organ Abolished

5.10 Once an administrative organ is abolished, its original administrative capacity is either lost or transferred to another administrative organ. No matter which is the case, the concrete act adopted by the abolished organ before its abolition is still effective and can therefore be subject to administrative reconsideration. The issue is which organ will have jurisdiction over such cases. The RAR provides that the case shall be under the jurisdiction of the administrative organ at the next higher level over the administrative organ which has succeeded in the functions and powers of the administrative organ abolished.¹⁷ The question then becomes which organ is the administrative organ succeeding to its functions and powers. It could be the organ which exercises, after its abolition, its original authority or takes over its assets. On the other hand, if the administrative authority is merely transferred, *e.g.* through merging of two administrative organs, the merged organ will be the one. It may also be the case that the original functions may, after its abolition, be split between two different administrative organs. Then jurisdiction will be determined according to the rules on joint jurisdiction as discussed above.[18]

Jurisdiction Transfer

5.11 When an administrative reconsideration organ finds that a case it has accepted is not under its jurisdiction, it shall transfer the case to an administrative organ which has jurisdiction over the case. Such transfer is similar to the transfer of cases between different people's courts. Transfer may happen between different departments of the same people's government, or between different people's governments at the same level, or between different administration reconsideration organs at different levels.

Several conditions have to be met before transfer. Firstly, the case should have already been accepted by the administrative reconsideration organ. Secondly, the administrative organ concerned has found that it does not have jurisdiction over the case. Thirdly, the administrative organ to which the aforesaid case has been transferred should have jurisdiction over the case. However, the initiative to transfer the case shall be made by the original administrative reconsideration organ. Though the original reconsideration organ believes that the organ to which the case is transferred has jurisdiction, it may well be the case that its decision is wrong. Even that is the case, the organ to which the case is transferred cannot send the case back or transfer it to another administrative reconsideration organ.[19] The main purpose for this provision is to prevent undue delay in the examination of the case concerned. But the administrative reconsideration organ to which the case is transferred may request the administrative organ at the next higher level to designate jurisdiction.[20] Such provision may prevent undue delay in the hearing of administrative reconsideration cases. In so doing, it shall provide appropriate protection to the applicant's legitimate interest and impose effective supervision over administrative organ.

Designation of Jurisdiction

5.12 Designation of jurisdiction will only happen when a dispute arises between administrative organs over jurisdiction for reconsideration and it cannot be resolved by the parties to the dispute through consul-

JURISDICTION

tation. It is because the allocation of responsibilities among different administrative organs is often not clearly set out and the relationship between different administrative organs are not clearly defined in legislation. What often occurs are disputes between two or more working departments under the same people's government. Then the administrative organ at the next higher level above the two parties shall designate one of the administrative organ to take the case.

Priority of Jurisdiction

5.13 The issue of priority of jurisdiction will not arise if the applicant will only apply to one administrative reconsideration organ. However, it is not a legal obligation which the applicant should undertake. He is not prohibited from making application for administrative reconsideration to two or more administrative organs. Then the issue of priority of jurisdiction shall arise as only one of them should hear the case. It is provided that the case shall be under the jurisdiction of the administrative organ that first receives the application for reconsideration.[21] As to how to determine which organ receives the application first, it could either be decided according to the registration date of application, or through the consultation between different administrative organs to which the application has been sent to, or through designation by administrative organ at the higher level.

Complaint to the Correspondence and Reception Department and Administrative Reconsideration

5.14 It is an important political task in China for state organs at different levels to handle correspondence from ordinary citizens and receive their visits. At present, a special correspondence and reception department is usually set up in all people's governments at or above county level. Many complaints to the correspondence and reception department are concerned with some concrete administrative acts of administrative organs. The correspondence and reception department has therefore certain function to resolve administrative disputes. It should, however, be noted that correspondence and reception is different from administrative reconsideration. They are supplementary to each other and neither of them can replace the other. As far as the function of dispute resolution and supervision is concerned, administrative reconsideration is more speedy, normative and effective. Moreover, most administrative reconsideration decisions are subject to judicial review, which strengthens the justice of administrative reconsideration.

As administrative reconsideration system only started to function in 1991, many people are not familiar with it. People therefore are still used to opting for correspondence and reception. In order to make full use of the system of administrative reconsideration, the RAR provides that where citizens, legal persons and other organizations make complaints to the correspondence and reception department which are still within the time limit for administrative reconsideration, the correspondence and reception department shall immediately notify the complainants to file an application for reconsideration to the administrative organ that has jurisdiction for reconsideration.[22] As there are certain conditions for bringing a case for administrative reconsideration, it is natural that only some of complaints brought to the correspondence and reception department will meet the requirements for administrative reconsideration. Only for those cases shall the correspondence and reception department notify the applicants of their opportunity to apply for administrative reconsideration. The failure to do so is misconduct of the correspondence and reception department.

Other Jurisdiction

Apart from various issues discussed above with regard to jurisdiction, the RAR has also provided a catch-all provision which provides that "other cases involving jurisdiction for reconsideration shall be handled according to the provisions of the laws, regulations and rules."[23] It is mainly because of the complexity of administrative activities themselves. It is impossible for the RAR to cover all kinds of cases. If there are provisions in the RAR, then they should be complied with. If there are not provisions in the RAR, then other laws, regulations and rules may make supplementary provisions. In so doing, this provision also has the function to harmonize the relationship between other legislation and the RAR.

5.15

Notes

[1] Fang Xi, *Xing Zhen Fu Yi Zi Nan* (Guidebook to Administrative Reconsideration), Part Five, at pp. 77–88, Legal Science Press, Beijing, 1991; Huang Shuhai, *Xing Zhen Fu Yi Tiao Li Jiang Zuo* (Lectures on the Regulation on Administrative Reconsideration),

Lecture Four, pp. 49–67, China People's Public Security University Press, Beijing, 1991; Yu Gang, *Jian She Xing Zhen Fu Yi Guan Xia Zhou Yi* (Comment on the Establishment of Jurisdiction of Administrative Reconsideration in the Overview of Administrative Reconsideration), Li Peichuan, at pp. 147–52, China Legal System Press, Beijing, 1993.

[2] There are several books discussing the governmental structure in China in detail. In addition, administrative structure is often discussed in books on Constitutional Law.

[3] s. 48 of The Organic Law of the Local People's Congresses and Local People's Governments.

[4] s. 51 of the same law.

[5] s. 55 of the same law.

[6] s. 59 of the same law.

[7] Su Meifeng, *Xing Zhen Fu Yi Ruo Gan Wen Ti Zhi Guan Jian* ("Opinions on Several Issues relating to Administrative Reconsideration") in *Collection of Legal Essays 1991*, Vol. 2, pp. 94–100, at pp. 96–97.

[8] This has been argued to be one of the principles of administrative reconsideration. Refer to the section on principles.

[9] See Fang Xi, pp. 79–81.

[10] This is stipulated in s. 11 of the RAR.

[11] According to the information from the State Council the people's government's jurisdiction of reconsideration has become common practice when the Administrative Reconsideration Law is enacted.

[12] See Sheyi, pp. 43–44.

[13] This last argument does not seem to be that persuasive as many cases have shown that administrative organ at the higher level would be equally biased.

[14] See Sheyi, pp. 46–47.

[15] See Sheyi, p. 52.

[16] See Sheyi, p. 54.

[17] See s. 17 of the RAR.

[18] Refer to the section on joint jurisdiction.

[19] See s. 17 of the RAR.

[20] Resignation of jurisdiction shall be discussed in the next section.

[21] See s. 20 of the RAR.

[22] See s. 21 of the RAR.

[23] See s. 22 of the RAR.

CHAPTER SIX

HEARING OF RECONSIDERATION CASES AND THE RELATED ISSUES

Many issues relating to the hearing of administrative reconsideration cases are similar to those of administrative litigation cases. Both administrative reconsideration and judicial review aim at the control of maladministration and enhancement of administrative efficiency. They are nevertheless different in nature as one is administrative activity, while the other is judicial activity. This chapter intends to examine the main issues relating to the actual hearing of administrative reconsideration cases and also those related issues. Comparison with administrative litigation will be made wherever possible and necessary.

6.01

The Format of Reconsideration

As mentioned above, administrative reconsideration is a kind of administrative activity and it should therefore reflect the principle of efficiency in administration, which is an essential difference between administrative reconsideration and judicial review. The principle of efficiency has two aspects: one is convenience to the parties concerned; and the other is convenience to the speedy and concise hearing of reconsideration cases by administrative organs.[1] One way to incorporate this principle into the RAR is to provide that administrative reconsideration be conducted by applying the system of reconsideration by written documents.[2] This means the administrative reconsideration organ will only review the written documents submitted by the parties concerned and it does not have to summon the parties or witness to the hearing. This is the main form of hearing of reconsideration cases. But it is by no means the only way. When the administrative reconsideration organ deems it necessary, other forms of hearing of reconsideration cases may also be adopted. For example, if the material facts of the case are not clear from the written materials

6.02

submitted, or it is convenient for the parties to come to the actual hearing to explain certain issues, or the parties concerned request to be present, or the administrative reconsideration organ believes there exist other circumstances which render adjudication by written documents appropriate, then a form similar to court hearing may be adopted.

The Effect of the Concrete Administrative Act under Reconsideration

6.03   The general principle governing the effect of the concrete administrative act under reconsideration is that the execution of the action shall not be suspended in the course of hearing. This means a concrete administrative act is lawful and can be executed before it is annulled, changed or declared invalid by the administrative reconsideration organ according to legal procedure. This provision is similar to section 44 of the ALL. The reasoning behind this provision is also the same. That is, if the execution of the concrete administrative act will be suspended, the applicant may submit an application whenever it wants to suspend the concrete administrative act concerned. Such kind of abuse of the right to application will prevent the concrete administrative act from coming into effect in time. As a result, the efficiency of administration will be seriously hampered. The state and public interests will be unavoidably damaged.

However, this does not mean that a concrete administrative act can never be suspended. Such an extreme provision may also be against the purpose of the administrative reconsideration system, *i.e.* the protection of legitimate interests of the parties concerned.[3] A balance needs to be achieved between the requirement of efficiency and the protection of the interests of the aggrieved parties. There are four situations under which suspension may be allowed.[4] The first is the defending party deems the suspension necessary. This is not an arbitrary exercise of discretion. The administrative reconsideration organ will review the decision of the administrative organ and will recommend suspension if one of the following situations is revealed, *i.e.* the normative documents relied upon have either not come into effect or have lost its effect, the neglect of the conditions which lead to lenient handling, etc. obvious abuse of authority or excess of power, mistake in the facts upon which the applicant's action was deemed illegal, and the illegality of the applicant's action needs further evidence and imposition of penalty may cause damage to the applicant which can never be restored.

Secondly, the administrative reconsideration organ deems the suspension necessary. If any of the above-mentioned situations occurs, the defending party should request suspension. If it fails to do so, the administrative reconsideration organ may demand the suspension. This is one of the remedies and purposes of application for reconsideration. If the administrative reconsideration organ should, but fails to, make such a decision to suspend the concrete administrative act, then the supervisory authority and the remedies provided will be incomprehensive.

The third situation is where the administrative reconsideration organ believes that the application for suspension of a concrete administrative act is reasonable and therefore decides to suspend the execution. This will only happen when the defending party and the administrative reconsideration organ deem suspension unnecessary, but the applicant applies for suspension of execution. In order for the administrative reconsideration organ to change its original belief, two extra conditions need to be satisfied. One is that the execution of the concrete administrative act may cause losses to the applicant which is not remedial; the other is that the suspension of the concrete administrative act will not be contrary to the state's and public interests.[5]

The last situation is where suspension is stipulated by the relevant provisions of the laws, regulations and rules. Suspension of execution is a complicated issue and usually provided for in specific legislation, of which there are three types, *i.e.* laws, regulations and rules. Such provisions should be recognized by the RAR. One example is section 40 of 1986 Regulation of the People's Republic of China on Administrative Penalty for Public Security, which provides that:

> The original ruling shall continue to be executed during the time a petition or suit against the penalty for violating the administration of public security is taking place.
>
> In case a guarantor can be found or bail has been paid according to regulations by the detainee or his family, the original ruling can be suspended temporarily during the time a petition or suit is taking place. When the ruling is revoked or starts to be enforced, the bail shall be returned according to regulations.

The failure for the defending party to suspend execution of a concrete administrative act will lead to possible administrative penalty upon the legal representative of the administrative organ concerned under the RAR.

HEARING OF RECONSIDERATION CASES & THE RELATED ISSUES

Withdrawal of Reconsideration Application

6.04 Withdrawal of a reconsideration case by the applicant before a decision is made by the administrative reconsideration organ is an issue relating to not only the exercise of the applicant's rights, but also the other persons' rights or public interests. It is because indulgence of unlawful or inappropriate concrete administrative act may adversely affect the public interests. A balance needs to be struck between the individuals' rights to withdrawal and the protection of other persons' rights or public interests. Only under two situations may withdrawal be allowed. One is that the applicant withdraws its application before a decision is made by the administrative reconsideration organ; the other is the defending party of the application has changed the concrete administrative act and the applicant agrees and applies for its withdrawal.[6] In order to ensure that the withdrawal is not coerced, the withdrawal needs the approval of the administrative reconsideration organ and shall be recorded on its file. In so doing, the administrative reconsideration organ may refuse those involuntary withdrawal of application.

Once an application is withdrawn, the applicant may not apply for reconsideration again for the same facts and reasons. This provision mainly intends to maintain the seriousness of administrative reconsideration.

Applicable Legislation (Law)

6.05 What should be the applicable legislation (law) is an important issue, not only to administrative reconsideration, but also to judicial review.[7] The word "law" in the phrase of "applicable law" in its broad sense covers the laws enacted by the NPC, the administrative regulations adopted by the State Council, local regulations and rules promulgated by local legislatures, the decisions and orders with a general binding force formulated and promulgated by administrative organs at higher levels according to law, and the regulations passed by autonomous regions. The legal effects of these normative documents are different. The issue is whether they are all applicable by the administrative reconsideration organ in handling cases. There hardly exist any arguments with regard to the applicability of laws, regulations and local regulations. Controversy is mainly on the applicability of rules, and decisions and orders with a general binding force formulated and promulgated by administrative organs at higher levels according to laws and administrative regulations. The issues relating to applicable legislation in administrative reconsideration are mainly similar to those relating to judicial review and they will be discussed in details in the part on judicial review. However, different views exist with regard to the legal effects of rules, decisions and orders with a general binding force, *i.e.* whether or not they should be relied on, instead of being taken only as reference, by administrative reconsideration organs. Most scholars adopt the view that they should be relied on by administrative reconsideration organs.[8]

As far as regulations are concerned, the Constitution and the Organic Law on Local People's Congresses Local People's Governments provide that certain administrative organs have the authority to make universally binding regulations. They include various ministries and commissions of the State Council, Provinces, Autonomous Regions and Municipalities under direct control of the central government. These regulations will usually work out the details of the laws and administrative regulations and therefore play an essential role in the implementation of the laws and administrative regulations in social life and the enhancement of administrative efficiency. They also contribute to the administration according to law or the application of rule of law principle in administration.[9] Practice also reveals that a large quantity of concrete administrative acts are undertaken by relying on various rules. In certain areas more than 70 per cent of the normative documents are regulations. Given this fact, administrative reconsideration has to apply those regulations. Otherwise, there will not be any applicable legislation in many cases. This will lead people to doubt the legal effect of regulation, especially when concrete administrative acts are undertaken according to the regulation. Therefore the RAR provides that regulations should also be applied by the administrative reconsideration organ. One pre-condition is of course that the regulations must be made according to laws and are therefore lawful and effective regulations.

The next issue is about decisions and orders. They play an important role in filling the vacuum left by laws, administrative regulations and regulations, especially in those cities which do not have the authority to make regulations. However, it should also be noted that existing decisions and orders from different departments or governmental organs often contradict each other and no sound system has been developed to improve the making of decisions and orders. The RAR has provided that they should be relied upon when an administrative reconsideration case is considered by administrative reconsideration organ.[10] Its theoretical ground seems to be the principle governing administrative organizations, *i.e.* the lower administrative organs should obey the decisions and orders from a higher administrative organ, rather than a solid legal ground. That is understandable bearing in mind that administrative reconsideration is itself an administrative act governed by law. Nevertheless, there do exist legal sources to support such argument. The Organic Law on Local People's Con-

6.06 gresses and Local People's Governments provides that local people's governments at or above county level should implement the decisions and orders of administrative organs at a higher level.[11]

Concern has been expressed[12] about the difference, in this aspect, between administrative reconsideration and judicial review. The ALL only provides that laws and administrative regulations can be relied on whereas regulations can only be referred to.[13] Then will the issue of application of different standards arise in dealing with the same case? This concern certainly has its merits as the issue will arise automatically when a case is brought up for judicial review if the aggrieved party is not satisfied with an administrative reconsideration decision. Having acknowledged the problem, one has to find a way out, *i.e.* is it possible to reconcile the difference of those provisions in practice?

The essence seems to be whether or not the decisions or orders relied upon by the administrative reconsideration organ are themselves lawful or effective. If the answer is affirmative, then those decisions or orders are consistent with and have merely provided details to the laws and administrative regulations. The result coming out of administrative reconsideration by relying on those decisions or orders will not be contrary to the laws and administrative regulations, *i.e.* will not be illegal. The reliance upon the decisions and orders will make it easier to resolve the case in dispute. Even if the case will be later brought for judicial review, it will not have a chance to succeed due to the lack of illegal element. Therefore the difference in the scope of applicable law is very unlikely to lead to unfairness due to the application of different remedial procedures, *i.e.* administrative reconsideration and judicial review.

This leads us to a more complicated issue, which is very likely to happen. That is, what the administrative reconsideration organ is supposed to do if it finds that the regulations, or decisions or orders with a general binding force, which serve as the basis for a concrete administrative act, are in conflict with the laws, administrative regulations and regulations or, other rules, decisions or orders with a general binding force?

It is clear that no application for reconsideration can be lodged against any decisions or orders, with a general binding force because they are abstract administrative acts. Even worse, they need to be relied upon by the administrative reconsideration organ. Neither is it possible to bring a case for judicial review against those decisions or orders.[14] Therefore no judicial remedy is available. However, there do exist remedies to redress such problems. The first is administrative remedy, basing on the supervisory role played by a higher administrative organ or people's government over a lower administrative organ or people's government. If the decisions or orders fall within the scope of functions and powers of the competent administrative reconsideration organ, it shall then decide on the nullification or change of the decisions or orders according to law as a separate issue. It should be emphasized that there is an implied condition, *i.e.* the decisions or orders relied upon are made by a people's government or an administrative organ under the supervision of the competent administrative reconsideration organ.[15]

6.07 If the rules or decisions and orders with a general binding force, which serve as the basis for a concrete administrative act, are made by an administrative organ or people's government enjoying a higher status than the administrative reconsideration organ, it will not have the power to handle the situation and has to report to administrative organ at the next higher level, which shall handle according to law. If the administrative organ at the next higher level does not have the power to handle the case either, the case shall be submitted to an organ which has the power to handle.[16] Assuming what is involved (a decision or order) is the contradiction between a municipal people's government in a province and an administrative regulation from State Council, then only State Council has the power to determine the validity of the decision or order with a general binding force. We know that the State Council will not handle any actual reconsideration cases. The logical answer is that only the contradiction between different normative documents other than laws and administrative regulations will be submitted for determination. Once the validity of the regulation, decisions or orders is determined, the hearing of the case should be resumed by the original administrative reconsideration organ. That possibly also explains why it is provided that the administrative reconsideration organ shall cease its hearing of the said case during that period of determination.

It may sound complicated, but in fact it is not, especially for those who are familiar with China's Constitutional Law. It is well defined in the Constitution and the two organic laws on State Council and local governments, what is the hierarchy among normative documents and how the conflict among different normative documents is supposed to be resolved. It is simply the application of that set of rules in the process of administrative reconsideration.[17] Therefore, even if there is no such provision as in section 43 of the RAR, the set of constitutional rules should still be applied. In the following two cases, the issue of applicable legislation and possible conflict between them has been dealt with.

Wholesale Department Store of Electronic Goods v. Measurement Bureau in X City[18]

A major quality check campaign was conducted throughout the whole country on April 20, 1991. The Measurement Bureau in X City (defendant) examined certain samples, namely some wires obtained from the plaintiff. The sampling showed that the products were of poor quality, according to Standard Law, Regulation on Industrial Products Quality Responsibility, Document No. 32 from State Council and sections 3(2) and 7 of the Interim Regulation on the Investigation and Penalty for Fake and Low Quality Commodities issued by the province. According to relevant legislation, the defendant imposed administrative penalties on the plaintiff. They included the criticism on newspaper, imposition of a fine of 12 per cent of the total value of the commodities, an imposition of a fine of RMB2,500 on the responsible person, and sealing up of some commodities for further disposition.

Dissatisfied with the decision, the plaintiff filed an action to the people's court, on June 4, based on the reason that the defendant was wrong and that the decision was made without a legal basis.

6.08 The people's court held that the Interim Regulation was a local regulation which cannot be relied on by the defendant to impose administrative penalties. It revoked the decisions of the defendant and ask the defendant take a new concrete administrative act. The defendant appealed to the Intermediate People's Court which held, that the quality check was made with sufficient evidence in imposing administrative penalties on the plaintiff for selling poor quality products. It is appropriate to apply the Interim Regulation. However, the third penalty was a repetitive one which was not consistent with the general legal principle that no double penalties for the same wrong. The fourth one was obviously inappropriate. Therefore, the first two administrative penalties were upheld, while the last two were revoked.

Zhang v. Education Bureau and Public Security Bureau in X City[19]

Zhang, aged four, went over to her neighbour's house and played with Jiang, aged 14, in the afternoon of June 29, 1991. Knowing that there was no one else in the house, Jiang molested Zhang. Zhang went home crying and told her parents what had happened. After an investigation jointly made by the Education Bureau and the Public Security Bureau in X City, Based on the grounds that Jiang had molested the plaintiff, they made a joint decision to transfer Jiang to a rehabilitation school according to the Regulation on the Protection of Juveniles in that city. Dissatisfied with the decision, Jiang, represented by his parents, applied for administrative reconsideration to the Country People's Government. It decided that although the molest did in fact occur, the decision was made inadequately based on merely one instance of molest; the decision was also contradictory to the order issued by higher administrative authorities which have binding effect. The order provides that those who molest or assault women many times shall be sent to rehabilitation school. This order provides detailed explanation of the Regulation.

Having understood the intention of reconsideration organs, the decision was voluntarily removed, followed by the withdrawal of the plaintiff's action. After investigations conducted by the provincial people's government, it decided to approve the application for withdrawal.

Participants of Reconsideration

There are three kinds of participants in administrative reconsideration, *i.e.* applicants, the defending parties and the third parties. The applicants are those who have the right to bring a case for administrative reconsideration. They may be citizens, legal persons or other organizations. If the citizen with a right to apply for reconsideration is incompetent or with limited capacity for conduct, his or her legal representative may apply on his behalf. The incompetency or limited capacity is mainly defined in sections 12 and 13, and sections 15 and 16 of the General Principles of Civil Law. If the citizen has passed away, his near relatives may apply for reconsideration on his behalf. The meaning of near relatives is the same as the definition provided in the Family Law, *i.e.* the parents, foster parents, spouse, adult children, brothers and sisters. They, in fact, apply in their own names instead of the deceased.

As far as legal persons or other organizations are concerned, their capacity to lodge an application may change if the legal persons or other organizations cease to exist, or have been taken over by other legal persons or organizations. Then those administrative organs replacing them will be qualified to bring a case for administrative reconsideration.

The defending party is the administrative organ whose concrete administrative act has been challenged by an applicant under administrative reconsideration. For an administrative organ to be qualified as a defending party, certain qualifications need to be satisfied. Firstly, it should be granted external administrative power by either laws or regulations. Secondly, it should have undertaken a concrete administrative act which is believed by the applicant to have infringed upon its lawful rights or interests. Thirdly, it is notified by the administrative reconsideration organ to participate in the reconsideration.

If the concrete administrative act is a joint one, *i.e.* taken in the name of two or more administrative organs, each organ shall be responsible for its activity. Then they shall be the joint defending parties of an application.[20]

Sometimes a citizen, legal person or organization is neither an applicant nor a defending party. But it has an interest in the concrete administrative act, against which an application for reconsideration is already filed. It may then, with the approval of the administrative reconsideration organ, file a request for participation in the reconsideration as a third party. There are certain elements which should be met for a party to become a third party to a reconsideration case. Firstly, the party should have an interest in the outcome of the case; secondly, the reconsideration has started, but is not yet finished; thirdly, the approval of the administrative reconsideration organ is required. Such procedural requirements are there to prevent those who are not qualified to be third parties to get involved so as to ensure the proper operation of the reconsideration process. As the third party is usually familiar with the concrete administrative act, its participation may contribute to the proper identification of material facts and provide a full picture of the case so that any illegal or inappropriate aspects of the concrete administrative act may be rectified and the legitimate interests of the applicant can be protected.

There may be two kinds of third parties: those who have direct interests in the case, and those who have indirect interests in the case. They should all be invited as third parties to the administrative reconsideration. A related issue which should be discussed is the legal status of third parties in administrative reconsideration. Only when there is already an administrative reconsideration case, can third parties apply, or be requested by the reconsideration organ, to join in the reconsideration.[21]

Remedies

6.10 As far as a concrete administrative act is concerned, if the application of laws, administrative regulations, regulations, as well as the decisions and orders with a general binding force is correct, the facts are clearly ascertained and the statutory limits of authority and procedures are duly complied with, then the applicant shall not have a case for administrative reconsideration. As a result, the concrete administrative act will then be sustained. On the other hand, if the applicant has a case,[22] there are various kinds of remedies available through administrative reconsideration. The defending party may be required to rectify procedural inadequacies, or a fixed time be set for the defending party to perform its duty, or the concrete act be annulled or changed or even specific performance be required of the defending party. This section will discuss these remedies.

Order of Rectification

6.11 The defending party is supposed to undertake the concrete administrative act in accordance with legal procedure. The pre-condition is that there should be legal procedure available. However, there does not exist any systematic or comprehensive system on administrative procedure because China does not have a uniform set of administrative procedural law. As a result, there are no existing procedures to be followed for the undertaking of many administrative activities. This is one of the main reasons for administrative organs to neglect procedural requirements. But if there are procedural requirements in legislation, they should be followed. The failure to do so is deemed to be procedural inadequacy. It usually refers to such situations as failure for the defending party to reveal its own identity, or failure to inform the applicant of its rights, or mistake of the date in the written decision, etc. But if the ascertaining of facts and application of laws are correct, and the breach of procedural requirements have not directly affected the legitimate rights of the applicants, the defending party will only be required by the administrative reconsideration organ to make up or improve the procedural inadequacy in the concrete administrative act, which remains effective.

This is quite a difference between the Western and Chinese legal systems where procedural justice in the former is so cherished that breach of procedural legal requirements will lead to the voidness of the act concerned. It is because procedural fairness is the only thing which can definitely be achieved and everybody is equal before the same procedural requirements. Whereas different people will have different perception of substantive justice which is influenced by a lot of factors such as ideologies, social and economic background, religious belief, and so on.

Now the importance of procedural legality has gradually been realized. With the promulgation the Administrative Penalty Law, it has been suggested that violation of the procedural requirements for the imposition of administrative penalties may cause the decision to be challenged. The order of rectification is a demand for the administrative organ to rectify its wrongs. The order is not restricted to procedural illegality or inappropriateness. If the administrative organ made a mistake in the applicable legislation, or identification of material facts, or abuse of power, or excess of power, an order of rectification can always be issued so long as it is the appropriate remedy.

Specific Performance

If the defending party fails to perform the obligations imposed by the laws, administrative regulations and regulations, it is a derelict activity. There could be two situations. One is that the defending party's refusal to perform the obligation; the other is that the undue delay on the side of the defending party to perform the duties falling within its

6.12

scope of obligations. The administrative reconsideration organ may set a fixed time for the defending party to perform the duty.

Nullification or Change of the Concrete Administrative Act

6.13 If the defending party commits substantive mistakes in the process of undertaking a concrete administrative act, the act shall be annulled or changed, or the defending party may be required by administrative reconsideration decision to undertake a concrete administrative act anew. Those substantive mistakes include ambiguity of the main facts, erroneous application of the laws, regulations, rules, or decisions and orders with a general binding force, violation of legal procedures, which affects unfavourably the lawful rights and interests of the applicant, the excess of authority or abuse of powers, and obvious inappropriateness of the concrete administrative act.

Clear identification of material facts is the prerequisite and basis for the administrative organ to apply the proper legislation. These material facts affect directly the result of the concrete administrative act. Mistakes with regard to minor facts are unlikely to lead to the nullification or change of the concrete administrative act. Instead, an order of rectification may be issued.

As far as defending party is concerned, it may have applied one legislation instead of another, or the wrong sections of the same legislation, or the legislation which has lost its effect, or the legislation which has not come into effect yet, or rules or the decisions and orders with a general binding force, which are, nevertheless, contradictory to the laws and administrative regulations.

As discussed above, sometimes breach of procedural requirements may not affect the legitimate substantive interests of the applicant. But other times it may affect the legitimate substantive interests of the applicant. If that is the case, the administrative reconsideration organ has the power to annul the concrete administrative act.

Any administrative power is granted by legislation and therefore has its scope or limit. If the administrative organ undertakes a concrete administrative act in excess of its authority, it will be illegal. Whereas abuse of authority or powers in a broad sense is also a kind of act in excess of powers authorized. But to be more specific, it is the use of powers for a different purpose, which is not the aim of the legislation at all. It is similar to the taking into account irrelevant consideration or failure to take into account relevant consideration. Such kind of concrete act should be annulled or changed by the administrative reconsideration organ.

Obviously inappropriate concrete administrative acts may also be amended or changed by reconsideration organ. It refers mainly to the exercise of discretionary powers by administrative organs, *i.e.* the administrative organ undertakes an unreasonable concrete administrative act within the scope of its discretion. Whether a concrete administrative act is reasonable or not depends on the administrative measures or provisions adopted by the specific administrative organs. For example, the imposition of a fine upon those who breach food hygiene law. The standards of the fine imposed are provided in the regulations. If the fine imposed by the administrative organ has deviated from the standard very much, then that concrete administrative act would be deemed to be unreasonable or inappropriate. In the following case, the original administrative decision was changed by the administrative reconsideration organ.

Ma v. Public Security Station on X Harbour[23]

6.14 Yu, the third party, a tourist travelling in a steamer departing from Wuhan to Shanghai in November 1990, forced himself into a female rest room, and having put his hands over the victim's mouth, indecently assaulted Ma, who was having a shower. Afterwards Yu escaped through the door while pushing the victim away. In order to catch Yu, Ma rushed through the door and chased Yu alone and naked. She eventually went as far as nine metres from the rest room. She screamed for help while chasing Yu who was finally caught by the police. Yu was then transferred to the police station situated on the steamer. The police questioned Yu about the incident in which Yu claimed to have mistakenly gone to the wrong rest room. Yu was later asked to write down what had happened.

Ma, together with a few people, requested the police to punish Yu. Intending to settle the whole thing out of court, Yu's leader was asked by the police to make an apology for him, which was not acceptable to Ma. The case was transferred to the police station located at the harbour. Based on the information supplied by the police on the boat, Yu was charged with humiliating and insulting women and was fined RMB50. Feeling that the penalty was too light, Ma applied for administrative reconsideration.

The administrative reconsideration organ found out that the facts of the incidence were clear and there was sufficient reason for Ma to apply for reconsideration. Yu violated the Regulation on Administrative Penalty for Public Security and the penalty was too trivial. The administrative reconsideration organ changed the penalty to seven-day custody.

It should be noted that which of the above remedies would be granted will be determined on a case-by-case basis with the intention of achieving justice and fairness. If necessary, the administrative organ may even undertake a concrete administrative act, replacing that of the defending party.

Relationship between Administrative Reconsideration and Judicial Review

6.15   Administrative reconsideration and judicial review are different means to redress wrongs committed by administrative organs and to restore justice to the applicant, while at the same time protect the lawful exercise of executive authority by administrative organs. Sometimes the provisions of some laws and regulations stipulate that a person concerned shall first apply to an administrative organ for reconsideration and then bring a suit before a people's court if the person concerned does not accept the reconsideration decision. If that is the case, administrative reconsideration is compulsory and a pre-requisite for judicial review. That means all administrative remedies should be exhausted before resorting to judicial remedies. It has been suggested that it will enable the administrative organ at a higher level to supervise those at a lower level, make full use of special expertise to solve these specific problems. The relatively simple procedure is convenient to the parties and reconsideration can help reduce the burden of the people's courts by solving most administrative disputes at the level of administrative reconsideration. If the applicant does not accept the decision made by the administrative reconsideration organ to reject the application, the applicant may, within 15 days from the date of receiving the written decision on the rejection of the application, bring a suit before the people's court. If the laws or regulations provide otherwise, then those provisions have to be followed. For example, if the laws provide that the administrative reconsideration decision will be final, no application for judicial review will be accepted.

The second situation is that the laws or regulations do not stipulate administrative reconsideration as the prerequisite for judicial review. The applicant shall then have the choice, to either lodge an application or bring a case to the people's court for judicial review. If an application for judicial review has already been accepted, then no application for reconsideration will be accepted. On the other hand, if the applicant has lodged an application for administrative reconsideration which has been accepted, then no application for the same case can be filed before the people's court within the statutory time limit for conducting reconsideration.

Conclusion

6.16   Administrative reconsideration has been implemented for many years in China and the RAR has also been in force for five years. In the first two years after the promulgation of the RAR, many cases were brought up for reconsideration. But the figures have been decreasing since then.[24] It has been acknowledged that the reconsideration system has contributed to the resolution of many administrative cases. The scope of administrative reconsideration has expanded to cover many aspects of administration, including public security, planning, real estates, land, public utilities, environment, labour, customs, administration of industry and commerce, transportation, electricity administration, culture, and so on.[25] However, there also exist many problems which need to be solved. The existence of bias or the applicant's perception of potential bias has a discouraging effect upon the applicant to bring cases for reconsideration. A survey has also revealed some problems with the existing system. Most people would prefer bringing cases to local people's government rather than to the administrative organ at the next higher level, especially when they are located in another city. In order to improve the system and its legal effects, the system itself has to be improved first; this issue has been dealt with by the 1994 amendment to the RAR, which now generally keeps the choice open to the applicant unless the law provides otherwise. Then we also need qualified personnel to run the system in order to achieve its legislative objective.[26] While these suggestions may help solve some problems, it has to be borne in mind that the nature of administrative reconsideration is only an internal supervision with certain judicial characteristics. While acknowledging that improvements need to be made, it should not be expected to be as impartial as the judiciary.

Notes

[1] See Sheyi, p. 99.
[2] This is regarded as one of the principles of administrative reconsideration. For detailed discussion, refer to the section on the principles.
[3] See s. 1 of the RAR.
[4] This is provided for by s. 39 of the RAR.
[5] See Sheyi, p. 100.
[6] See s. 40 of the RAR.
[7] There is one chapter in Part Four of this book which is on applicable law. For detailed discussion, refer to that chapter.
[8] See Shu Meifeng, p. 100; see also Li Yiming, *Du Shi Yong Gui Fan Xing Wen Jian Shen Li Xing Zhen Fu Yi An Jian Zhi Qian Jian* ("View on the Application of Normative Documents in Adjudication of Administrative Reconsideration Cases") in *Collection of Legal Essays (Administrative Law) 1991*, Vol. 2, pp. 112–14.
[9] See Shu Meifeng, p. 100.
[10] See s. 41 of the RAR.
[11] See s. 35(1) of the Organic Law of the Local People's Congresses and Local People's Government.
[12] See Sheyi, p. 112.

[13] For detailed discussion of applicable law in judicial review, refer to the relevant chapter in Part Three.
[14] Refer to the chapter on applicable legislation in Part Three.
[15] For details, see Sheyi, p. 121.
[16] See s. 43 of the RAR.
[17] For those who are not familiar work the hierarchy of legislative in China, refer to Albert Chan, "Introduction to the Chinese Legal System", Butterworths, 1992, chapter 6.
[18] See Li Peichuan, pp. 335–37.
[19] See Li Peichuan, pp. 348–51.
[20] See also Sheyi, p. 79.
[21] See Zhou Huijun, *Xing Zhen Fu Yi Zhong Di San Ren De Fa Lu Di Wei* ("The Legal Status of Third Parties in Administrative Reconsideration"), in *Collection of Legal Essays 1993*, Vol. 4, at pp. 55–56.
[22] It means that the applicant successfully challenges the relevant administrative organ on one of the grounds discussed above.
[23] See Li Peichuan, pp. 352–54.
[24] See Huang Shuhai, *Xing Zhen Fu Yi Zhi Du De ShiShi Qing Kuang Ji Si Kao* ("The Implementation and *Thought on the Administrative Reconsideration System*",) in *Collection of Legal Essays 1993*, Vol. 4, pp. 47–50.
[25] See Huang Shuhai, p. 47.
[26] See Huang Shuhai, pp. 48–50.

PART 3

ADMINISTRATIVE LITIGATION (JUDICIAL REVIEW) IN CHINA

CHAPTER SEVEN
THE STRUCTURE OF ADMINISTRATIVE LITIGATION

Introduction

Administrative litigation refers to the litigation activity under which a citizen, legal person or other organization, believing that his legitimate rights or interests have been infringed by concrete administrative act[1] of an administrative organ or its personnel, apply to the people's court according to law for judicial protection and the court will exercise its power to review the administrative act concerned and adjudicate upon it.[2] It is judicial control over the exercise of administrative power by the executive branch of the government for the resolution of administrative disputes, of which one party is administrative organ or its personnel. The necessity and importance of judicial review in the supervision of the exercise of administrative power by the executive branch of the government and the protection of people's legitimate rights and interests have been acknowledged in China, where the executive branch of the government enjoys enormous power.[3] The function of administrative litigation is very much the same as judicial review in common law jurisdiction.[4]   7.01

Different countries have, due to their different historical, political and cultural reasons, different constitutional structures. The relationship between the three main branches of the government, *i.e.* the legislature, executive and judiciary, differs from one country to another. Judicial control of executive power is concerned with the relationship between the judiciary and the executive, which is determined by the constitutional structure of a country. Therefore, it is quite natural that the structures of judicial review may vary from one country to another. For example, the organs responsible for judicial review, the scope, grounds and remedies available may differ from one another. Though the scope and degree of control exercised by the judiciary over the executive may be different, in essence, it is all about the check and balance exercised by the judiciary over the executive branch of the government.

On the other hand, judicial review is an important judicial procedure for the resolution of disputes relating to public administration for the purpose of protecting the legitimate rights and interests of the citizens, legal persons and other organizations. In this sense, it is treated at least equally, if not more important as civil and criminal procedures.[5] This part of the book will discuss in detail the theory and practical operation of judicial review in China. It will start with the historical development of judicial review in China, which will contribute to the understanding of some unique characteristics of the system in China. It then moves on to discuss all the important issues relating to judicial review in China, such as the objectives, scope, grounds, jurisdiction and available remedies of judicial review. The difference between judicial review in China and common law jurisdiction will be highlighted wherever possible and necessary.

Development of Judicial Review in China[6]

7.02 Judicial review in a modern sense started in the Republic of China, after it overthrew the Qing Dynasty. Dr. Sun Yatsen, the first president of the Republic of China, made it clear in the temporary Constitution that administrative litigation would be provided for by other legislation. When the Republic of China was formerly founded, a regulation on administrative litigation was promulgated, which was afterworlds changed to administrative litigation law. It has later been amended three times and had been in use up to the founding of the People's Republic of China in 1949.[7]

When the Communist Party took over power, it abolished all the legislation and legal system of the Republic of China and started afresh. In its first constitutional document entitled the "General Principles of the People's Political Consultative Committee of the People's Republic of China", section 19 provided that "people and people's organizations have the right to appeal to the people's procuratorate and judicial organs against any state organs or their personnel for their unlawful and derelict behaviour." This was confirmed with slight changes by section 97 of the 1954 Constitution of the People's Republic of China, which states that "any citizens of the People's Republic of China have the right to appeal orally or in written form to state organs at different levels against any state organs or their personnel for their unlawful and derelict behaviour."[8] The main difference here seems to be the expansion of the supervisory organs as the term "state organs" also include administrative organs. That is to say, appeal may also be brought to administrative organs. The right to challenge the state organs or their personnel was confirmed as a constitutional right.

However, that right was only implemented in very limited areas through legislation.[9]

In 1978, the Communist Party held its Third Plenary of 11th Meeting and stated in its final report that socialist democracy and legal system should be strengthened and people's rights and interests, as promised under the Constitution, should be undoubtedly protected and nobody should be allowed to infringe on them.[10] Encouraged by the report, legal scholars started to conduct research to analyze the necessity of administrative legislation and the establishment of administrative litigation system in China. From 1978 to 1982, scholars had revealed the shortcomings of the available remedial measures at that time, *i.e.* appeal to administrative organs at higher level. That was obviously inadequate to protect the legitimate rights and interests of the citizens against the encroachment by administrative organs. The necessity and importance to establish an impartial administrative litigation system in China had been advocated.[11] That period was regarded as the preparatory period in theory for the establishment of administrative litigation system in China to address the complaints brought up by ordinary citizens against the government or its personnel for unlawful exercise of administrative power.

7.03 In practice, administrative litigation was adopted in several legislation promulgated in that period. Section 25 of the 1979 Election Law of the National People's Congress and Local People's Congresses of the People's Republic of China provides that "anyone who has an objection to the roll of voters may appeal to the election committee. The election committee shall make a decision on the appeal within three days. If the appellant is not satisfied with the decision, he may bring a suit in the people's court. The judgment of the people's court shall be final." Section 15 of the 1980 Income Tax Law of the People's Republic of China for Chinese-Foreign Equity Joint Ventures provides that "in case of a dispute with the tax authorities over tax payment, a joint venture must pay tax according to the relevant regulations before applying to higher tax authorities for reconsideration. If it does not accept the decision made after such reconsideration, it may bring a suit in the local people's court." These were just piecemeal provisions and may be treated as exceptional. In general, lawsuits against administrative organs were still rare during that period because they depended on the specific authorization of specific legislation as mentioned above. Without clear legal authorization, an ordinary citizen or legal person or other organization may not bring a case to the people's court to challenge any administrative organs.

That period was brought to its end by the enactment of the 1982 Civil Procedure Law of the People's Republic of China (for trial implementation) (CPL), which started a new period from 1982 to 1986.[12] Section 3(2) of the CPL provides that "the provisions of this Law are applicable to administrative cases that by law are to be tried by the people's courts." This provision formally acknowledges that there is a category of cases called administrative cases. This section also implies that laws enacted by the National People's Congress or its Standing Committee can provide for the people's courts to accept and adjudicate administrative cases. It also grants the people's courts the authority to adjudicate administrative cases according to the CPL. That is why some scholars regard the enactment of the 1982 CPL as the formal beginning of administrative litigation system in China.[13] This provision is therefore a very important development of administrative litigation system in China. It provides, for the first time, the procedures to be followed in administrative litigation.

7.04 In the following several years from 1982 to 1988, more than 130 laws and administrative regulations provided for the hearing of administrative cases.[14] Professor Jiang Mingan classified these legislations into nine categories. Apart from the 1986 Regulation on Administrative Penalty for Public Securities of the People's Republic of China, which grants ordinary citizens the right to challenge the decisions of public security bureaus to impose administrative penalties upon them, there were eight kinds of economic administrative activities which could be challenged by ordinary citizens according to respective legislation, including food hygiene administration, land administration, forest administration, industrial and commercial administration, intellectual property administration, taxation administration, medical administration and environmental administration.[15] These cases were more or less related to economic activities and were heard by the economic adjudication panel of the people's court.

However, those public security cases were neither criminal, nor economic, nor ordinary civil cases, it was inappropriate for either divisions of civil law, criminal law or economic law to deal with them. Therefore, some local courts started to establish a special division of administrative law to hear administrative cases. By the end of 1988, the Supreme People's Court also established a division of administrative law and more than 1,400 local people's courts established such panel to hear exclusively administrative cases.[16]

7.05 The next stage is the drafting period of the ALL, which started in 1986. In 1986 a research group composing of legal scholars was established to conduct research on administrative legislation, especially the urgency of and necessity of administrative litigation law. At that time, civil law, civil procedural law, criminal law and criminal procedure law were all enacted. There were also many administrative legislations governing various aspects of economy and society. But there was no administrative procedural law. It was a gap in Chinese procedural legislation. Therefore the group of experts started the drafting of the ALL. At the beginning, the group intended to draft a comprehensive administrative law, including both substantive and procedural administrative law. But that was proved to be too ambitious and difficult and no consensus could be reached among the group members as to the scope of the draft. The team finally gave it up and, after consultation with the Legislative Affairs Commission of the National people's Congress, settled down to draft administrative litigation law for which the conditions were already ready and the legislation would be more practical and feasible. The team completed its drafting by August 1988 and the draft was submitted to the Legislative Affairs Commission (LAC). From then onwards, the LAC formally became involved in the drafting of the Administrative Litigation Law. After wide consultation with various governmental organs, both at central and local levels, the judiciary, procuratorate, legal experts, research institutes and ordinary people, the ALL was approved on April 4, 1989 with effect from October 1, 1990.[17]

Objectives of the ALL

Section 1 of the ALL states clearly the legislative objectives. It mentions two kinds of objectives, *i.e.* procedural and substantive ones. Procedural objective ensures the correct and prompt handling of administrative cases by the people's courts. The ALL, in essence, is a procedural legislation stipulating the procedures for the handling of administrative cases. It has laid down mainly detailed requirements as to the scope of acceptable cases, courts' jurisdiction, parties to judicial review proceedings, evidence, the conditions to bring and accept a case, execution of judgment, available remedies, and the special procedures for foreign-related judicial review. It has not only defined the authority of the courts in adjudicating administrative cases, but also laid down certain restrictions on the exercise of judicial control of administration. Most of these provisions were missing from the 1982 Civil Procedural Law, which only had three provisions concerning the adjudication of administrative cases.[18] The enactment of the ALL has provided the people's courts with clear legal source on the procedures for the adjudication of administrative cases. In that sense, the ALL will contribute to achievement of correctness and accuracy of adjudication of administrative cases.

7.06

However, procedural legislation is there to ensure the proper application and implementation of substantive legislation and to rectify wrongs caused by any wrongful application or implementation of substantive legislation through the adjudication of the courts. A specific procedural legislation has its substantive objectives to achieve. The ALL has two specific substantive objectives which are stated in section 1. The first is to protect the lawful rights and interests of citizens, legal

117

persons and other organizations from unlawful infringement by any administrative organs or their personnel. As one party to any administrative relationship is an administrative organ and exercises statutory power, its legal status is unequal with the other side, which is normally in a weaker bargaining position. The ALL is enacted to provide proper legal protection to the weaker party to administrative relationship. If the legitimate interests or rights of the citizens, legal persons or other organizations are indeed infringed by the concrete acts of administrative organs or their personnel, then the people's courts should grant the victim appropriate remedies.[19] The other substantive objective is to safeguard and supervise the exercise of administrative powers by administrative organs in accordance with the law. It has two aspects. The first is the supervisory function exercised by the people's courts through adjudication, *i.e.* to ensure that any concrete administrative acts undertaken by administrative organs are in accordance with both substantive and procedural administrative legislation. The second is to safeguard those lawful concrete administrative acts from undue interference. The judiciary may achieve this objective by sustaining concrete administrative acts undertaken according to conclusive evidence, correct legislation and proper legal procedures.[20]

The two substantive objectives of the ALL are in theory compatible with, not contradictory to, each other. But they have different emphases. In practice, it is very difficult to achieve the balance between the two. Judicial practice has shown that the proper exercise of authority by the administration has often been overemphasized.[21] Which substantive objective is more important was also a main issue over which different views existed. The final version of section 1 combined the protection of rights with supervision of administractive organs.[22]

The relationship between the substantive and procedural objectives should also be noted. There exist various channels to achieve the two substantive objectives. However, we are concerned here with the substantive objectives of administrative litigation, *i.e.* judicial review. The achievement of the two substantive objectives not only depends on but also is restricted by the procedural objective of the ALL. Through the control of administrative power by the judiciary in the form of the adjudication of administrative cases, those two substantive objectives can be achieved. Specifically speaking, the people's courts will examine the legality of concrete administrative acts undertaken by the administrative organs. For some categories of concrete administrative acts, the courts may review their reasonableness.[23] If the acts undertaken are unlawful or sometimes unreasonable, the courts have the responsibility to rectify them and exercise their authority accordingly by annulling or repealing those concrete administrative acts and prescribe relevant remedies to the applicants. In so doing, the courts can supervise whether or not the administration has complied with the principle of rule of law in undertaking administrative acts. If the acts undertaken are lawful, then the courts should maintain them and require the applicant to perform their obligations imposed by the relevant administrative organ under substantive administrative legislation. That will ensure that the administrative organs can exercise its legal authority without undue or improper interference.

Reasons for the Late Adoption of Judicial Review in China

7.07 The above discussion shows that the establishment of administrative litigation (or judicial review) system, in its modern sense, is quite a recent event in China, compared with judicial review in common law jurisdiction, such as the United Kingdom and the United States, or continental legal systems, such as France and Germany. There are many reasons contributing to this late development of judicial review in China. They include constitutional, political, economic and cultural reasons, which can be summarized as follows.[24]

Constitutional Reason

7.08 Under China's Constitution, there is no separation of powers. In other words, the necessity of check and balance between the three main organs of the government, *i.e.* executive, judiciary and legislature is not accepted. The Chinese National Legislature, the National People's Congress, enjoys the supreme authority, including both executive and legislative power, and plays a supervisory role over the other two branches of the government, *i.e.* the State Council (executive) and the Supreme People's Court.[25] They are allocated respective powers to administer and adjudicate independently.[26] But the judiciary is not empowered to exercise check over the executive. And in fact, the executive branch of the government is, in practice, half a level above the judiciary at the same level. Judiciary is not completely independent of the executive.[27] Moreover, the judiciary is funded by the executive branch of the government at the same level, not directly from the national reserve. Therefore, China's different constitutional structure and lack of funding from the state purse all contribute to the non-independence of the judiciary.

However, it has been realized that certain types of cross-control and cross-supervision among the three main organs of the government, especially judicial control and supervision, is also necessary in China because of the possibility of abuse of both executive and legislative powers.[28]

Political Reason[29]

7.09 The judicial review system is closely associated with modern democracy and the rule of law principle. However, the Chinese Communist Party had not paid sufficient attention to democracy and rule of law for many years in the past. It had always been in the leading position and in control of all the three major organs of the government.[30] The administration of state affairs mainly depended on the policies issued by the Party rather than laws. The supervision regarding the question as to whether or not the administration had complied with the Party's policies was the capacity or function of the administration at the next higher level or the organization of the party issuing the policy, rather than the function of the courts. Even if the administration had breached the policies, the courts could not interfere because there was no law granting them the authority to interfere.

Only since 1978, the Communist Party itself has realized the importance of law and gradually started to establish a modern legal system in China. It has also become aware of the fact that running the country merely according to policies will give the party members too much power, which is the direct reason for abuse of power and corruption. Mere internal supervision by the party or the administration is not sufficient. External legal supervision of public administration is more effective. The Communist Party, at its recent meeting, the Fourteenth Plenary, has made it clear that it is essential to strengthen China's legal system, including the administration according to law.

Economic Reason[31]

7.10 The development of a legal system depends on the necessity of the economic development of the society. Only when the economy develops to a certain extent, will the necessity arise for the government or its organs to regulate various economic activities through registration, license, approval, examination or imposition of penalties in order to maintain the proper order of social and economic development.[32] However, during the process of governmental regulation of the economic development, it is unavoidable that disputes may arise between the government on the one side and those to be regulated on the other side. A dispute resolution channel is then required to solve those disputes. Courts are the ideal ones because of their impartial status.

After the Communist Party came into power in 1949 in China, it adopted a centrally planned economic system. As a result, the whole country was regarded as a big family and everything was owned by the State. No distinction was made between the Party and the administration, the administration and enterprises. Enterprises and other organizations did not have any independence or autonomy in their business operation. All citizens did not have much choice for their career because those living in the cities would be allocated jobs by the state. Therefore, the state, enterprises and individuals were all within a big family. The state was the head of the family and it could issue orders to all the members of the family, which had to be obeyed by the members in the big family. Under such a system where individuals did not enjoy independent rights, there was not need to resort to the courts.

Since the start of China's opening up to the outside world in 1978, enterprises have gradually been granted more autonomy in their business operation and individuals can also choose their own jobs. Disputes between administration and those to be administered have appeared. Especially since the Fourteenth Plenary of the Communist Party held in 1994, it has been determined that China will adopt a market economy. Direct governmental control by issuing orders will be changed to indirect regulation in different ways, including the licensing system. Such regulating authority may be abused. Therefore there exists the necessity for the establishment of legal control of the exercise of governmental regulating authority.

Cultural Reason[33]

China's feudal system had been in existence for over 2,000 years and the feudal monarchy ideology has deeply influenced Chinese culture and become part of it. Obedience to governmental officials was one element. As a result, the feudal concept that citizens should not bring legal action against the government or governmental officials was deep in the mind of ordinary citizens. The government or its officials were regarded as superior to ordinary citizens, and the government and the citizens were not equal. Therefore citizens should not sue the government. To bring a case to the court or to be brought to the court is not a glorious thing in the mind of many Chinese.[34]

7.11

The Communist Party claimed that a socialist system was established since 1949. The government is the people's government which serves the people of the country and represents the interests of the people. People should always love and support its own government. Such an understanding in theory has prevented the establishment of an administrative litigation system in China.

All those reasons have contributed to the late establishment of judicial review procedure in China. After the adoption of the Open-Door Policy in 1978, it has been realized how easily governmental powers may be abused and governmental officials may be corrupted. Eventually, the necessity of a control mechanism was realized and has been put into practice.

Sources of Judicial Review

7.12 As China mainly adopts a continental legal system, there does not exist the concept that the courts have certain inherent power. The jurisdiction of the courts over any lawsuits, including those against administrative organs for their exercise of administrative power, has to be prescribed by legislation. Otherwise, the courts will not have jurisdiction over matters for which no legal provisions stipulate that they are under the courts' jurisdiction. This is different from the common law approach towards judicial review, as adopted in the United Kingdom and Hong Kong, where the source of judicial review is common law. That is to say, the High Court has the inherent authority under common law to review the legality of the behaviour of the executive.[35] There are several legal sources for judicial review in China.

Constitutional Source

7.13 There exists a consensus among Chinese scholars that the current constitutional source for judicial review in China is in paragraph one of section 41 of the 1982 Constitution.[36] It provides that "Citizens of the People's Republic of China have the right to criticize and make suggestions regarding any state organ or functionary. Citizens have the right to make to relevant state organs complaints or charges against, or exposures of, any state organ or functionary for violation of the law or dereliction of duty; but fabrication or distortion of facts for purposes of libel or false incrimination is prohibited." Here the term "relevant state organs" should include the judiciary (the People's Courts). Though the Constitution confirms the citizens' right to judicial review, citizens in China cannot rely on any provisions in the Constitution to bring a lawsuit directly to the courts because constitutional rights cannot be directly enforced. The Chinese Constitution is not directly operative and the people's courts in China do not have the authority to pass a decision on whether or not a matter is unconstitutional. Such authority is in the hands of the Legislature, National People's Congress or its Standing Committee.[37] In order to bring any constitutional provisions into operation, including the right to judicial review, other specific legislation has to be enacted. Such legislation will be regarded as direct legal source.

Direct Source of Judicial Review

7.14 The direct legal source of judicial review in China has developed over the years. At the beginning, judicial review was based on the 1982 CPL.

However, the CPL did not provide for the categories of administrative activities which could be subject to judicial review. From 1982 onwards to the promulgation of the ALL, many other specific legislation, especially those relating to public administration, has provided the aggrieved party the opportunity to bring a case for judicial review. Those legislation were also legal source for judicial review before the adoption of the ALL. Starting from October 1, 1990 when the ALL came into effect, the ALL has become the formal legal source for judicial review.[38] The ALL has two advantages: one is that it has laid down the procedural requirements concerning administrative litigation; and the second is that it has defined the scope of acceptable cases. However, the ALL states that there may also be other legal sources by which citizens may bring a case for judicial review. That is to say, other legislation may stipulate that citizens may challenge a new type of concrete administrative acts through the courts.[39] Previous legislation shall still be valid and useful if those cases do not fall within the scope of acceptable cases under the ALL.

Conditions for Judicial Review[40]

7.15 Section 2 of the ALL provides for the conditions under which citizens, legal persons or other organizations may bring a case for judicial review. It has been given an academic term by Chinese scholars as the right to sue.[41] It is similar to the concept of locus standi in common law jurisdiction. It refers to the qualification of an individual or legal person or an organization to apply for judicial protection.[42] Section 2 of the ALL provides that:

> If a citizen, a legal person or any other organization considers that his or its lawful rights and interests have been infringed upon by a concrete administrative act of an administrative organ or its personnel, he or it shall have the right to bring a suit before a people's court in accordance with this Law.

This provision is essential in the sense that it has provided for the three essential components for a case to qualify as an administrative litigation case.[43] Firstly, the plaintiff must be those who believe that their lawful rights or interests have been infringed upon by concrete administrative acts of administrative organs or their personnel. Here the test is an subjective test. It is sufficient if a plaintiff believes genuinely that his lawful rights or interests have been infringed upon. It does not matter whether or not the plaintiff has, in practice, got a true case against the administrative organs or their personnel. That is an issue the courts will find out and determine through the process of adjudication. In one case, the plaintiff is a joint venture. Its major busines was the manufacture of television parts and components for export. It imported the raw material, semi products and other packing materials from foreign countries. It sold those products which are not up to the standards to a Chinese domestic company. That was discovered by the defendant, the Customs office in that city. The defendant imposed customs duty, consolidated tax and also administrative penalty on the plaintiff, according to section 41 of Customs Law and section 6 of the Regulation on the Exemption of Customs Duty for Imported Goods by Joint Venture, for not going through the proper legal examination and procedures for selling products in the Chinese market. The plaintiff brought a case for judicial review to challenge the decision of the defendant on the grounds that they sold the products at a very low price. The people's court upheld the decision of the defendant.[44] In this case, the plaintiff believed that the defendant's imposition of customs duty and penalty on it had infringed its legitimate interests. Though he did not have a real case to win, he had satisfied the requirement to bring a case to the people's court.

An important issue concerning the qualification as a plaintiff in administrative litigation is whether or not the plaintiff should be the person under the administration of the defendant or it suffices for the plaintiff to have direct interests in the concrete administrative acts undertaken by the defendant, or it depends on legal provisions.

Secondly, the defendant must be an administrative organ or its personnel which/who is authorized to exercise administrative power. Only an administrative organ can become a defendant in judicial review cases. No judicial organs, legislative organs, Party's branches or military organs can be sued against as defendant. Another point here is the element of unlawfulness. That is to say, the act undertaken must be an unlawful one.

Thirdly, the administrative acts to be sued against must be concrete administrative acts. The ALL does not provide any definition as to what a concrete administrative act is. But section 1 of the Opinions of the Supreme People's Court on the Interpretation of the Administrative Litigation Law (hereinafter as Opinions on the ALL) states that:

> A concrete administrative act is a unilateral act undertaken by a state administrative organ or its personnel, legally authorized organizations, or organizations or individuals entrusted by an administrative organ, in exercising administrative power in the process of conducting administration, targeting at specific citizens, legal persons or other organizations with regard to their rights and obligations.

7.16 There are four points in this definition which should be noted. Firstly, the act must be a unilateral act of the administrative organ concerned, not a bilateral act between the plaintiff and the administrative organ undertaking the act; secondly, the act must be the result of the exercise of an administrative power, not any contractual rights or collective rights by the administrative organ or its personnel; thirdly, the act must target at a specific person (either natural or legal), not an act applicable to the general public, which will be regarded as abstract administrative act; fourthly, it must affect the legal rights or obligations of the specific persons. Only when those four elements are satisfied can an administrative act be classified as a concrete administrative act and be challenged through administrative litigation.

Section 41 adds two more conditions for a case to qualify as an administrative case. Firstly, is that the case must fall with the scope of acceptable cases.[45] If the case falls outside the scope, the people's court cannot accept the case. Secondly, the case must be within the jurisdiction of the people's court to which the case is accepted. Otherwise, the court may refuse to accept.[46]

Notes

[1] The concept of concrete administrative act is one of the most important concepts in the procedural administrative law in China. For detailed discussion of the concept, refer to the theory part and later sections in this chapter.
[2] See Ying Songnian, pp. 1–2.
[3] See Luo Haocai 1993, p. 1.
[4] In this book, administrative litigation and judicial review have the same meaning and will be used interchangeably.
[5] See Luo Haocai and Ying Songnian, *Administrative Litigation Law*, 1990, p. 1.
[6] For detailed discussion of historical development of judicial review system in China, refer to Luo and Ying 1990, pp. 65–75; Pi and Hu, pp. 11–15; Jiang Mingan, pp. 28–37; Xu and Pi, pp. 1–7; Zhang and Zhang, pp. 396–400.
[7] See Luo and Ying 1990, pp. 65–70.
[8] See Luo and Ying 1990, pp. 70–71.
[9] For example, 1950 Land Reform Law provided that peasants who were not satisfied with the evaluation of their class by the township people's government might appeal to the county people's court. Apart from that legislation, there was hardly any other legislation stipulating the right to challenge any administrative decisions.
[10] See Jiang Mingan, p. 32.
[11] See Jiang Mingan, p. 32.
[12] Different opinions exist as to whether or not this period should be from 1982–88.
[13] See Jiang Mingan pp. 33–34; Luo Haocai and Ying Songnian, Administrative Litigation Law, pp. 71–72.
[14] This information is provided by Luo and Ying in their book.
[15] See Jiang Mingan, pp. 34–35.
[16] See Pi and Hu, p. 30.
[17] See Jiang Mingan, pp. 35–36; Luo Haocai and Ying Songnian pp. 73–74.
[18] s. 3(2) of the 1982 Civil Procedural Law provides that "The provisions of this Law are also applicable to administrative cases that by law are to be tried by the people's courts".
[19] See Zhong Hua Ren, *Ming Gong He Guo Xing Zhen Su Song Fa Quan She* (Comments and Interpretation of the ALL of the PRC) (hereinafter as Quan She), pp. 6–7.

20 Those are the conditions laid down in s. 54(1) of the ALL to sustain a concrete administrative decision.
21 See Quan She, p. 7.
22 See Jiang Mingan, pp. 37–38; Quan She, pp. 5–9.
23 Fro details, refer to the section on judicial review of discretionary power.
24 Professor Jiang Mingan has suggested political, economic and cultural reasons for the late development of judicial review system in China. While agreeing with him that those three are indeed important reasons, the author of this book believes constitutional structure is the main legal reason.
25 Section 57 of the Constitution states that "The National People's Congress of the People's Republic of China is the highest organ of state power. Its permanent body is the Standing Committee of the National People's Congress." s. 67(6) provides that the Standing Committee of the National People's Congress exercises the function and power to supervise the work of the State Council, the Central Military Commission, the Supreme People's Court and the Supreme People's Procuratorate. S. 92 maintains that "The State Council is responsible and reports on its work to the National People's Congress or, when the National People's Congress is not in session, to its Standing Committee."
26 S. 85 of the Constitution states "The State Council, that is, the Central People's Government, of the People's Republic of China is the executive body of the highest organ of state power; it is the highest organ of state administration." S. 126 of the Constitution stipulates that "The people's courts exercise judicial power independently, in accordance with the provisions of the law, and are not subject to interference by any administrative organ, public organization or individual." S. 128 provides that "The Supreme People's Court is responsible to the National People's Congress and its Standing Committee . . ."
27 See *The Law on Judges in the PRC 1996.*
28 See Jiang Mingan, pp. 63–64.
29 See Jiang Mingan, pp. 29–30.
30 The situation shall remain so for the near future because no other parties are allowed to compete with the Communist Party for Power, which is provided in the Constitution.
31 See Jiang Mingan, pp. 27–28.
32 This is the typical Marxist political economics.
33 See Jiang Mingan, pp. 30–31.
34 See Chen Youxi, *Dui Xing Zhen Su Song Kun Jing De Hong Guan Si Kao* ("Reflection on the Dilemma of Administrative Litigation"), in *Collection of Legal Essays on the ALL*, pp. 26–31.
35 See H.W.R. Wade and Forsyth, *Administrative Law*, pp. 38–39, seventh edn, 1994, Clarendon Press, Oxford.
36 It may be assumed that s. 19 of the "Common Principles" and s. 97 of the 1954 Constitution were the constitutional sources.
37 S. 62 of the Constitution provides, "The National People's Congress exercises the following functions and powers:
   (2) to supervise the enforcement of the Constitution;
   (3) to enact and amend basic laws governing criminal offences; civil affairs, the state organs and other matters; . . ."
   S. 67 of the Constitution provides, "The Standing Committee of the National People's Congress exercises the following functions and powers:
   (2) to enact and amend laws, with the exception of those which should be enacted by the National People's Congress;
   (3) to partially supplement and amend, when the National People's Congress is not in session, laws enacted by the National People's Congress provided that the basic principles of those laws are not contravened;
   (4) to interpret laws; . . ."
38 For detailed discussion of those legal sources, refer to the previous section on the development of judicial review system in China.
39 Refer to the section on the scope of judicial review.
40 See also "Guan Yǔ Xing Zhen An Jian De Shou Li" in *Xing Zhen Shen Pan Shi Jian Yu Yan* ("The Practice and Study of Administrative Adjudication"), Jiu Huang Jie and

Li Daoming, China Legal System Press 1991, pp. 101–108. See Chen Guosheng, *Xing Zhen Su Song Zhong Yuan Gao De Jie Ding* ("The Determination of the Plaintiff in Administrative Litigation") in Collection of Legal Essays 1993, pp. 46–47.

[41] The conditions to sue are likely to be broader than the concept of *locus standi*.
[42] See Quan She p. 10; Liu Wei, *Tan Xin Zhen Su Song Yuan Gao Zi Ge De Jie Ding*, Comment on Qualification of Plaintiff in Administrative Litigation in *Collection of Legal Essays (Administrative Litigation Law) 1993*, pp. 56–59.
[43] See Wu Xielin, *Xing Zhen Su Song Yuan Gao Zo Ge Xing Lun* (A New Approach to the Qualification of the Plaintiff in Administrative Litigation), in *Collection of Legal Essays (Administrative Litigation Law)* 1993, pp. 48–52; Liu Quanzhu, *Lun Xing Zhen Su Song De Yuan Gao Zi Ge* (Comment on the Qualification of the Plaintiff in Administrative Litigation), in *Collection of Legal Essays (Administrative Litigation Law) 1993*, pp. 53–55;
[44] See Zhang Qiuke, *Zhong Guo Xing Zhen Su Song Shi Yong Da Quan*, p. 274.
[45] Scope of acceptable cases shall be discussed in the next chapter. In this book the term of "scope of acceptable cases" will be used interchangeably with the term of "scope of jurisdiction".
[46] The issue of jurisdiction shall be discussed in Chapter 8 of this book. See Luo and Ying, *Xing Zhen Su Song Fa Xue* (Administrative Litigation Law), chapter 4, pp. 96–117; Pi and Hu, *Xing Zhen Su Song Fa Jiao Chen* (Textbook on Administrative Litigation Law), Chapter 5, pp. 62–74; Jiang Mingan, Chapter 7, pp. 106–130.

CHAPTER EIGHT
SCOPE OF JURISDICTION IN JUDICIAL REVIEW

8.01   Section 2 of the ALL only provides for the three general conditions under which a person may bring a case to the people's court for judicial review. They are the legal reasons why people can apply for judicial review. That section must be read together with section 41. One of the extra conditions under section 41 is that the case must be within the scope of acceptable cases. That is to say, not all administrative acts which meet the conditions under section 2 are judicially reviewable. Instead, only certain kinds of concrete administrative acts, as stipulated under section 11 of the ALL, are subject to judicial review.

   The concept of the scope of jurisdiction is concerned with the categories of administrative acts which are, or are not, subject to judicial review. As far as the plaintiff is concerned, the scope of jurisdiction is about the scope within which he can seek judicial protection and obtain judicial remedies for the breach of its lawful rights or interests by the relevant administrative organ.[1] There do not exist any jurisprudential reasons as to why other concrete administrative acts satisfying the conditions of section 2 are not judicially reviewable. The determination of the scope of jurisdiction is purely based on the principle of convenience, the legal system involved and the demand of the society. It reflects to what extent the judiciary has control over the executive. Before the enactment of the ALL, China did not have much experience in judicial review. In order to ensure that the adjudication of administrative cases can be held properly, the legislature decided to limit the scope of jurisdiction at the beginning. It can later gradually expand the scope when more experience is obtained.[2]

8.02   The ALL is one of the three main procedural legislation in addition to civil and criminal procedural laws. It has a specific chapter listing the categories of administrative acts which are both subject to and not subject to judicial review. But in the other two pieces of procedural legislation, there are no provisions listing the cases which are subject to civil or criminal litigation. That shows the difference between administrative litigation on the one hand, and civil and criminal litigation on the other hand. Several reasons have been suggested by Chinese scholars.[3]

Firstly, administrative litigation is concerned with the relationship between executive power and judicial power. According to the allocation of powers principle under the Chinese Constitution, executive branch and judicial branch of the government are allocated executive and judicial authority respectively. Executive authority is subject to the supervision and check of the judiciary to a certain extent. But the nature of executive activities has determined that it cannot be subject to judicial review unconditionally. That means certain executive activities should not be subject to judicial review. For example, some administrative acts may relate to state and public interests and need to be kept secret. If they are subject to judicial review, the openness nature of the judicial process may leak its secrecy; some administrative acts may be especially urgent and need to be dealt with as soon as possible whereas judicial review process is usually time-consuming and may improperly delay the process and cause serious result; some other administrative acts may be of strong political characteristics and are very subtle and changeable under different conditions. If they were dealt with through judicial process, the courts would not be able to find appropriate legal criteria upon which to adjudicate. Discretion is one of the features of administrative power. But if discretion is granted to the judiciary in the application of legal principles, that will confuse the allocation of work among different governmental branches, especially between the judiciary and executive. Therefore, executive activities need to be subject to judicial review; but not all executive activities should be subject to judicial review due to those reasons mentioned above. It is therefore necessary to lay down in the ALL whether or not a specific category of administrative acts is subject to judicial review.

Secondly, judicial review is only one of many kinds of legal supervision over the executive activities. Others include the supervision exercised by the legislature, people's procuratorate, administrative supervisory organ, audit organs and the mass media. In order to better use each kind of machinery available effectively and avoid overlapping, the scope of judicial review should be clearly distinguished from the areas which are subject to the supervision of other legal machineries. That is the practice in China. For example, the legislature mainly supervise legislative activities and other abstract administrative activities, such as the issue of rules or orders by the administrative organs which affect the general public. Procuratorate mainly supervises the administrative activities by administrative personnel which are in breach of criminal law. Clear legal provision of the scope of judicial review can demarcate the areas which are subject to different kinds of supervisory machineries.

Thirdly, judicial review is one of those remedial procedures available in administrative law. Others include complaint to the administrative organ concerned, administrative reconsideration procedure and state compensation procedure. The scope of remedies available under judicial review should also be distinguished from the scope of other remedial procedures so that they will constitute a comprehensive and effective remedial structure for people to challenge the legality or reasonableness of administrative activities undertaken by administrative organs.

These are the three main reasons to justify the necessity to lay down in the ALL the scope of judicial review.

Categories of Administrative Acts Subject to Judicial Review

8.03 The general principle is that the people's courts can only accept lawsuits against those concrete administrative acts which are stated to be judicially reviewable by legislation.[4] If a concrete administrative act is not specifically mentioned either by the ALL or any other legislation as reviewable, then it will not be subject to judicial review. Section 11 of the ALL lists eight categories of concrete administrative acts which are reviewable. The Opinions on the ALL provide more detailed provisions with regard to the scope of jurisdiction. The categories of concrete administrative acts subject to judicial review are almost the same as those for administrative reconsideration. The RAR was enacted in 1990, one year later than the ALL. On the basis of incorporation of all judicially reviewable cases as administratively reconsiderable ones, the RAR has expanded the scope a bit further.[5] As scope of administrative reconsideration has been discussed in great detail in previous parts of this book, this part will only mention those categories briefly and analyze possible differences.

Administrative Penalty

8.04 Administrative penalty is the first category of concrete administrative act subject to judicial review. It is a kind of legal sanction imposed by administrative organs on citizens, legal persons or other organizations for their violation of laws and regulations. Section 11(1) lists five of them, including detention, fine, rescission of a license or permit, order to suspend production or business or confiscation of property, which one refuses to accept.⁶ The 1996 Administrative Penalty Law (APL) has also laid down the procedures concerning the imposition of administrative penalty which must be followed.

Detention

Detention is a penalty restricting personal freedom. It refers to administrative detention executed by the public security bureau for the violation of the Regulation on Administrative Penalties for Public Security. Administrative detention is different from criminal detention. Though both of them are executed by the public security bureaus, their legal sources of authority are different. Criminal detention is based on the breach of criminal law. According to sections 9 and 10 of the 1996 Administrative Penalty Law, only laws may create penalties restricting personal freedom.

8.05

Imposition of Fine

The imposition of a fine is a proprietary penalty. It mainly refers to the situation under which a person is required by the administrative organ to pay a certain fine as a penalty for this breach of laws or regulations. With the promulgation of the APL in 1996, the administrative organs which have the authority to create new kinds of administrative penalty, including fines, have been clearly defined or restricted. These organs which have not been legally authorized to impose fines will no longer be able to do so.⁷

8.06

In one case concerning a Sino-Japanese joint venture company, the company imported 20 vehicles in 1987. The Customs department exempted the customs duty and consolidated tax on the vehicles according to the Regulation on the Supervision and Exemption of Customs Duty on Goods Imported and Exported by the Sino-Foreign Cooperative Enterprises. Two years later, the company sold five vehicles to a Chinese domestic company. Customs ordered the company to go through the formalities. It confiscated the income obtained by the company from the sale of the five vehicles and imposed a fine on the company. The company brought the case for judicial review. As section 9 of the regulation provides that the imported vehicles by a joint-venture company cannot be sold unless permission is obtained and customs duty is paid. Otherwise a penalty may be imposed.⁸

Rescission of Licence and Suspension of Production

Rescission of a licence or permit, suspension of production or business are penalties restricting the capacity of performance. Revocation of

8.07

valid licences by the administrative organs lawfully obtained a permanent prohibition of the licensees to undertake those licensed activities. It is a very serious sanction. Suspension of production or business is only a temporary suspension of approved activities. Apart from these two, there are also other kinds of sanctions restricting the capacity of performance, such as the cancellation of certain privileges, imposition of additional conditions on licensees, and so on. Whether or not they are also subject to judicial review is hardly a question as most Chinese scholars agree that all administrative sanctions are within the scope of judicial review.[9] Under the 1996 APL, revocation is regarded to be more serious than other penalties restricting the capacity of performance. It can only be created by laws or administrative regulations.[10]

In another case relating to a joint venture, the plaintiff, a medicine manufacturer made a proposal to the relevant authority in the province to establish a joint venture with a Japanese partner. Its proposal was approved and a business licence was issued by the defendant, the Administration Bureau of Industry and Commerce. The defendant discovered later that the registered capital was not adequate and decided to revoke the licence. The plaintiff brought a case for judicial review against the decision of the defendant. The court held that the legitimate interests of all parties shall be protected by the laws. In this case, section 7 of the Rules on the Contribution of Registered Capital of Sino-Foreign Cooperative Joint Ventures grants the authority to the defendant to revoke the approval when certain conditions are not met. The defendant's decision was upheld.[11]

Confiscation

8.08 Confiscation of property is treated as a remedial penalty in China. Such a penalty is usually imposed with the intention to stop the infringing activity or to restore the infringed rights or interests. Apart from confiscation of property, it may also take the form of an order to do or not to do some specific activities.

Warning

Section 11(1) only mentions the above five administrative penalties which are often encountered in daily life. They fall into four types but they do not represent a comprehensive list of the four types of administrative penalties. These five sanctions are only used as examples. Citizens, legal persons or any other organizations may bring a lawsuit against any other types of administrative sanctions, except those clearly excluded from the scope of judicial review. Chinese scholars classify administrative penalty into five types. The fifth type is any kind of warning issued by the administrative organ to those breaching law. A warning will normally state that the violator's behaviour has breached the law and inform the violator not to do the same again. It may be in the form of direct warning, criticism through circulation by paper, and so on. The main purpose is to enable the violator to learn lessons from the past and at the same time to have an educational effect upon the other people that it is necessary to comply with laws and regulations. If a warning is used externally, it should still be subject to judicial review. But if it is used internally by administrative organs, it will be excluded from judicial review under section 12(3).

Compulsory Administrative Measure

A compulsory administrative measure refers to a measure taken by an administrative organ to restrict the freedom to exercise certain rights or to request the performance of certain obligations with the intention of achieving specific objectives. Section 11(2) lists four administrative compulsory measures which, again, do not constitute a comprehensive list.[12] It is generally agreed that all administrative compulsory measures should be subject to judicial review. They may take four different formalities. The first is preventive compulsory measure such as compulsory separation, treatment or education. Their purpose is to prevent the occurrence of improper behaviour which may endanger society or cause other kinds of undesirable results.[13] The second is a protective compulsory measure. It refers to the measures taken by an administrative organ, with the intention to ensure that it can or may in the future take an action against the illegal behaviour, such as compulsory investigation, search or temporary detainment of property. The third is a prohibitive compulsory measure. It refers to the measure to prohibit an illegal activity which has happened or is in implementation such as compulsory confiscation, destruction, imposition of duties or taxes, or prohibition to use, and so on. The fourth is an implementary compulsory measure. It refers to the measures taken by administrative organ to force a person to perform his duty imposed by a specific administrative law.[14]

8.09

Autonomy in Business Management

Economic reform has brought into existence different forms of enterprises, such as state-owned, collectively owned, foreign investment and privately owned enterprises. These four kinds of enterprises may all be established according to relevant legislation. In order to ensure that all enterprises can be run properly, legal protection and guarantee have been provided for under these legislations. One specific guarantee

8.10

is the autonomy in business management. The specific scope of power and degree of autonomy differ from one kind of enterprise to another because these four kinds of enterprises are different in ownership. But it mainly includes the autonomy in making decisions about production, the price of products, sale of its products, purchase of raw material, disposal of its assets, employment, wages and internal structure.[15] If a concrete administrative act of an administrative organ deprives an enterprise or an individual of its autonomy in its business operation, the enterprise or the individual may bring a lawsuit under the ALL for judicial review.

Refusal to Grant Licences[16]

8.11 Licences are certificates issued by administrative organs or their authorized representatives upon application according to legal provisions to grant the capacity or legal qualification to the applicant to undertake certain activities which usually cannot be undertaken unless with approval. There are many kinds of licences such as a licence for special kinds of business operation, *e.g.* hotel, travelling, licence permitting the use of special kind of tool, such as a gun or knife, licence to produce special kinds of industrial products, such as electrical goods and measuring tools, hygiene licence, licence to exploit natural resources, import and export licences, civil aviation licence, business licence, driving licence, and so on.[17]

Licences are essential for the lawful operation of business or proper undertaking of certain activities. It has been discussed above that the rescission of licence is subject to judicial review. The refusal to issue a permit or licence by an administrative organ or the failure of the administrative organ to respond to the application are also subject to judicial review. The condition is that the applicant must have applied to the appropriate licensing authority and the application is refused or the licensing authority fails to reply within the time limit or a reasonable time period if there is no statutory time limit.[18]

In one case, the plaintiff proposed to the Foreign Economy and Trade Commission in B province to establish a joint venture with a motor car company in Hong Kong in 1989. Relevant documents had been prepared. The defendant refused to approve the application on the grounds that: the division of profit was obviously in favour of the Hong Kong Company; and the managing director and the deputy managing director were all appointed by the Hong Kong partner. The defendant asked the plaintiff to amend the agreement, which the plaintiff did. But the commission still refused to approve the application.[19] It is not clear from the facts why the commission still refused to approve the application. If the defendant refused to approve because of its abuse of power or the refusal is obviously unfair, then the plaintiff can successfully challenge the decision of the defendant. Alternatively, the case may also be classfied into the category of failure to perform statutory duty to grant approval to qualified applicant.

Failure to Perform Statutory Duty

8.12 Section 11(5) is concerned with the failure of administrative organs in the performance of statutory duties to protect personal and proprietary rights of natural or legal persons. These personal or proprietary rights are recognized by China's Constitution and many other specific legislation. They include the right to life, freedom, name, reputation, portrait, to property, debts, succession, patent, copyright, and so on.[20]

There are several conditions which should be satisfied in order to bring a case for judicial review. The first is that personal or proprietary rights have been infringed or will be fringed; secondly, the person concerned has already applied to the administrative organ for protection; thirdly, the administrative organ has a statutory duty to provide the applied protection; and fourthly, the administrative organ refuses to perform its statutory duty or fails to respond.[21]

Failure to Pay Subsidy or Pension

8.13 The ALL is concerned with a specific kind of pension, *i.e.* the pension granted according to law by the civil affairs department or other relevant administrative organs to disabled soldiers or public servants or the direct relatives of the soldiers or public servants who died for the country. This kind of pension is an essential financial help to the disabled ones or the direct relatives of the deceased. The failure to grant a pension will disturb the normal life of the persons concerned. They can bring a lawsuit against the administrative organ concerned under the ALL.

It should be noted that here we are concerned with the duty of the administrative organ to pay such kind of pension. There must be legal provision for the payment of pension by the relevant administrative organ. If the law or administrative regulation provides only for the enterprise concerned to pay a pension, then the failure to pay the pension will lead only to civil lawsuit between the applicant and the relevant enterprise, rather than administrative litigation.

Unlawful Request for Duty Performance

8.14 An administrative organ may be entitled to require citizens, legal persons or other organizations to perform certain kinds of duties as imposed by a specific piece of administrative legislation. If the duty is imposed by law or administrative regulation, and it is enforced by the administrative organ according to proper legal procedure, then it should be performed properly. Otherwise, the request for the performance of duty, *e.g.* without legal provision or without following legal procedure, will be an infringement of lawful rights of the person concerned.

What is exactly the scope of unlawful request for duty performance is subject to different interpretations. Unlawful requests can be classified into those in violation of substantive and procedural legislation, and further classification is also possible. For example, an administrative organ may impose a fee according to its own rule or notice upon enterprises such as security fee, education fee or request enterprises to provide labour for certain kinds of work such as construction of roads and schools. If their own rules are not consistent with national laws and administrative regulations, then their request may be regarded as unlawful ones in violation of substantive legislation. The requests for performance of duty without following proper legal procedure, *e.g.* legal conditions, criterion, quota or time limit, may also infringe the lawful rights of citizens, legal persons or other organizations. They are all subject to judicial review.[22]

Infringement of Other Personal or Proprietary Interests

8.15 Apart from the seven categories of concrete administrative acts mentioned above which may infringe personal or proprietary rights,[23] there exist many other kinds of concrete administrative acts which may also infringe other kinds of personal or proprietary rights of citizens, legal persons or other organization. The Opinions on the ALL have given some examples.[24]

Section 4 of the Opinions on the ALL states that if a person is not satisfied with the verdict reached by an administrative organ concerning compensation to him, he may bring a case for judicial review. Some legislation authorizes administrative organs to make a verdict through administrative methods on disputes over civil compensation between equal parties. Such verdicts are reached through unilateral exercise of executive power in the process of administration and can be enforced if performance is not voluntarily carried out. It is therefore a concrete administrative act and should be subject to judicial review. Such kind of verdicts should be distinguished from another kind of verdict where administrative organs only act as a mediator or conciliator according to laws or administrative regulations to arbitrate and reach a verdict accordingly. Then the parties cannot bring the case for judicial review. Instead, they are only entitled to bring a case as a civil case rather than a judicial review case.[25]

Section 5 of the Opinions on the ALL stipulates that if a person is not satisfied with any compulsory indemnity decisions made by an administrative organ according to its authorization, he can bring a case for judicial review. Administrative indemnity refers to monetary compensation granted by an administrative organ to the person whose lawful rights or interests have been infringed by any lawful concrete administrative acts undertaken by administrative organs. The compulsory purchase of land by an administrative organ according to law is one of such examples.[26] Usually, indemnity may be determined in one of two different methods: one is through negotiation of the parties, an agreement is reached as to the amount of compensation; the other is that the administrative organ unilaterally makes a decision as to the amount of compensation. Only against the second kind of compensation may the citizens, legal persons or other organizations bring a lawsuit under the ALL as a judicial review case.[27]

Section 7 of the Opinions on the ALL provides that a person may bring a lawsuit under the ALL if he is not satisfied with a decision concerning ownership of or the right to use land, mineral resources, forests and any other natural resources made by the administrative organs in charge. It is because relevant administrative organs have been authorized under the Land Administration Law and Mineral Resources Law to handle disputes concerning the ownership of or the right to use those natural resources. Their decisions can be enforced through judiciary if the party concerned neither complies with it nor brings a lawsuit against the decision. Decisions concerning the ownership to real properties made by relevant administrative organs will directly affect the proprietary interests and rights of the related persons. Such decisions are also judicially reviewable.[28]

The Opinions on the ALL only list the above three as examples of other concrete administrative acts affecting other personal or proprietary rights or interests. There may be more. The effect of section 11(8) is that any concrete administrative acts infringing on personal or proprietary rights are judicially reviewable, except those excluded under section 12 of the ALL.

Administrative Acts Reviewable under Other Legislation

Apart from personal and proprietary rights and interests, people enjoy many other kinds of rights and interests, such as the freedom to march, association, assembly, speech, publication, and belief, and the right to employment, rest and education. It is also possible that these rights or interests of people may be infringed by concrete administrative acts undertaken by administrative organs. Section 11 thus provides, in addition to those eight categories discussed above, that the people's

8.16

courts shall accept other administrative lawsuits which are brought in accordance with the provisions of relevant laws and regulations. In other words, so long as other laws or regulations provide that a new concrete administrative act is subject to judicial review, then it will be. The reason to incorporate such a provision in the ALL is to enable the scope of judicial review to be expanded gradually when the circumstances become appropriate and necessary.[29]

Such an open-ended provision leaves behind a practical problem which needs to be dealt with. Suppose one kind of concrete administrative act was not subject to judicial review. Now a new legislation, either a law or an administrative regulation, provides for the right to bring a case for judicial review to challenge that kind of concrete administrative act. If the activity conducted by the person was before the implementation of the new legislation, but the concrete administrative act is undertaken by the administrative organ after the new legislation comes into force. The problem is whether or not the person is entitled to bring a judicial review case to challenge the concrete administrative act if he is not satisfied with the act. Neither the ALL itself nor the Opinions on the ALL provides an answer. A reply issued by the Supreme People's Court in 1989 provides the solution. The reply states that in order to protect the lawful rights and interests of the person concerned and as long as the case is brought within the time limit, the person should be entitled to bring a case for judicial review.[30] Such a reply is also consistent with general legal principles. As the administrative act is undertaken after the new legislation, then the legislation is obviously binding on the administrative organ.

A related issue concerning the scope of judicial review is the conflict between legislation at different levels. Suppose a law or administrative regulation provides that a concrete administrative act is subject to judicial review. Some administrative rules or other normative rules issued by the administrative organs do not state that the concrete administrative act is judicially reviewable. What should the court do under such a circumstance? If this is the case, then according to the hierarchy of legislation, a law or an administrative regulation prevails over administrative rules or any other normative rules. A person's right to sue as provided for under a law or administrative regulation cannot be unduly deprived by any administrative rules or other normative rules.[31] That is to say, the person can still bring a case for judicial review.

8.17   There are several reasons why the scope of judicial review is finally determined as such. The first reason is the necessity to protect the legitimate rights and interests of citizens, legal persons and other organizations. That is the objective of any legislation and therefore is also one for the enactment of the ALL. In order to ensure the effective protection against unlawful infringement by administrative organs, it is necessary to give people the right to challenge those categories of administrative acts which are very likely to affect their fundamental (especially personal and proprietary) rights and interests. As the scope of public administration is expanding all the time, it is natural to make it possible for the scope of judicial review to be expanded whenever it is necessary for the protection of lawful rights and interests.

The second reason is the maintenance of a proper relationship between the judiciary and the executive.[32] In his explanation of the draft ALL to the Standing Committee of the National People's Congress, Wang Hanbing, the Deputy Chairman of the Standing Committee of the NPC, states that people's courts should adjudicate administrative cases according to law, but should not interfere with administrative acts undertaken within the limits set by laws and regulations, should not substitute administrative organs to exercise administrative power because of the necessity to maintain effective administration by the administrative organs. Judicial supervision of administrative acts is only one means of supervision. Apart from that, there is still legislative and administrative supervision. Moreover, the judiciary also has a duty to ensure that any lawful exercise of administrative power shall not be unnecessarily interfered with. It is also commented that apart from exceptional cases, the people's courts, in adjudicating judicial review cases, should not substitute the decisions of administrative organs with their own decisions.[33]

The other reason is that the scope of jurisdiction can only be gradually expanded with the increase and accumulation of experience in adjudication of judicial review cases because of the political, historical and cultural reasons. The trend of expansion can easily be observed for the period from 1982 with Civil Procedural Law (for trial implementation) to 1989 with the Administrative Litigation Law. There is no doubt that with the development of democracy, balance of powers and rule of law in China, the scope of judicial review will be further extended.

Acts Not Subject to Judicial Review

Apart from the categories of concrete administrative acts which are subject to judicial review, section 12 of the ALL provides that there are four kinds of administrative acts which are not subject to judicial review. They are the acts of the state, abstract administrative acts, internal administrative decisions and administrative decisions which are final as provided by law. 8.18

Act of State[34]

8.19 An act of state is not interpreted either in the ALL or the Opinions on the ALL. There exist two different views, a narrow one and a broad one, on the scope of act of state. The narrow view holds that acts of state only include acts of national defence and foreign affairs.[35] The broad view maintains that acts of state include acts of government or acts of the ruling body, related to all kinds of decisions made by the central government of a country through exercising its sovereign function to the outside world, as well as inside the country.[36]

The broad view is supported by some scholars. For example, Professor Jiang Mingan argues that acts of state are also called governmental acts, governing acts or political acts. They refer to the acts performed in the name of the state by either the head of the state, the executive branch of the central government, or the national legislature. In the case of China, they refer to the acts of the President, the State Council and the National People's Congress. Under the Chinese Constitution, any acts undertaken by the President and the National People's Congress (NPC) in the name of the state are immune from judicial control. There is therefore no need to exclude them through any other legislation such as the ALL.[37]

The narrow approach also has its followers. A well articulated one is provided by the Interpretation of the ALL.[38] It states that acts of state only refer to acts undertaken by state organs, according to the authorization of the Constitution and laws and in the name of the state, concerning the relationship between states, national security and other important national issues of which the legal responsibility shall be borne by the state directly.

There are four ingredients in the definition of act of state. Firstly, an act of state is concerned with either inter-state relationship, or the security of the state involved or any other important national decisions, not with ordinary administrative affairs of the state. Secondly, an act of state is a political act executed in the name of the state. Thirdly, an act of state is, in essence, an act to exercise national sovereignty and therefore, under general principle of law, should not be subject to legal control within a state. Fourthly, any consequences caused by an act of state shall be borne directly by the state.[39]

There is consensus between the two approaches that an act of state is an exercise of sovereignty and represents the highest interest of the county and has a strong political characteristics in nature. The only difference is whether or not acts of state include solely external acts or both external and internal acts. Specifically speaking, whether or not acts relating to public interest should be treated as acts of state. The ALL only lists two categories of acts of state, *i.e.* the acts of national defence and foreign affairs. The acts of the state in the area of national defence are normally undertaken in order to protect national sovereignty, especially in the areas of territorial integrity or national security. Actual decisions made by the state relating to military activities will fall into this category. Acts of state in the areas of foreign affairs include the establishment or severance of diplomatic relationship between states, conclusion of international treaties, and so on. However, following the interpretative approach adopted for section 11, it is fair to say that acts of state under section 12(1) should cover more than the two listed types. They are not the only two categories of acts of state. It has been suggested that other important acts undertaken by the executive branch of the state concerning national public interests should also be classified as acts of state. For example, the order issued by the State Council to implement martial law in certain areas within a specific province, autonomous region or municipality directly under the control of the central government.[40] The enforcement of martial law in certain geographical regions, special measures adopted for dealing with emergency or of major disaster relief should be regarded as acts of state.[41]

It should be emphasized that any act of state must be concerned with national sovereignty and important national interests. They do not include all acts undertaken by the administrative organs in the areas of national defence or foreign affairs. Certain concrete decisions, such as whether or not a person should serve in the army, a diplomatic passport should be issued, an overseas visit should be approved and so on, concern neither national sovereignty nor important national interests. They are concrete administrative acts and should be subject to judicial review if they fall into the scope of section 11 of the ALL. Neither does it include any other decisions made by local people's governments.[42] Therefore the only criterion for the determination of whether or not an act is an act of state is whether or not it is the exercise of sovereign power concerning important national interests, both externally and internally.

Reasons for the Exclusion

Several reasons have been put forward to explain why acts of state are excluded from judicial review.[43] Firstly, an act of state has a certain degree of emergency.[44] Any lawsuit against an act of state may cause delay in the performance or implementation of the act of state. It may result in the loss of an important opportunity and lead to grievous loss of national interests. Secondly, some kind of act of state requires certain degree of secrecy. But the judicial process requires openness which may lead to the leakage of secrecy. Thirdly, an act of state is often undertaken under political or policy consideration rather than on strict legal grounds. Though any act of state should generally be under-

8.20

taken according to law. But under extreme circumstances, legal restrictions may be disregarded and approval from the legislative authority be sought later and the judiciary should not interfere, neither before nor after the act of state.[45] The main reason put forward by Professor Luo is that acts of state are related to the exercise of sovereignty and most countries in the world grant immunity to acts of state in national courts. Furthermore, they are also related to the interests of the country as a whole and the interests of the people.[46]

Abstract Administrative Acts

8.21 An abstract administrative act is a term in contrast to concrete administrative act. It refers to, under section 12(2) of the ALL, administrative rules and regulations, regulations, or decisions and orders with general binding force formulated and announced by administrative organs. It can be classified into two categories: one is administrative legislative acts, including the promulgation of administrative regulations and rules according to its granted legislative authority; and the other refers to orders and decisions which have general binding effect.[47] These orders and decisions are issued for the implementation of laws, administrative regulations and rules. Though they are not administrative legislative activities, they are nevertheless abstract administrative acts because the essence of abstract administrative act is its scope of application.[48]

Compared with a concrete administrative act, an abstract administrative act differs in the following aspects. Firstly, it aims at people in general or one kind of people rather than a specific person; secondly, it targets at one type of situations rather than a specific event; thirdly, it has a general effect after it comes into force whereas a concrete administrative act will have no effect upon any similar acts happened either before or after the concrete administrative act.[49]

Legal Control of Abstract Administrative Acts

8.22 However, it is by no means, suggesting that abstractive administrative acts shall be subject to no legal control or supervision. Under the Chinese Constitutional structure, abstract administrative acts are subject to different kinds of legal controls. The control may be either exercised by the legislature or the administrative organ at the next higher level depending on the categories of abstract administrative acts. If it is an administrative regulation, or order or decision issued by the State Council, then it is subject to the review of the Standing Committee of the National People's Congress. Section 67 of the Constitution states that the Standing Committee of the National People's Congress has the power to annual those administrative rules and regulations, decisions or orders of the State Council that contravene the Constitution or the law; and to annul those local regulations or decisions of the legislature of provinces, autonomous regions, and municipalities directly under the central government that contravene the Constitution, the law or the administrative rules and regulations. Section 89 of the Constitution provides that the State Council has the authority to alter or annul inappropriate decisions and orders issued by local organs of state administration at various levels. If it is an administrative regulation, rule, decision or notice issued by local people's governments or their functioning branches, it will be subject to the review of the administrative organ at the next higher level or the people's congress at the same level or the people's congress at the next higher level. Section 7 of the 1980 Organic Law of the Local People's Congresses and Local People's Governments of the People's Republic of China states that local people's congresses at and above the county level shall have the power to alter or annul inappropriate resolutions and orders of the people's governments at the corresponding levels, and to alter or annul inappropriate resolutions of the people's congresses and inappropriate resolutions and orders of the people's governments at the next lower level.

Does section 12(2) mean that the people's court can never review the legality of abstract administrative act under any circumstances? Suppose a concrete administrative act is undertaken by an administrative organ relying on an order issued by a superior administrative organ. A case for judicial review is then brought to the people's court to challenge the legality of the concrete administrative act. Under such circumstances, the legality of the abstract administrative act is the precondition of the legality of the concrete administrative act. The issue is whether the court can review the legality of the order concerned if the applicant also challenges the legality of the order. One scholar suggests that the court can, though not qualified to annul the order concerned, nevertheless rule on the issue of legality of the order concerned under such circumstance.[50] It has been argued that the people's courts may, instead of applying the order, choose to apply directly laws or other administrative regulations or orders at a higher level. They may also recommend the administrative organ with authority to repeal the order in issue. Any abstract administrative order can only affect a person (both natural and legal) or other organization through a concrete administrative act. Even though an abstract administrative act is excluded from the scope of judicial review, it may still be subject to the judicial supervision by the people's courts in their process of examining the legality of concrete administrative acts.[51]

143

Internal Administrative Acts

8.23 Internal administrative acts refer to those undertaken by administrative organs towards other administrative organs or their own working staff or internal matters. The relationship between one administrative organ and another is usually an issue to be dealt with under organic law. Apart from that, section 12(3) stipulates four types, including decisions of awards or punishments of their staff, or decisions of appointment or relief of duties of their staff. Chinese scholars hold different views as to whether or not they are the only four types of internal administrative acts.[52] The broad approach holds that internal administrative activities cover both abstract and concrete administrative acts. Since the ALL has clearly excluded abstract administrative acts from judicial review under section 12(2), it is not necessary to mention them under section 12(3). All those administrative acts mentioned under section 12(3) are undertaken through the exercise of administrative power and affect only the persons or matters concerned. They are in nature within the category of concrete administrative acts. But these decisions are targeted at the internal staff or affairs of those administrative organs, not decision targeting at external persons (both natural and legal) or organizations.

There does not seem to exist any legal justification for the exclusion of those internal administrative acts from judicial review as they completely satisfy the definition of concrete administrative act and easily fit into the scope of section 11. Several reasons have been suggested for the exclusion. The first reason is that judicial review is still a quite new topic and legal machinery available in China. The judiciary has not gained sufficient experience and therefore should not be overloaded with sophisticated work. Secondly, as to the management of civil servants, China is still at the stage of developing its own legal system to govern the operation of the civil service.[53] The system is therefore not stable yet and subject to change from time to time, depending on the policy decision of the central government. Thirdly, internal administrative acts are mainly concerned with administrative policy issues and therefore not appropriate for the people's courts to handle.[54] These reasons for the exclusion are purely based on policy consideration, not jurisprudential reasons.[55] Professor Luo argues in his book that the main reason for their exclusion from judicial review is to ensure the proper exercise of administrative power, and the requirement of efficient public administration.[56]

The exclusion of those internal administrative acts from judicial review does not mean that civil servants will not be able to address their grievance against the administrative organs in charge of them. Instead, they may resort to different remedial means such as an appeal to the administrative organ at the next higher level, or to the supervisory organs, or to the personnel department. That is to say remedial means have already been provided within the administrative structure. However, internal remedial means are part of the executive branch of the government in nature. They do not enjoy the independence and impartiality as the people's courts do. It is logical for the aggrieved party to cast doubts about the result coming out of internal remedial means, especially when the results are not in their favour. In theory, the achievement of administrative efficiency should only be one of the reasons to be taken into account in the determination of the scope of judicial review. Other factors such as justice and reasonableness should also be taken into account. Whether or not the achievement of administrative efficiency should supersede the necessity of justice and reasonableness is highly questionable.

There are some administrative acts which may be border-line between abstract and concrete administrative acts. If that is the case, it has been suggested that the people's courts should, according to the general principles and objective of the ALL, exercise its discretionary power to determine whether or not the act should be subject to judicial review.[57]

Concrete Administrative Acts as Final

8.24 Section 12(4) of the ALL provides that any concrete administrative acts which are provided for by laws to be finally decided by administrative organs will not be subject to judicial review. Here the term "laws" is used. Section 3 of the Opinions on the ALL states clearly that "laws" only refer to the normative documents issued by the NPC or its Standing Committee. They do not include any administrative or local regulations. If an administrative decision is regarded as final, that is a restriction upon one of the fundamental rights of a person, *i.e.* the right to resort to the judiciary for the resolution of disputes he is involved in. Such kind of restriction should only be provided by laws, not by any secondary legislation. If any administrative regulations or local regulations provide that certain kinds of concrete administrative acts shall be final and cannot be challenged in the people's courts, these provisions will be treated as void and the aggrieved party can ignore their existence and bring a case to the people's courts for judicial review.[58]

The main reason for such a provision, as professor Jiang argues, is based on the complexity of administration. Some administrative acts involve highly technological issues and require special knowledge, technology or experience. The people's courts may not be well equipped to handle such cases. It is therefore more appropriate for the relevant administrative organs to handle those cases. Some other administrative acts may be undertaken to deal with emergencies or of political nature and therefore need to be handled flexibly and quickly.

Then the courts will not be the appropriate forum to resolve such issues.

In essence, finality of administrative acts is really an issue about the relationship between the executive and the judiciary. The attitude of the judiciary in the United Kingdom and Hong Kong towards the legal effect of finality clauses has changed over the years. The modern case of Anisminic is the leading case in this area.[59] In that case, British Foreign Compensation Act 1950 provides that any decisions of the Foreign Compensation Commission, a statutory body on compensation shall be final. The court held that the decision will only be final if it is made lawfully. The court can still review whether or not the decision is a lawful one. Since that case, it has been well established that the judiciary no longer accepts that finality clauses will actually mean that the administrative act concerned shall be final. Instead, the House of Lords holds that the true intention of Parliament is that those administrative decisions will only be final on the condition that they are lawful ones. Such an interpretation of the effect of finality clauses will allow the courts to review the legality of those acts which have been provided for as final by both primary and secondary legislation. This is the result of active judicial interpretation in common law, as practised in the United Kingdom and Hong Kong.

In China, however, the whole constitutional arrangement is different. The final authority of statutory interpretation is in the hands of the legislature, not the judiciary. It is therefore impossible for the people's courts to be as active as the courts in the United Kingdom or Hong Kong. The Chinese national legislature, *i.e.* the NPC, has decided to reserve itself the right to determine how to maintain the balance between the executive and judiciary in order to ensure the harmony between the interests of the state and the interests of individuals.

8.25   Finality provisions in laws actually deprive the aggrieved parties the right to resort to judicial protection when they believe their lawful rights or interests are infringed. The scope of finality provisions should be strictly limited.[60] Currently, there are only two types of legislative provisions which have provided that certain kinds of concrete administrative acts shall be final. One is that if a person is not satisfied with an administrative decision he may bring a case either for administrative reconsideration or judicial review. But if he chooses administrative reconsideration, then the decision of the administrative reconsideration organ shall be final. For example, section 15 of the 1985 Law on the Control of Exit and Entry of Citizens of the People's Republic of China provides that:

> If a citizen subject to the penalty of detention by a public security organ refuses to accept the penalty, he may, within 15 days of receiving notification, appeal to the public security organ at the

next higher level, which shall make the final decision; he may also directly file suit in the local people's court.

Section 29 of the 1985 Law on Control of Exit and Entry of Aliens of the People's Republic of China provides that:

> If an alien subject to a fine or detention by a public security organ refuses to accept the penalty, he may, within 15 days of receiving notification, appeal to the public security organ at the next higher level, which shall make the final decision; he may also directly file suit in the local people's court.

The above examples show that the aggrieved parties are given two alternatives to address their grievance. Only if the aggrieved parties prefer to administrative reconsideration will the decision of administrative reconsideration become final. It cannot then argue that justice or fairness is sacrificed for the sake of administrative efficiency.

The other one is that if a person is not satisfied with a specific administrative act he may only bring a case for administrative reconsideration and the decision of administrative reconsideration organ shall be final. For example, the 1993 Trade Mark Law of the People's Republic of China has the following provisions:

> Section 21: if an application for trademark registration has been rejected and the trademark is not to be publicly announced, the Trademark Office shall notify the applicant in writing. If the applicant does not agree with the rejection, it may apply for a re-examination within 15 days after receiving the notification, and the Trademark Review and Adjudication Board shall make a final decision and notify the applicant in writing.

> Section 22: if an objection is filed against a trademark which has been given preliminary examination and approval and has been publicly announced, the Trademark Office shall hear the opponent's and the applicant's statements of the facts and reasons and shall, after investigation and verification, make a decision. If a party disagrees with the decision, it may apply for a re-examination within 15 days after receiving notification of the decision, and the Trademark Review and Adjudication Board shall make a final decision and notify the opponent and the applicant in writing.

> Section 28: after the Trademark Review and Adjudication Board has made the final ruling upholding or revoking a registered trademark, it shall notify the parties concerned in writing.

Similarly, paragraph 3 of section 43 of the 1992 Patent Law of the People's Republic of China provides:

The decision of the Patent Re-examination Board in respect of any request, made by the applicant, the patentee or the person who made the request for revocation of the patent right, for re-examination concerning a utility model or design shall be final.

Paragraph 3 of section 49 of the same Law provides: "The decision of the Patent Re-examination Board on a request to invalidate the patent right for a utility model or design shall be final." These examples are all concerned with highly technological issues which require expertise in certain areas. It is therefore much better to leave them in the hands of experts so as to achieve efficiency and fairness.[61]

Notes

[1] See Jiang Mingan, p. 106.
[2] See Quan She, p. 31; also Luo and Ying pp. 99–101. Luo argues that constitutional structures, political, economic factors, democracy ideology and request for legal protection.
[3] See Jiang Mingan, pp. 106–09; Luo and Ying, pp. 102–06; Pi and Hu, pp. 62–67.
[4] Legislation includes both the ALL and any other specific enactment which provide for a catergory of cases to be subject to judicial review.
[5] Refer to the chapter on scope of jurisdiction in the second part, administrative reconsideration, of this book.
[6] They are exactly the same as those under the 1996 APL.
[7] Refer to the section on administrative penalty.
[8] See Zhang Qiuke, *Zhong Guo Xing Zhen Su Song Shi Yong Da Quan* (Practice Guide to Administrative Litigation in China), Changchun Press, 1991, p. 275.
[9] See Ying Songnian, pp. 450–501.
[10] See ss. 9, 10, 11 of the APL.
[11] See Su Song Da Quan, above n. 8, p. 319.
[12] For detailed discussion of each of those four administrative compulsory measures, refer to the relevant section in administrative reconsideration.
[13] It can be argued that those with *aids vires* may be compulsorily segregated and treated.
[14] For detailed discussion, please refer to the relevant section of Administrative Reconsideration in this book; it should also be noted that sheltering for examination has been formally abolished by the 1996 amendments to Criminal Procedure Law.
[15] The autonomy of state-owned enterprises is stipulated in the State-Owned Industrial Enterprise Law of the People's Republic of China and the Regulation on the Transition of Business Management of State-Owned Industrial Enterprises; the autonomy of collectively owned enterprises is stipulated in the Regulation on Urban and Township Collectively Owned Enterprises in the People's Republic of China and the Regulation on Rural Collectively Owned Enterprises in the People's Republic of China; the autonomy of privately owned enterprises is stipulated in the Interim Regulation on Privately Owned Enterprises in the People's Republic of China; the autonomy of sole proprietors is stipulated in the Interim Regulation on the Management of Urban and Township Sole Proprietors in the People's Republic of China; the autonomy of foreign investment enterprises is stipulated in the relevant foreign investment legislation.
[16] In the ALL, both licence and permit are mentioned. But no distinction is made between the two. Chinese scholars do not think there is any clear distinction between the two. In this book, the two terms mean the same thing and will be used

interchangeably. For detailed discussion of licencing system, please refer to the relevant section in chapter two of the first part of this book.
17 See Luo and Ying 1990, pp. 169–70.
18 See Luo and Ying 1990, p. 170.
19 See Su Song Da Quan, above n. 8, pp. 319.
20 See Quan She, pp. 43–44.
21 See Jiang Mingan, pp. 121–122; also Ying Songnian, Yang Xiaojun and Fang Shirong, *Xing Zhen Su Song Fa Xue* (Administrative Litigation Law), China University of Political Science and Law Press, Beijing, 1994, pp. 78–80.
22 See Quan She, pp. 46–53.
23 One scholar has argued that the first seven categories mentioned in s. 11 of the ALL may infringe upon not only personal and proprietary rights but also other kinds of rights. Any other kinds of concrete administrative acts will only be subject to judicial review if they infringe upon personal or proprietary rights or interests. For details, see Jiang Mingan, p. 124. The author does not agree with Professor Jiang's second argument because it is not consistent with s. 11(9) which allows future legislation to proscribe any kinds of concrete administrative acts, not necessarily only those infringing upon personal or proprietary rights or interests, to be subject to judicial review.
24 See ss. 4, 5 and 7 of the Opinions on the ALL.
25 This is provided for by s. 6 of the Opinions on the ALL.
26 For more detailed discussion of compensation for lawful activities, refer to the chapter on State Compensation Law.
27 The replies from the Supreme People's Courts dated October 10, 1989 and December 1, 1992 state that disputes over indemnity decisions on medical accidents and traffic accidents by relevant administrative organs are judicially reviewable. See Quan She pp. 50–52.
28 This is confirmed by the 1993 reply from the Supreme People's Court. See Quan She, pp. 52–53.
29 It has been a tradition of China's legislation to have such an open-ended section so that amendments can be added when they are required. it is possible that a final expansion will be to abstract administrative act which would be a major amendment to the ALL. Though it may not be possible in the near future, it is certainly the trend and scholarly writing has appeared in Chinese legal journal.
30 See the reply from the Supreme People's Court dated January 23, 1989.
31 This is an issue concerning applicable law before the start of judicial review, which is different from the topic of applicable law (legislation) in the process of judicial review. The latter shall be discussed in a separate chapter.
32 See Luo Haocai 1993, p. 45.
33 See Quan She, p. 47.
34 Professor Wang Guiguo has summarized Chinese scholars' views on act of state in his article entitled "A Comparative Study on the Act of State Doctrine — With Special Reference to the Hong Kong Court of Final Appeal" which is a book chapter in the book by Wang Guiguo and Wei Zhenying (ed) "Legal Developments in China", Sweet & Maxwell, 1996, pp. 273–76.
35 Those are the two clearly mentioned in s. 12(1) of the ALL.
36 See Professor Luo Haocai 1993, p. 308.
37 See Jiang Mingan, p. 126.
38 See Quan She, pp. 53–54.
39 See Luo Haocai 1993, pp. 308–09.
40 In 1989 order was issued in both Beijing and Tibet to implement curfew because of the student movement.
41 See Luo Haocai 1993, p. 309. Luo offers a different approach suggesting that they are not acts of state, but still not subject to judicial review. See Wang Guiguo, p. 275.
42 See a latter case.
43 See Jiang Mingan, p. 127. Luo Haocai 1993, pp. 309–10.
44 Emergency may be argued to be an exceptional case and should not be regulated by ordinary legislation. See Mo Jihong and Xu Gao, *Jing Ji Zhuang Tai Fa Xue* (Law on Emergency), China Public Security University Press, Beijing, 1992, chapter 4.
45 See Jiang Mingan, p. 127. It happened in one British case where later legislation was passed to overrule a court decision concerning state compensation.

SCOPE OF JURISDICTION IN JUDICIAL REVIEW

46 See Luo Haocai 1993, pp. 310–11.
47 The issue of classification of regulations and normative documents has been discussed in the section on administrative legislative acts in administrative law theory.
48 See Jiang Mingan, p. 127; Luo Haocai 1993, pp. 310–11. Discussion is also made on abstract administrative act in the section on classification of administrative acts in Chapter 2 on administrative law theory.
49 See Quan She, p. 55.
50 See Jiang Mingan, p. 128.
51 See Jiang Mingan, p. 128. Also refer to the latter chapter on applicable legislation.
52 See Luo Haocai 1993, pp. 312–14.
53 China's civil service is mainly based on the Regulation on Civil Service, which provides for certain grievance-addressing means.
54 See Jiang Mingan, p. 130.
55 See Sheyi, p. 55.
56 See Luo Haocai 1993, pp. 313–14; see also Jiang Mingan, p. 130.
57 See Jiang Mingan, p. 130.
58 This is provided by s. 3, para. 2, Opinions on the ALL.
59 *Anisminic Ltd v. Foreign Compensation Commission* [1969] 1 All ER 208; [1969] 2 AC 147 (HL(E)).
60 In practice, the use of finality clauses in Chinese legislation is also restricted which shall be revealed from the following discussion.
61 See Quan She, pp. 56–57; also Jiang Mingan, pp. 130–131.

CHAPTER NINE
JURISDICTION OF THE PEOPLE'S COURTS

Jurisdiction of the people's courts for judicial review cases discusses the allocation or division of workload among courts at different levels and from different geographical locations for the hearing of judicial review cases as courts of first instance. In China there are four levels in the hierarchy of the courts. The basic courts (those at the bottom level) are District People's Courts (in urban areas) and County People's Courts (in rural areas). The next level is Intermediate People's Courts. The third is the Higher People's Courts. The fourth is the Supreme People's Court.[1] Unlike in the United Kingdom and Hong Kong where judicial review is the inherent power of the High Court, there is no such concept in China. Whether or not a court can accept what kind of cases purely depends on legislation. The ALL has one chapter prescribing the jurisdiction of the people's courts in the adjudication of judicial review cases. There are mainly two issues concerning jurisdiction. One is vertical jurisdiction, *i.e.* the allocation and division of work and authority among the people's courts at different levels. The other is horizontal jurisdiction, *i.e.* the allocation and division of work and authority among the people's courts at the same levels but in different geographical locations.

9.01

Vertical Jurisdiction[2]

Jurisdiction of Basic People's Courts

The general rule is, as stated in section 13 of the ALL, that judicial review cases should be heard by the basic people's courts as courts of first instance. The basic people's courts, *i.e.* County People's Courts and District People's Courts, are usually situated at the place where the plaintiff and defendant are located or where the concrete administrative acts are undertaken. Section 11 of the Opinions on the ALL

9.02

provides that the place where plaintiff is located include the plaintiff's domicile, the place he often stays in, or where his personal freedom is restricted. The grant of jurisdiction to them as courts of first instance shall be convenient to the parties concerned to take part in the litigation and exercise their right to solve their disputes through the judiciary. It will also reduce their economic burden and time as the Intermediate People's Courts, the Higher People's Courts and the Supreme People's Court are usually situated in different cities from where the parties reside. It is also convenient for the adjudication of those cases as the people's courts adopt an inquisitorial approach and sometimes the judges need to conduct interviews and collect evidence by themselves. In fact, most of judicial review cases are heard by basic people's courts. It has been stated clearly by Wang Hanbing, in his explanation on the draft of the ALL, that such a provision is based on the consideration of these two conveniences.[3]

There are, however, several exceptions to this general rule. Certain kinds of judicial review cases are prescribed under the ALL to be heard by either the Intermediate People's Courts, or Higher People's Court or the Supreme People's Court as courts of first instance, which will be discussed in the following sections. The main reason is to ensure the quality of adjudication.[4]

Jurisdiction of the Intermediate People's Courts

9.03 There are three types of judicial review cases under the jurisdiction of the Intermediate People's Courts as courts of first instance. The first type is the case concerning the confirmation of patent rights of invention and the administrative decisions reached by the Customs office on the imposition of administrative penalties, destraintment decisions, and orders on the payment of Customs duties.[5] The confirmation of patent rights of invention is concerned with the identification of whether a claimed invention is scientifically a true invention. That is a highly technological issue and requires expertise in the evaluation and judgment. Similarly, matters handled by the Customs office are usually very technical and difficult and also requires expertise. Moreover, the patent offices and customs are often located in intermediate or big cities. It is convenient for the adjudication if such cases are prescribed to be dealt with by the Intermediate People's Courts.

The second type of case is concerned with concrete administrative acts undertaken by departments under the State Council or by the people's governments of provinces, autonomous regions or municipalities directly under the central government.[6] The departments under the State Council refer to all the ministries, commissions, bureaus and offices directly under the administration of and responsible to the State Council. Application for judicial review may be brought either against an administrative decision reached on a specific matter by those administrative organs mentioned above or against an administrative reconsideration decision reached by those administrative organs. Such cases are usually very complicated and difficult, and highly influential in the region. The relevant judgments will have a considerable social impact. In order to ensure the quality of adjudication and reduce potential administrative interference, it is more appropriate for the Intermediate People's Courts to hear these cases as courts of first instance.[7]

The third type of case are those grave and complicated cases in the areas under the jurisdiction of the Intermediate People's Courts.[8] Neither the ALL nor the Opinions on the ALL has provided any definition or guidelines as to what kinds of cases may be regarded as grave and complicated cases, or which court should have the authority to determine whether or not a case is within this type. As to the first issue, it has been suggested that cases affecting the interests of many people or affecting public interests should fall into this type.[9] As to the second issue, there could be two possibilities. One is that a case may be submitted by a basic people's court to an Intermediate People's Court for adjudication if it believes the case is a grave or complicated one. The other is that the Intermediate People's Court may issue an order requiring a basic people's court to submit a case if it believes the case is a grave or complicated one. In judicial practice, both may occur.

Jurisdiction of the Higher People's Courts

The Higher People's Courts are mainly responsible for the supervision and issue of instruction concerning adjudication work of the people's courts at lower levels within its geographical jurisdiction, and hear appeal cases against judgments of Intermediate People's Courts. But section 15 of the ALL also provides that they shall have jurisdiction as courts of first instance over grave and complicated judicial review cases in areas under their jurisdiction. One source suggests that grave and complicated cases refer mainly to those cases challenging concrete administrative acts undertaken by the State Council, cases affecting major public interests and having wide media attraction, and other extremely complicated cases.[10] It is in practice very rare for a judicial review case to be directly brought to a Higher People's Court as a case of first instance.

9.04

Jurisdiction of the Supreme People's Court

9.05 The Supreme People's Court is the highest judicial organ within the court hierarchy in China. Its main function is to supervise and give instructions on the adjudication of all other people's courts in China, and to provide judicial interpretation with regard to how legislation may be implemented in judicial practice. Again, section 16 of the ALL provides that the Supreme People's Court may have jurisdiction to hear a judicial review case as court of first instance if the case is a grave and complicated one in the whole country. It has been suggested that cases having great influence over national politics or economy or being trans-provincial may fall within this type.[11]

Transfer of Jurisdiction among Courts at Different Levels

9.06 A people's court may find that a case it has accepted is not within its jurisdiction or is more appropriate for a people's court at higher or lower level to adjudicate. If that happens, section 23 of the ALL has made it possible for the people's court concerned to transfer that case to the appropriate people's court. But a decision can only be made by the people's court at the higher level. Three conditions need to be satisfied for the transfer of a case either way. Firstly, the case must have already been accepted as a case in the first instance. Secondly, the people's court to which the case is transferred must have jurisdiction over the case. But there is neither legal provision nor judicial interpretation as to who has the authority to determine whether or not the court to which the case is to be transferred has jurisdiction over the case.[12] If the court to which the case is transferred does not believe it has jurisdiction, a practical resolution is to submit the case to a higher court above both of them to designate a court for jurisdiction.[13] The third condition is that the two people's courts concerned must be directly related to each other in the court hierarchy.[14]

Horizontal (Geographical) Jurisdiction[15]

9.07 Horizontal jurisdiction is concerned with the allocation of jurisdiction among the courts at the same level as courts of first instance. The general rule concerning horizontal jurisdiction is that a judicial review case should be heard by the people's court in the location of the administrative organ that initially undertakes the concrete administrative act.[16] Apart from this general principle, there also exist two kinds of special geographical jurisdiction. One is concerned with judicial review applications against an administrative decision concerning real property. Such cases should be subject to the jurisdiction of the people's courts where the real property is located.[17] The other is concerned with judicial review cases against administrative compulsory measures restricting personal freedom which should be heard by the people's courts where either the plaintiff or the defendant is located.[18] The second special geographical jurisdiction leads us to the question of common jurisdiction, *i.e.* two or more courts have jurisdiction over the same case.

Common Jurisdiction

Sometimes it is possible that more than one court is qualified to have jurisdiction over one judicial review case. Such a situation may arise because the assets of the plaintiff(s) or defendant(s) are located in several different regions or the wrongs have been committed by the administrative organ in several different places or the wrongs have effects in several different places. Sometimes legislation may grant jurisdiction to different courts. For example, section 18 of the ALL allows the applicants to bring a case for judicial review against administrative compulsory measures restricting their personal freedom either to the people's court where the defendant is located or to the people's court where the plaintiff is located. It is very likely that the applicants will choose the courts where they are situated because of the convenience. Section 11 of the Opinions on the ALL explains that the place where the plaintiffs are located includes three possibilities, *i.e.* the domicile of the plaintiff, the place where the plaintiff actually resides, or the place where the plaintiff's personal freedom is restricted.[19] At least three courts are entitled to have jurisdiction over the case.

9.08

Under such circumstances, it is up to the plaintiff(s) to choose the suitable and convenient people's court to lodge his application. If an application for judicial review has been brought to more than one people's court, the court which first receives the application should have jurisdiction over the case.[20]

The case of *Li v. The Management Committee of Rehabilitation through Labour in X City*[21] is concerned with the issue of common jurisdiction. In this case, on January 3, 1992 Li (the plaintiff) committed theft in one vegetable market and was discovered by the people there. He threw the purse on the floor and ran away. Because he was not familiar with the roads and was caught by the people and the public security officer. The public security bureau sheltered the plaintiff for investigation the next day. After investigation, it was found the

Li was taken into custody for three months by the public security bureau because of theft in 1982. In 1983, the penalty of rehabilitation through labour for two years was imposed by the public security bureau in S Town. In May 1985, the plaintiff was found guilt for theft and imprisoned for one year by the District People's Court in S City. In December 1986, the plaintiff again was found guilty for theft and rehabilitation through labour for three years was imposed by the Managing Commission for Rehabilitation through Labour. On February 9, 1992, the public security bureau in X City reported the matter to the Managing Commission for Rehabilitation through Labour, the Commission made the decision to impose a penalty on Li of rehabilitation through labour for three years on February 25, 1992. Li was not satisfied with the decision and applied for administrative reconsideration. The Managing Commission on March 27, after reconsideration, made a decision to sustain the penalty. Li then, on March 29, 1992, brought a lawsuit to the People's Court located at his domicile . The People's Court there accepted the case in accordance with the laws.

In this case Li could bring a case to at least two courts: the court located at his domicile; and the other is the court where he is taken into custody, *i.e.* where his freedom is restricted.

Jurisdiction over Reconsidered Cases

9.09 If an administrative decision, before it is brought for judicial review, has been through the process of administrative reconsideration, then there are two possibilities. One is that the administrative reconsideration organ may maintain the original decision. If that is the case, then application for judicial review shall still be brought to the people's court in the locality where the original decision-making administrative organ situates.[22] That is what happened in the case of *Li V. Managing Commission of Rehabilitation through Labour in X City*. If the original decision has been amended partially or completely by the administrative reconsideration organ, then application for judicial review may also be lodged to the people's court in the locality where the administrative reconsideration organ situates. It will become an issue of common jurisdiction and should follow the relevant rules for the handling of common jurisdiction cases.[23]

What amounts to an amendment of original concrete administrative acts (or decisions) is not defined in the ALL. The Opinions on the ALL provide the explanation. There are three different kinds of amendments to the original decisions. The first is that the administrative reconsideration organ finds that the identification of material facts by the original decision-making administrative organ was wrong and makes relevant changes accordingly. The second is that the administrative reconsideration organ finds that the original decision-making administrative organ applied wrong legislation and therefore changes the applicable law accordingly. The third is that the administrative reconsideration organ changes the original decision by revocation, partial revocation or direct change of the original decision.[24] If one of the three conditions is satisfied, then the application for judicial review may also be lodged to the people's court at the place where the reconsideration organ is located.

Horizontal Transfer of Jurisdiction

If a people's court finds, after accepting a judicial review case, that it does not have jurisdiction over the case, it may transfer the case to the people's court in another geographical location which has jurisdiction. The rules and problems facing horizontal transfer of jurisdiction are the same as those facing vertical transfer of jurisdiction. The same conditions need to be satisfied for the transfer of the case.[25]   9.10

It is possible that a dispute may arise over jurisdiction if the court to which the case is to be transferred does not think it has jurisdiction. If this happens, the two courts concerned should first try to resolve the dispute through consultation.[26] If consultation cannot resolve the dispute, then it should be reported to a people's court superior to the two courts in dispute for the designation of jurisdiction.[27]

In the case *of Paper Mill in County A v. EPB in County A, and EPB in County B*,[28] a private paper mill in County A (the plaintiff) caused a serious water pollution in the river nearby because of problems occurred to its pollution control technology in December 1989. That adversely affected the water supply of the Water Factory of County A. Because the river also passed through County B, and that section of river in County B was also polluted. The Environmental Protection Bureau of both County A and County B then made respective decision to impose fines upon the plaintiff, at RMB10,000 and RMB5,000 respectively. The plaintiff was also ordered to suspend its production. The plaintiff was not satisfied with the decision and lodged administrative reconsideration applications to the bureau at the next higher level of the Environmental Protection Bureau of Counties A and B respectively. The reconsideration organs made written decisions to sustain the original penalties. The plaintiff was still not satisfied, then it lodged lawsuits to the People's Courts in Counties A and B on the ground that the penalties were extremely heavy, both the People's Courts in County A and County B refused to accept the case because each of them believed the case should be under the jurisdiction of the other. Then consultation was conducted for several times but no agreement was reached. Finally, they reported to the Intermediate People's Court for designation of jurisdiction. The Intermediate People's Court then designated the People's Court in County A to have jurisdiction over the case. The People's Court of County A accepted the case on October 30.

The designation of jurisdiction may also occur if a people's court which has jurisdiction over a case is unable to exercise its jurisdiction for special reasons. What would constitute special reasons is not defined in either the ALL or the Opinions on the ALL. One source provides two kinds of special reasons, *i.e.* factual and legal reasons. Factual reasons include such things as natural disaster, war or any other unforeseeable natural events which have made impossible the exercise of jurisdiction by the court concerned. Legal reasons include situations such as the adjudicators (judges) in the courts concerned may be biased or likely to be biased so as to affect the fairness of the judgment, or the judges concerned applied for withdrawal which leads to the result that nobody is capable to hear the case.[29]

Notes

[1] The court structure is laid down in the 1979 Organic Law of the People's Courts of the People's Republic of China.
[2] For detailed discussion of vertical jurisdiction, refer to Pi and Hu, pp. 83–85; and Jiang Mingan, pp. 133–34; Luo and Ying 1990, pp. 118–39.
[3] See part 3 of the Explanation in Jiang Mingan, pp. 278–79.
[4] See Pi and Hu, p. 84.
[5] See s. 14 of the ALL.
[6] This is provided for by s. 14(2) of the ALL.
[7] If such cases will be heard by the basic people's courts, it is very likely that the administrative organ concerned will try to use its administrative authority to influence the basic courts' hearing of the case. As discussed above, people's courts are funded by the local people's governments, there is a high possibility that they may be unduly influenced by the people's government at the same level or an administrative organ at a higher level.
[8] This is provided in s. 14(3) of the ALL.
[9] See Quan She, p. 62.
[10] See Quan She, pp. 63–64.
[11] See Quan She, p. 64.
[12] See s. 21 of the ALL and Quan She, pp. 71–72.
[13] See s. 22 of the ALL and Quan She at pp. 72–75.
[14] See Sheyi, pp. 75–77; and also Pi and Hu, pp. 90–92.
[15] Horizontal jurisdiction and geographical jurisdiction mean the same thing and will be used interchangeably in this book.
[16] See s. 17 of the ALL.
[17] This is provided for under s. 19 of the ALL.
[18] This is discussed in the next section on common jurisdiction.
[19] See Quan She, p. 69.

NOTES

[20] See s. 20 of the ALL.
[21] See Quan She, p. 69.
[22] See s. 17 of the ALL.
[23] Refer to the section on common jurisdiction in this book.
[24] See s. 10 of the Opinions on the ALL.
[25] Refer to the section on vertical transfer of jurisdiction discussed above.
[26] It is also possible that both courts concerned want jurisdiction over the same case, then the same rules will apply, which is provided by section 22 of the ALL.
[27] *Ibid.*
[28] See Quan She, p. 74.
[29] See Quan She, p. 73.

CHAPTER TEN
GROUNDS FOR JUDICIAL REVIEW[1]

10.01 Grounds for judicial review refer to the legal basis or reasons upon which certain concrete administrative acts may be lawfully challenged by the aggrieved parties in the people's courts. To put it in another way, they are the legal grounds upon which the judiciary may review the legality of concrete administrative acts. In so doing, the people's courts can supervise and control the exercise of power by administrative organs and ensure that they shall fulfil their obligations properly. The fundamental principle of judicial review is legality from which many detailed grounds have evolved. This chapter will first examine the principle of legality in the context of judicial review and then consider four specific grounds as mentioned in the ALL in detail. Three other grounds shall be discussed in the next chapter on judicial control of discretionary power.

The Principle of Legality[2]

10.02 Section 5 of the ALL provides that the people's courts, in handling administrative cases, shall examine the legality of concrete administrative acts. This section has confirmed the status of the principle of legality in judicial review. This means the people's courts shall usually only review, whether or not an administrative organ has acted lawfully in undertaking any concrete administrative acts. Strictly speaking, the people's courts will not review the reasonableness of any concrete administrative acts because whether or not a concrete administrative act is reasonable is supposed to be handled through administrative reconsideration. Therefore, only when discretionary power is exercised will the people's courts examine the reasonableness under very restricted circumstances.[3]

Several reasons have been put forward for this general provision.[4] The first is that executive and judicial powers are exercised respectively by the executive and judiciary according to law. They are independent of each other. The judiciary is most experienced in making decisions on whether or not an administrative act is lawful, which is within the scope of adjudication. Whether or not an administrative act is appropriate or reasonable within the limits of law falls into the scope of executive power. In order to ensure that administrative organs may handle properly large amounts of complicated administrative matters efficiently, they have been granted certain discretion in the exercise of their power, which is essential for the proper public administration. Any complaints against the appropriateness of the exercise of discretionary powers should be handled through administrative reconsideration within the administrative system rather than judicial review.[5]

Secondly, judicial review has two objectives. One is to protect the legitimate interests of citizens, legal persons and other organizations through the examination of the legality of the exercise of administrative power. The other is to ensure that administrative organs may exercise their administrative authority without improper interference and administrative decisions can be implemented properly if they are lawful decisions. The judiciary achieves these two objectives by upholding lawful administrative decisions and overruling unlawful administrative decisions respectively. These two objectives are equally important. While emphasizing the first one, the judiciary should not ignore the second one. Instead, it should try to achieve a balance between the two.[6]

Though the review of administrative decisions by the judiciary should generally be limited to illegality, it is by no means to say that the people's courts can never review inappropriate administrative decisions. There are two circumstances under which the people's courts may be able to review the reasonableness of concrete administrative acts. Firstly, while it is easy to distinguish, in theory, issues on legal, policy, and factual matters which are supposed to be determined by different organs, in practice, there exist grey areas among the three kinds of issues which have been generally recognized in different jurisdiction. Those falling within the grey area may be treated both as either factual or legal issues. If they are deemed to be legal issues with factual elements, then the people's courts will be able to review them. In this respect, the people's courts have discretion. As a result, less discretion will be left to the administrative organs.[7] Secondly, the people's courts have been granted certain jurisdiction under the ALL to scrutinize the improper exercise of discretionary power.[8]

Legality and Judicial Review

Judiciary in its adjudication of judicial review cases shall adhere to and apply the principle of legality in its examination of concrete adminis- 10.03

trative acts. It will review the legality of both the substance of the concrete administrative acts and the procedures for the undertaking of those acts. Whether or not the substance of any concrete administrative acts is lawful depends on several factors.[9] Firstly, the subject of administrative relationship should be lawful. Specifically speaking, the decision-making administrative organ must be lawfully established and authorized to make the decision and the decision is targeted at the right person or matter. If either side to administrative relationship is unlawful, then the substance of the act will not be lawful. Secondly, the administrative organ is not *ultra vires* in undertaking the concrete administrative act. If an administrative organ exercises the power belonging to another organ, either administrative, supervisory or even judicial, or exceeding its geographical or administrative jurisdiction, it will be deemed *ultra vires*. The act undertaken accordingly will be unlawful. Thirdly, the administrative organ should not abuse its power.[10] Fourthly, the administrative organ is not derelict. This refers to administrative inaction, which is also regarded as unlawful because the relevant administrative organ must fulfil its obligations.

The principle of legality also requires administrative organs to undertake concrete administrative acts according to legal procedures. Though there is no uniform administrative procedural law as such in China, specific procedural requirements have been incorporated into various legislation for the undertaking of both concrete and abstract administrative acts. For example, the 1986 Regulation on Administrative Penalties for Public Securities has provided for the relevant procedures for the imposition of administrative penalties on those in violation of this regulation. Those procedural requirements have to be followed by the police officers. The 1996 Administrative Penalty Law of the People's Republic of China has provided for the procedures for the creation and imposition of various administrative penalties which have to be followed by the administrative organs. Likewise, those statutory procedural requirements should be complied with by the relevant administrative organs in the creation and imposition of administrative penalties.

Illegality as Grounds of Judicial Review

10.04 Legality is the fundamental principle of judicial review in China. Illegality is therefore the general ground for judicial review. Because of the broadness of the concept of legality as revealed, the scope of illegality is also wide correspondingly. Illegality is not a simple ground of judicial review. Instead, it is a concept to describe the legal feature of several specific grounds as revealed by section 54 of the ALL. There are altogether seven specific grounds listed in section 54. They include insufficiency of evidence, inaccuracy in the application of legislation, failure to comply with legal procedure, *ultra vires*, abuse of power, failure or delay in the performance of statutory duty, and obvious unfairness.[11] Among them, the first grounds actually grant the judiciary the power to review the facts of the case, which is quite different from the concept of judicial review in Western countries.[12] The following three can be argued to belong to another category, *i.e.* illegality.[13] The concept of illegality seems to be much wider than its counterpart under English administrative law where illegality is only one of the three main grounds for judicial review.[14] The last three grounds[15] shall be put into the third category in this book, *i.e.* the grounds to control discretionary powers.[16]

Another difference worthy of comment is that under common law jurisdiction, as practised in the United Kingdom and Hong Kong, judicial review is quite different from appeal. Judicial review is regarded as the inherent power of the High Court to review the legality of executive. Grounds for judicial review is not restricted by any legislation and the courts may expand the grounds for judicial review from time to time. It is a common law right. The right to appeal is a statutory right, which has to be prescribed by legislation.

But China basically adopts a continental legal system where both the right to judicial review and right to appeal have to be prescribed by legislation. Without legal authorization, a person will not be entitled to bring a case to the people's courts. Having examined the principle of legality and the general grounds of illegality for judicial review, it moves on to discuss the first four specific grounds one by one, *i.e.* insufficiency of essential evidence, wrongful application of legislation, failure to comply with legal procedure and *ultra vires*. The other three grounds are related to the control of the exercise of discretionary power and will be discussed in the next chapter.

Insufficiency of Essential Evidence

Insufficiency of essential evidence is the first ground for judicial review in China. The undertaking of any concrete administrative acts has to be based on facts which, in turn, need to be supported with evidence. The existence of sufficient evidence is directly related to the legality of any concrete administrative acts undertaken by administrative organs. Essential evidence has been held to be the precondition and basis for the legality of concrete administrative acts.[17]   10.05

According to the nature and importance of evidences, they can be classified into ordinary and essential evidence.[18] Ordinary evidence refers to those which can be used to prove the existence of non-material facts for the undertaking of any concrete administrative acts.

Essential evidence refers to those which can prove the existence of material facts upon which the concrete administrative act is undertaken. Essential evidence should satisfy three requirements. Firstly, it must be objective. That is to say the evidence is in actual existence, not imagined. Secondly, it should be related to the material facts and be able to prove the existence of the latter. Otherwise it will not be regarded as essential evidence. Thirdly, it should be lawful. It means that the evidence should have been obtained, collected and submitted according to proper procedural legal requirements. If the methods adopted to obtain the evidence is unlawful, then the evidence, even though essential, should not be relied upon for the undertaking of any concrete administrative acts.[19]

Here the legal requirement is that the essential evidence must be sufficient. That has been suggested to mean that there must be plenty of conclusive evidence to prove the existence of all the material facts for the undertaking of any concrete administrative acts.[20] There is both quantity and quality requirements. In quantity, there must be enough evidence so as to prove the existence of the facts. In quality, the evidence must be able to prove the existence of material facts, not non-material facts. If any of the material facts cannot be proved by evidence, then the evidence provided to support the undertaking of concrete administrative acts will be regarded as insufficient as far as the concrete administrative acts are concerned.

Section 32 of the ALL provides that the defendant shall bear the burden of proof for any concrete administrative acts it has undertaken and shall provide the evidence upon which the acts have been undertaken. If the defendant fails to provide the court with the essential evidence upon which the concrete administrative acts are undertaken or the evidence provided does not include the essential evidence, the people's court may annul the concrete administrative acts. If the defendant only submits evidence which is to its own advantage, then the plaintiff may rebut by providing his own evidence.

10.06 There are two issues worthy of discussion. One is when the defendant is supposed to discharge its burden of proof and whether late submission of evidence should be accepted. Section 43 of the ALL states that the defendant shall provide the people's court with the documents on the basis of which concrete administrative acts have been undertaken and file the pleadings of defence within 10 days of receiving the copy of plaintiff's pleadings. It is clear that the defendant is required to submit evidence before the actual hearing. However, section 30 of the Opinions on the ALL allows the defendant to submit evidence at any time before the completion of the trial at the first instance. That is a contradiction between different sources of law. According to the hierarchy of Chinese legislation, the provision in the ALL should prevail over those in the Opinions on the ALL.[21] A more subtle but essential question is what is the criterion to determine whether or not the defendant has discharged its burden of proof. Does it have the burden to provide evidence to its own disadvantage? This is a highly practical issue. In one case in Shangdong Province, a plaintiff was beaten by police officers for failing to pay fines. He brought the case for judicial review. The case has been with the people's court for eight months because the defendant denies the accusation. But the plaintiff has no witnesses except a medical certificate that he had been beaten.[22]

The other issue is whether or not the evidence, that was obtained illegally, can be admitted by the people's courts. Different opinions exist on this point. One argues that the strict application of the rule of law principle does not allow the admission of any evidence obtained by unlawful means.[23] The second opinion represents the attitude of the people's courts, which maintains that a practical approach should be adopted. If the evidence is not a key one, the people's court will not admit it. If the evidence is an essential one, it is suggested that the people's court may, after scrutiny, admit it. The people's court may then issue judicial recommendation to the administrative organ concerned requesting investigation or correction later.[24] The second approach actually adopts double standards in the determination of admission of evidence obtained unlawfully, which is not consistent with the requirement of rule of law principle.

Insufficiency of essential evidence has two possibilities. Many cases brought to the people's courts on the grounds of insufficiency of essential evidence are based on the argument that either the defendant (an administrative organ) fails to provide any evidence or is unable to provide essential evidence for the confirmation of the existence of material facts. Because the insufficiency of essential evidence often implies wrongful identification of facts. This will then lead to wrongful application of legislation. This is why it is often invoked, together with another ground, wrongful application of legislation. If it is proved that an administrative act is undertaken due to insufficiency of evidence, the judiciary can repeal partially or completely the original act and order the relevant administrative organ to undertake a new administrative act.

Failure to Provide Evidence

The following five cases are about the failure to provide evidence.   10.07

He Xiguang v. Administration Bureau of Industry and Commerce in Shanwei City[25]

On August 23, 1988, the plaintiff went back to his hometown in Fujian from Hong Kong. He took a bus in Shenzhen, which passed through

Haifeng on August 25. The officers of the Administration Bureau of Industry and Commerce in Haifeng discovered that the plaintiff was in possession of US$38,736 and HK$158,900. The officers examined the plaintiff's visa and found that the plaintiff had only declared the possession of US$1,000 and HK$3,000 respectively.

The bureau detained part of the plaintiff's Foreign exchange amounting to US$32,736 and HK$150,000. The detained foreign exchange was submitted to the People's Bank to change to renminbi of which 50 per cent was confiscated. The reason was that the plaintiff had not obtained the approval from Customs, according to the Implementation Regulation Regarding the Punishment for Violation of Foreign Exchange Control of the PRC and the Regulation Regarding the Punishment of Profiteers and Speculators.

The plaintiff claimed that he had obtained approval from Customs. He claimed that his confession that he was involved in foreign exchange speculation was a result of violence inflicted on him by the officers. The plaintiff had applied for administrative reconsideration to the Administration Bureau of Industry and Commerce in Shanwei City (the defendant), but the decision of the Bureau of Haifeng was sustained on the basis that the plaintiff's claim at administrative reconsideration contradicted his own admission. When the plaintiff made the admission to the officers of the Haifeng Bureau, the plaintiff said that he brought the money to buy a house in Fujian and the money was given by his father who was in Singapore. However, when the plaintiff applied for administrative reconsideration, he said that he obtained the money from investment and he planned to buy a house in Shenzhen.

Then the plaintiff brought a lawsuit to the people's court. The people's court held that the plaintiff had made some contradictory admissions and caused the delay of the investigation. However, there was evidence that Customs had approved the plaintiff's possession of foreign exchange because the written approval from Customs was produced. Therefore the plaintiff did not violate the law and the accusation by the defendant lacked of essential evidence and the administrative decision was annulled.

Nanjing Zhuangyuanlou Restaurant v. Nanjing Branch of National Bureau of Foreign Exchange Control[26]

10.08 The plaintiff was a joint venture and it borrowed money from a third party, an investing company. When the third party gave the agreed amount to the plaintiff, the third party alleged that it did not have renminbi and had only US dollars. The plaintiff signed a loan contract for US$200,000 and entrusted the third party in writing to exchange the US dollars into renminbi on its behalf. The Nanjing Branch of the National Bureau of Foreign Exchange Control (the defendant) then penalized the plaintiff for unlawful exchange of foreign currency because the third party exchanged the US dollars to renminbi with its own renminbi, which was prohibited by the laws on foreign exchange control. The plaintiff then applied for administrative reconsideration, but the National Bureau upheld the decision of the Nanjing Branch.

The plaintiff applied to the court for judicial review and claimed that the plaintiff had the authority to entrust the third party to act as its agent to exchange the foreign currency under section 63(1) of the General Principles of Civil Law. The plaintiff also contended that the defendant's allegation that foreign currency was not exchanged through the foreign exchange centre was groundless. Moreover, it was only the third party's liability that it used its own RMB to exchange the foreign currency which violated the laws on the foreign exchange control.

The court of first instance held that the application of laws and regulations by the defendant was correct and dismissed the plaintiff's application and the plaintiff did not have the authority to entrust an agent to exchange the foreign currency on its behalf.

The plaintiff appealed. The court of second instance was of the opinion that section 63 of the General Principles of Civil Law states that citizen and other legal entities have the authority to entrust a third party as agent, and the defendant's contention that the plaintiff did not the have this authority to entrust an agent was groundless. Moreover, the third party should be solely liable for its act in excess of its authority as an agent to convert the US dollar to renminbi with its own currency, which was unknown to the plaintiff. In conclusion, the plaintiff's act was lawful and the decision of the defendant was lack of evidence and the laws were mistakenly applied.

In this case, the defendant failed to provide any evidence that the plaintiff had violated legislation on the foreign exchange control. This means there is lack of material facts to prove the defendant's allegation. If the plaintiff did not violate the law on foreign exchange control, its application is obviously wrongful.

The above two cases were about the defendant's failure to provide any evidence to prove that the plaintiff unlawfully engaged in foreign exchange transaction. There are some cases which are argued solely for lack of essential evidence.

Zhang Xizheng and Medicine Purchase Station in Lin Tai County v. Land Administration Bureau in Lin Tai County[27]

10.09 In 1980, a medicine shop was allocated to the medicine purchase station (the second plaintiff) and the staff of the medicine shop moved into the medicine purchase station. The five houses and five apartments with land of 408.5 square metres originally occupied by the medicine shop was left empty. In 1985, the original manager of the station arranged a sale of the 10 houses on the land to the first plaintiff for RMB3,000. The plaintiff then demolished the houses and built 13 new houses. The second plaintiff did nothing to stop the first plaintiff. When the Land Administration Bureau in Lin Tai started the registration of land, the second plaintiff did not report its right to use that land, the transaction of the right over the land to the Land Administration Bureau. Both plaintiffs admitted the transaction of houses. Zhang Xizheng also admitted that she paid RMB1,000 for the land, which she later denied. The plaintiffs were charged with illegal sale and purchase of state-owned land.

The defendant made a decision on April 22, 1991, according to the Constitution and the Regulation on Requisition of Land for State Construction to confiscate the RMB1,000 generated through the sale of land. The first plaintiff was ordered to demolish the 13 houses illegally built on the land within one month and pay a fine of RMB100. The land-use right obtained by the first plaintiff was taken back by the state. The first plaintiff claimed that she only obtained the buildings on the land, but not the land itself. Moreover, she claimed that the regulation was already abolished on January 1, 1987, which the defendant should not apply in 1991. The second plaintiff claimed that the allegation of illegal buying and selling of state-owned land was groundless.

The court of first instance held that there was actually a transaction between the two plaintiffs for the sale of land and the first plaintiff had admitted the transaction of the land to the defendant. The evidence showed that the land-use right was also transferred to the first plaintiff because the plaintiffs confessed there was a transaction of the title of the land which they denied after the imposition of administrative penalties.

However, the court of second instance held that the transaction was only a transaction of title of the houses on the land and the plaintiffs had revoked their confession of the land transaction. The defendant could not provide evidence to prove its allegation of illegal sale and purchase of state-owned land between the two plaintiffs. The defendant's decision should be annulled for lack of essential evidence and wrongful application of law. Moreover, the Constitution cannot be directly invoked by the people's court in adjudication.

Jiayuguan Branch of Xiliu Engineering and Construction Corporation v. Jiayuguan Municipal Taxation Bureau[28]

10.10 On June 5, 1987, the plaintiff signed a contract for the restoration of the Jiayuguan Tower with Great Wall Office the third party. The project commenced on June 8, 1987. Since 1985, the construction units issued receipt whenever they received funds from the third party and it became a custom to issue receipt which the plaintiff followed. It bought the receipt from Jiuquan and issued it when the unit received funds for the project. It received from the third party a total sum of RMB403,640. In June and July, Xiao, a tax collector of Jiayuguan Township Tax Office, asked the chief of the third party to inform all the construction units that they should pay tax at the Tax Office of Jiayugan Township. The third party suggested a lump-sum should be paid when the project was completed. Xiao agreed with the suggestion and the third party notified the plaintiff to do so. On December 16, 1987, the Jiayugan Tax Bureau (the defendant) issued a notice that from January 1, 1988, all construction units should use a new invoice with the seal of the defendant. The plaintiff immediately went to buy the invoice from the defendant after it was notified by the third party. However, Xiao, the person in charge of the invoice, was on leave when the plaintiff went to buy the invoice and Zhang, an accountant of the Tax Office sold half a book of invoices to the plaintiff, of which the other half had been used by Zhang. Four days later, the plaintiff met Xiao. He sold a book of invoices to the plaintiff. In June 1988, the third party informed the plaintiff that the method of tax payment was varied and the plaintiff had to pay the tax each time when it received the payment. On June 27, 1988, the defendant investigated the plaintiff's accounts according to a report to the defendant.

The defendant found that the plaintiff had four acts which violated the law. First of all, the plaintiff had not reported its income within the time limit. Secondly, the plaintiff had violated the Provisional Procedures for the Control Over Nation-wide Commercial Invoices. Thirdly, the plaintiff had obtained income without submitting the proper invoice paper to the tax office. Finally, the plaintiff had concealed information about its income and had not reported its tax payment according to the tax regulation. The plaintiff was ordered to pay the tax and the fine.

The plaintiff applied to the Provincial Tax Bureau for administrative reconsideration after it paid the tax and fine. However, the reconsideration organ did not make any decision for two years. The plaintiff brought a lawsuit to the people's court.

The court of first instance found that the plaintiff did not apply to Jiayugan Tax Office on time for tax payment registration and used an unofficial receipt bought in the market. The plaintiff actually violated the Provisional Regulation of the PRC on the Administration of Taxation and Levies (Provisional Regulation) and the Provisional Procedures for the Control Over Nation-wide Commercial Invoices on the first two counts against it. However, the fourth was the plaintiff's violation of section 37(3) of the Provisional Regulation by concealing that the actual income for the purpose of escaping from the tax liability, which was groundless because of the agreement reached between Xiao and the third party, and the fact that the construction project was not completed. The court of first instance held that the first two decisions should be upheld, but the fourth was with insufficient evidence, which caused a misapplication of laws and regulations by the defendant. Therefore the penalty should be annulled accordingly.

The defendant appealed. The court of second instance dismissed the appeal.

Chen Jiayou v. The Real Property Administration Bureau of the Liuzhou City[29]

10.11 The Real Property Administration Bureau of the Liuzhou City (the defendant) was of the opinion that the plaintiff had sublet his public housing unit to two persons, Liu and Ling, for rent, violating section 11 of the Provisional Regulation of the Real Property Administration of Liuzhou City which stated that the lease should be terminated when the law is violated. The defendant terminated the lease with the plaintiff and ordered the plaintiff to remove all properties from the unit within seven days. The plaintiff applied for administrative reconsideration, but the reconsideration organ sustained the defendant's decision. Then the plaintiff applied to court for judicial review and contended that the decision of the defendant was lack of evidence. The plaintiff also claimed that the two said persons had conspired to tell lies in order to obtain the lease of that housing unit from the defendant.

The court of the first instance found out that the plaintiff had been granted a housing unit for business purposes from the bureau under the administration of the defendant in 1980. The plaintiff had applied to strike off the original business licence and then carried on the catering business from 1989 without the approval of the Real Property Administration Bureau. The plaintiff then sublet the unit to Liu and Ling. The plaintiff had varied the purpose of the unit and violated the regulation by subleasing the unit. Therefore, the termination of the lease by the defendant was correct.

However, the court of second instance held that the defendant had merely based its judgement on the report of the above two persons and reached the decision that the plaintiff had violated section 11 of the regulation. The report alone did not amount to sufficient evidential basis. Moreover, although the plaintiff had actually varied the purpose of the unit, the defendant was not able to draw any inference that the plaintiff had sublet the unit to Liu and Ling. The allegation of the sublease by the defendant was lack of essential evidence.

The court of second instance annulled the decisions of the defendant and the court of first instance, and ordered the defendant to make a new decision in one month after receiving this judgment.

Failure to Provide Essential Evidence

10.12 There are some other cases which can be argued on both failure to provide evidence and lack of essential evidence. In this category, the defendants usually provide some evidence, but not enough to prove the existence of material facts. The following are examples.

Wang Shijiang and Wang Shihai v. the People's Government of Huang Fa Town[30]

The plaintiffs' house was endangered by a brick factory and the brick factory agreed to compensate the plaintiffs for the removal of their home. The plaintiffs then applied to the village for the occupation of a plot of abandoned land to build a dwelling house on October 30, 1990. The village approved the application on November 5 and the plaintiffs then applied to the People's Government of Huang Fa Town (the defendant) for approval. Su, the chief of one district office of the defendant approved the application on November 17. Su then went to the main office of the defendant for the town planning licence and the construction licence on November 20. The two licences were issued and Su then applied for land-use permit. Han, an officer of the main office told Su that there was no problem for the application of the land-use permit and Su could make the application a few days later. However, Su's employment contract was terminated by the local people's government later. On December 4, the plaintiffs gave the licences to the construction team and said that the land-use permit would be accepted. The construction was completed in May 1991. The defendant alleged that the plaintiffs had unlawfully occupied the land for the purpose of building dwelling houses without a land-use permit and ordered the plaintiffs to demolish the houses and return the land. The plaintiffs claimed that the building was approved by the officers under the defendant. The plaintiffs also applied for the permit to the land administration bureau.

The court of first instance held that the evidence was clear and the application of laws was correct and rejected the plaintiffs' argument. The plaintiffs appealed and the court of second instance held that when Su signed the approval, he actually approved the application on behalf of the defendant. Moreover, the plaintiffs had obtained the approval of the village and the two licences, the building did not amount to an unlawful occupation of land for house building. However, it was improper for the plaintiffs to merely rely on Su's verbal representation and believe the land-use permit would be accepted. In conclusion, the allegation of the defendant for the unlawful occupation of land by the plaintiffs was lack of essential evidence.

In this case the failure to obtain a land-use permit was a fact. But it did not amount to the allegation that the plaintiffs unlawfully occupied the land. The defendant failed to provide sufficient essential evidence to prove that the plaintiffs did not obtain approval of the Township People's Government, which is the essence of this case.

Yie Ronghua (first plaintiff) and Ning Hong Hotel (second plaintiff) v. The Tax Bureau of Xiu Shui County[31]

10.13 The Ning Hong Hotel, the second plaintiff, was a collectively owned enterprise. The hotel started the service on January 1, 1990 before the construction work was completed. On February 1, the Tax Office of Yi Ning Town carried out an investigation of the hotel for tax purposes. The second plaintiff did not report any income or pay any property tax to the Office until December 24, 1990 when the investigation was carried out. That was due to the valuation of the hotel building and the taxation date were not yet ascertained. During this period, the office did not inform the plaintiff to report its income or urge the plaintiff to pay tax. On December 24, Fan, a tax collector from the office discovered that the second plaintiff had not paid the tax and ordered Gan, the legal representative of the hotel, and Chen, the accountant of the hotel, to the Taxation Bureau to calculate property tax which amounted to RMB11,760. Chen said to Fan that the hotel was in debt and asked Fan to exempt the property tax. Fan was sympathetic and agreed to exempt the tax. Then a new taxation report was filled. Fan said to Chen that Fan had some quarrels with Ye, the first plaintiff. Fan asked Chen to invite Ye to discuss the issue. When Chen asked Ye to go, he refused and took away the taxation report from Chen. Ten days later, Ye met Fan in the hotel and Ye told the second plaintiff not to pay property tax to Fan because Ye was of the opinion that Fan had cheated them. Ye had also said some words against Fan. On April 23, 1991, the second plaintiff paid the tax on request. Ye had also confessed that he had made mistakes on this matter.

The tax bureau of the county (the defendant) issued a notice and held that the hotel refused to pay tax and the first plaintiff, as the person in charge, should bear the responsibility. The hotel was ordered to pay the property tax of RMB11,760 and fines were imposed on the two plaintiffs respectively.

The plaintiffs applied for administrative reconsideration, but the defendant's decision was sustained by the reconsideration organ. The plaintiffs then lodged a lawsuit to court. The court of first instance held that the defendant had erroneously identified the legal representative of the hotel. Gan was actually the legal representative of the hotel, but he had not refused to pay taxation. Therefore the fine on the hotel was inappropriate because of lack of evidence. Moreover, although the first plaintiff had misbehaved, however, he was not the representative of the hotel and his fine for acts against taxation was illegal.

The defendant appealed. The court of second instance upheld the judgment of the court of first instance. In this case, several grounds had been relied on by the people's court: in the main, there are lack of essential evidence and abuse of powers.[32]

Zhu Jinru v. State Land Administration Bureau in Huizhou City[33]

10.14 The plaintiff belonged to the Oil and Chemical Industrial Company of Heizhou, and the company acquired the forest land of 100 mu (one mu equals $1/15$ hectare) from the forest station, a third party to this case. The forest station then suggested the company to exchange the land with a car. The forest station required the company to buy a car worth RMB200,000. On that day the company and the forest station signed the "Contract for Exchange of Property". The plaintiff acting in the names of a restaurant and a third person also signed another contract with the same contents with the forest station. Then the forest station suggested that the plaintiff should pay RMB200,000 in instalments and the forest station would buy the car itself. The State-Owned Land Bureau of Heizhou County (the defendant) was of the opinion that the plaintiff had dishonestly acquired the land in the names of the company, the restaurant and the third person. This was in violation of section 47 of the Land Administration Law and section 5 of the Implementation Procedure on the Land Administration in Guangzhou Province. The defendant made the decision that the land which the plaintiff acquired shall be confiscated by the State government. The plaintiff claimed that he only acted in the capacity of the representative of the company to enter into the transaction and the allegation by the defendant was lack of evidence.

The court found out that the plaintiff did not have the authority to represent the first company. The first contract between the company and the forest station was void. But the documents had shown that the plaintiff had actually acquired the land on behalf of the restaurant, because the contract bore the seal of the restaurant. Moreover, the defendant reached its decision by merely basing on the contracts that the plaintiff unlawfully acquired the land without carrying out any proper investigation. Therefore the allegation by the defendant was lack of essential evidence. Moreover, the defendant's imposition of penalty on the plaintiff without any investigation on the matter was also a violation of legal procedure as well.

Xu Deliao v. Patent Administration Bureau in Hu Bei Province[34]

10.15 In 1987, the plaintiff invented a kind of technology which could be applied to the production of shoes. The plaintiff then signed a contract applying the new technology with the third party who was a manufacturer producing a part of a shoe. In 1991, the plaintiff applied to the National Patent Bureau for the patent of the technology to produce that part of a shoe. In 1992, the third party also applied to the Patent Administration Bureau of Hubei Province (the defendant) for the patent of that part. The defendant held, according to section 8 of the Patent Law and section 32 of the Technology Contract Law, that the plaintiff and the third party were joint owners of the patent because the plaintiff and the third party had co-operated with each other to invent that part.

The plaintiff brought a lawsuit to the intermediate people's court in Wu Han. The evidence had shown that the plaintiff had actually invented the product and the third party was only a contracting party to manufacture the product. The defendant had not clarified the relationship between the plaintiff and the third party, and made its decision merely on the third party's application. According to law, the inventor of a product is entitled to register the product and obtain a patent over it. The defendant's decision was lack of evidence.

There are a couple of issues to be noted in this case. One is whether or not the case should be regarded as an administrative case or a civil case. The second issue is on what grounds the plaintiff challenges the defendant's decision. As what was under challenge was the decision of the defendants, it should therefore be regarded as an administrative case.

Liu Chen Lian Hua Electronic Company in Ping Nan County v. Fishery Administration Station in Ping Nan County[35]

10.16 According to the Regulation on the Implementation of the Fishery Law in Guangxi Autonomous Region, it was unlawful to manufacture, sell and use fishing instruments which were either prohibited or not up to the standard as stipulated by the provincial regulations. The plaintiff was a factory which was licensed to manufacture electricity generators, batteries and other kinds of metal products (except televisions). On May 18, 1993, the Fishery Administration Station of the Ping Nan County (the defendant), based on the reports from others that the plaintiff had produced forbidden fishing instruments, investigated the plaintiff's factory and the home of Chen, an employee of the plaintiff and who was not in the Province at the time. The officers of the defendant detained 33 fish electrocuting machines, tools for the machines, parts of them, posters of the machines, other letters and information. The properties detained were stored in the Station. However, the defendant did so without issuing any legal documents for the detention, the defendant only gave a list of the detained properties to Chen's family. On May 20, the defendant gave a verdict that the plaintiff had violated section 10(4) of the regulation for producing forbidden fishing instruments. The defendant imposed on Chen a fine of RMB20,000 and seized the tools of the plaintiff. When the verdict was delivered to Chen's home on May 21, Chen's wife refused to sign the receipt of the verdict and the defendant simply left the verdict in Chen's house.

Chen only realised that the defendant imposed administrative penalty on him when he returned on May 24. He contended that the products which the defendant seized were electricity generators instead of fish electrocuting machines. The plaintiff and Mo, the licence holder of the factory, applied to the Marine Product Bureau of the Yulin Area for administrative reconsideration on June 3. However, the bureau refused to reconsider the defendant's decision because the plaintiff made the application when the time limit had expired. The plaintiff and Mo then lodged a lawsuit to the court.

The court held that first of all, the licence holder of the factory was Mo not Chen. It was lack of essential evidence to impose a fine on Chen on the grounds that the plaintiff had illegally manufactured forbidden instruments. Moreover, the time limit for the plaintiff to apply for administrative reconsideration had not expired as the calculation of time limit only starts when the plaintiff was aware of the penalty. Here the defendant violated procedural requirements by leaving the verdict with Chen's family without seeing Chen. The detention of the properties was lack of legal basis. Therefore, the fine on the plaintiff and the seizure of the factory's tools were also lack of essential evidence. Furthermore, the defendant's action to send the seized products to be tested during the litigation was also in violation of legal procedure. The results obtained cannot be relied on as evidence. Therefore, the defendant's decision should be annulled.

It is also possible that the administrative organ did not have sufficient evidence when it undertook the concrete administrative act. When a judicial review case was brought to the people's court, the administrative organ then went to collect evidence. This would be regarded as insufficiency of essential evidence. That is what also happened in this case. Apart from lack of essential evidence, violation of legal procedures is another ground relied on by the people's court in this judicial review case.

Xie Junzhong v. People's Government in Tinzi Township in the Suburb of Nan Ning City[36]

In 1985, the plaintiff applied to the production team which he belonged to for the construction of a house on a plot of abandoned land which belonged to the team. The team approved the application. The plaintiff then applied to the local government for the permit to do the business of selling miscellaneous products and also applied to the Tabacco Administration Bureau for the permit to sell cigarettes. In the course of the application, the plaintiff had produced the permit by the team. His application was approved. In the same year, the plaintiff built a house on the same land of which the area was 40 square metres. When the plaintiff started the construction, the Land Administration Law and the Regulation on Road Administration in Guangxi were not yet implemented.

In 1989, the defendant held that the plaintiff built the house on the

10.17

collectively owned land without permit in contrary to section 45 of the Land Administration Law and ordered him to demolish the premises on the land. The plaintiff contended that the construction of the house was approved by the relevant governmental organs and there was no requirement of law for the application of permit at the time he built the house. During the litigation, the defendant went to the Road Administrative Bureau to collect evidence.

The court found that the house was constructed prior to the implementation of the Land Administrative Law and pre-existing requirements were satisfied. Therefore the allegation of the defendant was lack of evidence and the administrative penalty should be annulled. Moreover, the application of section 45 of the Land Administration Law was an erroneous application of legislation. The defendant appealed but the court of second instance dismissed the appeal. The court of second instance held that defendant's application of the legislation which was not implemented at the time the plaintiff did the act amounted to an erroneous application of laws and regulations. The collection of evidence by the defendant during the process of litigation was against legal procedures. Nor was there evidence to prove that the plaintiff had violated any legislation.

The Interpretation of Evidence

10.18 There are cases where both the plaintiff and the defendant do not have any disputes with regard to the evidence. The difference arises around the interpretation of the evidence. The next case is an example.

Li Yunxiang and others v. Shanghai Municipal Real Property Administration Bureau[37]

In 1990, the third party and her son applied to the Real Property Administration Bureau of Shanghai (the defendant) for the registration of their ownership over the house in question. The third party also made a declaration in the newspaper about the loss of the original document of the property right over the said house. After investigation, the defendant issued the property right certificate to the third party on May 26, 1992.

However, before the certificate was issued, the plaintiff had applied to the branch of the defendant for a decision of ascertaining the property right over the house in question. The plaintiff contended that the house was originally owned by her husband who had already died and she was entitled to inherit the house under law. Moreover, she claimed that she had applied for confirmation of title several times before the issue of the certificate to the third party and therefore the defendant had infringed her lawful right.

The court, after reviewing the documents, found out that the premises actually belonged to the plaintiff's husband before his death. Moreover, according to section 8 of the Provisional Procedure Concerning the Registration of Title Over the Premises in City and Town, the certificate should only be issued when it was clear that there was no dispute over the title of the premises. The defendant should not issue the certificate to the third party until the plaintiff's application was dealt with. In the present case, the defendant had disregarded the plaintiff's application for confirmation of her title over the house and made the decision, to grant title to a third party. Its administrative act was lack of essential evidence. The court of first instance annulled the decision of the defendant.

The defendant and the third party appealed, but the court of second instance dismissed the appeal and upheld the judgment of the court of first instance.

Combination of Insufficiency of Essential Evidence and Wrongful Application of Law

10.19 The grounds for insufficiency of essential evidence is often invoked by the plaintiff in conjunction with the grounds of wrongful application of legislation. It is logical because lack of essential evidence usually equals to wrongful identification of essential facts or the persons concerned which leads to the wrongful identification of material facts. As material facts are usually mentioned in relevant legislation for their application. Therefore wrongful identification of material facts will naturally lead to wrongful application of legislation. The following cases are examples.

Luo v. Food Hygiene Inspection Bureau in X County[38]

The plaintiff had been contracted to run the business of a tea shop for a third party. The Food Hygiene Centre of the County (the defendant) later found out in an investigation that the restaurant was operated without the required licences and the facilities were not up to standard. The defendant ordered the business of the tea shop to be suspended until the condition was improved. The plaintiff disregarded the order and carried on the business, which he did after three warnings. The plaintiff was finally fined RMB1,000, but he claimed that the penalty should be imposed on the third party. The court held that the penalty was unfair and should be amended. In fact, the defendant had erroneously identified as the person to whom the fine should be imposed because the actual owner of the tea shop was the third party. Therefore the administrative decision was lack of essential evidence, which led to an erroneous application of law.

The case of *Mao Yunbing v. Gangdong Township People's Government* is another example where several grounds were relied on. The case is concerned with the unlawful occupation of land. The defendant asked the plaintiff to return the land, which he legitimately occupied, to the collective owner and also applied the wrong section of the Land Administration Law to reach its decision.[39]

When a case is brought up to the people's courts, it is quite natural for the defendant to provide evidence to its own, not to the plaintiff's, advantage. But that is quite natural and cannot be used as a justification to challenge the decision of the administrative organ concerned. Instead, the plaintiff should provide its own evidence to rebut the evidence of the defendant.

On the other hand, the supply of evidence obtained unlawfully can be regarded as one possibility of insufficiency of essential evidence. It is most likely to happen in judicial review cases brought against public security bureaus (the police). Judicial practice shows that there are not many cases falling within this category in other areas of public administration.

Inaccuracy in the Application of Legislation[40]

10.20   The exact meaning of inaccuracy in the application of legislation is not explained, either in the ALL or in the Opinions on the ALL. Chinese scholars have given different interpretations which have been summarized by Professor Luo Haocai in his book.[41] Most scholars agree that inaccuracy in the application of legislation should be restricted to the inaccuracy in the application of substantive legislation.[42] However, Professor Luo suggests in his book that application of legislation should refer to the application of both substantive and procedural legislation. The people's courts should review not only the errors in the application of substantive legislation, but also errors in the application of procedural legislation.[43] It is correct to say that legislation includes both substantive and procedural ones. There is no legal justification why this should be restricted only to inaccuracy in the application of substantive legislation. However, statutory interpretation has to be done in its context. By putting section 54(2)(b) in the context of the ALL, especially together with section 54(2)(c), it seems more logical to restrict the erroneous application of legislation under section 54(2)(b) to substantive legislation. It is because section 52(2)(c) puts the violation of legal procedure as separate grounds for judicial review. In other words, the inclusion of both substantive and procedural legislation under section 52(2)(b) would make the provision of section 52(2)(c) redundant. The relevant remedy shall be a partial or complete repeal of the original administrative act, and an order, if necessary, for the administrative organ to undertake a new administrative act.

Reasons for the Inaccuracy in the Application of Legislation

Inaccuracy in the application of legislation may be caused by various factors. Three main factors have been suggested.[44] Firstly, China adopts a unilateral legal system and there is legislation enacted at different levels and with different effect. There are laws, administrative regulations, regulations, administrative rules and various normative documents with legal effect. They may be enacted by the National People's Congress or local people's congresses, by the Central People's Government or local people's government, and various administrative organs at different levels.[45] It happens occasionally that the two pieces of legislation will be contradictory to each other. If that is the case, the administrative organ concerned has to choose one to apply. If the two pieces of legislation are at different levels in the hierarchy, then the one at the higher level should prevail. The choice will become a difficult task, especially when the two pieces of legislation are at the same level of the legal hierarchy. Moreover, different scopes of applicability of different legislation may further complicate the issue.[46]

10.21

Secondly, Chinese legislation is, compared with legislation in the United Kingdom or Hong Kong, very general and many legal provisions only lay down the principles in the areas concerned and usually lack detailed provisions. On the one hand, it has something to do with the tradition of a continental legal system which usually emphasizes the importance of legal principles. On the other hand, it is impossible for any country to have detailed legal provisions on everything. It is because the society is changing all the time and public administration is so dynamic. It is even more true in China as it is at present still in the transitional period from a planned economy to a market economy and its legal system is also in a transitional period. During this period, it is not surprising that gaps in legislation may exist. The administration has to rely on general legal principles to make decisions. It is therefore unavoidable that errors may occur in the process of application of law.

Thirdly, the quality of law enforcement officers is also essential to the accurate application of legislation because any legislation has to be implemented by people. If the law enforcement officers misidentify the nature of the facts as discussed in the previous section, or ignore the relevant factual elements, or misinterpret the relevant legislation or is unfamiliar with the legislation, then he may commit an error in the application of legislation.[47]

Categories of Inaccuracy in the Application of Legislation

10.22 Different classifications have been suggested. Three, five and six categories have all been suggested.[48] Here Professor Luo's classification will be adopted for its simplicity, *i.e.* to classify inaccuracy in the application of legislation into three categories. They are the application of correct legislation to wrong subjects, application of wrong legislation, and application of wrong provisions of correct legislation.

Application of Correct Legislation to Wrong Subject(s)[49]

10.23 It mainly refers to situations under which the administrative organ either grants rights to the subjects who are not entitled to or imposes obligations or administrative penalties upon those who are not responsible. The issue of licence to unqualified person(s) or failure to issue licence to qualified person(s), and improper imposition of tax are examples. Many of the cases examined in the previous section on the grounds of insufficiency of essential evidence are also examples of application of correct legislation to wrong subject(s).

Li Guoguang v. Huolong Township People's Government[50]

In 1990, the plaintiff was approved by the Huolong Township People's Government (the defendant) to build a single-storey house not exceeding 75 square metres. The plaintiff had actually built a two-storey house of 69.4 square metrs.

When the defendant discovered that, it served a notice to the plaintiff and an order to the plaintiff to suspend the construction work. The defendant sent the order twice but the plaintiff ignored it. The plaintiff was then ordered by the defendant to demolish the second floor in accordance with section 45 of the Land Administration Law. The plaintiff claimed that he was originally approved to build a two-storey house. However, the documents of approval were destroyed by his neighbour and he was only approved to build a single-storey house when he made the second application.

The court held that section 45 of the Land Administration Law was only applicable to the unlawful occupation of land. However, the plaintiff had not violated section 45, even though he built the second floor without approval. The defendant's imposition of penalty on the plaintiff according to section 45 was an erroneous application of legislation.

This is again an application of wrongful legislation, more appropriately, it may be regarded as wrongful identification of material facts.

In the case of *Jiayuguan Branch of Xiliu Engineering & Construc-*

tion Corporation v. Jiayuguan Municipal Taxation Bureau,[51] the plaintiff did not have the intention to evade the payment of tax. Nor did he objectively do anything to cheat or evade the payment of tax. Therefore the application of the Interim Methods on the National Administration of Invoice amounted to the application of correct legislation to the wrong subjects.

The *Nanjing Zhuangyuanlou Restaurant v. Nanjing Branch of National Bureau of Foreign Exchange Control* case is another example in this category.[52] In this case, it is the third party not the plaintiff who violated the relevant legislation on foreign exchange control. The penalty should be imposed on the third party instead of the plaintiff. Therefore, it is the application of correct legislation to wrongful subjects.

Application of Wrong Provisions of Correct Legislation

There are two possibilities. One is that the administrative organ should apply one section or subsection, but it actually applies another section or subsection. The second possibility is that the administration should apply several sections in the legislation, but it only applies to one of them. The following are several examples.

10.24

Mao Yunbing v. Gangdong Township People's Government in Cong Ming County[53]

In 1975, the plaintiff was approved by the tenth production team to which he belonged, to build a residential house on a plot of collectively owned land owned by the nineth production team. In 1979, the production team reviewed the record of the land and discovered that the plaintiff had a plot of land of which the area was 14.5 metres by 10.3 metres. In 1987, after obtaining approval of the defendant, the plaintiff used the land he owned to build some huts for chicken rearing and later he used the huts to rear cows. In late 1991, the County People's Government carried out an investigation and held that the plaintiff had unlawfully occupied collectively owned land to build houses, which violated section 38 of the Land Administration Law and amounted to unlawful occupation of land.

The plaintiff was ordered by the defendant to restore the land he occupied to the village and demolish the huts built on the land. The plaintiff claimed that he had the right of use over the land and refused to follow the defendant's decision. He made an application to the court.

The court had found out that the plaintiff was given the right to use the land by the production team. The court held that the defendant had erroneously applied that law because the defendant had not first of all solved the dispute over the right to use the land in question between the plaintiff and the nineth production team according to the stipulation of section 13 of the Land Administration Law. The defendant imposed a penalty on the plaintiff based on unclear facts. The defendant made the decision without going through the procedure to ascertain the right over the land under section 13 of the Land Administration Law. It also amounted to a violation of legal procedure.

In this case, three grounds can be relied on by the people's courts. The first is lack of essential evidence to prove that the plaintiff unlawfully occupied the land. The second is that the defendant applied the wrong section in the Land Administration Law. The third is failure to follow the legal procedure.

Chen Cunmei v. Tobacco Bureau in Zhen Yang County[54]

10.25 The plaintiff was a seller of cigarettes. On September 26, 1990, she went to another county to collect the money owed by Wan (a third party) to her. Wan did not have money and he paid the plaintiff in terms of locally produced cigarettes.

When the plaintiff passed Ching Yan County, the Tobacco Administration Bureau (the defendant) found out that the plaintiff was in possession of the cigarettes without the permit of transportation and detained the cigarettes which were later returned to the plaintiff. However, the plaintiff was then penalized for the sale of cigarettes contrary to section 17 of the Regulation on Exclusive Right to Sell Tobacco. The defendant, based on section 49 of the Implementation Rules of the Regulation, compulsorily purchased the cigarettes of the plaintiff and a fine amounting to 18 per cent of the total value of the cigarettes of RMB1398.78 which was also imposed on her. The defendant alleged that the plaintiff sold the cigarettes without permission and sold them in other regions which was prohibited by the law. The plaintiff claimed that the defendant had wrongly applied the two provisions and the penalty was obviously unfair.

The court of first instance held that the plaintiff had actually sold cigarettes without permission, but she had not sold the cigarettes in other regions. Therefore, the offence she committed was not serious because the cigarettes were not foreign cigarettes and the fine should only be 10 per cent of the total value according to section 19 of the Implementation Rules. It was obviously unfair to the plaintiff that the defendant applied section 17 of the Regulation and section 49 of the Implementation Rules. Therefore the administrative penalty should be amended accordingly. However, the court of second instance held that the application of section 17 of the Regulation amounted to a misapplication of legislation and the fine imposed in excess of the limit of that section amounted to an excess of authority. The application of section 54(4) of the Administrative Litigation Law by the court of first instance was inappropriate.

There are two grounds relied on in this case by the court of second instance. One is the misapplication of legislation. The other is *ultra vires*. Different opinions were expressed by the courts of first and second instances as to whether or not obvious unfairness is also grounds for judicial review in this case. It seems that obvious unfairness can also be argued in this case.

Liu v. Administration Bureau of Industry and Commerce in X City[55]

The plaintiff obtained business licences from counties A and B. The scope of his business was bicycle repairing. In 1986 the plaintiff sent his employee to B county to buy bicycle parts. The Administration Bureau of Industry and Commerce (the defendant) discovered that the parts lacked invoices and a certificate of quality. The defendant subsequently discovered that the plaintiff had also produced 58 bicycles of a fake brand and 51 out of 58 bicycles were sold. The defendant transferred the case to the Administration Bureau of Industry and Commerce in county B. The bureau in county B imposed a fine on the plaintiff for unlawful extension of the scope of business. The defendant subsequently imposed a fine on the plaintiff for violation of the Trademark Law.

The plaintiff brought a lawsuit to the court, and the court of first instance found that the defendant had applied wrong section of the Trademark Law. Instead other sections of the law should be applied. However, the court of second instance held that both the defendant and the first instance court had erroneously applied the laws because the bureau in county B had already dealt with the matter and the plaintiff should not received repetitive punishments.

10.26

Application of a Wrong Piece of Legislation

Application of a wrong piece of legislation may also be caused by different factors. The first is that the administrative act undertaken is according to legislation A, while the applicable law should be legislation B. This may occur when several pieces of legislation govern the same kind of administrative activities, or one legislation granting either different authorities to more than one administrative organ or several authorities to the same administrative organ. Therefore it often happens that one kind of activity is governed by several pieces of legislation, or several administrative organs. Then it is easy for the administrative organ to make an error in the application of legislation if the quality of decision maker is not up to the standard.

10.27

GROUNDS FOR JUDICIAL REVIEW

Shanghai Huxi Liang You Transaction Department v. The Administration Bureau of Industry and Commerce in Bao Shan District in Shanghai[56]

10.28 In 1991, the Administration Bureau of Industrial and Commercial (the defendant) confiscated 150 tons of wheat from the plaintiff. The wheat was owned by a third party in another province who imported the wheat from Australia, but the third party found that the wheat did not satisfy its need. Then it entrusted the plaintiff to sell the wheat to a flour factory with the permission of the Hu Nan Provincial People's Government. The defendant carried out an investigation and found out that the plaintiff had not obtained a permit of export under the rules of the control of foods by the Shanghai Municipal People's Government. The plaintiff claimed that the business was lawful and no permit of transportation was needed according to the relevant regulations issued by the Ministries of Railway, Commerce and Transportation. The case was brought for administrative reconsideration. The reconsideration organ failed to make a decision within two months and the plaintiff brought the case to the people's court.

The court held that the wheat actually belonged to the third party in the other province. The sale of the wheat is with the permission of the people's government in that province and was not under the jurisdiction of the defendant. Therefore, the rules of the Shanghai Municipal People's Government was inapplicable. The defendant had misapplied the legislation.

This was a very influential case in Shanghai when it was adjudicated. It was highly controversial and showed the complexity of the issue of whether or not the administrative organ had applied the correct or wrongful legislation. It is also an issue of applicable legislation.

Lu Yunyang v. Administration Bureau in Lin Gui County[57]

10.29 The case was also mentioned in the discussion of the grounds of insufficiency of essential evidence. The plaintiff was a worker of the forest station, it was his duty to purchase timber for the station. The defendant fined the plaintiff for an illegal timber transaction by the plaintiff, which was in contrast to the local law in Guangxi Province. The local law stipulated that timber was a monopolized commodity and could only be bought and sold by the authorized departments. The defendant did so without following the investigation procedure and the evidence was inadequate to show the plaintiff had committed the offence. Therefore the application of the local legislation was inappropriate because the plaintiff did not actually commit the offence.

The second possibility is that the administrative organ has applied the legislation which had not come into force. The following cases are of this category.

INACCURACY IN THE APPLICATION OF LEGISLATION

Xie Junzhong v. People's Government in Tinzi Township in the Suburb of Nan Ning City[58]

The plaintiff was found to have unlawfully built houses on the collectively owned land, in contrast to section 45 of the Land Administration Law. He was ordered to demolish the houses within seven days. The plaintiff claimed that he had obtained approval from the relevant government departments. Moreover, the most crucial thing was that the plaintiff built the house prior to the implementation of the Land Administration Law of the PRC. Therefore the requirements of the law should not be applicable to the plaintiff. The court found that the plaintiff had obtained approval and the requirements at the time he built were satisfied. Moreover, the law only came into force after the building of the house. The application of section 45 of the law was inappropriate. The court of second instance was of the same opinion with the court of first instance.

10.30

This is a case where the administrative organ applied the legislation which had not come into effect when the plaintiff constructed the house.

Zheng v. Grassland Administration Bureau in Inner Mongolia[59]

The plaintiff was entrusted to buy plant medicine and he bought 1,779 kg of various kinds of medicine from the local farmers who obtained them in the protected national grassland. When the Grassland Administration Bureau found out, it imposed a fine on the plaintiff according to the Regulation on the Administration of Grassland in the Autonomous Region of Inner Mongolia, which had not come into force at the time the plaintiff bought the medicine, for damaging the national grassland by the plaintiff.

10.31

The court of first instance held that the Law of the PRC on Grassland prohibited the collection of wild plant medicine in the protected national grassland. But the plaintiff only bought from the local people. He should not be penalized under the law. Moreover, the local regulation had not come into force at that time, the defendant's application of the regulation amounted to an erroneous application of laws and regulation.

The third possibility is that the administrative organ has, in undertaking the concrete administrative act, applied the legislation which had already lost its legal effect.

The fourth possibility is that the administrative organ had applied the legislation which it does not have the authority to apply. Usually, every piece of legislation will stipulate its law enforcement organ to exercise administrative authority. That organ is empowered to apply the relevant legislation within the scope defined by the legislation to undertake concrete administrative acts. If an administrative organ has,

185

in undertaking a concrete administrative act, applied a legislation which it is not authorized to apply, then it will be deemed to commit an error in the application of legislation.

The fifth possibility is that the administrative organ intentionally avoid the application of an appropriate piece of applicable legislation. It often occurs when there exists several legislation, one is to its advantage and the others are not. Then it may choose the one to its advantage. For example, the administrator chooses to apply one legislation at a lower level of the legal hierarchy instead of another applicable legislation at a higher level; or the administrative organ is supposed to apply special legislation, but it applies the ordinary one. The following cases are in this category.

Bao Huiqing v. Labour Bureau in Yangpu District in Shanghai[60]

10.32 In May 1992, the plaintiff was dismissed by the textile factory where she worked. The factory issued the certificate on February 4, 1993 to certify that the plaintiff had left the original working position. The plaintiff, on March 25, 1993, brought the certificate to ask the defendant to provide her the job waiting insurance benefit under the local provisional regulation regarding the job waiting insurance policy, which came into force on November 1, 1992. However, the officer of the defendant refused and a certificate of job waiting was issued. The defendant contended that the provisional regulation was inapplicable because the plaintiff was fired before the implementation of the provisional regulation. It contended that the situation should be governed by the previous legislation and the plaintiff would not be entitled to the right to enjoy the benefit as stipulated in the new provisional regulation.

The court of first instance was of the opinion that section 31 of that provisional regulation stated that after its implementation, when there was any inconsistency between the old legislation and the provisional regulation, the provisional regulation should prevail. Therefore the defendant had erroneously applied the legislation because the plaintiff applied for the benefit after the implementation of the regulation. In this case, the administrative organ failed to apply a local legislation which had already come into effect.

Min v. The Hygiene and Epidemic Prevention Station in X City[61]

10.33 This case concerns inconsistency between national law and local regulation. The plaintiff was a sole proprietor who manufactures soft drinks. The Hygiene Station of the County (the defendant) found the hygiene of the plaintiff's factory was not up to standard. The defendant imposed on the plaintiff a fine of RBM1,000 and his licence was revoked by the defendant according to the Law of Food Hygiene and other local regulations.

The court held that the RMB1,000 fine was lawful. However, according to national law, only the people's government at county level or above can revoke the licence, but the local regulations changed the requirements and enabled the defendant to revoke the plaintiff's licence. The court was of the view that the national law should prevail and the defendant had erroneously applied the legislation.

Fujian Provincial Electronic Products Supervision and Testing Institute v. Fujian Provincial Bureau of Standard Measurement[62]

10.34 In 1988, the plaintiff was entrusted by the Electrical Industry Company of Fuzhou Province to carry out an authentication test of a kind of refrigerator. In 1989, the authentication test was completed and a report was presented to the Electrical Industry Company in an authentication conference.

The defendant made a decision that the plaintiff had exceeded its competency and authority of authentication to certify a refrigerator. The plaintiff was ordered to stop authentication evaluation of refrigerators and a fine of RMB1,000 was imposed on the plaintiff according to sections 36 and 55 of the Implementation Rules for the Metrology Law (Implementation Rules), section 22 of the Metrology Law and the Regulation on Metrology and Authentication of Products Quality Testing Institute. The plaintiff claimed that section 55 of the Implementation Rules only refers to those institutes that provide notarization service without proper certificate. The plaintiff, however, had been granted the certificate by the State Measurement Bureau and approved by Fujian Measurement Administration Bureau. Moreover, the test was within the plaintiff's capability and the test was done according to the Metrology Law. The facts were that the plaintiff was commissioned to test a brand refrigerator and a report was presented to the conference on the refrigerator held by the company which entrusted the plaintiff to conduct the test.

The court of first instance held that the plaintiff violated section 22 of the Metrology Law which stated that the institutes that provide notarization service to the public must be approved by measurement authorities at the provincial level or above in terms of capability and reliability. Moreover, when the plaintiff expanded its scope of business, it must follow the procedures in the Implementation Rules which had not actually been followed by the plaintiff. Therefore the defendant's decision should be sustained.

However, the court of second instance was of the opinion that the report was not a kind of notarization and the issue of a report by the plaintiff was only a usual act within its function. The plaintiff had not actually expanded its business. A retrial was ordered. In the retrial the court sustained the decision of the court of first instance because the decision of the court of second instance was lack of evidence and contradicted the facts.

This case was eventually heard by the Higher People's Court in Fujian Province according to judicial supervision procedure as stipulated in the ALL. The judgment of the court of first instance was sustained. This is a positive case under which the challenge based on application of wrongful legislation failed.

Nie v. Shang Xin Township People's Government in X County[63]

10.35 In 1982, the plaintiff's grandfather was granted a plot of land of which the area was 5 mu (1 mu equals $1/_{15}$ hectare) permitted by the Shang Xin Township People's Government (the defendant). The plaintiff built four small houses on the land. In the subsequent few years, the plaintiff had extended the area and built other premises on it without the approval of the Township People's Government. The plaintiff was found to be in unlawful occupation of collectively owned land in 1988. The defendant relied on the rule of the local people's government at county level to order the plaintiff to demolish the buildings on the land. When the time limit was due, the defendant discovered that the plaintiff had passively resisted the order. The defendant compulsorily carried out the order and the plaintiff's property was demolished. The plaintiff applied to the court for judicial review and claimed compensation.

The court held that the plaintiff had violated the legislation to build and the defendant's penalty was correct. The issue here is whether the defendant should have applied section 45 of the Land Administration Law or the rule issued by local people's government. In practice, it does not make any difference in this case because they are consistent.

Violation of Legal Procedure

10.36 There are different kinds of legal procedures and the discussion in this section is restricted to those specific methods and steps which are supposed to be followed by administrative organs in undertaking concrete administrative acts. Any administrative decisions need to be made through one or another kind of procedure. Administrative procedures may be classified in different ways. Broadly speaking, it may be classified into legal procedure, *i.e.* the procedure laid down in legislation, and non-legal procedure, *i.e.* customs or tradition formulated from time to time by the administrative organ in practice for making particular administrative decisions. According to the classification of administrative acts, as discussed above,[64] administrative procedures may also be classified into administrative legislative procedure, administrative enforcement procedure and administrative judicial procedure.[65]

China has been a country ruled by man rather than by law for over 2000 years, so people have more belief in the importance and necessity of a great leader rather than a well-established legal system. Chinese history has shown that the administration had not, in implementing legislation, paid much attention to procedural legal requirements in the past. The traditional belief was that so long as the substantive contents of any administrative decisions are correct, any defects in administrative procedures should not affect the validity of the decision.[66]

It has been suggested that the rule of law principle as stated by section 5 of the Chinese Constitution, together with some other constitutional provisions, has laid down the requirements to comply with legal procedures.[67] However, the implementation of those constitutional principles need their incorporation into more specific legislation. For many years, not enough attention has been paid to the legislation on procedural requirements for administration. It is true that most substantive administrative legislation such as those on the administration of commerce and industry, taxation, customs, public security, and so on, has incorporated certain procedural requirement on the exercise of administrative power. Those procedural legal requirements are mainly very general and lack of detail. There are often more procedural requirements on those under administration than on the administration itself. Consequently, some important administrative procedures have not been incorporated into any legislation.

The ongoing economic and legal reform has revealed the importance of compliance by the administration with proper legal procedures. Chinese scholars have realized that the rule of law principle requires administration to be conducted according to legislation, including both substantive and procedural legislation.[68] In fact, substantive and procedural rights are closely related to each other. A concrete administrative act in violation of procedural requirements cannot be guaranteed to comply with substantive legislation. In other words, failure to comply with proper legal procedures may lead to infringement of substantive legal rights. Moreover, it has gradually been realized that people are also entitled to procedural rights apart from substantive rights. The violation of procedural legal requirements is itself an infringement of the legitimate rights of those under administration.

10.37 More recently, legislatures at both national and local levels have paid more attention to the enactment of legislation incorporating more detailed legal procedures for public administration. The Regulation on Administrative Penalties for Public Securities stipulates certain procedures for the imposition of administrative penalties in public security cases. The ALL provides that the people's courts may review whether or not the administrative organs have followed the required legal procedures in undertaking concrete administrative acts. A more recent example is the enactment of Administrative Penalty Law of the People's Republic of China in 1996. That legislation has provided for more detailed procedural requirements on the establishment and imposition of administrative penalties.

Different opinions exist on the effect of concrete administrative acts in violation of legal procedures. It has been generally accepted that the long-term objective is for the people's courts to annul any concrete administrative acts which are undertaken in violation of legal procedures. Due to the existence of various practical issues,[69] however, judiciary has treated violation of procedural requirements differently according to the seriousness of violation. It may be summarized as follows.[70] Firstly, violation of customary procedures will not affect the legal effect of any concrete administrative acts concerned unless the violation amounts to abuse of power.[71] Though those customs formulated over the years in practice and are by no means arbitrary, whether or not they are followed in undertaking concrete administrative acts will not, in principle, affect the validity and effect of the decision made. Compliance with non-legal procedural requirements are purely voluntary. Secondly, minor violation of legal procedures will not be regarded as violation of legal procedure as stipulated under section 54(2)(c) and therefore will not affect the legal validity of the relevant concrete administrative acts. It has not been clarified by Chinese scholars as to what will amount to minor violation. It may refer to those concrete administrative acts which, though undertaken in violation of legal procedures, do not cause any harm to the substantive rights of those under administration or only marginally affect the substantive rights of those under administration.[72] Thirdly, there are other kinds of violation of legal procedures, including disorder in compliance of legal procedures, violation of compulsory legal procedures, and so on. Any concrete administrative acts undertaken with such violation should be annulled regardless of whether or not they have affected the substantive rights of those under administration.

The classification of violation of legal procedures can be made according to different standards. New species is bound to come up from time to time. But the following ones are generally accepted by scholars and most frequently encountered by the judiciary. They include the missing of one in a series of procedural requirements for the undertaking of a concrete administrative act,[73] *e.g.* disorder in compliance with legal procedures, lack of legal formalities, and violation of time limit requirements.[74]

If legal procedure is violated, the judiciary can repeal the original administrative act partially or completely and order the administrative organ to undertake another act.

Violation of Compulsory Legal Procedure[75]

Mao Yunbing v. Gangdong Township People's Government in Cong Ming County[76]

One of the grounds relied on by the people's court in this case is the failure of the defendant to follow the procedure as stipulated is section 13 of the Land Administration Law. It states: 10.38

> Disputes concerning ownership of land and the right to the use of land shall be solved through consultation between the parties. If no agreement can be reached through consultation, they shall be decided by the people's government.
>
> Disputes concerning ownership of land and the right to the use of land between units under ownership by the whole people, between units under collective ownership, and between units under ownership by the whole people and units under collective ownership shall be decided by people's governments at or above the county level.
>
> Disputes concerning the right to the use of land between individuals, between individuals and units under ownership by the whole people, or between individuals and units under collective ownership shall be decided by people's governments at the township or county level.
>
> If a party refuses to accept the decision of the relevant people's government, it may file a lawsuit in a people's court within 30 days from the date of receiving notification of the decision.
>
> Before a dispute concerning ownership of land or the right to the use of land is solved, no party may alter the existing condition of the disputed land or destroy anything attached to it.

When the defendant imposed administrative sanction on the plaintiff, it failed to follow the legal procedure as required by section 13 to determine the land-use right before the imposition of the sanction.

Wang Wenping v. One Branch of Zhi Cheng Municipal Public Security Bureau[77]

The plaintiff has a dispute with a third party, Zhou, over the payment for the purchase of coal. After Zhou reported to the defendant that the plaintiff had deceived him, the plaintiff was detained for deception by the Municipal Public Security Bureau (the defendant). The plaintiff's wife was required by the defendant to pay back the deceived money and the fine for the plaintiff's assault on other persons, which proved to be untrue. The defendant also withdrew an amount of money from 10.39

the plaintiff's account. The plaintiff claimed that it was a pure economic dispute between Zhou and him and not the alleged deception, and brought a case to the people's court for unlawful infringement of his personal freedom and proprietary rights. The court found out that the evidence was clear that it was a purely economic dispute in nature. The main point here is that the defendant withdrew an amount of money which was said to be the amount the plaintiff deceived Zhou and gave it to Zhou before the issue was clarified. The defendant did it in an arbitrary manner, the court held that it was a violation of legal procedure. Moreover, it has also exceeded the authority of the defendant and amounted to abuse of power.

This is a case related to both the missing of legal procedure and disorder in compliance with legal procedure. In this case, the defendant did not follow either the procedure in the Regulation on Administrative Penalty nor Procedural Regulations on the Handling of Criminal Cases by the Public Security Bureau. Moreover, it is a civil dispute in which the public security bureau is not supposed to interfere.

Failure to Act Within Time Limit

Zhang Peirong v. Public Security Bureau in Akesu District[78]

10.40 On July 25, 1992, the plaintiff disputed with the officers of the Municipal Tax Bureau when the plaintiff was selling watermelon in the market. Then the plaintiff was detained by the Public Security Bureau under the defendant. On July 29, Liu, the officer of the bureau, delivered to the plaintiff the verdict to detain the plaintiff for 10 days. The plaintiff refused to sign the receipt of the verdict, but the officer said that the plaintiff must sign it and the plaintiff was entitled to made an "application" for administrative reconsideration within five days if he was not satisfied with the verdict. On the same day, the plaintiff wrote a document without stating that it was an "application" for administrative reconsideration and submitted it to Liu, but Liu did not transfer it to the bureau. On August 9, when he was released, the plaintiff made the second application to the defendant for administrative reconsideration. The defendant rejected the application on the grounds that the time limit had passed.

The defendant claimed that the first application was rejected because of the lack of words expressing the intention of application for administrative reconsideration. When the second application is filed, the time limited had expired.

The court of first instance found that the plaintiff had actually made the first application when he was in custody. It was the fault of the officers in the detention centre not to pass the application to the

VIOLATION OF LEGAL PROCEDURE

defendant. And the error of the first application was caused by the plaintiff's ignorance of the procedure. The defendant should have dealt with the application but failed. The failure to undertake administrative reconsideration amounted to a violation of legal procedure. It may also be argued to be the failure to perform statutory duty of administrative reconsideration. The court of second instance was of the same opinion.

Liu Chen Lian Hua Electronic Company in Ping Nan County v. Fishery Administration Station in Ping Nan County[79]

This case has already been discussed on the grounds of insufficiency of essential evidence. The plaintiff's machines were detained by the defendant for manufacturing the prohibited fishing instrument. This is a case where the plaintiff won the case purely on procedure. The main issue here is that the plaintiff had first of all applied for administrative reconsideration. The defendant rejected the application for the reason that the time limit expired. However, the plaintiff did apply for reconsideration within the time limit. But the defendant, without proper investigation, took compulsory measures and imposed penalties on the plaintiff, which was in violation of legal procedure because the defendant denied the plaintiff's right to resort to administrative reconsideration. The second violation of legal procedure is the defendant's collection of evidence in the process of litigation which is prohibited by relevant legislation. 10.41

Supply and Sales Department in X City v. Price Inspection Bureau in X City[80]

The plaintiff was penalized by the defendant for its violation of the price control. The plaintiff applied for administrative reconsideration to the administrative organ at higher level. However, no decision was made within the time limit. The plaintiff brought a lawsuit to court. The court held that the plaintiff had actually violated the law. But, the defendant had also violated some legal procedure. 10.42

First of all, the defendant seized material for evidence without producing warrant which violated the regulation regarding the investigation of the offence against price control. Moreover, when the defendant imposed a fine on the plaintiff, it had erroneously calculated the account.

Inaction

Failure to handle a case has been held to amount to violation of legal procedure. Failure to investigate has also been held to be a kind of violation of procedural requirement. The next two cases are similar and are both related to the failure by the defendant to conduct required investigation.

The case of *Zhu Jinru v. State Land Administration Bureau in Huizhou City*[81] has been discussed above. It is also relevant here. The main relevant point here is that the defendant had not carried out any investigation and made the decision against the plaintiff arbitrarily. The court held that the lack of investigation was a violation of legal procedure.

In the case of *Lu Yunyang v. Administration Bureau in Lin Gui County*,[82] the plaintiff and two other people were found to have carried out an unlawful timber transaction which was a monopolized commodity and the sale of it was restricted. The defendant penalized the plaintiff under the local regulation without any investigation. The court of first instance held that it amounted to a violation of legal procedure as well as lack of essential evidence. But in the retrial, the court held against the defendant based only on lack of essential evidence.

Excess of Legal Authority (Ultra Vires)

10.43 Various attempts have been made by Chinese scholars to define the concept of *ultra vires* in China. Some define the concept according to the contents of *ultra vires*, while others define it according to the categories of different kinds of *ultra vires* activities.[83] There are mainly two different views. One approach holds that the concept of *ultra vires* refers to the concrete administrative acts undertaken by the administrative organs, or its personnel, or other organizations either legally authorized or entrusted by those administrative organs which exceed the scope of authority either legally prescribed or authorized or entrusted.[84] The other approach maintains that *ultra vires* refers to the circumstances under which the administrative organs either exercise administrative power, which is not legally granted to them, or exceed the scope of legally authorized administrative power.[85]

The main difference between the two approaches is whether or not the concept of *ultra vires* should include "no authority", which refers to the situation that the administrative organs have exercised administrative authority that is neither within their jurisdiction nor entrusted to them by other administrative organs.[86] But both approaches agree that *ultra vires* is only about substantive *ultra vires*, which means that the administrative organs have actually undertaken activities which are in excess of their legal authority.[87]

Most Chinese scholars have not referred to the concept of procedural *ultra vires*. Professor Luo Haocai has mentioned the concept of procedural *ultra vires* and discussed the concept briefly.[88] However, it seems more logical to restrict the concept of *ultra vires* under section 54(2)(d) to substantive *ultra vires*, based on the argument raised previously, *i.e.* a statutory provision has to be interpreted in its context. Section 54(2)(c) actually equals to the concept of procedural *ultra vires*, though the ALL uses a different expression. If section 54(2)(d) is interpreted broadly to cover both substantive and procedural *ultra vires*, then section 54(2)(c) would become redundant and no longer necessary.

Therefore, the concept of *ultra vires* under judicial review in China is much narrower than its counterpart under judicial review, as practised in the United Kingdom and Hong Kong where the concept of *ultra vires* is the general principle. It covers both substantive and procedural *ultra vires*, which can be further divided into subcategories. All the grounds for judicial review in the United Kingdom and Hong Kong derive from the doctrine of *ultra vires*.[89]

According to the above discussion on the concept of *ultra vires*, *ultra vires* administrative activities may be classified firstly into two categories. One is the exercise of authority which is not related to the functions of the administrative organs concerned (no authority). The other is the exercise of authority which is within the types of authority the administrative organs may exercise, but exceeds the scope of the jurisdiction of the specific administrative organ. The second may be further divided into vertical *ultra vires*, *i.e.* lower administrative organ usurps the authority of the higher administrative organ, or vice versa; horizontal *ultra vires*, *i.e.* one administrative organ usurps the authority of another administrative organ at the same level, either because they are at different geographical locations or they are in charge of different administrative functions; and *ultra vires* in content, *i.e.* the exercise of administrative power exceeds the legal scope.[90]

The remedy available for *ultra vires* is the same as that under the three grounds discussed previously.

No Authority

The following two cases are about no authority. Here the relevant administrative organ exercised the authority of judiciary which were clearly in excess of administrative power.

10.44

Jinghua Research Institute of Machinery and Technology in Shanghai v. The Administration Bureau of Industry and Commerce in Chang Ning District in Shanghai[91]

The plaintiff had a dispute with a third party company about a joint-venture contract. In April 1990, they applied to the economic contract arbitration committee in Chang Ning District for an arbitration, in accordance with the Regulation on Arbitration of Economic Contract of the PRC. The committee was required by the third party company to freeze the plaintiff's account. Then the Administration Bureau of Industry and Commerce in Chang Ning District in Shanghai (the defendant) delivered a notice to the Bank of Industry and Commerce of China to freeze the plaintiff's account for three months. However, no notice of the defendant's act was delivered to the plaintiff. The plaintiff did not realize that its account was frozen until May 3, 1991.

The plaintiff claimed that the defendant did not have the qualification to do this because the parties only required the arbitration committee to conduct the arbitration. Moreover, the defendant did not have the authority, in the capacity as an administrative organ, to freeze the plaintiff account according to the regulation. Therefore, the defendant had infringed the plaintiff's legitimate right.

The court of first instance held that the defendant was not qualified to freeze the plaintiff's account because it was not the defendant, as an administrative organ, who should deal with the dispute and the matter of freezing the bank account. The relevant legislation provides that the arbitration committee set up under the defendant has the authority to handle the case. However, the Joint Notice by the Supreme People's Court and the People's Bank of China only states that only the people's court has the authority to freeze bank account and provides for the procedure. But it does not stipulate that any administrative organs have the power to do it when they deal with disputes over economic contract. The defendant had done it without any legal basis and it was an act which exceeded its authority.

The defendant appealed and the court of second instance dismissed the appeal and upheld the judgment of the court of first instance.

This is a case of no authority. The defendant had exceeded its authority in two aspects: one is that it handled the case by usurping the power of the arbitration committee; and the other is that it exercised the power to freeze a bank account, which is an authority only granted to the judiciary.

Zhang Sheyou v. Wangzai Township People's Government[92]

10.45 The plaintiff was a sole proprietor who ran the business of selling food in Wangzai Township. On May 26, 1993, the security team under the People's Government of Wangzai Township (the defendant) held that the plaintiff engaged in criminal enterprise for burglary, and provided information to the criminals. The security team brought the plaintiff's wife and son to the team's station and detained the cigarettes in the plaintiff's shop. On May 27, the plaintiff was asked to pay the team RMB6,000 as fine and security, and the team released the cigarettes and a receipt was issued. On May 28, the defendant imposed on the plaintiff an extra fine of RMB2,000.

The plaintiff claimed that the security team under the defendant had made its decision without evidence and the imposition of the fine and the deposit was lack of legal basis. The defendant had exceeded its authority. As a result, the plaintiff suffered economic loss from the defendant's act.

The court held that only the public security bureau had the authority to impose a fine on anyone who violated the Regulation on Administrative Penalties for Public Security. The defendant was only an administrative organ and had no authority either to fine the people who violated the regulation or to detain the goods. The defendant had acted in excess of its authority. Moreover, the court held that the defendant's decision was lack of essential evidence.

Horizontal Ultra Vires

10.46 This category of cases is concerned with the exercise of administrative power which is within the geographical jurisdiction of either the same or a different kind of administrative organ in another region. Some scholars have classified this category of cases as *ultra vires* in content.

Dong Tai Sea Product Rearing Company v. Public Security Bureau in Xieyang[93]

On February 17, 1991, the plaintiff entered into an agreement with a third party for a transaction of five tons of baby fish for the plaintiff's fishery. However, when the plaintiff took the baby fish, the third party had provided 9.79 tons. But the plaintiff only had a permit for five tons. When the Public Security Bureau in Xieyang County (the defendant) discovered this, it held that the plaintiff's transportation of baby fish amounted to smuggling and its public security officers detained all the fish and the RMB11,200 which was also with the staff on the vehicle. On March 23, the defendant made a decision to release the 4.79 tons of extra fish, but the plaintiff was fined RMB11,200 and the third party for RMB10,000 for smuggling baby fish. On May 9, the defendant issued a receipt of confiscation of 6.424 tons of baby fish instead of a fine of RMB11,200. The plaintiff then applied to the people's court for judicial review.

The plaintiff claimed that the responsibility for the extra amount of fish was on the third party and the plaintiff had not been smuggling the baby fish. The defendant did not have the authority to impose a fine either. Moreover, it was inappropriate for the defendant to issue a receipt for the confiscation of baby fish (which it did not do) instead of a receipt for a fine of RMB11,200.

The court of first instance held that the defendant did not have the power to impose a fine on the plaintiff, because the authority to impose a fine is with the Fishery Bureau under the Fishery Law of the PRC. Moreover, the act of the plaintiff did not amount to smuggling, although it had violated the relevant laws and regulations. During the trial, the plaintiff was persuaded to withdraw the case from the people's court.

The Public Procuratorate applied for a retrial on the grounds that the plaintiff did not withdraw the case voluntarily and the concrete administrative act of the defendant was unlawful. The Intermediate People's Court accepted the argument of the Public Procuratorate and revoked the permission for the plaintiff to withdraw the case, and designate another county people's court to hear the case. The court held, among other issues, that the imposition of a fine was *ultra vires*, for which the defendant should be liable.

Yang Xinlan v. Urban Branch of Yingchuan Municipal Administration Bureau of Industry and Commerce[94]

The main issue here is that in the retrial. The court held that the plaintiff's son had insulted the officers of the Administration Bureau of Industry and Commerce which was an act that interfered with the peace and order of the bureau, but it should be dealt with by the Public Security Bureau because the plaintiff's son had actually violated the Regulation on Administrative Penalty for Public Security. The defendant's punishment of the plaintiff was an act in excess of its own authority.

Zheng v. X Forest Public Security Bureau[95]

10.47 The plaintiff was a retired worker. With the approval of the Administration Bureau of Industry and Commerce, the plaintiff set up the "Iron and Wood Processing Factory". The licence stated that the scope of business of the factory was the sale of small tools as its major business, and transportation as auxiliary business. Since the factory site had not been completed, the plaintiff removed 170 cubic metres out of 370 cubic metres of wood rolls he bought earlier to another place. It was discovered by Chi, a police officer, and had quarrelled with the plaintiff.

The remaining 200 cubic metres of wood rolls were detained by the Public Security Bureau (the defendant) and a fine of RMB2,000 was imposed on the plaintiff. Moreover, the plaintiff was detained for investigation for 40 days. The business licence of the plaintiff was also revoked by the defendant.

The court held that the defendant had exercised the power of the Administration Bureau of Industry and Commerce by revoking the plaintiff's licence. In doing so, the defendant had acted in excess of its authority. Moreover, even the defendant had the authority to detain the plaintiff for investigation, this administrative penalty was inapplicable under this situation. It was held that the defendant had also abused its power.

One Branch of the Construction Company in Po On County v. Guangming Branch of Shenzhen Municipal Public Security Bureau[96]

10.48 On March 20, 1990, the plaintiff purchased some timber in Donggaun Town for the construction project it had undertaken in another town. When the plaintiff transported the timber to the destination, it had only the receipt of payment, but not the invoice for the timber. The Public Security Bureau of Guangmin Town (the defendant) discovered this and seized the plaintiff's timber and a fine of RMB1,350 was imposed on the plaintiff because the plaintiff did not have either the invoice for the timber or the permit of transportation of the timber. Afterwards, the plaintiff produced the invoice and the permit to prove the timber was obtained legally. However, the defendant still insisted on the penalty.

The plaintiff then brought a lawsuit to the court. The plaintiff claimed that it had only had a receipt of payment when transporting the timber. The timber was lawfully obtained and should not be seized.

The court held that the defendant did not have the authority to investigate the transportation of timber and the defendant was not conferred the power to impose fine on such an offence. It was the authority of the Forest Affairs Bureau under section 33 of the Forest Law of the PRC to impose a fine. Therefore it was an act in excess of the authority of the defendant.

Chen Cunmei v. Tobacco Bureau in Zhen Yang County[97]

10.49 The facts have been stated in another section of this chapter. It is a case concerning the transportation and sale of cigarettes which need special permit. But the plaintiff did not have this permit. The Implementation Rules for the Regulation on the Exclusive Sale of Tobacco stated that if the offence committed was not serious, then only 10 per cent of the total value of the cigarettes should be fined. In this case, the court found that the plaintiff had transported the cigarettes without any permit, but her act did not amount to the transportation of cigarettes to another "region", therefore only a fine of 10 per cent of the total value should be imposed. It amounted to an excess of power to impose a fine on the plaintiff, which was heavier than the stipulations in the legislation.

Li and others v. Phoenix Township People's Government[98]

10.50 The facts were stated in the next chapter. In this case, one kind of the payment imposed on the plaintiffs was premiums for an insurance policy. According to the Regulation on Property Insurance, the parties must make the agreement voluntarily. The defendant, by compulsorily requesting the plaintiffs to buy an insurance policy had therefore acted in excess of its authority.

Li v. Nan Ming Branch of Public Security Bureau in X City[99]

10.51 The plaintiff, because of illness, entrusted Xiu to operate his marketing station of which the business was to purchase abandoned metal. The Public Security Bureau of X County (the defendant) found that Xiu's licence belonged to Li when the defendant carried out an investigation of theft nearby. Then the defendant seized the licence and 60 tons of metal because Xiu operated the business without a licence. Subsequently, the metal was sold to another marketing station at a discount and the licence was returned to Li after two months.

The court held that the defendant had violated sections 5, 6, 17 and 22 of the Interim Regulations on the Administration of All Urban and Rural Industrial and Commercial Entities, and the defendant had exceeded its authority by seizing the licence and confiscating the metal.

The defendant appealed and contended that the metal repurchase was a special business and the public security had the authority the administer it and the penalty was not imposed in excess of its power. Moreover, the plaintiff should not be qualified to sue because it was Xiu, not Li, on whom the penalty was imposed. The decision of the court of second instance was not known yet.

Vertical Ultra Vires

Che Fengying v. Rural Planning Administration Bureau in Xuzhou City[100]

10.52 On December 28, 1992, the Countryside Planning Bureau of Xuzhou City (the defendant) issued a permit of construction to a third party, Chen, to demolish his original three-bedroom house and build a new two-storey house on the same plot of land; the area of the house was 197 square metres. However, the distance stated in the building plan between the planned house and the plaintiff's house was only one metre. The defendant also issued the construction licence to the third party without the consent of the City Planning Bureau of Xuzhou City.

The plaintiff claimed that the defendant had infringed his legitimate right. His right to light and passage will be affected. Furthermore, the defendant was only authorized by the City Planning Bureau to approve the application, but was not authorized to issue a construction licence. Therefore the defendant had exceeded its authority and the decision should be annulled.

The court of first instance held that the distance between the plaintiff's house and Chen's house did not satisfy the requirements stipulated in section 66 of the No.6 Document (1992) issued by the City

Planning Bureau. Moreover, the defendant had not reported to the City Planning Bureau for their consent and the defendant issued the construction licence without the bureau's consent. The defendant had therefore exceeded its power to grant approval. The court held that the licence in question should be revoked. The defendant appealed, but the court of second instance dismissed his appeal and upheld the original decision according to section 61(1) of the ALL.

In this case, the administrative organ at the lower level exercised the power of the administrative organ at the next higher level.

Sun v. Wu Xin Township People's Government in the Suburb of Beijing[101]

The plaintiff's father was approved by the committee of the village he lived in, to build a house. Thirteen years later, the plaintiff applied to use the land nearby to extend his house due to the housing shortage. The committee of the village agreed and reported to the Wu Xin Township People's Government in the suburb of Beijing (the defendant) for approval. Without an accurate investigation, the defendant's approval and permit was issued.

10.53

Subsequently, the defendant found out that approval was inappropriate. It then entrusted the committee to retract the permit and inform the plaintiff not to build. The committee did not do so. Although the defendant had notified the plaintiff several times, the plaintiff still built on the land. In the following year, the defendant issued a written decision against the plaintiff and resumed the land which the plaintiff occupied under sections 45 and 48 of the Land Administration Law.

The court of first instance delivered its judgment against the plaintiff on the grounds that it was correct for the defendant to make such a decision and the plaintiff appealed. The court of second instance held that the defendant had violated sections 41 and 48 of the Land Administration Law because section 41 stipulated that only the people's government at county level or above had the authority to approve the use of collectively owned land. Therefore the defendant had acted in excess of its authority. Section 48 stated that all permits issued by the administrative organ in excess of its authority was null and void. Therefore the approval by the defendant was void.

Notes

[1] Professor Luo Haocai has spent six chapters in his book to discuss the six grounds for judicial review in China. Up to now his book is the most comprehensive and detailed

GROUNDS FOR JUDICIAL REVIEW

publication to discuss the grounds with the approach similar to that adopted in common law jurisdiction.
2 The principle of legality as one of the two fundamental principles of administrative law has been discussed in the second part of this book on the theory of administrative law in China. Here the principle of legality will be discussed in the context of judicial review, which is really a discussion of the same principle from a different angle.
3 Judicial review of the reasonableness of concrete administrative acts is stated to be an exception to the principle of legality. However, judicial practice reveals that many cases brought to the people's courts under the ALL are concerned with the reasonableness of the exercise of discretionary power by administrative organs. For detailed discussion, refer to the chapter on judicial control of discretionary power. This point is also mentioned by Wang Hanbing in his explanation on the draft of the ALL.
4 See Quan She, p. 18.
5 See Jiang Mingan, pp. 70–72.
6 Refer to s. 2, Cap. 1 of this part on the objectives of the ALL.
7 See Zhou Hanhua, *Lun Xing Zhen Su Song Zhong De SiFa Nen Dong Xing* ("Evaluation of Judicial Initiative in Administrative Litigation") in *Collection of Legal Essays on Administrative Litigation Law 1993*, at pp. 1–8.
8 Refer to the chapter on judicial control of discretionary power.
9 See Luo Haocai 1993, pp. 38–42.
10 Detailed discussion of what constitutes abuse of power will be discussed in the chapter on judicial control of the exercise of discretionary power.
11 S. 54 provides that:

> After hearing a case, a people's court shall make the following judgments according to the varying conditions:.
>
> (1) If the evidence for undertaking a specific administrative act is conclusive, the application of the law and regulations to the act is correct, and the legal procedure is complied with, the specific administrative act shall be sustained by judgment.
>
> (2) If a specific administrative act has been undertaken in one of the following circumstances, the act shall be annulled or partially annulled by judgment, or the defendant may be required by judgment to undertake a specific administrative act anew:
>
> a. inadequacy of essential evidence;
>
> b. erroneous application of the law or regulations;
>
> c. violation of legal procedure;
>
> d. exceeding authority; or.
>
> e. abuse of powers.
>
> (3) If a defendant fails to perform or delays the performance of his statutory duty, a fixed time shall be set by judgment for his performance of the duty.
>
> (4) If an administrative sanction is obviously unfair, it may be amended by judgment.

12 See Luo Haocai 1993, p. 4.
13 Some scholars maintain that illegality also includes abuse of power, and failure or delay in the performance of statutory duty.
14 Lord Diplock classified the grounds for judicial review in the GCHQ case into three categories, *i.e.* illegality, irrationality and procedural impropriety. He stated the ground of illegality in this way:

> By "illegality" as a ground for judicial review I mean that the decision-maker must understand correctly the law that regulates his decision-making power and must give effect to it. Whether he has or not is par excellence a justiciable question to be decided, in the event of dispute, by those persons, the judges, by whom the judicial power of the state is exercisable.

See *Council of Civil Service Unions v. Minister for the Civil Service* [1985] AC 374 at 410.
[15] The ground of obvious unfairness seems to be based on the principle of reasonableness. For detailed discussion, refer to the chapter on judicial control of discretionary power.
[16] This classification is purely the author's innovation and is up to discussion.
[17] See Luo Haocai 1993, p. 324.
[18] S. 31 of the ALL classifies evidence into seven categories, including documentary evidence, material evidence, audio-visual material, testimony of witnesses, statements of the parties, expert conclusions, and records of inquests and records made on the scene. This classification is made according to the external characteristics of evidences.
[19] With regard to this point, scholars and judicial practice hold different views.
[20] It seems that Chinese scholars have combined ss. 54(1) and 54(2)(a) to explain the meaning of s. 54(2)(a) of the ALL. See Luo Haocai 1993, pp. 331–32.
[21] Though the answer to this question in legal theory is quite clear-cut, the judicial practice seems to suggest a different answer. Courts are more willing to follow the Opinions on the ALL.
[22] The author is told of this case shortly before the completion of this book by an official from the State Council who conducted investigation in Shangdong recently.
[23] See Jiang Mingan, p. 150.
[24] See Luo Haocai 1993, p. 349.
[25] See *1992 China Law Report* (in Chinese, published by the China People's Security University Press), pp. 1248–51.
[26] See *1992 China Law Report*, pp. 1292–97.
[27] See *1992 China Law Report*, pp. 1208–13.
[28] See *1992 China Law Report*, pp. 1237–43.
[29] See *1994 China Law Report*, pp. 1599–602.
[30] See *1993 China Law Report*, pp. 1158–63.
[31] See *1993 China Law Report*, pp. 1199–203.
[32] The court of first instance also relied on violation of legal procedure, a point on which the author does not agree.
[33] See *1994 China Law Report*, pp. 1505–08.
[34] See *1994 China Law Report*, pp. 1562–65.
[35] See *1994 China Law Report*, pp. 1576–79.
[36] See *1994 China Law Report*, pp. 1464–68.
[37] See *1994 China Law Report*, pp. 1475–78.
[38] See Jiang Mingan et al., *Analysis of Administrative Cases*, China People's Public Security University Press, 1991 p. 125–27.
[39] For facts and detailed discussion, refer to the next section on in the application of legislation.
[40] Many Chinese scholars have discussed this for judicial review in their books. Refer to Luo Haocai 1993, Chapter 16 of Judicial Review in China; Ma Yuan (ed) *Encyclopaedia of Judicial Review*, Beijing Teacher's College Press, 1990, pp. 187–89; Jiang Mingan, *Administrative Litigation Law*, pp. 199–201.
[41] Some scholars start the definition from the meaning of accurate application of legislation, *i.e.* positive approach (see Ma Yuan, p. 182); others define the grounds directly; see Luo and Ying 1990, and Jiang Mingan, pp. 194–224.
[42] See Luo Haocai 1993, p. 351.
[43] See Luo Haocai 1993, p. 352.
[44] See Luo Haocai 1993, pp. 352–54.
[45] For the discussion of the variety of legislation in China, refer to the chapter on applicable legislation in judicial review.
[46] For detailed discussion as to the hierarchy of various legislation in China, refer to the chapter on applicable legislation.
[47] See Luo Haocai 1993, pp. 352–54; Jiang Mingan, pp. 200–01.
[48] Ma Yuan suggests five (see p. 187), which is supported by Sheyi (see p. 181); Jiang Mingan suggests six by adding the sixth, p. 200; Luo Haocai suggests three, pp. 354–63. There does not seem to be much difference between different classification because what has been covered by the three different classification are almost the

same. The only difference is that Professor Luo will further divide the three categories.
49 See Luo Haocai 1993, pp. 360–64.
50 See *1994 China Law Report*, pp. 1461–64.
51 See *1992 China Law Report*, pp. 1237–43.
52 See *1992 China Law Report*, pp. 1292–97.
53 See *1992 China Law Report*, pp. 1214–16.
54 See *1992 China Law Report*, pp. 1288–92.
55 See Jiang Mingan et al., *Analysis of Administrative Cases*, pp. 215–18.
56 See *1993 China Law Report*, pp. 1248–53.
57 See *1994 China Law Report*, pp. 1516–20.
58 See *1994 China Law Report*, pp. 1464–68. Refer to the same case under . . .
59 See Jiang Mingan et al., *Analysis of Administrative Cases*, pp. 201–03.
60 See *1994 China Law Report*, pp. 1592–95.
61 See Jiang Mingan et al., *Analysis of Administrative Cases*, pp. 128–30.
62 See *1992 China Law Report*, pp. 1269–74.
63 See Jiang Mingan et al., *Analysis of Administrative Cases*, pp. 279–82.
64 Refer to the section on administrative acts in the chapter on theory of administrative law in China.
65 All three classifications include both legal and non-legal procedures. The legal effect of non-legal procedures shall be discussed in later sections.
66 See Luo Haocai 1993, p. 373.
67 It has been argued that the requirement of simplicity and efficiency for administration under s. 27 of the Constitution may be contradictory to the requirement under s. 5 of the Constitution and therefore the requirements under the two sections need to be balanced. But the ALL does not mention the requirement of simplicity and efficiency. It may therefore be argued that the requirement of legality prevails if the two conflict. It has been suggested that the principle of democracy, *i.e.* making a decision through a democratic method (the implementation of this principle in practice may still take quite a long time), the principle of administration according to legislation and the principle of respecting the basic rights of citizens all imply procedural legal requirements. For details, please see Luo Haocai 1993, pp. 370–372.
68 See Luo Haocai 1993, pp. 33–35.
69 Those issues include no uniform administrative procedural legislation, lack of procedural provisions in many legislation, existence of large amount of traditional procedural requirements, lack of a comprehensive system on time limit, and lack of provisions on liabilities for violation of legal procedures. For detailed discussion of those issues, see Luo Haocai 1993, pp. 384–86.
70 This categorization has been suggested by Professor Luo. See Luo Haocai 1993, p. 383.
71 See Luo Haocai 1993, p. 383; Jiang Mingan, p. 203; for more detailed discussion of abuse of power, refer to the chapter on judicial control of discretionary in this book.
72 See Jiang Mingan, p. 202.
73 For example, the Regulation on Administrative Penalty for Public Security prescribes the following legal procedures: summon, hearing, investigation, verdict, service, appeal, and enforcement.
74 See Luo Haocai 1993, pp. 379–381.
75 Disorder is the compliance with legal procedure falls within violation of compulsory legal procedures.
76 See *1992 China Law Report*, pp. 1214–16.
77 See *1994 China Law Report*, pp. 1430–37.
78 See *1994 China Law Report*, pp. 1440–43.
79 See *1994 China Law Report*, pp. 1576–79.
80 See Jiang Mingan et al., *Analysis of Administrative Cases*, pp. 39–42.
81 See *1994 China Law Report*, pp. 1505–08.
82 See *1994 China Law Report*, pp. 1516–20.
83 See Luo Haocai 1993, pp. 387–88.
84 This definition is provided by Professor Luo Haocai in his book. It represents the narrow approach towards the concept of *ultra vires*. See Luo Haocai 1993, p. 388.
85 This is the broad approach and is supported by Quan She at pp. 181–82, and Ma Yuan at p. 190. Because Ma Yuan is the deputy chief justice in the Supreme People's Court

and both books are actually written by the judges, it is fair to say that this approach represents the approach adopted by senior judges in China and therefore the view of Chinese judiciary.

86 See Luo Haocai 1993, p. 389.
87 See Sheyi, p. 182.
88 Professor Luo Haocai raises the concept in his book on *Judicial Review in China* and points out two possibilities, *i.e.* exceeding the time limit for the exercise of administrative power and failure to follow compulsory legal procedures as provided by legislation. For details, see Luo Haocai 1993, p. 392.
89 See Wade and Forsyth, *Administrative Law*, Oxford University Press, 7th ed. 1994, pp. 41–49.
90 Different classifications have been suggested by Chinese scholars. For example Professor Luo provides one classification (see pp. 389–94). Ma Yuan and Lin Zhun (Sheyi) provide another (see Ma Yuan, pp. 190–93; Quan She, p. 182). It seems more appropriate to combine the two to form a third one, which is what this book adopts.
91 See *1993 China Law Report*, pp. 1243–48.
92 See *1994 China Law Report*, pp. 1428–30.
93 See *1993 China Law Report*, pp. 1154–58.
94 For detailed description of the facts, refer to the next chapter on judicial control of discresionary power. See *1994 China Law Report*, pp. 1523–29.
95 See Jiang Mingan et al., *Analysis of Administrative Cases*, pp. 276–78.
96 See *1992 China Law Report*, pp. 1154–56.
97 See *1992 China Law Report*, pp. 1288–92.
98 See *1993 China Law Report*, pp. 1206–11.
99 See Jiang Mingan et al., *Analysis of Administrative Cases*, p. 3.
100 See *1994 China Law Report*, pp. 1482–86.
101 See Jiang Mingan et al., *Analysis of Administrative Cases*, pp. 272–75.

CHAPTER ELEVEN
JUDICIAL CONTROL OF DISCRETIONARY POWER

Background

11.01 The practice of feudal autocracy for thousands of years has put administrative organs in a superior position in China. The administrative organs enjoyed both executive and judicial powers, and possessed enormous discretionary power.[1] The traditional concept that officials may rule people and people are supposed to be obedient to officials instead of suing them still has wide influence over the people in modern China.[2] People would usually pray for wise, smart and caring leaders (or rulers) at both national and local levels instead of trying to establish any legal measures in order to restrict the powers enjoyed by the rulers because democracy is not part of Chinese culture.

After the Communist Party took over power in 1949, it enacted some legislation, such as the Constitution and some others, though not in great numbers. Apart from this limited number of legislation, the administration heavily relied on policies issued from time to time by various administrative organs, which were usually under the leadership of the Communist Party as provided in the Constitution.[3] In making policies, those administrative organs enjoyed wide discretionary powers which were hardly subject to any sort of legal control. Both policies and legislation usually only laid down the general principles and guidelines and lacked detailed provisions. Administrative organs were responsible for the implementation of policies and legislation. They enjoyed enormous discretionary power in undertaking any concrete administrative acts according to those policies and legislation. Such discretion was again subject to little control. That was why stories of misuse or abuse of discretionary power were often heard though hardly litigated in China's history.[4]

China used to be a planned economy under which everything was planned and decided by the state, *i.e.* various administrative organs.

206

The administrative organs enjoyed enormous power and discretion in making decisions, while those under administration had little choice except to obey orders. China has undertaken economic reform and legal reform for more than a decade and half since 1978. It has now formally adopted the policy of a socialist market economy under which principles for the proper operation of a free market is given due weight. In other words, it is pledged that unnecessary and unhealthy governmental interference with the operation of a market economy will be reduced as much as possible. It does not mean that the government will not regulate the development of the economy at all. Even in those well-recognized market economies, administrative regulation of the market is unavoidable to a certain extent.

As for China, it is still in the transitional period from a planned economy to a market economy, and the regulating power enjoyed by the administrative organs is still quite strong due to several reasons.[5] Firstly, a historically unnecessary regulating authority has not been completely abolished yet. Secondly, state-owned enterprises still constitute more than 50 per cent of the enterprises which need state regulation. Thirdly, state regulation or interference with the economy is required in modern society. The exercise of these regulating powers is very much discretionary. For the development of a healthy market economy, it is necessary to restrain over-control of the market through administration. It is by no means trying to deny the role of administration in regulating the economy. In order to achieve a balance between over-control and insufficient regulation, it is suggested that a legal framework should be established for the operation and regulation of economy. In so doing, both the market and the regulators will have rules to comply with. The administration can use legal methods to regulate the market.

Discretionary Power and its Development

Administrative discretionary power refers to the power of administrative organs to selectively undertake concrete administrative acts which they believe to be accurate based on the purpose and fundamental aims prescribed by the law in undertaking the concrete administrative acts within the scope prescribed by law.[6] Chinese scholars generally hold the position that discretionary power and its judicial control is a phenomenon of modern Western society and the product of constitutional doctrine of separation of powers. In history, sovereigns in Western countries were the same as those in Eastern countries like China. They were supreme and enjoyed absolute powers in legislation, administration and adjudication. With the development of capitalism,

11.02

a *laissez faire* economy and the modern industrial revolution, the separation of powers took root and the state government was requested not to interfere, or to interfere as little as possible, with the economy. As a result, the administration did not enjoy much discretion. However, the development of modern society in the twentieth century has made social life more complicated and there is a great demand for the government to take positive action in many areas such as social production, development, safety, welfare, culture and many other aspects. In response to this request, the scope of administration of the government has been broadened and their functions have been strengthened. Much administrative work has become highly technical and requires expertise. Therefore the legislature no longer has enough time and sufficient expertise to enact feasible, detailed and well-thought-about legislation to meet the requirements in every aspect of administration. Furthermore, more and more new activities are undertaken by the state from time to time. If the legislature cannot provide detailed legislation governing those aspects, their regulation will be left to the administration to handle discretionally. That is to say, both by law and in reality, the discretionary power enjoyed by the administration is necessary.

11.03 In China, various political movements after 1949 had made the state and people realize the importance of the rule of law principle. Many legislation has been enacted since 1978. Due to lack of experience, however, much legislation lays down only the framework and general principles. The administrative organs enjoy wide discretionary powers, not only in undertaking concrete administrative acts, but also in undertaking abstract administrative acts. The exercise of discretionary power in undertaking abstract administrative acts is not subject to judicial control in at the moment.[7] Instead, it is subject to legislative and administrative controls. We will only discuss legal control of the exercise of discretionary power by the administrative organs in undertaking concrete administrative acts.

An overview of Chinese legislation will reveal that many administrative organs enjoy wide discretionary powers. For example, the administration bureau of industry and commerce at various levels, enjoy discretion in making decisions on whether or not to issue or revoke a business licence of an enterprise, and the amount of fine to be imposed for failing to comply with relevant enterprise registration regulations.[8] Taxation bureaus at various levels enjoy discretion in the imposition of fines on persons for illegal evasion of tax liabilities. The land administration bureaus enjoy discretionary power in deciding whether or not to grant a land-use right certificate and building certificate and the imposition of a penalty for illegal construction and occupation of land. The public security bureaus enjoy discretionary power in enforcing compulsory measures against citizens, especially those restricting the liberty of people, *e.g.* detention. Environmental agencies enjoy the discretion in determining the amount of a fine imposed on those in violation of environmental legislation and cause environmental pollution or destruction of natural resources. The food and hygiene authority enjoy discretion in determining the amount of a fine imposed on those failing to meet the food and hygiene requirements. There are plenty of other examples. All these discretionary powers, if not properly exercised, will infringe upon legitimate rights and interests of those under administration.

Those are just some examples of different kinds of discretionary powers granted under legislation to administrative organs in undertaking concrete administrative acts. They are far from a complete list of discretionary powers enjoyed by the administrative organs. Scholars in China have made efforts in the classification of discretionary powers. Different classifications have been put forward.[9] It seems that most scholars agree that discretionary power can first be classified into procedural and substantive discretion. Difference mainly exists with regard to sub-classification of either procedural or substantive discretion.[10]

Substantive Discretion

Substantive administrative discretion refers to the freedom to make decisions concerning the substance of a matter. It can be further classified as follows.

Discretion within the Limits set by Legislation

This is the most common species of discretionary power exercised by various administrative organs. It occurs when a piece of legislation provides for several kinds of compulsory measures for the administrative organ concerned to choose to apply to a category of activities. For example, the Regulation on Penalties against Public Securities provides that warning, fine or detention may be imposed on the violators of public securities regulation, depending on the degree and seriousness of the violation of legislation. That is to say, the public security officer may impose either a warning, a fine or detention. If the public security officer chooses detention, it also enjoys discretion in deciding the duration of detention.

Alternatively, a piece of legislation may set the range of penalty to be imposed and the administrative organ shall have the discretion to determine the exact amount of penalty. The Food and Hygiene Law provides that the penalty for violation of food hygiene legislation is between RMB20 to RMB30,000.

It often happens that the relevant administrative organs, in exercising their discretion, may fail to exercise or misuse their authority for various reasons. This will lead to the violation of the lawful interests of the person(s) involved.

Discretion in Determining the Essential Legal Elements

11.05 This is concerned with the determination of the nature and the characteristics of the activities undertaken by the person subject to administrative control. The nature and characteristics are related directly to the specific decisions to be made by the administrative organs. It could be the case that the administrative organ has to exercise its discretion to determine the nature of an activity because of the vacuum left by the legislation. For example, there is no provision in the Regulation on the Administrative Penalties for Public Security on how to deal with the situation of interference with public affairs through the use of force or threat, which is not up to the degree of constituting a crime. But it is more serious than interference in public affairs without the use of force and threat. If the latter shall be dealt with according to the regulation, the former should obviously be under similar legal control. As a result, the public security bureau has to exercise its discretion to fill in such a gap, which is admissible by law. It may also be the case that legislation stipulates what the administrative organs should do if the circumstances are "serious", or "especially serious", or "frivolous". These terms are very ambiguous. Usually, there are no detailed legal conditions, or understanding of them. Their exact meaning needs to be determined by the law enforcement organs, usually administrative organs, through its exercise of discretionary power.

Procedural Discretion and the Necessity of Judicial Control of Discretionary Power

11.06 Procedural discretion is concerned with the freedom of administrative organs in choosing the appropriate method, procedure or time limit to undertake a concrete administrative act when either alternatives are provided in law or there are no legal provisions.[11]

Administrative discretionary power is a kind of administrative power. It has the common features of any other administrative activities such as being unilateral, unequal and compulsory. The administrative organ has the authority to request the person (natural or legal) concerned to do or not to do something. The latter has the obligation to follow such a request. The relationship between them is therefore unequal. Because those under administration do not enjoy any bargaining power, improper exercise of discretionary power may infringe upon the legitimate interests of the person concerned.[12]

Secondly, administrative discretionary power is very flexible as the administrative organ is granted the authority to choose from different alternatives and the relevant legislation usually does not provide clear guidance with regard to which alternative should be chosen and how to choose. This feature has been claimed to be the essence of discretionary power.[13] Because of this flexibility, an administrative organ may arbitrarily exercise its discretionary power, which may lead to obvious unfairness or abuse of its authority. Both of them are the grounds recognized under the ALL by which a concrete administrative act may be challenged through judicial review.

The necessity to keep the exercise of executive power within its legal limits is omnipotent. It is because discretionary power is authorized by law. Its exercise should be within its defined legal scope and its exercise should be consistent with the objective and fundamental aim of the legislation concerned.

In China, the concept of administration according to law has been promoted by the central government and generally accepted, though it is still a relatively new one.[14]

The Principles Governing the Control of Discretionary Power

Principle of Legality

The fundamental principle of judicial review in China is stated in section 5 of the ALL, *i.e.* the principle of legality. Specifically speaking, in handling judicial review cases, the judiciary (people's courts) shall only examine the legality of concrete administrative acts undertaken by administrative organs. Literal interpretation and application of section 5 of the ALL will lead to the conclusion that the judiciary is excluded from the examination of the appropriateness or reasonableness of any concrete administrative act. This is in line with the traditional approach towards judicial review.

11.07

The traditional approach is that the exercise of discretionary power is always lawful in formality. The issue of unlawful exercise is out of the question. The exercise of discretionary power can only be appropriate or inappropriate. Therefore discretionary power is not subject to judicial control.[15] This approach is no longer popular and has been discarded by most Chinese administrative law scholars. The current approach is that there are certain legal requirements upon the exercise of discretionary power. For example; the exercise of discretionary power should be within its legal scope and consistent with the legislative objective and fundamental principles. If the exercise of discretionary power exceeds the legal scope or is against the legislative objective or fundamental principles, then that exercise of discretionary power should be regarded as illegal.[16] Apart from illegal exercise of discretionary power, there also exists the inappropriate exercise of discretionary power, which is not usually subject to judicial control. This does not mean no remedies are available to redress inappropriate exercise of discretionary power. If any person has any complaints in this aspect, he is supposed to bring the case to the relevant administrative organ at the next higher level for administrative reconsideration.[17] Under exceptional circumstances, the judiciary will examine the reasonableness of the exercise of discretionary power.

The Principle of Reasonableness[18]

11.08 Some scholars have also argued that apart from the principle of legality, the principle of reasonableness should also be regarded as a basic principle of judicial review in China. It should be an important component of the rule of law principle. The experience of foreign jurisdiction reveals the necessity and feasibility for the judiciary to apply the principle of reasonableness to review the exercise of discretionary power. Moreover, the application of the principle of reasonableness is in accordance with legislation and subject to strict restriction of judicial procedure. It is by no means an arbitrary supervision.[19]

Wang Hanbing, the Deputy Chairman of the Standing Committee of the National People's Congress, states in his explanation of the ALL that the review of reasonableness of concrete administrative acts is an exception to the general principle of legality.[20] Nevertheless, he confirmed the existence of the principle of reasonableness in judicial review in China. But its application is restricted and most unreasonable concrete administrative acts are supposed to be dealt with through administrative reconsideration.

It has been suggested that the contents of the principle of reasonableness should include:

1. the intention of the exercise of discretionary power should be consistent with the legislative objective, that is, it should be for the interests of the state and the people, comply with the specific legislative objective and be out of goodwill;
2. it should be based on proper consideration, *i.e.* to take into relevant consideration and not to take into account irrelevant consideration;
3. the contents of the concrete administrative act should be reasonable; and

4. the administrative act should follow the reasonable procedures and methods.²¹

If any of these requirements is not satisfied, then there may be a possibility that the concrete administration acts will be challenged before the people's courts. In essence, the administrative decision should be not only within the conditions or scope as defined by legislation, but also in compliance with the objective and purpose of the legislation.

Relationship between Legality and Reasonableness

The concept of legality under Chinese administrative law has to be interpreted broadly as far as judicial control of discretionary power is concerned. As mentioned previously, the issue of illegality may also arise when discretionary power is exercised. However, the principle mainly relied on by the judiciary to challenge the exercise of discretionary is the principle of reasonableness. This is why the principle of reasonableness has a very important role to play.

Discretionary power is the authority granted under legislation to the administrative organs. It can be exercised by the authorized administrative organs. However, whether or not its exercise is lawful depends on whether or not the authorized administrative organs have used the granted authority reasonably. In common law jurisdictions such as the United Kingdom and Hong Kong, the principle of reasonableness has been firmly established as a legal requirement for the exercise of discretionary power by administrative organs.²² Therefore, the unreasonableness in the exercise of discretion will turn the concrete administrative act to be unlawful and therefore breaches the principle of legality.²³

11.09

Grounds for Judicial Control of Discretionary Power

Judicial control of administrative discretion has developed over the years and many legal principles have been well established by the judges in common law countries. Whereas in continental countries, such as France and Germany, there also exists a set of comprehensive legal rules on the control of discretionary powers.

In China, section 54 of the ALL has also incorporated reveal specific grounds under which the exercise of discretionary power can be judicially challenged. They are abuse of powers, obvious unfairness, and failure or delay in the performance of statutory duty.²⁴

11.10

Abuse of Powers[25]

11.11 Abuse of powers in administrative law refers mainly to abuse of administrative discretionary powers.[26] Usually, an administrative organ is granted the discretion to undertake concrete administrative acts when certain legal conditions are satisfied.[27] The discretion is about the undertaking of the final activities rather than the identification of facts. Discretion may be granted in the undertaking of all kinds of administrative activities. It can be about whether or not to undertake a concrete administrative act, what kind of acts should be chosen, the measures to be chosen, the scope of choice, the time limit or the methods of activities, and so on.[28]

The exact meaning of abuse of power is defined neither in the ALL nor in the Opinions on the ALL. Scholars have provided different definitions. Professor Luo holds that abuse of power occurs when the administrative organs or their personnel intentionally undertake any concrete administrative acts which are within their jurisdiction, but not in compliance with the legislative objective, spirit or principle.[29] According to the authors from the Supreme People's Court, abuse of powers refers to the situation when a concrete administrative act undertaken by an administrative organ is, though within its discretion, against the purpose and principle of the law and unreasonable.[30] Both definitions agree that the following three conditions need to be satisfied in order to bring a judicial review case successfully on the ground of abuse of power. Firstly, a concrete administrative act, constituting abuse of power, is still within the jurisdiction of the relevant administrative organ in formality. Secondly, the concrete administrative act is against or deviates from the legislative objective, spirit or principle. Thirdly, the concrete administrative act is only related to the exercise of discretionary power.[31]

Scholars hold different views with regard to other essential elements of abuse of power. One view is that the concrete administrative act must be unreasonable, which is caused by improper exercise of power by the administrative authority concerned.[32] This view emphasizes the objective result of the concrete administrative act. The judiciary may then rely on the principle of reasonableness to examine the consequence. The test is an objective one, and the judiciary may determine what is meant by reasonableness by taking into account relevant factors in a specific case.

The other view proposes an alternative fourth element, i.e. the administrative organ must have the intention to abuse its authority.[33] This is a subjective criterion. In other words, negligent administrative act can never be classified as abuse of power.[34] This criterion has its practical problem in implementation. The ALL puts the burden of proof upon the defendants in judicial review, i.e. administrative organs. The defendants can easily avoid the submission of this evidence, showing that they had improper intention in undertaking any concrete administrative acts. However, Professor Luo argues that the intention refers mainly to the intention to violate the legislation objectives, spirit and principles, and the existence of such an element distinguishes abuse of power from any other grounds of judicial review.[35] If this element is to regarded as an essential element of the abuse of power, the judiciary may request the relevant administrative organs to provide evidence to show that they have the genuine intention to comply with the legislative objectives, spirit and principles. Whether or not this can be done is not clear as the Opinions on the ALL do not provide any guidance in this respect.

A third approach in the definition of abuse of power focuses on the principle of reasonableness. It believes that abuse of power is a general concept referring to all kinds of exercise of discretionary power in violation of the principle of reasonableness.[36] This approach has the advantage of simplicity in the sense that the judiciary needs only to examine whether or not this sole criterion has been satisfied. The determination of whether or not the administrative act is reasonable depends on other factors such as the intention, spirit and principle of the relevant legislation.[37] Therefore in judicial review of the exercise of discretionary power, it is unavoidable to examine the objective and spirit of the relevant legislation and the intention of the decision makers. Apart from unreasonableness, it also proposes that abuse of power has two more characteristics. One is that it is an unlawful administrative activity. The other is that abuse of power only occurs within the scope of the exercise of administrative discretion.[38] This approach is not really more simplified than other approaches in the application.

11.12   Different categorizations of concrete administrative acts amounting to abuse of power have been proposed. Most scholars agree that inappropriate motivation and purpose, pursuit of unfair enrichment, inappropriate consideration (including taking into account irrelevant consideration and failing to take into account relevant consideration) shall amount to abuse of power.[39] Capriciousness in undertaking concrete administrative acts,[40] abuse of procedures[41] have also been suggested to be considered as abuse of power. Professor Luo also maintains that obviously unfair concrete administrative acts should be regarded as abuse of power.[42] Another scholar has suggested seven major forms of abuse of power, including unlawful objective, irrelevant consideration, failure to consider relevant consideration, unlawful intention, unlawful delay, inconsistency and inappropriate procedure.[43] According to a sensible rule of statutory interpretation, especially contextual approach, it seems more appropriate to limit abuse of power to the first four categories. Obviously, unfair concrete administrative acts are unreasonable but may not amount to abuse of power. They may be challenged on the grounds of obvious unfairness rather than grounds of abuse of power. Similarly, unlawful delay is also a separate ground for judicial review under the ALL. Inappropriate procedure may be put on the grounds of violation of legal procedures (procedural *ultra vires*).

It should be noted that it is just an academic interpretation. It seems that these grounds do correspond to the grounds developed in common law countries by the judiciary to control the exercise of discretionary power. This is not surprising as judicial control of discretionary power is a new concept to the Chinese legal system and most scholars have looked to Western countries to borrow experience and are naturally influenced by both their judicial practice and academic writings. Now this section will move on to examine judicial practice in China to see how Chinese judiciary has relied on these grounds to conduct judicial review and what are the categories which have been recognized by the Chinese judiciary.

If an administrative act is found out to be an abuse of power, then the judiciary can repeal partially or completely the administrative act concerned, and issue an order requesting the administrative organ to undertake a new act.

The most frequently invoked category seems to be the undertaking of concrete administrative acts by the personnel in administrative organs for improper motivation. The following cases are in this category. The first case has actually touched several grounds and several categories of abuse of power.

Unlawful Intention

Li Guangru and others v. The People's Government in Phoenix Town[44]

11.13　In 1992, the people's government in Phoenix town (the defendant collected agricultural tax, agricultural special products tax, etc., according to the Regulation on the Farmers Burdens in Sichuan Province from 25 peasants (the plaintiffs). The defendant also requested the plaintiffs make some other payments, including tobacco tax, the money for school construction, medical insurance charge for domestic animals, highway maintenance fee and a house insurance premium. The plaintiffs claimed that the defendant violated the Regulation on the Farmers' Burden in Sichuan Province by imposing those five extra tax burdens on them. They also argued that the defendant's imposition of the extra five kinds of payment lacked legal basis. The defendant contended that those five extra tax burdens were imposed according to some other normative documents issued by the local county or district people's government and should be lawful administrative acts.

The court held that the defendant's imposition of the five extra tax charges had seriously violated the provisions of the Regulation on

Costs Borne by the Peasants and Labour Management issued by the State Council and the Regulation on the Farmers' Burden in Sichuan Province and were unlawful administrative acts.

The tobacco tax was not a kind of mandatory tax. According to the Sichuan Regulation, whether or not to grow tobacco should be voluntary, and only those who grow tobacco should pay tobacco tax according to the amount of tobacco they grow. However, a normative document was issued by the local county people's government, according to which the defendant in 1992 allocated tobacco tax to all families of the peasants, regardless of whether or not they grew tobacco.

In 1992, after collecting money for school construction from the plaintiffs according to the Sichuan Regulation, the defendant demanded and compulsorily collected extra payment, with the excuse of improving the standard of the school. This is in clear violation of Section 22 of the Sichuan Regulation which stipulates that the collection of any payment from the peasants must be voluntary, and should follow the proper procedure by getting the approval of the Provincial People's Government. In this case, the defendant neither consulted the peasants nor obtained approval of the Provincial Government. Instead, it imposed the payment upon the peasants unilaterally, which was held to amount to abuse of power.

According to section 25 of the Sichuan Regulation, the medical charge must be paid voluntarily by the plaintiffs, based on the principle that whoever benefits should pay. Service charges should be determined through consultation and cannot be imposed compulsorily. In 1992 the defendant unilaterally issued service contracts to the plaintiffs and collected service charges compulsorily. In fact, the plaintiffs did not conclude any contracts with the defendant. Nor did they get any service or benefits. The defendant's collection of service charge turned out to be an abuse of power.

Section 15 of the Sichuan Regulation provides that peasants, classified as labour force, have the duty to construct and maintain the highways. Peasants who cannot provide service can apply to the relevant authority and pay contribution upon approval in lieu of service. Only males between 18 and 55 and females between 18 and 50 are classified as the labour force in the countryside. However, the defendant expanded the scope of labour force to children and elderly people aged over 55 (for male) and 50 (for female). It was also held to be an abuse of power.

According to the Regulation on Property Insurance of the People's Republic of China, property insurance should be on voluntary basis and through conclusion of contract. The defendant, since 1990, compulsorily collected insurance premiums from the plaintiffs without providing the plaintiffs any receipts, according to relevant normative documents issued by the Phoenix Township People's Government. In so doing, the defendant exceeded its authority.

JUDICIAL CONTROL OF DISCRETIONARY POWER

In this case, the court held that the collection of the first four kinds of extra payments amount to abuse of power. Specifically speaking, the imposition of tobacco without legal grounds, the imposition of highway construction and maintenance fee without following legal standards, the imposition of extra school construction without following proper legal procedure, and the imposition of medical charges in violation of legal provisions, are all regarded as abuse of power. The main legislative objective of the Sichuan Regulation mentioned in this case is to reduce the financial burden of the peasants and various powers granted under the regulation should be exercised to achieve such legislative objectives. Here the exercise of the granted discretionary power by the defendant was against such legislative objective. In essence, the Phoenix Township People's Government has those discretionary powers, but its exercise of that power was clearly against the legislative objective.

Zhang Xueju v. Administration Bureau of Industry and Commerce in X District of Xizhang (Tibet) Autonomous Region[45]

11.14 On August 28, 1988, Jiu, the head of the defendant, which was the Administration Bureau of Industry and Commerce in Tibet, and five other officers investigated the business of sole proprietors in a cement factory, including the plaintiff. On the request of the officers, the plaintiff produced her business licence and the receipt of the management fee for Industry and Commerce Administration in June. The plaintiff told the officers that the management fee in July had already been paid but the receipt was kept by a third party so she was not able to produce it. The officers ordered the plaintiff to pay it again because no evidence proved she had paid it and a receipt was issued. However, Jiu said that the plaintiff should pay a fine for the 28 days delay of payment, plus a fine which was four times the administration fee. The plaintiff disputed with Jiu and the officers on this matter. Finally, Jiu seized the plaintiff's licence. The plaintiff later went to the office of the defendant and produced the receipt for the management fee in July. Jiu then said that no fine was necessary. However, he insisted that the plaintiff had exceeded his scope of business by carrying on other business, including selling torches and batteries which were not included in the licence, and an additional management fee should be paid for selling torches and batteries. The plaintiff was not satisfied with Jiu's decision and said Jiu was corrupt, then left Jiu's office. The defendant revoked the plaintiff's licence. On September 1, 1988, the defendant found that the plaintiff's husband, Wang, was in the shop and the shop was open. The officers of the defendant questioned Wang as to why he still ran the business without a licence. The defendant disregarded Wang's explanation that he did not run the business. He was only having a break from work and went back to see whether his children were all right or not. The defendant imposed a fine of RMB500 on Wang for carrying on the business without a licence.

The plaintiff applied for administrative reconsideration of the defendant's decision. The defendant held that Wang should be fined RMB200. Moreover, it fined the plaintiff RMB200 for exceeding the permitted scope of business. The defendant also notified the plaintiff that after the execution of the penalty, the defendant should return the licence to the plaintiff and allow her to carry on the business on her request. However, the defendant required the plaintiff to apply for the licence again after the plaintiff had already paid the fine. The plaintiff brought a lawsuit to court.

The court held that, according to the classification of goods in the conventions and the Regulation of the Business of Enterprises, as well as common practice, torches were categorized in the group of miscellaneous products, not metal products. The licence of the plaintiff stated that the plaintiff could sell miscellaneous products and therefore the plaintiff had not violated the relevant legislation. The defendant disregarded the conventions and the law, and its act was an abuse of power. Moreover, the defendant imposed a fine on the plaintiff for carrying on the business without a licence, merely based on hearsay evidence that the plaintiff made a representation that she had opened the shop on August 29 and 30 to check stock. That was the day the defendant discovered Wang was there, which was supported by other citizens' reports. The accusation was not supported by evidence. In this case, the imposition of fines was arbitrary and not supported by evidence. Even if Zhang had relevant evidence that she did not exceed the scope of business, the defendant still refused to give back the fine. It can be inferred that it was an abuse of power.

Zhang and Chen v. Public Security Bureau in X City of Jiangsu Province[46]

It was an abuse of power to impose sanction on a citizen who was not an object that the law intended to punish.

The plaintiffs, Chen and Zhang, were water transportation sole proprietors. They took a petrol tank on Chen's vessel to a repair centre to do some repair work to the tank. In the course of repairs, the tank exploded and Wang, a worker in the centre, and the plaintiffs, suffered grievous injury. Wang died six days after the explosion. The defendant, the Public Security Bureau, then detained the plaintiffs' licences and their vessels. The plaintiffs asked the defendant to return the vessels and the licence several times. The defendant insisted that the plaintiffs had to pay Wang's medical and funeral fees. The plaintiffs refused to pay because the explosion was not their fault.

The court, according to section 44 of the ALL, ordered the defendant to return the licences. However, the defendant then refused to execute

11.15

the court's order and argued that the incident constituted a criminal offence and should be regulated by section 115 of the Criminal Law and sections 16 and 18 of the Regulation on the Administration of Dangerous Chemicals. The case should not be dealt with under the ALL. Later on, the defendant made a supplementary application to detain the plaintiff's licences. Meanwhile, the Committee of Politics and Law of that city persuaded the defendant to return the licences to the plaintiffs. In this case, it is clear from the facts of what the defendant did towards the plaintiffs amounted to administrative compulsory measures, which infringed the legitimate interests of the plaintiffs. The accident of the explosion was caused by the third party rather than the plaintiffs. It was argued that the imposition of a penalty on the plaintiffs, who did not commit the offence, amounted to abuse of power.[47] It was not clear from the facts provided that the defendant had the intention to misuse its power. If there was no intention, then it would not amount to abuse of power. If that is the case, wrongful application of legislation can still be argued.

Chen (first plaintiff) and Economic and Technology Corporation in X County in Zhejiang Province (second plaintiff) v. Price Control Bureau in X District[48]

11.16 In early 1990, each of the two third parties, Li and Wang, who were officers at the Price Control Bureau of X County, bought a television from the second plaintiff. But they were requested by the second plaintiff, at the same time, to buy something which they did not want, which led to a quarrel between the two third parties and Chen, the first plaintiff. In January and September 1990, the second plaintiff purchased two types of bicycles and reported their proposed retail price (of RMB240 and RMB238 respectively) to the Price Control Bureau in X County. Li and Wang refused to approve the retail price on the grounds that the proposed prices were too high. The second plaintiff then sold the bicycles at prices between RMB223 and RMB247 without approval. In July 1990, the second plaintiff purchased 50 television sets for sale. The Price Control Bureau in X County set the retail price at RMB3,140. But the second plaintiff sold them at prices between RMB3,180 and RMB3,250. In December 1990, knowing that there would be a large-scale price control investigation, Li and Wang took back the approval form from the second plaintiff concerning the retail price of the television sets. They then held that the purchase and sale of both bicycles and television sets by the second plaintiff was without approval and made a decision to impose fines on both plaintiffs. It imposed on the second plaintiff a fine of RMB10,000 and confiscated RMB133,590 obtained by the plaintiff in the course of selling the television sets on the grounds of violation of the Regulation on Price Control which states that the sale of the television sets without approval is subject to penalty. A fine of RMB200 was also imposed on the first plaintiff as he was the person in charge. The plaintiffs applied to the defendant for administrative reconsideration. The defendant changed the total amount of unlawful income obtained by the second plaintiff RMB12,309. But the other two fines were sustained. The plaintiff brought a lawsuit to court.

The plaintiffs claimed that the defendant had approved the retail price for the television sets at RMB3,140 but the defendant subsequently took back the written approval which was issued to the plaintiff. Then the defendant imposed a fine for selling without approval. Moreover, the plaintiffs claimed that they were entitled to sell the bicycles because they applied for the confirmation of the retail price, but the Price Control Bureau in X County refused to approve it. The court of first instance delivered the verdict that the amount to be confiscated should be RMB11,673.32 but upheld the two fines. The court of second instance held that the plaintiffs had actually violated the laws. However, the act of the defendant was improper because it should have stated the retail price of the bicycles. Moreover, the defendant took back the approval for the television sets and then imposed a fine on the plaintiffs for selling without approval, which amounted to an abuse of power because the acts of the two officers were not to rectify any unlawful acts. Instead, they tried to punish the plaintiffs for personal reasons. It is a clear-cut case of unlawful intention. The intention element, *i.e.* revenge, could be argued to be an irrelevant consideration.

Di v. Standard Measurement Bureau in X County[49]

In 1988, two officers of the defendant pretended to buy some goods from the plaintiff's shop in order to investigate the measuring instruments. The plaintiff told the officers that the original weighing instrument was inaccurate and another one should be used. The officers insisted on the use of the original one and then produced their identification and imposed a fine on the defendant in accordance with the Metrology Law of the PRC. The plaintiff claimed that the officers had used inappropriate means to investigate and the court held that it was a type of abuse of power. It is because the purpose of the Metrology Law was to modernize the use of measuring instruments for technology improvement. However, the officers used improper means to trap the plaintiff and fined the plaintiff which was a clear contradiction of the law.

Inappropriate Consideration

The following cases either take into account irrelevant consideration or fail to take into account relevant consideration.

11.17

11.18

Guo Debing v. Public Security Bureau of Jinghe County in Xinjiang Uygur Autonomous Region[50]

Guo Debing (the plaintiff) led a team of workers, including Fan, to undertake a construction project in Jinghe County. He received part of the payment for the project of about RMB8,000. Due to some dispute over the distribution of the money between the plaintiff and Fan, the plaintiff left Jinghe without paying Fan RMB3,500 out of the RMB8,000 which Fan deserved. Fan and other workers reported the case to the Public Security Bureau of Jinghe County (the defendant). The defendant suspected the plaintiff of running away with the money which would constitute an offence of deception. It issued an order of shelter for examination. The plaintiff brought a lawsuit to the court, claiming that the dispute between him and Fan was purely economic in nature. He challenged the issue of the order of shelter for examination because the suspicion of deception was groundless. The plaintiff also alleged that the defendant had infringed his legitimate interests by sheltering him from examination and violated the Circular Regarding the Integration of the Measures of Forced Labour and the Measures of Shelter for Investigation into Rehabilitation Through Labour, issued by the State Council (The Circular) in 1980.

The first issue is whether or not the plaintiff may bring a case for judicial review. According to section 2 of the Opinions on the ALL, citizens may bring a case for judicial review if they are unsatisfied with a public security bureau's decisions of compulsory shelter for examination.

The main issue in this case is whether or not the defendant may issue an order of compulsory shelter for examination. According to The Circular, shelter for examination was applicable only to those suspects who committed ordinary offences and refused to tell their true names, residential addresses and those who may have committed offences at different places. This condition for the adoption of shelter for examination is further stressed by the Notice Strictly Restricting the Use of Shelter for Examination (The Notice), issued in July 1985 by the Ministry of Public Security. In this case, the identity of the plaintiff is very clear and the application of shelter for examination against the plaintiff is in violation of The Circular and The Notice.

Furthermore, the Ministry of Public Security, the Supreme People's Procuratorate and the Supreme People's Court jointly issued the Circular on Illegal Detention in Commercial and Trade Actitivities on September 8, 1990. It states that some local public security bureaus and procuratorates for the protection of their local economic interests exceed their authority and unlawfully detain people in purely economic cases in the name of investigating economic crime. Such illegal activities have seriously infringed on the personal freedom of the people concerned and interrupted social and economic order. Public security bureaus, people's procuratorates and courts should pay sufficient attention to this matter and take appropriate measures to prevent or rectify the matter. In this case, the defendant's issue of an order of shelter for examination falls into the category of unlawful interference with economic disputes, which is supposed to be dealt with through civil procedure on an equal basis. The court held that the defendant's issue of the order amounted to an abuse of power and, based on section 54(2)(1) and 54(5) repealed the decision of the defendant.

In this case, the defendant used the authority of issuing an order of shelter for examination to the wrong person, on wrongful activity and for wrongful purposes. That has been regarded by the court as abuse of power. This case can also be argued to be the application legislation to wrong persons.

Zhu v. Land Administration Bureau in X County in Jiangxi Province[51]

In order to open a road-side restaurant, in 1990 the plaintiff started to build a house on the left side of the front door of a factory nearby without the approval of the Land Administration Bureau (the defendant). The house would obstruct the sight of the road user and cause accidents, had it been built. The factory had negotiated with Zhu many times and informed him of the possible consequences. But the plaintiff continued to build the house, regardless of the objection by the factory. Several traffic accidents occurred after the construction of the house because the sight of the driver was obstructed by the house. The defendant issued an order to the plaintiff, according to section 45 of the Land Administration Law, requesting the plaintiff to demolish the house within 15 days, seizing the land so as to give it to the state, imposing a fine of RMB300 on the plaintiff, and requesting the factory, the third party, to pay the plaintiff RMB400 as a demolition fee. The plaintiff applied to the court within the time limit after receiving the order from the defendant.

The court held that the plaintiff's construction of the house in question was illegal. Section 45 of the Land Management Law stipulates that the defendant could order the plaintiff to demolish the house. But the seizure of the land and the imposition of a fine are not stipulated in section 45 or any other provisions. The defendant had abused its power by making those two decisions without any legal basis because no legislation had granted the defendant that power. The request for the third party to pay RMB400 demolition fee was due to lack of legal grounds.

It should be noted that the ownership of the land belongs to a village of which the plaintiff is a resident and the Land Administrative Bureau does not have the authority to change the ownership under the Land Administration Law and should only order the return of the land to the

11.19

villagers under the Land Administration Law. To ask an innocent third party to pay the plaintiff RMB400 as demolition fee for the plaintiff's illegal act was due to lack of legal grounds and was too lenient on the plaintiff.

In this case, the defendant did not properly deal with the offence committed by the plaintiff according to law. Instead it asked an innocent party, the factory, to bear partial responsibility for the plaintiff's offence. It can be argued that it is the wrongful exercise of discretionary power and account taken into has irrelevant consideration. Also, it is suggested to be an case of abuse of power.

Capriciousness or Unreasonableness

11.20 The first case was concerned with double penalties for the same offence. The second case is related to improper reasons for the change of the original decision. The third case is an obviously unreasonable decision and related to both the first and third categories. Each of these three kinds of administrative decisions has been challenged under the ground of abuse of power.

Yang Zhongsheng v. Public Security Bureau in JianYang County[52]

The plaintiff ran a tea house where he also played video films. He obtained relevant licences. He rented a video tape and played it for 10 minutes. He then found out that it was an obscene video and immediately stopped playing it. The plaintiff's video tape recorder and television were seized by the Public Security Bureau in Jian Yang County (the defendant) in a door-by-door action by the defendant to search for the persons playing obscene videos. The defendant questioned the plaintiff on the matter and the plaintiff made a true statement of what happened and the fact that he immediately returned that obscene video tape and never played any other obscene video tapes again. A fine of RMB2,000 was nevertheless imposed on the plaintiff by the defendant because the plaintiff had shown an obscene video. A verdict and receipt for the fine was duly served on the plaintiff. But at the same time the plaintiff was requested to pay RMB1,100 to have his television set and video tape recorder returned. When the plaintiff requested a receipt from the defendant, he refused and they quarrelled. After the plaintiff's second request, he was reluctantly given an informal receipt by the defendant. The RMB1,100 was returned to the plaintiff after his complaint to the superior of the defendant. Shortly after that, the defendant issued the second verdict to detain the plaintiff's television set and tape recorder again. The plaintiff applied for an administrative reconsideration, but the Public Security Bureau did not give any decision within the time limit. The plaintiff then brought a lawsuit to court and contended that he committed the offence unintentionally and the sanction of RMB2,000 fine was too heavy and wrongful. Moreover, he suffered direct economic loss from the administrative act. The defendant contended that the second verdict was not a public security penalty. It is a decision to confiscate property for which the duration for administrative reconsideration is two months and the plaintiff should bring the case for reconsideration first.

The court held that what the defendant did is a kind of public security penalty which was obviously unfair to the plaintiff. Sections 7 and 37 of the Regulation on Administrative Penalties for Public Security have conferred power upon public security bureaus to seize property, which should also be regarded as a kind of public security penalty. That is to say the time limit for administrative reconsideration is five days instead of one or two months. The defendant's identification of facts for the imposition of the penalty was also due to lack of grounds. The specific police officers had abused his power by imposing the penalty twice against the plaintiff for the same offence.

In this case, double penalties for the same offence were regarded as an abuse of power. The court had not dealt with the argument of unfairness in the decision.

Liang v. The People's Government in X Town in Zhejiang Province[53]

The plaintiff was permitted by the local people's government at township level (the defendant) to demolish a 40-square metre hut, where he formerly lived, and build a single-storey house of 55 square metres in the same location. The location of the house was ascertained and the plaintiff then built the house in accordance with the stipulations in the permit. However, a neighbour, Lin, on the east side of the plaintiff's house, stopped the plaintiff because the plaintiff had removed some soil near the foundation of Lin's house and caused the foundation of Lin's house to sink. The defendant tried to mediate the dispute between the plaintiff and Lin but the defendant's efforts failed. The defendant then seized and revoked the plaintiff's permit of construction for non-compliance to the requirements, but the plaintiff continued the construction work. The defendant finally made a decision and ordered the plaintiff to demolish the foundation of the house he built.

11.21

The court of first instance made a decision against the plaintiff because the plaintiff had disregarded the local government's decision.

Two different opinions exist among the judges of the court of second instance on how the matter be dealt with. The first one is that the plaintiff should first follow the defendant's decision and then apply for compensation. The plaintiff's refusal to follow the defendant's decision was inappropriate and therefore the judgment of the court of first instance should be sustained. The second opinion was that even if the defendant had the authority to revoke the permit, it did so without proper reason. This amounts to an abuse of power. Therefore the court of second instance should not support the decisions of the defendant and the court of first instance. Then the sanction should therefore be annulled. The court adopted the latter opinion and held that the variation of the original administrative decision, *i.e.* revocation of the permit without legal justification, was an abuse of power. This can be treated as a capricious decision.

Xiao Lianjie v. The Hygiene and Epidemic Prevention Station[54]

In 1991 Li, an officer of the Hygiene and Epidemic Prevention Station (the defendant) carried out a hygiene investigation in the plaintiff's restaurant and required the plaintiff to pay an investigation fee of RMB5. The plaintiff found that Li did not have the appropriate identification and suspected Li's identity as a true officer of the defendant. The plaintiff refused to pay the fee with the excuse that he had no income on that day and no money was available. The next day, Li came again and the plaintiff's wife intended to pay, but the plaintiff stopped her and he insisted that Li should produce the documents for collection of the fee. Then the plaintiff and Li had a serious argument and insulted each other. The plaintiff finally had not paid the fee. The defendant issued a warning to the plaintiff and ordered the plaintiff to pay the investigation fee within two days of RMB10 (twice the original fee) and another machinery operation fee of RMB20. The defendant stated that if the plaintiff did not pay then it would send an officer to collect the fee and the plaintiff would have to pay an additional transportation fee of RMB40. The plaintiff disregarded the warning. In the afternoon of that day when the fine was due, the defendant sent an officer to collect the fee. But the plaintiff only agreed to pay the RMB30 and refused to pay the transportation fee. The defendant then issued a notice which declared that the plaintiff had violated the Regulation on the Administration of Hygiene of Public Place and imposed a fine of RMB500, according to the Implementation Rules of the Regulation.

The court held that the Regulation and the Implementation Rules had not granted the defendant any right to collect the transportation fee and the machinery operation fee. The defendant had changed the investigation fee from RMB5 to RMB10. All these acts lacked legal basis and amounted to an abuse of power because of their violation of the purpose of the regulation to educate the offender. The defendant misused its power to create various kinds of fees.

In this case, the increase of the amount of the investigation fee and the collection of the transportation fee and machinery operation fee, without legal basis, were regarded by the court as an abuse of power. Strictly speaking, these may be better regarded as *ultra vires* acts. However, an examination of the motivation of the defendant to collect the fees will show that they are inconsistent with the objective of the legislation. This can be argued to be an abuse of power.

Li v. Bureau of Urban Construction in X County[55]

11.22 The plaintiff made an application for a reconstruction of his house. The defendant granted a licence and stated that the height of the house should not exceed 3.2 metres. Later, a third party, Shi, was allowed to build a house at a height of 3.6 metres. The plaintiff sued the defendant for violation of the regulations made by the provincial people's government. The defendant contended that the decision on the height was discretionary. The court held that the defendant had abused its power because it permitted the house to be built higher than 3.2 metres, only according to its own will without any legal basis, and the defendant had also refused to explain why it permitted the third party to build a house higher than 3.2 metres to the court. This is a typical capricious decision made by administrative organs, and has been treated as an abuse of power. Another interesting and important point in this case was that the failure to provide evidence and reasons was deemed to be an abuse of power.

Lack of Legal Grounds

11.23 The exercise of administrative power without clear legal bases has been held by the people's courts to be an abuse of power.

Li v. Office in Charge of the Street Affairs in X City in Guizhou Province[56]

In 1989, the officers in the Office for Street Affairs discovered that Li, the plaintiff, had placed an oven and 13 plastic buckets for sale on the street near his shop, which violated the relevant legislation. The officers removed the oven and the buckets. But Li quarrelled with them and tried to stop them. In the course of dispute, they used an electric rod to shock Li, who was then injured. The doctor in the hospital found that the plaintiff had suffered an injury to the layer of tissue under his skin. The defendant detained Li's goods according to the Regulation on Environmental Administration (Trial) of that town.

The court held that, firstly, the defendant had exceeded its authority to detain the plaintiff's goods under the Regulation of the Environmental Administration of that County. Moreover, the defendant's officer's use of electric rods had violated the stipulations in the Regulation on the Use of Weapon and Caution by the People's Police and amounted to an abuse of power. Moreover, under the Regulation on the Structure of Office for Street Affairs, the function of the defendant was to manage the work of the resident committee and to reflect the ideas and complaints of the residents to the higher level bureau. The defendant was not the bureau in charge of the administration of urban hygiene. It does not have the authority to impose the administrative sanction of detention of property. The court held that the defendant had exceeded its power to detain the plaintiff's goods. In this case, two grounds were invoked. One is the abuse of power by using electric rods, contrary to the relevant legislation. The second are the grounds of *ultra vires*.

Lu Yunyang v. Administration Bureau in Lin Gui County[57]

11.24 In July 1992, the plaintiff was ordered by the unit he belonged to, to purchase timber of 200 cubic metres. The plaintiff employed two other persons to buy timber. In October 1992, the People's Government of the province (the defendant) took an action to eliminate unlawful transaction of timber and found that the plaintiff did not have the receipt, invoice of the timber. The defendant held that the plaintiff had unlawfully bought timber for profit. A fine was imposed on the plaintiff and the two men on the basis that they carried out an unlawful timber transaction which violated sections 7 and 10 of the Order No.12 (1990) of the People's Government of the Guangxi Autonomous Region. After administrative reconsideration, the plaintiff brought a lawsuit to the court. The plaintiff claimed that he purchased the timber in the capacity of a worker of the forest work station. It was his duty and not unlawful. The defendant contended that the plaintiff had done it in the capacity of a forest worker, but for his own interest. The court, on the evidence that the plaintiff purchased timber in pursuant of his duty and he had done it in accordance with the instruction of the company he belonged to, held that the defendant had acted in abuse of its power and the acts were due to lack of essential evidence, as well as a misapplication of laws and regulations. However, the defendant appealed and the court of second instance held that the original judgment was based on a wrong procedure and ordered a retrial. In the retrial, the court was of the opinion that the concrete administrative acts should be annulled merely due to lack of essential evidence.

The court of first instance had not stated why the act of the defendant amounted to an abuse of power, though section 4(2)(d) of the ALL was quoted.

Yang Xiulan v. The Administration Bureau of Industry and Commerce in Ying Chuan City[58]

11.25 The plaintiff was a sole proprietor of a stall in a market. Her son sold fruit near the stall without licence, which was reported to the Administration Bureau for Industry and Commerce (the defendant). The defendant imposed administrative penalty, a fine, on the plaintiff's son. Her son was subsequently injured by the officers of the defendant after

GROUNDS FOR JUDICIAL CONTROL

they had quarrelled and insulted the officers of the defendant. The defendant was of the opinion that the plaintiff had violated the relevant stipulations of the Regulation on Trades in City and Towns and ordered the plaintiff to suspend the business for one month and wait for the final decision. But the plaintiff ignored the order and carried on her business before a final decision was made by the defendant. On January 6, 1989, the defendant compulsorily moved the plaintiff out of the market and detained her goods. On February 13, the defendant issued a written order to the plaintiff and asked her to collect her goods within 10 days otherwise the goods would be sold. The plaintiff refused to collect her goods. On September 18, 1989, the defendant then delivered a final written decision to the plaintiff and refused to compensate the plaintiff for the damage of the goods. The plaintiff claimed that she refused to collect the goods because their condition had deteriorated and the defendant refused to compensate her. The defendant claimed that the suspension was ordered in accordance with the Provisional Regulation on Individual Business. The court of first instance held that the defendant had abused its power by seizing the goods because it had not relied on any legislation to do so. The plaintiff appealed and contended that the defendant's acts were wholly illegal and the original judgment was wrong. The court of second instance dismissed the appeal. However, after reviewing the judgment by the intermediate people's court, a retrial was ordered by the Higher Court. It was held at the retrial that the plaintiff's son had violated the Regulation on Administrative Penalty for Public Security and should be handled by the public security bureau instead of the defendant. The defendant's act amounted to an excess of its power and the detention of goods was an abuse of power because the defendant had not relied on any legal basis to detain the goods. The defendant only did this to mainten public order, it said.

This case has been through adjudication three times: the court of first instance, the court of second instance and the retrial process. There are mainly two issues involved in this case. One is the applicable legislation, and the other is the nature of the defendant's act, whether it is an abuse of power or an excess of authority. It can be argued that authority in previous cases, *i.e.* the exercise of power without any legal grounds would amount to arbitrariness and lead to an abuse of power, is also applicable in this case.

Obvious Unfairness

Obvious unfairness is another ground upon which action can be taken to challenge the exercise of discretionary power. According to section 54(4), this ground is rather limited and can only be invoked to challenge administrative penalties, as mentioned in section 11(1) of the

11.26

ALL,[59] not any other kinds of concrete administrative acts. The condition for judicial review is that concrete administrative acts must be obviously unfair. The meaning of "obvious unfairness" is defined neither in the ALL nor in the Opinions on the ALL. One academic interpretation provided by the authors from the Supreme People's Court is that obviously unfair administrative penalties refer to penalties imposed upon wrongdoers which are, though within the scope of penalties provided by laws and regulations, extremely unfair and incompatible with the wrongs committed.[60] Professor Luo maintains that obviously unfair administrative penalties refer to those penalties which are within legal limit, but not in compliance with the principles of reasonableness, objectiveness and proportionality.[61] The third approach holds that obviously unfair penalties are those in violation of the principles of proportionality, equal application and compatibility.[62]

Obvious unfairness, in essence, refers to the consequences of concrete administrative acts. To examine the grounds of obvious unfairness independently, there does not seem to be any logical reason to explain why it is restricted to the exercise of discretionary power. Obviously unfair consequences may be caused by various reasons including those grounds discussed above. It has been argued that those obviously unfair administrative acts are within the legal scope of administrative organs and lawful in formality, but the results are obviously unfair to those under administration. If the administrative acts outside the legal scope of administrative organs, the ground of excess of power (*ultra vires*) may be invoked.[63] This approach has been generally accepted by Chinese scholars.[64]

Obviously unfair consequence caused by the imposition of administrative penalties may also be due to the inappropriate exercise or abuse of discretionary power. Several differences have been suggested between obvious unfairness and the abuse of power. Firstly, the subjective element is different. Obvious unfairness may be caused by both intention and negligence, whereas abuse of power must be intentional. Secondly, the scope of application is different. Obvious unfairness is limited to administrative penalties, while the abuse of power may occur in the exercise of any administrative power. Thirdly, the nature of the administrative acts covered is different. Obviously unfair administrative acts are, in essence, only in violation of the principle of reasonableness, while acts abusing power are in violation of lawful exercise of discretionary power. Fourthly, judicial remedies are different. The judiciary may only annul those abusing power, while it can change (or amend) the obviously unfair administrative acts.[65]

Apart from those differences, there also exists overlap between obvious unfairness and the abuse of power. It seems better to distinguish the two grounds in this way. Firstly, obvious unfairness may be regarded as a broader concept than the abuse of power, in the sense that it covers both intentional and negligent administrative acts. Secondly, the obvious unfairness requires that the consequence caused to those under administration must be obviously inappropriate and the degree of unreasonableness is higher than abuse of power which only requires evidence to show the existence of abuse and it does not matter whether or not the consequence is fair.[66]

There are three kinds of obviously unfair administrative penalties. **11.27** One is that the relevant legislation has provided for the range of administrative penalty. The penalty actually imposed appears obviously unfair, even though it is within the legal range. The Food and Hygiene Law of the People's Republic of China is one example which grants the administrative organ the discretion to impose a fine for violation of the law between the range of RMB20 to RMB30,000. If a penalty of RMB30,000 is imposed for a minor offence, it is obviously unfair. The second is that the relevant legislation provides for several penalties, but the administrative organ has chosen the one which is obviously unfair to those under administration. For example, the Medicine Administration Law of the People's Republic of China provides that for the sale of fake medicine, the administrative organ may impose the following sanctions, including a fine, suspension of production and revocation of business licence. Similar provisions also exist in the Regulation on Administrative Penalties for Public Security. The third one is that the legislation only grants the discretion of imposition of penalty to the administrative organ, but does not stipulate any legal limits. Many environmental legislation does not provide any range or varieties of administrative penalties.[67] The first two may be described as the exercise of more limited statutory discretion. For the third one, there is in fact no statutory limit at all.

Various types of reasons causing obviously unfair situation have been suggested by Chinese scholars.[68] They may be summarized as follows. The first is incompatibility of administrative penalty with the wrongs committed. It may be either too heavy or too light. It may also be the case that the same sanction is imposed for different offences or different sanctions are imposed for the same offence. The second is that double penalties are imposed for the same offence. Thirdly, inappropriate consideration may also be a reason leading to obviously unfair consequence.[69]

In order to determine whether or not a concrete administrative act is obviously unfair, the judiciary has to determine on a case-by-case basis due to the importance of the context of a concrete administrative act. Generally speaking, the following elements should be taken into account by the judiciary. They are the motivation of the decision maker, the principle of reasonableness, customs and traditions of the place where decision is made, the social impact and the relative autonomy of the decision maker.[70]

The above discussion reveals that the judiciary reviews mainly the appropriateness of any concrete administrative acts concerned, not its legality when the grounds of obvious unfairness is invoked. That may, according to the explanation provided by Wang Hanbing, be regarded as an exception to the principle of legality, as stated under section 5 of the ALL. But the ALL does not provide for what sort of situations should be included under this exception, which is the basis for amending the concrete administrative act. Query has been raised as to whether or not the court is better qualified than the administrative authority to make a more accurate and fair decision.[71]

It has been suggested that the exercise of discretionary power is not only an issue of appropriateness, but also an issue of legality. And certain kind of inappropriate exercise of discretionary power is also illegal which is judicially reviewable. The essence of this is whether or not the inappropriate exercise of discretionary power constitutes an illegal act.[72] It is not an easy issue to be determined. To be consistent with previous discussions and analyses, it may be appropriate to suggest that obvious unfairness should be restricted to the inappropriate exercise of discretionary power. Those obviously unfair and also unlawful administrative penalties may be challenged under other grounds such as wrongful application of legislation, and so on.

Judicial practice in China shows that incompatibility is frequently argued by the parties involved in judicial review cases to challenge the concrete administrative acts undertaken by administrative organs. The following are the cases in this category.

The remedy for an obviously unfair act is that the judiciary can actually change the decision made by the administrative organ concerned. That is quite different from the practice in the United Kingdom and Hong Kong.

Improportionality

11.28 There are two elements here. One is that the circumstances where the penalties imposed are not proportional to the wrongs committed. The other is that the degree of improportionality must be to the extent of obvious unfairness. This means a reasonable person can see that it is an improportional decision.

Luo Shufeng v. Public Security Bureau of TianJing City[73]

The plaintiff, Luo Shufeng, and Dong, the third party, were neighbours and their relations bad. It rained on July 14, 1990. Next morning, the plaintiff swept the dirty water in front of her door to the public drainage in order to discharge it. Dong was angry with the plaintiff because the dirty water passed through her front door. Dong, together with her son, Fan, and her daughter-in-law, Chen, then swept the water back to the plaintiff's side and in doing so, dirty water spilt on the plaintiff's clothes. In the course of the matter, Fan used obscenities to insult the plaintiff. The plaintiff was enraged and slapped Fan. Subsequently, the four people had a fight. Fan kicked the plaintiff. When the other villagers separated the parties, Dong and Chen prevented the plaintiff from leaving and continued to beat her until she fell down and fainted. The plaintiff suffered brain injury and was hospitalized for 15 days.

After the investigation by the local branch of the Public Security Bureau of Tanjan City (the defendant), administrative penalties were imposed on Fan and Chen, according to sections 22(1) and 22(3) of the Regulation of the PRC on Administrative Penalties for Public Security. The verdict was to detain Dong for 15 days and Chen for 10 days for assaulting the plaintiff, and to detain Fan for 15 days for insulting the plaintiff publicly. Dong, Chen and Fan applied for administrative reconsideration and the defendant changed the penalties and imposed on Dong and Fan a fine of RMB200 each and Chen a fine of RMB100 on the grounds that the plaintiff was also wrong to a certain extent.

The plaintiff then brought a lawsuit to court. The plaintiff claimed that she engaged in a fight with the three third parties because of a dispute initiated by one of the third parties. As a result, she had suffered a brain injury. She claimed that she was also publicly insulted by them and the penalties on them should not be so light. The defendant contended that the plaintiff had also contributed to the fight and she also insulted one of the third parties verbally. It would be too harsh to detain them. The court of first instance held that the dispute was initiated by Dong, and the plaintiff had suffered grievous injury. The misconduct of Dong and Fan was extremely serious and the administrative penalty of fine as imposed by the defendant was too lenient and incompatible to the seriousness of their offence. These concrete administrative acts were obviously unfair to the plaintiff. The court changed the defendant's decision accordingly by detaining Dong and Fan for 15 days.

The defendant appealed, arguing that the court's decision has interfered with the discretionary power of the public security bureau. The court of second instance was of the opinion that though the plaintiff had also misbehaved herself in the course of the dispute, the conduct of the three third parties was so serious, had caused serious consequences and also was a bad social influence. Therefore, the original judgment was upheld.

In this case, the reconsideration organ has changed the original administrative penalties to much lighter penalties, compared with the offence committed. This has been held to be obviously unfair to the plaintiff.

JUDICIAL CONTROL OF DISCRETIONARY POWER

Zhao Yongping v. Tianshan Branch of Uygur Municipal Public Security Bureau[74]

11.29 The plaintiff and the third party, Fu, had disputes with each other in the past. On November 25, 1992, the plaintiff went to market to buy pig food and met Fu. When the plaintiff passed Fu, she thought the plaintiff's coat touched her body and said some words to the plaintiff who quarrelled with Fu. In the course of their argument, the plaintiff slapped Fu on her face. Fu took a brick but did not use it to hit the plaintiff when she saw that the plaintiff's head was injured. The plaintiff pushed Fu towards a wall and Fu was injured.

Tianshan Branch decided to impose a penalty of 15 days detention upon the plaintiff, according to section 22(1) of the Regulation on Administrative Penalties for Public Security because he had assaulted Fu. The plaintiff brought the case to the defendant for administrative reconsideration and argued that he assaulted Fu because he was insulted by her first. The defendant sustained the decision of the Tianshan Branch. The plaintiff then brought the case to court for judicial review.

The court of first instance held that it was clear that the plaintiff's act was in violation of section 22(1) of the Regulation on Administrative Penalties for Public Security and that the plaintiff should be subject to administrative penalty. However, the dispute was caused by Fu and the injury Fu suffered was not so serious, and the plaintiff's offence was not so serious either. The court of first instance held that the imposition of the highest penalty of detention for 15 days was obviously too heavy. This should be amended, according to section 54(4) of the ALL. The defendant appealed, but the court of second instance upheld the judgment of the court of first instance, according to section 61(1) of the ALL.

This is a typical case where the plaintiff breached relevant legislation and should be subject to administrative penalty. However, the penalty imposed was obviously unfair to the plaintiff and not compatible to the offence he committed. In order to achieve justice, the penalty should be amended so that the legitimate interests of the plaintiff can be protected. It is about incompatibility of sanction with the offence committed.

Inappropriate Consideration

11.30 Inappropriate consideration occurs in cases where the administrative organs either fail to pay attention to some important factors which can affect the final decisions or make decisions by relying on some factors which should not be taken into account.

Ji v. Public Security Bureau in X City[75]

On October 17, 1990, the plaintiff's father had carelessly injured his leg and the bleeding could not be stopped. The plaintiff then went with his father to a hospital. He found that nobody was on duty in the emergency and registration section. The plaintiff then brought his father to the accommodation section where Doctor Ho was on duty. He said that they would not deal with the patient without registration. The plaintiff then returned to the emergency section, but there was still nobody there. He required the doctor to treat his father first and he would register later, but Ho refused. The plaintiff was angered and had an argument with Ho. Finally the plaintiff beat Ho once and Ho suffered an internal injury on his face. The Public Security Branch under the defendant imposed a fine of RMB70 on the plaintiff and ordered him to pay RMB50 as Ho's medical expenses. The plaintiff applied for administrative reconsideration and the defendant found that the offence committed by the plaintiff was serious and changed the fine to 10 days detention. The plaintiff brought a lawsuit against the decision of the defendant on the grounds that the penalty imposed by the administrative reconsideration organ was too heavy.

The court held that the plaintiff should be liable for his assault to Ho. However, the plaintiff would not have done so if somebody was on duty in the emergency section. Moreover, the plaintiff had only beat Ho once and the injury Ho suffered was also not serious. The 10-day detention was therefore improper and unfair to the plaintiff.

In this case, the penalty of 10-day detention imposed upon Ji is too heavy and out of proportion because the Public Security Bureau failed to take into account the factor that his father was seriously ill and no doctor was available. The result, *i.e.* the penalty imposed, is obviously unfair because the defendant failed to take into account the relevant factors, *i.e.* the reason Ji beat Ho.

He Zheng County Grain and Cooking Oil Trade Corporation v. The Administration Bureau of Industry and Commerce in Ning Xia Hui Autonomous Region[76]

11.31 The plaintiff was a state-owned enterprise with a proper business licence to engage in the trade of grain and cooking oil at market prices. The plaintiff did not have its own warehouse and used a state-owned warehouse where national reserves are stored, because the space in these warehouses is limited and could not store enough of the plaintiff's goods. From 1988 to 1989, the plaintiff borrowed several times from the national reserve to sell at the market price. Though it obtained the assistance and consent of the county food administration department, the nature of its activity is still in breach of relevant legislation, which requires examination and approval. Both the plaintiff and the county food administration bureau were at fault. The plaintiff sold the wheat and flour several times in order to solve the shortage of wheat in those areas. The plaintiff gained a profit of RMB161,112.8 from the sale of the wheat and flour from the national reserve. The Administration Bureau for Industry and Commerce (the defendant) discovered the matter in its investigation. It held that the plaintiff's activities constituted speculation and violated section 3(1) of the Provisional Regulation on Administrative Penalty for Speculation, which states that any behaviour interfering with the economy of the state and violating the state's laws and regulations for the purpose of gaining profit amounts to speculation. The defendant imposed a fine of 10 per cent of the total sale price of wheat at RMB32,409.8, removed the plaintiff from the company registration, and sent the case to the Public Security Bureau for investigation. The plaintiff claimed that his behaviour only amounted to an ordinary offence and he should not be penalized, according to the regulation. Moreover, he had not acted with the intention to gain profits.

The court of first instance held that even the plaintiff had earned a huge profit from the wheat transaction, it did not act to obtain huge profit, but to solve the shortage of wheat in some areas. Its behaviour did not amount to speculation. The administrative penalty imposed on him was obviously unfair. The defendant appealed but the court of second instance upheld the judgment of the court of first instance, based on the same legal reasons.

The main issue in this case is whether or not the plaintiff's activity of selling national reserve grain at market prices without going through the examination and approval procedures amounts to speculation. If this is true, then the administrative penalty imposed on it would be reasonable; otherwise, it would be unfair. As the plaintiff's main intention was not to gain huge profit, which is an essential component of speculation, then the penalty for speculation was not compatible with the wrong committed by the plaintiff. It was obviously unfair to the plaintiff. The decisions were repealed by the courts. In this case, obvious unfairness is caused by the failure of the administrative organ to take into account the relevant consideration, i.e. the motivation of the plaintiff.

Chi v. Public Security Bureau in X City of Zhejiang Province[77]

11.32 In 1990, the plaintiff and Lin drove motorcycles without driving licences. Some time later, the motorbikes collided with Zhao's bicycle, but Zhao fell down on the floor. However, Zhao did not suffer any physical injury or property damage from the accident. A dispute arose among the plaintiff, Zhao and Lin. In the course of the dispute among the three people, Zhao found that Lin tried to escape and then he used a broken glass to injure the plaintiff. The plaintiff suffered a serious injury on his face. The Public Security Bureau of Zhejiang Province (the defendant) then investigated this incident and discovered that the plaintiff had driven the motorbike without a licence. The defendant then detained the plaintiff for 15 days, according to section 27 of the Regulation on Administrative Penalty for Public Security. The plaintiff challenged the decision on the grounds of obvious unfairness.

Two different opinions existed among the judges on what administrative acts amounted to obvious unfairness. The first opinion was that unfairness means the penalty exceeded the limit stipulated by law. If the administrative organ imposed the penalty by exercising its discretionary power within the limits of the law, there would be no unfairness though the penalty was extremely heavy. The second opinion was that obvious unfairness meant the penalty was unproportionate to the offence which the plaintiff had committed, even though the penalty was imposed within the limit of the relevant provisions in the law. The court adopted the later view and varied the defendant's decision. The court held that although the plaintiff did not have a driving licence when he drove the motorbike, he did not cause any serious accident. Therefore, the 15-day detention was unfair to the plaintiff.

This is a case where serious sanction is imposed upon minor offence. It was held to be obviously unfair because the penalty was disproportionate to the offence committed.

Sha v. Public Security Bureau in X City of Jiangsu Province[78]

11.33 On January 12, 1991, the plaintiff was cleaning his tractor in the playground of a primary school in the town. The plaintiff saw a child was playing near his tractor. He feared that accident might occur and injure the child. He threatened the child who then left. The child was scared by the plaintiff and complained to his friends, Wei and Qin. Wei then said some impolite words to the plaintiff. The plaintiff was angered and chased Wei in order to catch him but the plaintiff failed to catch Wei. Then the plaintiff tried to catch Qin. When the plaintiff succeeded, he put his hands against the mouth of Qin. However, the plaintiff's act, because of his force, caused one of Qin's teeth to break and made one other unstable. Qin's mouth was bleeding and the blood ran out from his nose. Qin was hospitalized and the doctor found that the unstable tooth was normal for a child. The plaintiff agreed to compensate but the public security officers said the plaintiff should compensate RMB3,000 and also detained the plaintiff's tractor for 10 days.

In the administrative reconsideration, the Public Security Bureau of Jiangsu (the defendant) held that the plaintiff should be liable for both the damage and the instability of the tooth. However, the court held that the defendant had erroneously identified the facts and concluded that the instability of the teeth was also due to the plaintiff's fault. The

JUDICIAL CONTROL OF DISCRETIONARY POWER

defendant also erroneously held that the plaintiff had injured Qin's nose. The instability of the teath was merely a natural change for a child and the nose had not actually been injured. The defendant had mistakenly held that the plaintiff should be accountable and imposed a penalty accordingly, which was obviously unfair.

In this case, the defendant misidentified the material facts, and because of that, the defendant had imposed a heavier penalty on the plaintiff.

Lin v. X Branch of Shanghai Municipal Public Security Bureau[79]

11.34 The plaintiff and Chen were colleagues and formerly worked at the counter of soya bean products stall in the market. They were later moved to the vegetable counter. The plaintiff was not satisfied with the manager's decision and her bonus was deducted for her failure to obey the decision. One day, the plaintiff used a bamboo to hit the manager for revenge and the plaintiff also procured Chen to participate. It attracted a crowed of spectators to watch and look at what was happening, causing chaos.

The Public Security Bureau under the defendant penalized the plaintiff, according to section 19(1) of the Regulation on the Administrative Penalty for Public Security to detain the plaintiff for 10 days. The plaintiff applied for administrative reconsideration, but the defendant upheld the bureau's decision on the grounds that the plaintiff had assaulted the manager and she had caused an interference of public order.

The plaintiff then brought the case to court. The court held that the plaintiff had actually assaulted the manager and caused chaos in the market. However, the offence was not serious because the manager did not suffer from any serious physical injury and therefore the 10 day detention was unfair to the plaintiff because of its incompatibility with the plaintiff's offence.

This is quite similar to above cases as again, it is a serious penalty for a minor offence.

Inconsistency

Si Keiwei v. Hongkou Branch of Shanghai Municipal Public Security Bureau[80]

11.35 On June 21, 1991, the plaintiff had a dispute with a third party, Liao, on the matter of his transportation subsidy as to whether or not he was paid two months extra. Liao wanted the plaintiff to go to see the person in charge but the plaintiff refused. In the course of the dispute, Liao slapped the plaintiff, then the plaintiff kicked Liao, who suffered minor physical injury.

238

The defendant detained the plaintiff for 10 days, according to section 22 of the Regulation on Administrative Penalty for Public Security, which provides that detention of no more than 15 days, or a fine of no more than RMB200 or a warning may be imposed on any person assaulting the other person and causing the other person minor injury. The plaintiff claimed that he was provoked by Liao's words and only kicked Liao in self defence. The penalty imposed on him was too heavy and obviously unfair. After administrative reconsideration, the sanction was sustained by the Shanghai Municipal Public Security Bureau. The plaintiff then brought a lawsuit to the court.

The court of first instance held that both the plaintiff and Liao had misbehaved in the course of the dispute. The plaintiff should not be held to be solely accountable for Liao's injury because Liao insulted the plaintiff publicly and should also be subject to administrative penalty. But the defendant did not consider the whole process of the matter and the liabilities of both the plaintiff and Liao. Instead it only educated Liao through criticism but imposed the penalty of 10-day detention upon the plaintiff which was obviously unfair and should be amended accordingly in accordance with section 54(4) of the ALL. The court of second instance held that even the defendant had applied section 22(1) of the regulation correctly, however, it had failed to consider the liabilities of both parties to this incident. The penalty was obviously unfair according to section 54(4) of the ALL. Therefore the judgment of the court of first instance should be sustained.

In this case, unequal treatment by the administrative organ towards the two parties was held to be obviously unfair to one of the parties.

Liu Xuping v. The Urban and Rural Construction Committee in YiWu City[81]

11.36 The plaintiff applied to build the fourth floor of his house but the application was rejected by the Urban and Rural Construction Committee (the defendant). However, the plaintiff still built the fourth floor and the wall surrounding his house. The plaintiff's two neighbours also built the fourth floor at the same time without approval.

The defendant gave a notice to the plaintiff which stated that the plaintiff had illegally built the fourth floor, which violated section 32 of the Urban Planning Law of the PRC, and the walls of the fourth floor would be demolished unless the plaintiff paid RMB1,000. Subsequently, the defendant imposed a fine on the plaintiff for non-compliance with the procedure. A fine was also imposed on the plaintiff for the building of a fourth floor without a permit. The plaintiff claimed that the defendant had acted unfairly because other people nearby who violated the same law were ordered to pay a fine of a lesser amount. The defendant claimed that it had acted in accordance with section 32 of the City Planning Law.

The court of first instance held that the plaintiff should be punished under the City Planning Law for building without a permit, and the concrete administrative act of the defendant, *i.e.* the imposition of fines, was sustained by the court. However, the plaintiff appealed and the court of second instance held that although the plaintiff had violated the law, however, the penalty on him was obviously unfair because he was penalized much heavier than the others who also violated the same section. It was because the plaintiff was ordered to pay RMB75 as fine for each square metre he had built, but the others only needed to pay RMB10 as fine for each square metre. The penalties they received were not the same, although their misconducts were the same.

This case again falls into the first category, but it is about the imposition of different sanctions for the same kind of activities.

Luo v. Public Security Bureau in X City of Zhejiang Province[82]

11.37 In 1985, the plaintiff was approved to build three houses on a plot of land of 98.6 square metres in area. The locations and directions of the houses were ascertained and the foundations were built. However, the construction work was suspended for economic reasons. The third party was also permitted to build two houses in the next year. However, the third party varied the direction of the house. He also extended the area of the houses and built three houses without the approval of the relevant governmental department. The plaintiff was of the opinion that the third party's act would damage the fengsui (fortune) of the whole village and the distance between the house of the plaintiff and the third party's house was only about 1 metre. It caused an inconvenience to the villagers because the path was too narrow. The plaintiff tried to stop the third party and finally quarrelled with him. Later, the plaintiff resumed the construction work on his houses. The third party led his relatives to destroy some parts of the structure of the plaintiff's house because the plaintiff's house would obstruct the light supply of the third party's houses.

The officers in the village went to mediate between the plaintiff and the third party and an agreement was reached. Under the agreement, the third party should restore the direction of the house to the permitted one and compensate the plaintiff RMB150 for the damage. The third party was also ordered to build a new path because of his obstruction of the path. However, the third party had not actually restored the direction. When the plaintiff realized that, he went with some others to the third party's house and destroyed part of a wall of the defendant's house. The plaintiff's son threatened to do it again if the third party continued the work. The defendant detained the plaintiff for seven days for intentional damage of property belonged to other.

The court held that the penalty was obviously unfair because the third party committed the similar offence two years ago, but he was only ordered to compensate the plaintiff for the damage. However, the plaintiff was detained for seven days. The acts of the plaintiff and the third party were the same, but the punishments were not the same.

This case is about inconsistency, *i.e.* different sanctions for similar situations.

Lin v. Public Security Bureau in X County in Zhejiang[83]

The Zhou couple, are the neighbours of the plaintiff who was a taxi driver. He caused minor damage to the plaintiff's taxi when Zhou reversed his car negligently. Then the plaintiff had a serious argument with Zhou and his wife and they had a fight. Zhou's wife suffered an injury because the plaintiff slapped her and they were finally mediated by the neighbours. Subsequently, Zhou and two other persons entered the plaintiff's house with choppers. They assaulted the plaintiff and her husband. They entered the plaintiff's house again the next morning and damaged some property in the plaintiff's house. Subsequently, Zhou and the other persons entered the house of the plaintiff's sister and caused some damage to her property in the house.

11.38

The Public Security Bureau of Zhejiang Province (the defendant) made a decision according to sections 22 and 23 of the Regulation on the Administrative Penalty for Public Security to detain the plaintiff for 10 days for assault. Zhou was also detained for 10 days for damaging private property but the two other people were only given a warning. The plaintiff brought the case for reconsideration. The reconsideration organ sustained the decision. The plaintiff then brought the case to court.

The court held that the act of Zhou and the two others was serious and had serious consequences. The 10-day detention and warning imposed on the three people was obviously unfair. The court finally changed the penalty on Zhou to 15 days detention and imposed a fine of RMB200 on each of the other two persons.

Double Penalties

Huaxia Animal Medicine Co v. Agricultural and Fishery Burean[84]

This is a double sanctions case. The plaintiff purchased 800,000 units of a kind of animal medicine from another province. But the medicine lacked a certificate of quality. When the plaintiff sold the medicine, the Agricultural and Fishery Bureau (the defendant) found that the medicine was suspicious and conducted a test on it. The defendant found that the medicine was not up to standard. It then penalized the plaintiff according to sections 29(1) and 41 of the Regulation on the Control of Animal Medicine. The unsold medicine was seized by the

11.39

defendant and the defendant also imposed on the plaintiff a fine of RMB1,100. Moreover, a fine of RMB350 was also imposed on the manager of the plaintiff. The court held that the plaintiff had actually violated the law and should be penalized. However, the court held that it was obviously unfair for the plaintiff to pay a fine of RMB1,100 subsequent to the seizure. The plaintiff should not receive double punishment.

Failure to Provide Information

Wong v. Land Administration Bureau and Urban Construction Bureau in Shi Zu Shan City of Ningxia Autonomous Region

11.40   The plaintiff, Wong, had built premises which exceeded the approved area and he was ordered to apply for a supplemental approval, otherwise the premises would be demolished and the land would be resumed to the local government. The first defendant was later instructed by the court to investigate the matter again. Subsequently, the two defendants made a decision under the Land Administration Law and ordered the plaintiff to demolish the newly built toilet and pay a fine of RMB500. The court of first instance held that section 59 of the General Principles of Civil Law should be applied and ordered the plaintiff to demolish the premises built on the unlawfully occupied area. The defendants appealed and the court held that the administrative penalty was unfair because the defendants had not performed their duties to inform the plaintiff to comply with the procedure, therefore the mistake was contributory. The plaintiff should not solely bear the liability. Therefore, the penalty should be amended.

In this case, failure to inform the plaintiff of the necessary procedures which have been relied on by the administrative organ in undertaking the concrete administrative acts is held to be unfair to the plaintiff.

Failure or Delay in the Performance of Statutory Duty

11.41   The third grounds for legal control of discretionary power are the failure or delay in the performance of statutory power, which is stated in section 54(3) of the ALL. This ground is concerned with inaction of the relevant administrative organs. There is not much academic literature on this subject. Even in Professor Luo's book on judicial review, judicial review of administrative inaction was only mentioned briefly under other grounds while each of the other six grounds of judicial review is discussed in a separate chapter.[86] This is rather straightforward and simple in the sense that it is only related to the time when the concrete administrative act should be undertaken and nothing else.

But it is at least equally important as any other grounds because failure or delay in the performance of statutory duty may also infringe upon the legitimate rights of those under administration. Many legislation does not stipulate the exact time limit for the performance of statutory duties by administrative organs. They are granted discretion to determine when to undertake the concrete administrative act. If an administrative organ intentionally delays or fails to start the performance for inappropriate purpose, it will amount to the unlawful exercise of discretionary power.[87] That is against the principle of reasonableness. Such an exercise of discretion will not only affect the efficiency of administration, but also cause damage to those under administration.

Different opinions exist among Chinese scholars with regard to the forms of inappropriate or illegal exercise of discretionary power. Whether or not failure or delay in the performance of statutory power is one of the forms is arguable.[88] However, the scope of inaction which is subject to judicial review is closely related to the scope of judicial review, *i.e.* the categories of concrete administrative acts which are subject to judicial review. Most scholars generally agree that four kinds of administrative inactions are subject to judicial review. The first is the failure or delay in the grant of various licences or permits when the applicants have met the legal conditions; the second is that the failure or delay by the administrative organs in performing their statutory duties to protect personal and proprietary rights of the applicants; and the third is the failure or delay in providing subsidies. The fourth one is the failure or delay in performing any other statutory duties.[89]

There are several conditions which need to be satisfied in order to rely on these grounds to challenge the administrative organ concerned. The first is that the administrative organ must owe a statutory duty towards the applicant, either to issue a licence or to provide protection or anything else. Without the existence of statutory duty, the administrative organ cannot be sued on these grounds. Secondly, the statutory time limit has been passed or a reasonable time period has passed if there is not statutory time limit. Thirdly, the administrative organ must have refused or failed to respond during the time limit. Fourthly, there do not exist any defences.[90]

The next issue to be discussed is when the calculation of a time limit should start. It has been suggested that generally it should start from the time as stated by the applicant, provided that the defendant cannot provide any evidence to rebut the time put forward by the applicant. If there is inconsistent provisions in different legislation at different levels of the legal hierarchy, then the one at a higher level should be complied with. But if there is no clear statutory provision and the legislation only provides for a reasonable period, then the judiciary has to determine what will be the reasonable time period on a case by case basis and look into the specific circumstances relating to the concrete administrative act.

JUDICIAL CONTROL OF DISCRETIONARY POWER

If failure or delay in the performance of statutory duty is caused intentionally by the administrative organ concerned, then it may be classified as an abuse of power. If there is no intention on the part of the administrative organ but failure or delay is still caused, then the applicant can still apply for judicial review based on these grounds. As discussed in the section on abuse of power, abuse of legal procedures is also treated as an abuse of power. Logically, it may be better to treat this to be limited to failure or delay caused by any other reasons than intention. That shall be the consistent with the analysis and discussion of the other grounds for juridical review in this book. However, it should be noted that the judicial practice has not been consistent and has not treated grounds for judicial review as independent of each other. In fact, in many judicial review cases, several grounds are invoked basing on the same explanation. The relevant remedy shall be a court order for specific performance within a period of time.

Delay in Performance

Chen Jianfang v. Shanghai Municipal Public Security Bureau[91]

11.42 The plaintiff's husband was a research fellow of the Chinese Agricultural Science Institute and was sent to the United States in 1989 by the institute. He did not return as required. His son also went to the United States in 1990. In 1991 the plaintiff made an application to the Shanghai Municipal Public Security Bureau (the defendant) for passport and exit permit to the United States for visiting her son. She was granted a passport and an exit permit. She then applied and was granted the visa to visit her husband. She applied to the defendant again to change the exit permit to visit her husband. The defendant decided to defer the grant of exit permit because the institute informed the defendant that the plaintiff's husband had overstayed in the United States. Two months later, the defendant refused to grant the exit permit on the grounds that the plaintiff's reason for leaving China was different from the category of her visa. 12 days later, the plaintiff obtained the visa to visit her son and re-applied for exit permit. Under relevant legislation, the defendant is supposed to make a decision within three days. But the defendant neither approved nor refused the plaintiff's application though the plaintiff had asked for several times.

The plaintiff brought the matter to court and she claimed that she had the legitimate reason to apply for exit permit according to sections 5 and 8 of the Law on Control of the Entry and Exit of Citizens (the Law). The defendant should make a decision within the stipulated time limit. The defendant contended that it wanted to make a cautious decision which led to the delay. The defendant also claimed that because of the objection of the plaintiff's husband's institute, the application was rejected.

GROUNDS FOR JUDICIAL CONTROL

The court of first instance held that section 5 of the Law stated the Public Security Bureau should make a decision within the stipulated period of time. Moreover, the reason used by the defendant was inappropriate and the defendant violated the provision of section 5 of the Law by failing to make a decision within the time limit. The court ordered the defendant to make a decision within three days under section 54(3) of the ALL. The defendant appealed and its appeal was dismissed.

This is a simple case concerning the exercise of discretionary power within a time limit. The defendant has the authority to decide whether or not to issue an exit permit to the applicant. Such discretion is restricted in two senses. One is whether or not the applicant has met the conditions for the grant of exit permit. The second is that the discretion must be exercised within the time limit, *i.e.* three days. In this case, the defendant failed to perform its statutory duty to make a decision on whether or not to issue exit permit within three days without proper justification. This clearly falls within the category of section 54(3) of the ALL and the court can order the defendant to exercise its discretion within three days.

This is a case concerning the issue of passport which falls within the licence and permit category. Here, the Public Security Bureau in Shanghai improperly delayed the issue of an exit permit to the applicant without giving her any justification. The next case is also an undue delay case and the plaintiff won the case.

Shanghai Alcohol Factory v. The People's Government of Changning District in Shanghai[92]

11.43 The predecessor of the plaintiff obtained land-use rights to a piece of land in 1957. The People's Government of Chang Ning District in Shanghai (the defendant) issued the land-use certificate to the plaintiff in 1988. However, a third party challenged the plaintiff's land-use right in 1989. The Land Administration Bureau of Chang Ning District found that there were disputes over the land-use right. The plaintiff applied to the bureau for the resolution of the dispute so that its legitimate right can be confirmed. The plaintiff required the defendant several times to make a decision on the matter in accordance with section 13(1) of the Land Administration Law. But the defendant still failed to make decision six months after the plaintiff's application, although it had held a series of meetings within this six months. During that period, the plaintiff had sent a number of letters urging the defendant to make a decision. Then the plaintiff lodged a lawsuit to the people's court.

The plaintiff claimed that it had a right to ask for a decision under section 13 of the Land Administration Law of the PRC (the Law). The defendant had conducted conciliation disregarding the unwillingness

245

of the plaintiff. The defendant claimed that there was a convention to try conciliation before making a decision. The Law had not stipulated the length of time for not making a decision would constitute a failure to perform the statutory duty and the investigation work done should be regarded as performance of its statutory duty.

The court of first instance held that it was the duty of the defendant to make a decision under section 13 of the Land Administration Land without undue delay. Failure to make a decision within six months could be objectively regarded as an inaction. Furthermore, only an actual decision would amount to performance and the mere working process could not. In this case the plaintiff was unwilling to conciliate. It is therefore reasonable for the plaintiff to bring the case for judicial review because the defendant had failed to perform its statutory duty. The court ordered the defendant to make a decision within three months after the judgment came into force. The defendant appealed but it was dismissed by the court of second instance under section 61(1) of the ALL.

Tang v. Public Security Bureau in X County[93]

11.44 The plaintiff disputed with a third party concerning their children. In the course of argument the plaintiff suffered an injury on her head caused by the third party. At that night, the plaintiff and her husband went to the police station to report this matter and asked the Public Security Bureau to investigate it. Xie, the officer of the defendant, the Public Security Bureau of that county, went to investigate on the request of the plaintiff. The next day, the defendant made a decision according to relevant procedural requirement to deal with the civil disputes. The defendant ordered the third party to apologize and compensate the plaintiff RMB40 for medical expenses. The plaintiff was not satisfied with the decision and brought a lawsuit to court for the reason of non-performance of statutory duty. The defendant refused to answer in the court on the grounds that their handling of the case did not amount to non-performance.

In this case, the defendant had investigated the matter on request of the plaintiff without undue delay and made the decision according to section 5 of the Regulation on Administrative Penalty for Public Security, which allowed the defendant to conduct mediation if the matter was not serious. Therefore, the defendant had performed its duty. There was an element of neither delay, nor non-performance.

Failure in Performance

11.45 The next two cases are about failure to undertake concrete administrative acts.

Yang Feng and 504 Other Residents v. Urban Planning Bureau in Ping Ding Shan City[94]

In July 1992, the third party to this case, one economic and technological development centre, started the construction work of a four-storey building along the river in the city. The Urban Planning Bureau (the defendant) granted the third party a construction licence without consultation with the Water Bureau, which is, under section 24(3) of the Water Law, the organ in charge of the safety management of rivers in the city. The building was completed in June 1993. When the building was still under construction, some other corporations in the city planned to build eight more buildings on the river and started construction work in June 1993 without the approval from either the Urban Planning Bureau or Water Bureau. The plaintiffs were of the opinion that the buildings would adversely affect the control and prevention of flooding of the river because the river had flooded four times before. The plaintiff applied to the defendant requesting the termination of illegal construction on the river. But the defendant failed to do so. The plaintiffs then brought the case for judicial review.

The plaintiffs claimed that due to the seriousness of the possible consequences of building on the river, the defendant should exercise its statutory duty to stop illegal construction on the river. The defendant contended that the construction project of the third party was approved by the local government and construction licence was issued in accordance with the relevant regulations. Any other construction on the river was not approved by the defendant and it had in fact issued illegal construction notice to the offenders. Therefore it did not fail to perform its statutory duty.

The court held that the Urban Planning Law of the PRC had stipulated that no construction work could be carried out without a construction licence and the Water Law of the PRC also stipulated that no building could be constructed on the river unless with the approval of the relevant department, the Water Bureau. It was because the Water Bureau was the administrative organ for the river affairs. The defendant failed to take any action against the unlawful construction on the river, knowing that they had not obtained approval from the Water Bureau. Upon application of the plaintiffs, the defendant also failed to provide a satisfactory reply to the plaintiffs. All those amount to failure to perform its statutory duty. The Water Bureau also failed to perform its statutory duty as the administrative organ in charge of river management.

It is a typical case of failure to perform statutory duty. One issue here is the standing of the plaintiffs, *i.e.* whether or not the plaintiffs were entitled to bring the case for judicial review.

JUDICIAL CONTROL OF DISCRETIONARY POWER

Zhang and Liu v. X Branch of Pubic Security Bureau in X District of X City of Guizhou Province[95]

11.46 On January 2, 1988, the plaintiffs were hit by Wang's car and Zhang was hospitalized. The defendant, the Public Security Bureau of the district in that province, investigated the incident on that day. Zhang, the first plaintiff, stayed in hospital for 93 days and her daughter, Liu, who was the second plaintiff, stayed in hospital for 134 days. The plaintiffs had spent several thousands renminbi on hospital costs. The plaintiff asked the defendant to make a decision on the incident, but the defendant failed to do so for two years.

The plaintiff then applied to the people's court on the grounds of non-performance of statutory duty by the defendant. The court held that after the investigation, although the law did not stipulate the time limit for the bureau to make a decision, the defendant failed to make a decision for two years. It was obviously an undue delay of performance of statutory duty. The defendant was ordered to make a decision within two months.

Zhang Zhongnian v. Land Administration Bureau in HeLan County[96]

11.47 In 1985, the plaintiff and five other people, including the third party, Ti, agreed to establish a brick factory. The plaintiff was solely responsible for the management of the factory. Upon the approval of the County People's Government, a land-use certificate was issued for the factory to be built on a specified plot of land. However, the plaintiff actually built the factory on another piece of farmland which belonged to a village, without the approval of the defendant. In 1989, Ti and the other partners withdrew because of disputes among the partners and the plaintiff solely carried on the business. But the agreement for the use of that piece of land was not concluded between the factory and the village until 1990.

Due to the lack of soil, the plaintiff made an agreement with Tan (a villager) to remove soil from his farmland to manufacture bricks, to which the village only agreed two years later. From 1989 to 1990, the plaintiff removed soil from Tie's farming, which caused serious damage to the land and a drain of the soil. Tie had complained to the Land Administration Bureau (the defendant) several times since 1989. The defendant only made a decision in 1991 (a delay for two years). According to section 51 of the Land Administration Law and section 49 of the Method for the Implementation of the Law in NingXia Autonomous Region, the defendant imposed upon the plaintiff a fine of RMB2,045 for the damage caused to Tie's farmland of 409 square metres and ordered the plaintiff to restore Tie's land to its original status, to compensate Tie for not being able to use the farmland for half a year (RMB564). If the plaintiff failed to pay the relevant fines within 15 days, the fines would be doubled. The plaintiff applied to the court for judicial review of the defendant's decision.

The court of first instance held that the plaintiff had actually violated the Land Administration Law (the Law) and caused damage to the farm land. It was correct for the defendant to apply the Law and the method to penalize the plaintiff. However, there was lack of sufficient evidence for the defendant to hold that Tie's damaged land was 409 square metres and evidence showed that the land was bigger. Moreover, the court held that there was no legal grounds to hold the plaintiff to be liable for the loss suffered by Tie for half a year and to double the fines for failure to pay the fines within the time limit. These last two decisions were therefore annulled accordingly and the defendant was asked to make new decisions within one day after the judgment came into effect. The court of second instance adopted the evidence as identified by the court of first instance and dismissed the defendant's appeal.

The main issue in this case is that the plaintiff brought a lawsuit to the court on the grounds that the defendant had exceeded its power (the excess of power was not disputed) to penalize the plaintiff for damaging the farmland. However, the court held that the defendant's act lacked essential evidence and was an abuse of power. But Tie, the third party, who claimed that he suffered economic loss from the damage to the farmland caused by the plaintiff, applied to the defendant to order the plaintiff to compensate Tie and restored the land to its original status. However, the defendant had failed to deal with it for two years. The court held that the defendant should make a positive decision under section 54(3).

Notes

[1] See Luo Haocai, *Zhong Guo Si Fa Shen Ca Zhi Du* (Judicial Review System in China), Peking University Press, Beijing, 1993, p. 410; also Zhang Jinfan and Li Tie, *Zhong Guo Xing Zheng Fa Shi* (The History of Chinese Administrative Law), China University of Political Science and Law Press, Beijing, the Preface, pp. 1–14.
[2] Ibid., p. 410.
[3] The leadership of Communist Party has always been there in the four Constitutions in 1954, 1975, 1978 and 1982. The 1982 Constitution was amended in 1993 with no change to the leadership of the Communist Party.
[4] Only in 1982 was it made possible for an ordinary people to bring a legal action against an administrative authority.
[5] See Luo Haocai, *Zhong Guo Si Fa Shen Ca Zhi Du* (Judicial Review System in China), Peking University Press, Beijing, 1993, pp. 410–411; also Luo Haocai, *Examination of Issues Relating to Administrative Adjudication*, Peking University Press, Beijing, 1990, pp. 51–65.
[6] See Liu Jian, *Xing Zheng Zi You Cai Liang Quan Ruo Gan Wen Ti Tan Tao*

(Discussion of Several Problems Relating to Administrative Discretionary Power) in *Collection of Legal Essays (Administrative Law)*, 1992, Vol. 2, pp. 183–187.
7 One scholar Cui Zuolan has argued in *Legal Research* that it is necessary to expand the scope of judicial review to cover abstract administrative activities; see pp. 140–44, Vol. 18, No.1.
8 See Zhang Qiuhe, p. 135.
9 See Liu Jian, *Xing Zheng Zi You Cai Liang Quan Ruo Gan Wen Ti Tan Tao* (Discussion of Several Problems Relating to Administrative Discretionary Power) in *Collection of Legal Essays (Administrative Law)*, 1992, Vol. 2, pp. 183–187; Gao Jiawei, *Ye Tan Xing Zheng Zi You Cai Liang Quan* (Re-examination of Administrative Discretionary Power) in *Collection of Legal Essays (Administrative Law)*, 1992, Vol. 2, p. 194; Jiang Mingan, *Lun Zi You Cai Liang Quan Ji Qi Fa Lu Kong Zhi* (Examination of Discretionary Power and Its Legal Control) in *Collection of Legal Essays (Administrative Law)*, 1993, Vol. 3, pp. 116–122; Zhang Shufang and others, *Xing Zheng Zi You Cai Liang Quan Qian Tan* (A Brief Examination of Administrative Discretionary Power) in *Collection of Legal Essays (Administrative Law)*, 1992, Vol. 2, pp. 191–193.
10 *Ibid.*
11 See Zhu Xingli, *Faxueyanjiu* (China Legal Science), Vol. 3, No. 92, 1994, pp. 30–35; and Fu Guoyun, *Jurists*, Vol. 4, 1994, pp. 56–60.
12 See Hua Yang, *Guang Yu Si Fa Jian Du Kong Zhi Xing Zheng Zi You Cai Liang Quan De Si Kao* (Examination of Judicial Control of Administrative Discretionary Power), in *Collection of Legal Essays (Administrative Law)*, 1991, Vol. 2, pp. 92–93.
13 *Ibid.*
14 See Chen Quanshen, *Lun Xing Zheng Zi You Cai Liang Quan* (Discussion of Administrative Discretionary Power) in *Collection of Legal Essays (Administrative Law)*, 1990, Vol. 2, pp. 131–134.
15 This approach used to have its followers before the enactment of the ALL. See Hua Yang pp. 92–93.
16 *Ibid.*
17 See the chapter on administrative reconsideration.
18 "Reasonableness" and "appropriateness" have the same meaning in this book and will be used interchangeably.
19 See Luo Haocai, *Xing Zheng Shu Song Shen Pan Yan Jiu* (Study of Issues Concerning Judicial Review), Peking University Press, 1990, pp. 59–65.
20 See Zhou Pengcheng (ed), *Xing Zheng Zhi Fa Yu Xing Zheng Su Song Shi Wu* (Administrative Implementation of Law and Administrative Litigation Practice) Jilin People's Press, 1992, pp. 871–876.
21 See Luo Haocai 1993, pp. 62–64.
22 The leading case which is commonly held to establish the principle of reasonableness in the Commonwealth jurisdiction is the *Associated Provincial Picture Houses Ltd v. Wednesbury Corp* [1948] 1 K.B. 223 (C.A.).
23 This view is supported by Zhu Xingli, p. 32.
24 Different scholarly opinions exist. Some think obvious unfairness is the only ground for the judiciary to control the exercise of discretionary power, which is a minority opinion. Most Chinese administrative law scholars believe that the abuse of power and obvious unfairness are the two grounds to challenge the exercise of discretionary power. This book adopts the broadest approach by arguing that failure or delay in the performance of statutory duty is also a kind of abuse of power in the negative sense in addition to the other two grounds.
25 Many articles have been published to discuss this issue. Here are some examples. Jin Weifong, *Xing Zheng Lan Yong Zhi Quan De Ji Ge Wen Ti* (Several Questions Relating to the Abuse of Administrative Power) in *Collection of Legal Essays (Administrative Law)*, 1993, Vol. 3, pp. 133–136; Li Zhujun, *Lan Yong Zhi Quan Zhou Yi* (Discussion of Abuse of Power) in *Collection of Legal Essays (Administrative Law)*, 1993, Vol. 3, p. 137; Yang Xiaojun, *Lan Yong Zi You Cai Liang Quan De Fa Lu Si Kao* (Legal Analysis of Abuse of Discretionary Power) in *Collection of Legal Essays (Administrative Law)* 1991, Vol. 2, pp. 85–88.
26 See Yang Xiaojun, *Lan Yong Zi You Cai Liang Quan De Fa Lu Si Kao* (Legal Analysis of Abuse of Discretionary Power) in *Collection of Legal Essays (Administrative Law)*

1991, Vol. 2, pp. 85–88. This approach has been generally accepted by most Chinese Scholars.
[27] *Ibid.*
[28] See Yang Xiaojun, p. 87.
[29] See Luo Haocai 1993, p. 406.
[30] Quan She, p. 182.
[31] See Luo Haocai 1993, pp. 406–07 and pp. 414–15; also Sheyi, p. 182.
[32] See Quan She, p. 182.
[33] See Zhang Shangzhu, pp. 534–35; also Luo Haocai 1993, *Judicial Review*, pp. 406–07.
[34] *Ibid.*
[35] See Luo, p. 415.
[36] See Zhu Xingli, *FaXue Yan Jiu* Vol. 3, p. 32, 1994.
[37] That is possibly why Professor Zhu Xingli suggests that it is important to study the legislative intention in order to understand the meaning of abuse of power.
[38] The author also mentioned a fourth element of an abuse of power as a general concept, covering all administrative activities through the exercise of discretionary power which are in violation of the principle of reasonableness. This element raises nothing new from the third element mentioned above. Therefore, I do not think it should be a separate element or characteristics.
[39] See Luo Haocai 1993, pp. 407–08; Ma Yuan, pp. 193–94; Sheyi, p. 182.
[40] See Luo Haocai 1993, pp. 408–09; Ma Yuan, pp. 194–95.
[41] See Ma Yuan, p. 195.
[42] See Luo Haocai, 1993, pp. 409–10.
[43] See Yang Xiaojun, pp. 85–88.
[44] See *1993 China Law Report*, pp. 1206–10.
[45] See Jiang Mingan, *Case Analysis on Administrative Litigation Law*, China Democracy and Legal System Press, Beijing 1994, pp. 237–42.
[46] *Ibid.*, p. 243–46.
[47] See above, n. 45, p. 246.
[48] See above, n. 45, pp. 256–59.
[49] Jiang Mingan et al., *Analysis on Administrative Cases*, pp. 10–12.
[50] See *1992 China Law Report*, pp. 1177–80.
[51] See above, n. 45, p. 253.
[52] See *1994 China Law Report*, pp. 1407–10.
[53] See above, n. 45, pp. 247–50.
[54] See above, n. 45, pp. 250–53.
[55] See Jiang Mingan et al., *Analysis on Administrative Cases*, pp. 15–17.
[56] See above, n. 45, pp. 264–66.
[57] See *1994 China Law Report*, pp. 1516–20.
[58] See *1994 China Law Report*, pp. 1523–29.
[59] S. 11(1) of the ALL is not a comprehensive list and there may well be some other administrative sanctions either in existence or to be created by legislation. It is generally accepted that s. 54(4) will apply to any administrative sanctions.
[60] See Quan She, p. 185.
[61] See Luo Haocai 1993, p. 424.
[62] See Hua Yang, pp. 92–93.
[63] See Luo Haocai 1993, p. 436.
[64] See also Yuan Shuhong and Sha Qizhi, *Zi You Cai Liang Yu Si Fa Sheng Cha He Li Kong Jian De Jie Ding* (The Reasonable Demarcation between Discretion and Judicial Review, in *Collection of Legal Essays (Administrative Law)*, 1990, Vol. 2, pp. 144–149.
[65] See Luo, pp. 416–17.
[66] This argument is supported by Professor Luo, p. 417.
[67] See Luo Haocai 1993, pp. 424–25.
[68] For detailed discussion of the types of obvious unfairness, refer to Luo Haocai 1993, pp. 429–30; Quen She, p. 185.
[69] See Luo Haocai 1993, pp. 429–430; also Quan She, p. 185.
[70] See Luo Haocai 1993, pp. 430–33.
[71] See Yuan, p. 148.
[72] See Liu Jian, p. 166.

[73] See *1992 China Law Report*, pp. 1156–61.
[74] See *1994 China Law Report*, pp. 1400–03.
[75] See Quan She, pp. 192–93.
[76] See *1992 China Law Report*, pp. 1258–65.
[77] See above n. 45, pp. 335–37.
[78] See above n. 45, pp. 343–46.
[79] See above n. 45, pp. 346–49.
[80] See *1993 China Law Report*, pp. 1147–51.
[81] *Ibid*, pp. 1478–82.
[82] See above n. 45, pp. 341–42.
[83] See above n. 45, pp. 350–52.
[84] See above n. 45, p. 197.
[85] See above n. 49, pp. 236–38.
[86] See Luo Haocai 1993, pp. 168–186.
[87] See Huang Yang, p. 93.
[88] Evaluation and Summary of Research on Administrative Law, in Legal Research, Vol. 1, 1995, pp. 13–17, at p. 16.
[89] See Quan She, p. 184; Cui Zhenjun, "Preliminary Study of Administrative Inaction Cases", pp. 81–85; Lu Yanming, "A Study of Several Issues relating to Administrative Inaction Cases", in *Collection of Legal Essays*, 1992, Vol. 2, pp. 120–122.
[90] *Ibid*.
[91] See *1993 China Law Report*, pp. 1131–35.
[92] See *1993 China Law Report*, pp. 1183–87.
[93] See above n. 45, pp. 321–25.
[94] See *1994 China Law Report*, pp. 1490–92.
[95] See above n. 45, pp. 325–27.
[96] See *1992 China Law Report*, pp. 1199–203.

CHAPTER TWELVE
APPLICABLE LEGISLATION IN JUDICIAL REVIEW[1]

Introduction

In adjudicating administrative law cases, the people's courts shall review concrete administrative acts undertaken by administrative organs and decide whether or not the acts concerned are lawful. They will examine whether or not the administrative organs have complied with both substantive and procedural legislation in undertaking the concrete administrative acts. Those legislation used as criteria by the people's courts in determining the legality of concrete administrative acts is called applicable legislation.[2]   12.01

In China, there are different kinds of legislation with different legal effects, including national laws, administrative regulations, local regulations, departmental regulations and rules, and other normative rules and documents.[3] There are several important issues relating to applicable legislation, which need to be addressed. They include the variety of applicable legislation, the legal effects of different kinds of applicable legislation, the conflict between different applicable legislation, and their handling by the judiciary in the actual adjudication of judicial review cases.

Reasons for the Variety of Applicable Legislation

The variety of applicable legislation has been mentioned in sections 52 and 53 of the ALL. In fact the ALL has incorporated all types of legislation which may be enacted by the authorized bodies as provided under the Constitution and the Organic Law for People's Congresses at Different Levels. In theory, it is reasonable to include all kinds of   12.02

legislation as applicable legislation to be used as criteria by the people's courts in adjudication for the following reasons. Firstly, it is required by the fundamental principle of rule of law. Administrative organs, in undertaking concrete administrative acts, have to comply with relevant legislation. As administrative disputes arise from the exercise of executive power by administrative organs closely related to different kinds of administrative activities, such as food hygiene, medicine management, environmental protection, finance and taxation, trade mark and patent, calculation and statistics, and traffic and transportation, Customs and foreign exchange, mineral resources, labour disputes, construction, post and telecommunication, public security, and so on.[4] Unlike Chinese civil law and criminal law which have codes, there does not exist a unitary administrative code in China. Administrative functions are governed and regulated by different legislation. They may be national legislation, administrative regulations or departmental regulations or rules. If no other legislation, apart from national laws, are adopted as applicable legislation, then many administrative organs may not have any legal provisions in national laws to rely on in exercising administrative power to undertake various administrative activities. Therefore, the uniqueness and complexity of administrative cases require that all kinds of legislation be regarded as applicable legislation.

Secondly, with the progression of economic development, executive power of modern government has expanded gradually. Governmental organs play a very important role in various kinds of activities. In the case of China, it is at present in a transitional period, the functions performed by various administrative organs are also changing. It is not surprising that the national laws lag behind the economic development. On the other hand, it is also unrealistic for the national legislature to enact detailed legislation in every aspect. Therefore, while the conditions are not ready for the enactment of national legislation, it is common practice for the government to promulgate relevant administrative regulations or rules to meet the needs of social and economic development. Based upon China's present situation and possible future development, it is reasonable to endorse administrative regulations, departmental regulations and rules as applicable legislation in judicial review.[5]

The reason suggested to justify the adoption of local regulations and rules as applicable law in judicial review is the relationship between the power organ (people's congress) and people's courts. According to the provisions of Chinese Constitution, local people's congresses have the authority to promulgate local regulations which either provide details or supplement national legislation according to the specific situation or practical need of the locality. Those local regulations will only be applicable in the specific locality. The people's courts in the locality in handling administrative law cases should rely on those regulations as applicable law.

Basing on similar reasons, other normative documents issued by administrative organs should also be regarded by the judiciary as applicable legislation in the adjudication of judicial review cases.[6]

Variety of Applicable Legislation

The Constitution and Other National Laws

The Constitution, as the fundamental law of a country, is the highest law and represents and reflects the fundamental interests and will of the people in the country. Its status is higher than any other legislation. As the Constitution in China has only provided for principles on various aspects of legal structure in the country, its provisions need to be incorporated into specific legislation before they can be applied or complied with. That is to say, the Constitution cannot be invoked directly by the people's courts in the adjudication of judicial review cases.[7] In the case of *Zhang Xizheng v. Land Administration Bureau*, the two plaintiffs had a transaction of houses on a piece of land, and the defendant applied, in making its decision, the Constitution. It was held to be the wrongful application of law.[8] However, all national laws and regulations are promulgated upon relevant constitutional provisions and they are therefore the extension of the abstract constitutional principles. In that sense, it is fair to say that judicial review is an indirect review of whether or not a concrete administrative act is in accordance with constitutional provisions.

12.03

In China, the review of unconstitutionality is the task of the Standing Committee of the National People's Congress. Judicial review is much more restricted. The judiciary can only review the legality of concrete administrative acts undertaken by the executive, not even the legality of subsidiary legislation.[9] That is quite different from the judicial practice in the United Kingdom and Hong Kong where judicial review of subsidiary legislation is still possible.[10]

Other national laws refer to those normative legal documents passed by the National People's Congress and its Standing Committee. They include both substantive and procedural laws. Substantive applicable laws refer to those relied on by the people's courts in determining whether or not the substance of concrete administrative acts is lawful. Whereas procedural applicable laws refer to the laws relied on by the people's courts in determining whether or not the administrative organ has breached procedural legal requirements in undertaking concrete administrative acts.[11]

Administrative Regulations

12.04 Administrative regulations are those normative legal documents promulgated by the supreme national executive organ, *i.e.* State Council. Section 85 of China's Constitution provides that the State Council is the executive body of the highest organ of state power; it is the highest organ of state administration. It is responsible and reports its work to the National People's Congress or its Standing Committee.[12] The State Council enjoys the power to adopt administrative measures, enact administrative rules and regulations and issue decisions and orders in accordance with the Constitution and the laws (section 89(1)). As the legal status of the State Council is only lower than the National People's Congress, the status of its regulations and rules is also only lower than national laws. Though its regulations and rules cannot contradict the Constitution and other national laws, they have a general binding effect upon all state organs, social organizations and citizens. They may create new rights and obligations which are not provided for by the primary legislation, *i.e.* laws. They are classified as subsidiary legislation. On the one hand, they can be relied upon by the judiciary in judicial review. On the other hand, they are subject to the supervision and control by the legislature.

Sometimes the State Council, together with the Central Committee of the Communist Party, issue some normative legal documents, *e.g.* the Notice from the Central Committee of the Communist Party and the State Council upon the Establishment of Township Government and the Separation of Political and Administrative Function.[13] Those documents are both the Communist Party's policies and the state's administrative regulations and enjoy the same legal effect as any other administrative regulations.[14]

Local Regulations

12.05 Local regulations are those normative legal documents made by the people's congresses or their standing committees at the level of province, autonomous region and municipality directly under the control of central government, or at the level of relevant big cities authorized by the relevant province, autonomous region or municipality under direct control and then approved by the latter. As local regulations shall provide detailed provisions to the relevant legal norms as stated in national laws and regulations, they shall have a general binding effect upon the state organs, social organizations and citizens within that specified administrative region. Under section 53 of the ALL, local regulations can also be used by the people's courts directly as applicable legislation in reviewing the legality of concrete administrative acts.

Autonomous Regulations of Ethnic Autonomous Regions

They refer to various normative legal documents promulgated by the people's congresses in those ethnic autonomous regions. According to the relevant provisions of the Constitution and the Law on Ethnic Regional Autonomy, the people's congress in each ethnic autonomous region is granted the power to enact autonomous and separate regulations according to the characteristics of its locality.[15] Those autonomous and separate regulations will come into force after its approval by the people's congress at the next level above. They are only applicable in the autonomous region where they are enacted and they must be enacted according to the proper authorization and legal procedure and must not contradict the Constitution, national laws and administrative regulations. They shall also be applicable law relied upon by the people's courts in reviewing the legality of concrete administrative acts.

12.06

Regulations Issued by Ministries or Local People's Government

There are thousands of normative legal documents formulated and announced each year by ministries or commissions under the State Council in accordance with laws and administrative rules and regulations, decisions or orders of the State Council, by the people's governments of provinces and autonomous regions and municipalities directly under the central government, of the cities where the people's governments of provinces and autonomous regions are located, and of the larger cities approved as such by the State Council.[16] They constitute an important component of China's legislation and are a direct extension and detailization of laws and administrative regulations. There are four categories. The first are those enacted by various ministries and commissions under the State Council according to section 90 of the Constitution. The second category are local regulations including those enacted by local people's governments according to section 51 of the 1986 Organic Law of Local People's Congresses and People's Governments of the People's Republic of China. The third category includes those regulations enacted by the three special economic zones which have been authorized by the National People's Congress.[17] The fourth includes those regulations enacted by the people's governments of relatively large cities with the approval of the State Council.

12.07

It should be noted that the making of regulations must be properly authorized by national laws or administrative regulations, orders or decisions issued by the State Council. The essence here is the authorization. Without it, any documents issued by the same organs cannot be classified as regulations. Instead, they should be addressed as normative documents. They also fill in the gaps left by incomprehensive national legislation and are therefore supplementary to national laws and administrative regulations. They are generally followed by administrative organs in undertaking concrete administrative acts.[18]

A dilemma exists. On the one hand, if those regulations are completely ignored and not used by the people's courts as applicable legislation in judicial review, then in many situations no criteria can be used in evaluating whether or not a concrete administrative act is lawful. On the other hand, if all those regulations will be adopted as applicable legislation, chaos may arise because of the fact that many regulations are contradictory to one another. It is because there does not exist a uniform supervisory legal system to regulate the enactment of regulations and to ensure the consistency among various regulations. Moreover, the people's courts do not have the authority to examine the legality of regulations. Nevertheless, the ALL does not stipulate those normative documents to be applicable legislation.[19]

Normative Document

12.08 Normative documents refer to those documents issued by administrative organs, according to national laws, administrative regulations and departmental regulations, or according to their own statutory authorities, to achieve administrative objectives by taking into account practical circumstances of their region or department. They are general provisions targeting at persons or matters in general. Their status is lower than national laws, administrative regulations, and departmental regulations. Normative documents are applicable within the jurisdiction of the administrative organs which issue them. The rights and obligations provided for under normative documents should be within the scope of national laws, administrative regulations, and regulations. If this is true, normative documents should be complied with by administrative organs in undertaking concrete administrative acts. Otherwise, the relevant concrete administrative acts should be repealed.

Normative documents cannot be directly relied on as applicable legislation by the people's courts in the hearing of judicial review cases though many concrete administrative acts are undertaken according to normative documents. In reviewing concrete administrative acts, the judiciary cannot avoid the issue of illegality of normative documents, especially when the normative documents concerned are the sole justifications for the decision. As normative documents are abstract administrative acts in nature, the judiciary cannot, according to section 12 of the ALL, declare them either valid or invalid. There are two possible solutions for the judiciary, one is to avoid mentioning the normative documents in judgments; the other is not to treat normative documents as applicable legislation in judicial review but still discuss the legality of the normative documents. If the judiciary believes that the normative documents are unlawful, it can, some scholars suggest, express its views on the inconsistency between normative documents and legislation in the reasoning though it cannot declare them as unlawful. On the other hand, neither can the judiciary directly declare normative documents valid. Again the judiciary can only express its views about the consistency between normative documents and legislation in reasoning. It seems that Chinese judiciary is placed in a very awkward position as far as normative documents are concerned. One possible solution is to grant the judiciary the authority to review the legality of normative documents.

Legal Effect of Various Applicable Legislation

Though the ALL has stipulated that national laws, administrative regulations, local regulations, autonomous regulations, and regulations issued by Ministries or local people's governments, shall be applicable legislation by the people's courts in judicial review,[20] their legal effects are different in judicial review. Section 52 of the ALL provides that national laws and administrative regulations are absolutely binding upon administrative organs. That is to say, so long as there are clear provisions either in national legislation or in administrative regulations, the judiciary has to follow them. 12.09

When there are no national laws or administrative regulations available, then other applicable legislation may be invoked. Different views exist with regard to the legal effect of other applicable legislation. Section 53 of the ALL provides:

> The people's courts shall take, as references, the rules and regulations enacted, promulgated pursuant to the laws and administrative regulations, decisions, orders of the State Council by the various Ministries and Commissions of the State Council, and rules and regulations enacted and promulgated pursuant to the laws and administrative regulations of the State Council by the various provinces, autonomous regions, cities directly under the Central People's Government and cities where the people's governments of the province or autonomous region located in and people's governments of other larger cities which approved by the State Council.

The term "take as reference" has been subject to different interpretation. Professor Luo has summarized them into three different views.[21]

One view holds that "take as reference" means that the courts shall apply other applicable legislation as any review of the other applicable legislation by the people's courts shall contradict section 12(2), which provides that no abstract administrative acts shall be reviewable. The second view maintains that the term does not mean direct application. Instead, the people's courts should only take into account the spirit of regulations, but not the regulations themselves because the ALL does not provide that they may be applicable legislation and the quality of regulations is not that good. The third view takes the middle road by suggesting that the term actually means conditional application of regulation in judicial review. That is to say that the people's courts shall examine regulations first to see whether they are applicable.[22] It is a sort of selective application which gives the people's courts the discretion in this aspect. The third approach is supported by the judiciary. As one interpretation provided by the judges is that in adjudicating cases, the people's courts shall adopt those lawful (or legal) regulations (either departmental or local) as criteria or applicable legislation in reviewing the legality of any concrete administrative acts. As to those unlawful regulations, the people's courts shall not recognize their legal effects. In other words, they shall not apply them as applicable legislation in judicial review.[23] A related question is what will be regarded as a lawful regulation.

12.10 A lawful regulation must meet three conditions.[24] Firstly, the enacting authority must exercise its power in making regulation *intra vires*. Any regulations made *ultra vires* shall be unlawful. Secondly, proper legal procedures must be followed in the promulgation of any regulations. Thirdly, the substance of any regulations must not contradict the Constitution, national laws or administrative regulations. If one of the three conditions is not satisfied, the regulation made shall be regarded as unlawful and shall not be applied by people's courts in handling judicial review cases.[25]

It is therefore fair to say that the people's courts possess great discretion in deciding whether or not to make reference to any regulations (departmental or local). Different opinions exist with regard to whether or not it is appropriate to allow the people's courts to make reference to any regulations and to grant them the discretion to make the decision.[26] The reason for the existence of different opinions really comes down to one question, that is whether or not section 53 is contradictory to section 12(2) which provides that administrative rules and regulations, regulations, or decisions and orders with general binding force formulated and announced by administrative organs (abstract administrative acts) are not subject to judicial review.

No matter what the argument is, it is undeniable that the people's courts do possess the power to review the legality of departmental and local regulations under section 53, though that power is quite limited.

Firstly, only when a regulation is related to the determination of legality of a concrete administrative act can the people's court examine the legality of that regulation. No lawsuit can be brought directly to challenge the legality of any abstract administrative acts, including the legality of regulations directly. Secondly, even though the people's court determines that the regulation concerned is unlawful, it cannot announce that the regulation concerned is void and therefore repeal it. Instead, the people's court can only refuse to adopt that regulation as applicable legislation. Thirdly, the people's court cannot examine the reasonableness of the regulation concerned.[27]

Another issue is whether or not those normative documents issued by organs under direct control of State Council should also be taken as reference by the people's courts in handling judicial review cases. Those organs include State Administration Bureau for Industry and Commerce, State Commodity Inspection Bureau, General Customs and 13 other organs. Those organs are more directly related to business operation. Again, different opinions exist.[28] One approach believes that normative documents issued by those organs have already become part of norms and many of those organs also have compulsory enforcement instruments. If they may not be taken as reference, judicial review of cases concerning those organs will run into trouble.

A counter view is that those 16 organs are not within section 90 of the Constitution and therefore are not qualified to enact regulations. And section 53 of the ALL has also made it clear what kinds of organs may enact regulations. Furthermore, section 70 of the Opinions on the ALL has also strengthened the position that only those organs mentioned in section 53 of the ALL will have the authority to pass regulations.[29] However, it does not mean that those normative documents from those organs may not be referred to by the people's courts in judicial review at all. If the people's courts, after reviewing those normative documents, have not found any inconsistency between those normative documents and other applicable legislation, then they may be confirmed by the people's courts because they are lawful normative documents.

Conflict between Legislation

Conflict between Laws and Other Legislation

If any conflicts arise between national laws and other kinds of legislation, national legislation shall prevail and be complied with because national laws are higher than other kinds of legislation in the hierarchy of legislation.

12.11

Conflict between Regulations and Rules

For two regulations to conflict with each other, four conditions need to be satisfied. The first is that the regulations governing one type of administrative acts are enacted by different administrative organs; the second is that the different regulations have different provisions on one type of administrative act; the third is that application of different regulations may lead to different results; the fourth is that all regulations are legally effective at the same time.

There are many reasons for the existence of conflict between different regulations. It has been suggested that the main reasons include different jurisdictions of those administrative organs enacting regulations, unclear allocation of administrative legislative authorities, failure to annul or revoke invalid administrative regulations, the reflection of historical, economic and social differences among different localities in the regulations, local protection, and so on.[30]

Four specific have been suggested. One is to treat administrative regulations and regulations enacted by various Ministries and Commissions equally and apply the latter instead of the former when the two are both valid. The second is confusion of the nature, status and effect of local legislation and regulations enacted by various Ministries and Commissions. In the hierarchy of legislation, local legislation is higher than regulations enacted by different Ministries and Commissions.[31] Sections 52 and 53 of the ALL has confirmed this approach by stating that local legislation needs to be followed, while regulations enacted by various ministries and commissions should only be taken as reference in judicial review. The third is the confusion of the legal effect of regulations enacted by various ministries and commissions and local people's governments. As there is no legislation in China distinguishing the legal status between the two, it may be argued that they at the same level.[32] The fourth is the confusion of the difference between regulations and other normative documents, which is restricted to those documents relating administration and passed by administrative organs without legal authority to pass regulations.[33]

The conflict could be between regulations at different level, *e.g.* those at national and local levels and those at different local levels, or between regulations from different Ministries or Commissions, or between regulations enacted by different local people's governments.[34] Different conflicts should be resolved through different methods. For the first two kinds of conflict, section 53(2) of the ALL states clearly that:

> In case a people's court considers that there is an inconsistency among the rules and regulations enacted and promulgated by the local people's governments and the Ministries and Commissions

of the State Council, or inconsistency among the rules and regulations enacted and promulgated by the Ministries and Commissions of the State Council, the Supreme People's Court shall transfer the case to the State Council and invite the State Council to interpret and make a decision on it.

The people's courts may suspend the progress of judicial review when it submits through the Supreme People's Court to the State Council for interpretation. The adjudication may resume when the interpretation is made. If the interpretation states that there actually exists no conflict between the two regulations concerned, then the people's courts may rely on section 114 of the Opinions on the ALL, which states that "The people's courts shall refer to the Civil Litigation Law for matters which have not been raised by the Administrative Litigation Law, which shall always be followed by the people's courts, in the course of administrative litigation.

There are three relevant rules in the Civil Litigation Law which may be useful in judicial review when the issue of conflict of regulations is encountered. They are the differentiation of regulated objects, differentiation of scope of management, and the differentiation of authorities.[35]

As to the conflict between regulations from different localities, no rules are suggested in the ALL or the Opinions on the ALL. Therefore, only scholarly opinions have been expressed. Three rules have been suggested. The first is about those regulations relating to local public security, economic order and so on which should be regulated by regulations enacted in that locality. The second is related to those activities of the nature of crossing different localities which should be regulated either by administrative contracts or in the way as suggested by specific legislation. The third is about regulations concerning enforcement and the regulations where enforcement will be carried out should be adopted.[36]

The Implication of Section 53(2)

It has been suggested that the judiciary in China has inchoate authority to review the legality of other applicable legislation than national laws and administrative regulations.[37] The existence of such judicial authority is a matter of fact and there are several reasons to support its existence. Firstly, the enactment of regulations is in nature the exercise of executive power which should be controlled in order to prevent its abuse or *ultra vires* activities. Secondly, the Constitution provides for the system of people's congress and that the highest authority is in

12.12

the hands of the people's congress and the supervision of legislation is in the hands of the people's congress itself. That has excluded the possibility for the people's courts to review the constitutionality of legislation. But the Constitution does not exclude the possibility for the people's courts to review the legality of abstract administrative acts. What is only excluded under the ALL from the jurisdiction of the people's courts is the authority to declare any normative documents to be invalid. The ALL does not prevent the people's courts from selecting applicable legislation when they are in conflict. Thirdly, there is practical demand to grant the people's courts the authority to review applicable legislation in the adjudication of judicial review cases. It is because there are so many regulations and normative documents and many of them are in conflict with each other. It is unrealistic for the people's congresses or their standing committees to handle such a large amount of complicated cases relating to conflict of applicable legislation. It is therefore more appropriate to leave them for the people's courts to handle in actual adjudication of specific cases.[38]

There are three basic rules for the regulation of conflict of legislation. The first rule is that new legislation will prevail over old legislation. The second rule is that legislation at a higher level will prevail over legislation at a lower level. The third rule is that special legislation prevails over general legislation.

Notes

[1] It should be noted here that the term "laws" has special meaning. It refers to those legislation enacted by the National People's Congress or its Standing Committee. In order to avoid confusion, this book will use the term of applicable legislation instead of applicable law.
[2] See Luo Haocai 1993, p. 443.
[3] One important issue is what will be classified as legislation and especially whether or not departmental regulations and other normative rules will be classified as legislation. This issue has been discussed in the section on administrative legislative acts in the administrative law theory part.
[4] This is just a list of some major administrative functions performed by administrative organs and it is not comprehensive of all the functions performed by the executive branch of the government.
[5] However, the legal effects of different kinds of legislation are different.
[6] It should be noted that the legal effect of normative documents is quite different in nature from other kinds of applicable legislation. This will be discussed in the following section.
[7] In some countries, judicial review of unconstitutionality is possible.
[8] For details of the facts of this case, refer the chapter on grounds for judicial review.
[9] Whether or not the judiciary has any authority at all to review the legality of subsidiary legislation will be discussed in the latter section of this chapter.

NOTES

10 In one case, the Constitution was relied on, which was held to be a misapplication of law.
11 A different explanation is provided by Luo Haocai which the author believes is wrong. Professor Luo suggests that procedural law refers to the legislation upon which the judiciary relies on to conduct judicial review, which is the procedural law for the judiciary to comply with. Here it is concerned with the procedural requirements for administrative organs in undertaking concrete administrative acts. See Luo Haocai 1993, p. 448.
12 See section 92, 1982 Constitution.
13 See Luo Haocai 1993, p. 449.
14 This is something of a Chinese characteristic — the mixture of party and executive.
15 Section 116 of the Constitution provides:
   The people's congresses of national autonomous areas have the power to enact regulations on the exercise of autonomy and other separate regulations in the light of the political, economic and cultural characteristics of the nationalities in the areas concerned. The regulations on the exercise of autonomy and other separate regulations of autonomous regions shall be submitted to the Standing Committee of the National People's Congress for approval before they go into effect. Those of autonomous prefectures and counties shall be submitted to the standing committees of the people's congresses of provinces or autonomous regions for approval before they go into effect, and they shall be reported to the Standing Committee of the National People's Congress for the record.
16 The authority to promulgate regulations are provided for by relevant sections in the Constitution and the 1979 Organic Law of the Local People's Congress and Local People's Governments of the People's Republic of China, and relevant Decisions passed by the Standing Committee of the National People's Congress. The 1992 Decision of the Standing Committee of the National People's Congress on Authorizing the People's Congress of Shenzhen City and Its Standing Committee and the People's Government of Shenzhen City to Formulate Regulations and Rules Respectively for Implementation in the Shenzhen Special Economic Zone is one falling within the latter category.
17 See Luo Haocai 1993, pp. 464–65.
18 See Luo Haocai, *Zhong Guo Si Fa Shen Ca Zhi Du* (Judicial Review System in China), Peking University Press, Beijing, 1993, pp. 466–469.
19 See Luo Haocai, *Zhong Guo Si Fa Shen Ca Zhi Du* (Judicial Review System in China), Peking University Press, Beijing, 1993, p. 462.
20 It has been suggested by some scholars that statutory interpretation should also be regarded as applicable legislation. In fact, different kinds of statutory interpretation have different legal effects. Legislative interpretation is actually regarded as part of national laws as they may only be provided by the Standing Committee of the National People's Congress. Judicial interpretation does not have any formal legal status in the hierarchy of legal sources according to existing legislation. Since they are provided by the Supreme People's Court, in practice they are followed by the people's courts at various levels. Statutorily authorized administrative interpretation would have similar legal effects as the authorizing statute. Other kinds of administrative interpretation and academic interpretation would not have any binding effect. See Luo, pp. 453–56.
21 See Luo Haocai 1993, pp. 461–62.
22 For more detailed discussion of the three approaches, refer to Luo Haocai 1993, pp. 461–64.
23 See Quan She, pp. 175–76.
24 For detailed discussion of this, refer to the section on administrative leglislative acts is the part on administrative law theory.
25 See Quan She, ibid; see also Luo Haocai 1993, pp. 469–73.
26 See Luo Haocai 1993, p. 462.
27 See Luo Haocai 1993, p. 463.
28 See Luo Haocai 1993, p. 467.
29 Section 70 of the Opinions on the ALL provides:
   "When the people's court, in reaching its judgment or decision, needs to refer to regulations, it shall be expressly written as, "According to Section 53 of the

Administrative Litigation Law of the PRC, reference is made to the provisions of ... regulations".
[30] See Luo Haocai 1993, pp. 473-74.
[31] Different academic views exist with regard to the legal status of local legislation and regulations enacted by various ministries and commissions. One suggests that local legislation is enacted by local people's congresses which should enjoy higher legal status than regulations enacted by administrative organs. The second view is just the contrary as regulations enacted by various ministries and commissions are applicable throughout the country whereas local regulations are only applicable in those localities concerned. See Luo Haocai 1993, p. 478.
[32] If such a situation happens, it has been suggested that the conflict should be reported to the State Council via Supreme People's Court for interpretation and should not rely solely on the ranking of the administrative organs concerned. See Luo Haocai, p. 477.
[33] See Luo Haocai 1993, pp. 476-77.
[34] See Luo Haocai 1993, p. 474.
[35] See Luo Haocai 1993, p. 475.
[36] See Luo Haocai 1993, p. 474.
[37] See Luo Haocai 1993, p. 479.
[38] See Luo Haocai 1993, pp. 481-87.

PART 4

STATE COMPENSATION LAW

CHAPTER THIRTEEN
STATE COMPENSATION

Introduction

The State Compensation Law (SCL) of the People's Republic of China (PRC) was adopted by the Standing Committee of the Eighth National People's Congress (NPC) on May 12, 1994 and came into effect on January 1, 1995.[1] It has been hailed as another step forward in the protection of the citizens' lawful rights,[2] as the law has, for the first time in PRC history, clearly defined an operative legal basis for claiming compensation from state organs, including the scope and procedure of state compensation. The adoption of the SCL has not only contributed to the establishment of a comprehensive system of state responsibility in China, but also filled in the gap in the existing legislation of administrative law.[3]   **13.01**

This chapter examines and discusses the SCL. It begins with a review of the legislative development of the Chinese state compensation system leading to the passage of the SCL and provides some background information for further analysis. It then moves on to compare state compensation with civil compensation under the PRC General Principles of Civil Law (GPCL). It argues that state compensation, by its nature and function, can be regarded as a special kind of civil compensation. Thereafter, the chapter examines the scope of application of the SCL by discussing, firstly, why certain areas of the government's responsibilities have not been, and whether these areas should be, covered by the SCL; and, secondly, the two types of compensation provided by the SCL, namely administrative and criminal compensation. It then explores the procedure for claiming state compensation, commenting in particular on some of the unique features of the procedure of criminal compensation. The conclusion of this chapter notes the areas which may need further improvement, as well as the main contribution of the SCL to the evolving Chinese legal system.

Analysis of the SCL

Legislative Development

13.02 Chinese scholars claim that the necessity of state compensation was recognized soon after the founding of the PRC. Provisions on state compensation can be found in laws and regulations dating back to the early 1950s.[4] In fact, the principle that the state has the responsibility to pay compensation is stated in China's first constitution (1954). According to section 97 of that constitution, "Citizens who have suffered losses as a result of infringement of their civic rights by any functionaries of any state organizations have the right to compensation".[5] Though this principle is not adopted in the 1975 and 1978 Constitutions,[6] it reappears in the 1982 Constitution with only minor changes. The revised relevant provision reads, "Citizens who have suffered losses as a result of infringement of their civic rights by any state organ or functionary have the right to compensation in accordance with the law".[7] This is regarded as the constitutional basis for the establishment of a state compensation system. Unlike in many other jurisdictions, however, in China constitutional rights cannot be directly invoked by citizens and enforced by the People's Court. Specific laws and regulations are needed to implement the constitutional principle. The Economic Contract Law of the PRC (1981) and Regulation on Administrative Penalty for Public Security (1986) are two examples of those specific enactments, that have incorporated provisions on the state's responsibility to pay compensation. Section 33 of the Economic Contract Law provides that "If, due to the fault of higher-level leading authorities or of the department in charge of specialized work, an economic contract cannot be performed or cannot be fully performed, the higher-level leading authorities or the department in charge of specialized work shall bear liability for the breach of contract." Section 42 of the Regulations of the PRC on Administrative Penalties for Public Security states that "The public security organs shall admit their mistakes to those who are punished by mistake and return fines and confiscated property; in case the legal rights and interests of those who are so punished have been infringed upon, the loss shall be compensated for."[8] The GPCL (1986) reaffirms the same constitutional principle. Section 121 of the GPCL imposes civil liability on state organs or their personnel that, while executing their duties, encroach upon the lawful rights and interests of citizens or legal persons and cause damage. Thus through such incorporation, the constitutional principle has become invocable and enforceable in practice.

13.03 With the awakening of the rights consciousness in China, cases brought by both natural and legal persons against state organs have increased. However, in order to apply section 121 of the GPCL, many issues have still to be sorted and tested, such as the relations between state organs and their personnel concerning compensation, the liability of state organs for damages caused by public utilities, the necessity and procedure of compensation for illegal imprisonment, and so on. Those issues of common concern have perplexed the judiciary. It has become obvious that the broad constitutional principle and section 121 of the GPCL cannot meet the needs of the changing society. More detailed legal provisions are needed.

The enactment of the ALL in 1989 provides some guidance to the handling of lawsuits brought by citizens, legal persons or other organizations against government organs on "concrete administrative acts".[9] It contains several clauses on the liabilities of state administrative organs to pay compensation.[10] However, the ALL is in nature a procedural law and therefore focuses on procedural issues (such as the criterion for determining and method of calculating state compensation) rather than substantive provisions. Moreover, the ALL is restricted to concrete administrative acts only, and does not cover either abstract administrative acts or acts carried out by non-administrative organs which nevertheless participate in administration.[11] Therefore, in order to secure the implementation of the ALL soon after its adoption, the Legislative Affairs Commission of the NPC Standing Committee started the preparation for the drafting of the SCL. Through investigation and research conducted both in China and abroad, the draft SCL was made ready in October 1992 and distributed for consultation. The draft was revised in view of the opinions received from various branches of the government at both central and local levels as well as from the legal profession and the scholars. The revised draft was then submitted to the NPC Standing Committee for deliberation and discussion in December 1993. The SCL was finally adopted in May 1994.[12]

State Compensation and Civil Compensation under the GPCL

One of the most controversial issues accompanying the drafting process of the SCL is about the nature of state compensation. The question is whether, or to what extent, state compensation under the SCL is different from compensation for torts under the GPCL, especially section 121. The principle, scope and procedure are all said to be dependent on the understanding of and answer to this question.[13] Therefore a comparison will be made here between state compensation and civil compensation under the GPCL.

Different views were expressed in the legislative process.[14] Based on the adopted version of the SCL, victims can claim compensation from state organs if the latter or their personnel cause any harm or damages to the former through illegal exercise of authority.[15] The compensation

13.04

appears to be based on the breach of duty owed by state organs to the public to act lawfully and on the damages caused thereby. It can therefore be argued that state compensation is in nature a civil liability, similar to that provided by section 121 of the GPCL, though the scope of the latter is wider.[16] State compensation is concerned with some torts committed by state organs or their personnel only. In other words, the special status enjoyed by state organs gives rise to a special tortious liability, that can be distinguished from other kinds of tortious liability under the GPCL for the following reasons.

Firstly, the infringers in state compensation cases are state organs or their personnel. Due to the unequal status between the parties, many jurisdictions in the world have adopted special legislation to handle state compensation.[17] Interestingly, officials from the Legislative Affairs Commission have tried to draw the difference between state compensation and civil compensation by pointing out that the former falls within the field of public law, whereas the latter within the scope of private law.[18] This approach is in line with the understanding of public law in Continental Law countries such as France. Nevertheless, it is clearly contradictory to the doctrine generally accepted by many Chinese scholars and expressed in most textbooks, *i.e.* the socialist legal system does not recognize the distinction of public and private law. However, some Chinese scholars have recently argued for the necessity of the distinction between public and private law.[19]

Secondly, the parties liable to pay compensation are different in state compensation and other civil compensation cases. In civil compensation cases under the GPCL, the infringers bear the full responsibility to pay all compensation.[20] An examination of the SCL shows that state organs, not necessarily the actual infringers, are held liable to pay compensation for the damages or losses caused by state organs or their functionaries. This provision makes it possible for claimants to get appropriate compensation in time in cases where the infringers are financially unable to pay. Another difference is that only illegal exercise of authority by state organs or their functionaries will lead to state compensation, and compensation will only be paid if damages or losses can be proved. The actual infringers will only be required to pay if they intentionally committed errors or negligently committed grave errors.[21] The exact amount to be contributed, whether partial or all compensation, depends on the seriousness of the infringer's fault as well as his financial capacity. Furthermore, the SCL also provides that the infringers may be subject to disciplinary or even criminal sanctions in accordance with the SCL.[22] The following case shall illustrate the points mentioned above.

Zhang v. The County Hygiene and Epidemic Prevention Station[23]

13.05 Zhang had purchased about 85,000 kg of sugar cane from Guangxi in November 1994. He intended to sell it together with seven other people including Zhang. The partnership ended some time later and the remaining sugar cane was divided up among the parties according to their shares. Zhang received about 10,000 kg of sugar cane and sold them at home, in the neighbouring village, as well as the market. A lady who lived in village X and who was a customer of Zhang, was later hospitalized for food poisoning after consuming sugar cane from Zhang. The county hygiene and epidemic prevention station then, according to the information supplied by the patient's family, carried out an inspection on Zhang. They found out that Zhang did not have with him a health certificate, a hygiene approval certificate and a business licence. On February 16, 1995, the county hygiene and epidemic prevention station made a decision to destroy the remaining sugar cane that Zhang owned and to impose a fine of RMB5,000. They also ordered Zhang to compensate for the financial loss suffered by the patient.

Zhang, dissatisfied with the sanction decision, brought an action to the county people's court asking for the rescission of the decision that, in his point of view, was wrong. The hygiene and epidemic prevention station alleged that Zhang had violated the Food Hygiene Law by selling sugar cane without a health certificate, a hygiene approval certificate and business licence. The sugar cane was destroyed while the case was in trial.

The court held that Zhang had violated the Food Hygiene Law for selling sugar cane without proper licences. The hygiene and epidemic prevention station was thus correct in imposing a fine on Zhang. Nevertheless, the compensation order made by the station was *ultra vires* because the station did not have the authority to do so. The sugar cane destroyed by the station was also found to be of good quality and that the lady's food poisoning was caused by the consumption of another kind of food that had no direct relationship with the sugar cane sold by Zhang. This decision had thus violated the law. Zhang, based on the court decision, requested for compensation for the financial loss caused by the destruction of his sugar cane by the hygiene and epidemic prevention station.

The main legal issue in this case is whether or not Zhang can demand compensation from the station. That depends, firstly, on whether the station is a properly authorized law enforcement organ. The answer to this question is affirmative as the Food Hygiene Law stipulates that the station at county level or above is a law enforcement organ and should enjoy the rights and bear responsibility independently. Secondly, the exercise of administrative power must be unlawful. The action of destruction of the sugar cane, without proper reason, and the order for Zhang to pay compensation not caused by him, are clearly an unlawful exercise of power to impose administrative penalties that are within the jurisdiction of the county hygiene and epidemic prevention station. Thirdly, it is the county hygiene and

13.06

epidemic prevention station, not the person actually destroying the sugar cane, who is responsible to pay compensation. Though it is not mentioned in this case whether the fine of RMB5,000 is in proportion to the seriousness of Zhang's unlawful action, it is certainly a point that can be raised for the court to consider under the SCL. If it is obviously unfair, then it may also be challenged through judicial review on the grounds of obvious unfairness.[24]

Thirdly, the criteria for compensation, *i.e.* under what situations the liability to pay compensation arises, are different between state compensation and other kinds of civil compensation. Should compensation be based on fault, or illegality, or other criteria such as obvious unfairness? So far as state compensation is concerned, opinions differ.[25] The SCL adopts illegality as the basis for state compensation.[26] Whether individual functionaries (the direct infringers) should be held liable is fault based. The adoption of illegality as the criterion for state compensation is consistent with the provisions under the ALL. In fact, claims for compensation before the adoption of the SCL were based on illegality. The following two cases show that illegality has been adopted consistently for claim of administrative compensation.

Liu v. Public Security Bureau of X District[27]

13.07 In this case, Liu had complained about room problems many times in his working unit. He complained again in May 1995. One day after seeing Liu approaching the office, the manager of the working unit, who was sick of hearing the complaints, turned Liu down with the excuse that he did not have time. Being eager and desperate, Liu insisted that the manager solve his problem. Being annoyed, the manager pushed Liu out of the office. On his way out, Liu accidentally hit the desk and the cup on it fell over and broke. Water spilt all over the desk, damaging those documents on the desk. The manager was enraged and informed the police who arrested Liu without hearing his explanation. The next day, Liu was put into custody on the grounds of interference with the execution of public affairs. Liu brought legal action to the people's court. During the litigation process, the police then agreed to release Liu, but refused to make any compensation for his loss, arguing that the decision to put Liu under custody was a group decision and that the police were not at fault in that respect.

The issue here is whether or not the compensation is fault-based. The court held, relying on section 54(1) of the ALL, that the defendant were not clear about the facts and did not have conclusive evidence in making the decision to put Liu under custody. The decision should therefore be annulled. Whether or not an administrative organ should pay compensation depends on the unlawfulness of its decision, not its fault. The defendant should pay compensation under the SCL.

Wang v. Tax Bureau in X County[28]

This case further illustrates that illegality is the fundamental principle for the claim and determination of state compensation. Wang was a sole proprietor. He had bought cucumber and dried chilli from a nearby county and stored them in his house. Li is an officer at the tax bureau of X county and happened to pass Wang's house. Li asked Wang for his business licence and health certificate, and brought Wang back to the tax bureau. The director of the bureau, Zhang, examined the licence that covered agricultural by-products. Without checking up with the Administration Bureau for Industry and Commerce, Zhang arbitrarily believed that cucumber and dried chilli did not come within the category of agricultural by-products. He detained Wang's business licence. Wang was not satisfied with the decision and had an argument with Zhang. Without the licence, Wang was not able to sell the goods. He was forced to store up the goods. Later measures were taken by certain governmental departments for Wang to sell the goods, but Wang suffered a total loss of RMB3,000. Without a business licence, Wang was unable to conduct other business activities and suffered a daily loss of RMB500. Wang finally brought an action to the court, requesting it to annul the decision of the defendant with regard to the detention of his business licence and return the business licence to him, to determine what Zhang did was illegal and thus liable for his economic loss, of RMB3,500.

13.08

There are two issues in this case. One is whether or not the defendant had the authority to detain the business licence of the plaintiff. The second is whether the defendant should compensate for the plaintiff's economic loss. Under the Interim Regulation on Management of Individual Business Owner in Urban and Rural Areas issued by the State Council on August 5, 1987, such a business licence is issued by the relevant administration bureau for industry and commerce. Apart from the issuing authority, no other organizations or individuals have the authority to detain or revoke it. Here the defendant's decision to detain the plaintiff's business licence had exceeded its authority and therefore is illegal and invalid. Compensation should be made according to SCL. It is within the scope of compensation.

However, this emphasis on illegality does not mean that no damages can be recovered from the administrative organs for tortious acts arising from legal exercise of authority. In such cases, compensation will be paid pursuant to laws and regulations as administrative indemnity rather than as state compensation under either the ALL or the SCL.[29] The payment of indemnity is also essential to the protection of the legitimate interests of citizens from wrongful infringment by state organs. The case of *Li v. Public Security Bureau of X District*[30] proves this argument. Li parked his taxi in front of his house. Three police officers drove a car chasing another car driven by the suspect. While chasing the suspect, the police car crashed into Li's car while the police tried to avoid the passengers in the street. The accident left an obvious bump on the left side of Li's car and the paint on part of the car was scratched off. The police agreed to pay all the costs for the repair. But Li insisted on the replacement of the damaged part.

One of the issues here is whether or not the act of the police was unlawful. In this case, the three police officers were performing their duties when they had the accident which is an unforeseeable event and a kind of *force majeure*. The police did not breach any law. Then the plaintiff could not apply for state compensation. But he is nevertheless still entitled to indemnity. The final result of this case is that, after negotiation, the police agreed to pay all the costs for the repair and indemnified Li for his lost income while his taxi was under repair.

13.09   In this case it is not explained what the exact legal basis is for the payment of indemnity by the public security bureau to Li. It is clearly not illegality. Neither is it clear that it is the element of fault. The only thing which is obvious is the fact that Li suffered proprietory loss because of the act of the three police officers. It appears more beneficial for Li to bring the case for compensation under the GPCL as a civil tort. It should also be noted that quite frequently the payment of indemnity by state organs to those whose interests are affected is based on relevant statutory provisions, not on illegality or on fault.

State compensation and administrative indemnity constitute the major part of the Chinese state responsibility system at present. Whereas in civil compensation cases under the GPCL, criteria vary from one kind of tort to another. Most torts are fault-based, though there do exist strict tortious liabilities. Whether the torts are committed due to illegal exercise of power is not the concern. However, all torts are illegal and, so long as they are committed, compensation should be paid.

Fourthly, the methods to determine the amount of compensation are different. In ordinary civil compensation cases under the GPCL, the amount of compensation should generally cover both direct and indirect losses. For example, section 117 of the GPCL provides:

> "Anyone who encroaches on the property of the state, a collective or another person shall return the property; failing that, he shall reimburse its estimated price. Anyone who encroaches on the property of the state, a collective or another person shall restore the property to its original condition or reimburse its estimated price. If the victim suffers other great losses therefrom, the infringer shall compensate for those losses as well."

However, this rule should be taken in conjunction with another procedural rule, namely in civil litigation, the amount of compensation may be negotiated by the parties. The parties are encouraged to conduct conciliation both before and between proceedings, with the help of the judge. The court will make a decision if no agreement can be reached between the parties.[31]

On the other hand, state compensation, as provided by the SCL, may cover direct losses alone, or both direct and indirect losses, or a statutorily fixed amount per day, depending on the types of damage suffered.[32] Besides, due to the unequal status between the parties to state compensation, negotiation between the parties about the amount of compensation may be biased against the claimant. It is therefore not permitted under the SCL. The SCL also provides that a claim for state compensation should firstly be filed with the organ responsible for paying the compensation; such an organ is obliged to pay compensation within two months of the receipt of the claim, according to the relevant provisions under Chapter IV of the SCL. However, the amount of compensation shall be determined unilaterally by the organ. If the claimant is not satisfied with the compensation, he may file a lawsuit with a people's court within three months after the deadline.[33]

Finally, the relationships between the parties to state compensation and parties to compensation under GPCL are somewhat different. Under section 121 of the GPCL, any person can claim for damages so long as its lawful rights or interests have been encroached by a state organ or its personnel in execution of its duties. No special relationship, either administrative or of any other kinds, is required between the claimant and the state organ. Under the SCL, however, a person can only claim compensation if some sort of special relationship is proved to exist between the claimant and the state organ. That could be administrative relationship or any other type of special relationship evolved through state organs' activities, such as an investigation by the public security bureau, prosecution by the procuratorial organ, adjudication by the people's court, or prison management.[34] In theory, it is relatively easy to make the distinction. In judicial practice, however, it is rather a difficult task for the judges to undertake. The next case shows the difficulty.

Lin v. Highway Management Division (HMD) of X City[35]

In this case, the bridge situated at the heart of the city was damaged by a flood on the August 28, 1992. The HMD rushed to the scene for repair works immediately after the flood was over. Bars and wire gauzes were set up in order to obstruct and diverge traffic. A patrol team was also formed to make frequent inspections of the scene. On October 2, 1992, the mid-Autumn festival, when citizens went out to celebrate, there was a vast increase in traffic flow as well as people. The obstruction set up on the bridge was damaged by people using the bridge. At around 3:00 am next morning, when it was still dark, Lin drove across the bridge from the north without reducing

13.10

his speed. Without noticing that the bridge was still under repair, the car fell over the bridge and Lin suffered serious injury. The medical treatment cost a total of RMB20,000 and no settlement was made between the parties. The plaintiff brought the case to the people's court.

One of the issues raised in this case is the nature of the case, administrative tort or civil tort, and what will be the applicable law. One view is that this case falls within section 126 of the GPCL that states, "If a building or any other installation or an object placed or hung on a structure collapses, detaches or drops down and causes damage to others, its owner or manager shall bear civil liability, unless he can prove himself not at fault." The other view is that this is a case where omission of statutory duty has caused injuries and thus *ultra vires*. Sections 67 and 68 of the ALL should be applied.

It appears that the claimants under the SCL can also claim under the GPCL. However, based on two general principles of Chinese law, *i.e.* a specific legislation prevails over a general one and a later legislation prevails over an earlier one,[36] the provisions for state compensation under the SCL shall prevail over those under the GPCL. Therefore, the claimants who are qualified to claim compensation under the SCL can no longer bring a claim under the GPCL. This further proves that state compensation is a special kind of civil action. The case of *Lin v. HMD* supports this argument.

The above discussion shows that state compensation is similar to, but not the same as, civil compensation under the GPCL and therefore is a unique kind of civil compensation. Its separation from other kinds of civil compensation for tortious acts has led to the establishment of the state compensation system under the SCL. This, in turn, should contribute to better protection of the lawful rights and interests of both natural and legal persons.

Scope of Application

13.11 The scope of application of the SCL was a very controversial issue in the legislative process as it directly affected the structure of the SCL. Five years ago when the preparation just started for the drafting of the SCL, Professor Ying Songnian, a leading Chinese scholar in administrative law, proposed that the SCL should cover compensation in administrative, judicial, legislative and military fields.[37] However, many other scholars hold different views with regard to what should be covered by the SCL. This section shall examine, firstly, why certain fields are not, and whether they should be, covered by the SCL, and secondly, the exact scope of the SCL.

There were two opposing arguments as to the coverage of legislative compensation. One approach argues that the principle of rule of law requires that all state organs, including legislative organs, bear respective duties and responsibilities while enjoying authorities. Compensation should be paid if damages are caused by legislative acts.[38] The other approach argues that the people's congresses, the legislature in the PRC, are organs of state power and enjoy supreme authority at the respective levels. Judicial organs are only the enforcement organs of the people's congresses. They do not enjoy the authority to supervise the acts of the people's congresses. Furthermore, the scope of judicial review under the ALL only covers concrete administrative acts, not legislative acts.[39] Based on the necessity of consistency between legislation, the SCL should not cover legislative compensation. It has also been argued that few countries have covered legislative compensation in their state compensation legislation.[40]

The SCL does not include legislative compensation. Apart from the reasons mentioned above, several other concerns may also contribute to the exclusion of legislative compensation from the SCL. Firstly, it is common practice with legislation in the PRC that matters shall not be included if the legislators are not certain whether they should be covered and how they should be covered.[41] Secondly, legislative acts have been claimed by some scholars as state acts and therefore should be immune from responsibility for compensation.[42] Thirdly, compatibility with the ALL and other legislation may be another factor.

One possible result of this exclusion is the abuse of power by the legislature, for which victims have no remedy.[43] Moreover, the abovementioned reasons do not, in theory, constitute a serious obstacle to the inclusion of legislative compensation under the SCL. An examination of the Constitution of the PRC reveals that there exists a procedure for people's congresses to repeal legislation contradictory to the Constitution or laws of higher status. If such legislation can be repealed, logically, the damages caused thereby should also be compensated.[44] It has been common practice in some Western countries that subsidiary legislations are subject to judicial review and further actions for compensation can be filed following the results of judicial review.[45]

13.12 Different opinions have also been expressed with regard to whether military compensation should be covered by the SCL. Damages caused by military acts may be classified into three categories. One are those caused by military exercise or training, which are, according to one source, the main ones.[46] They are within the scope of civil disputes and can be recovered through civil claims, according to section 121 of the GPCL and the procedure laid down by the Civil Procedure Law (CPL).[47] The second concerns actual military action consisting of lawful acts, and therefore should not be within the scope of the SCL. The compensation for those acts should be provided through administrative indemnity.[48] The third category is concerned with the damages caused by illegal exercise of military power. It has been suggested that these may, in the future, be governed by a separate military law or other regulations.⁴⁹ The main reason for exclusion of provisions on military compensation, according to a distinguished scholar, Professor Pi Chunxie, is the exclusion of acts of national defence from the ALL.⁵⁰ However, as Professor Pi argues, military acts do not equal to acts of national defence,⁵¹ and furthermore, military organs have been put under state organs under the 1982 Constitution.⁵² It is therefore reasonable to subject them to the regulation of the SCL. It has also been claimed that doing so is beneficial to the unification and consistency of state compensation system nationwide.⁵³

Although the PRC is moving towards a market economy, many public utilities are still owned by the state. How to deal with the damages caused by mismanagement of the public utilities, such as roads and bridges, is essential to the protection of the lawful interests of the public. One argument is that there are some provisions in the GPCL on the compensation for damages caused by public utilities.⁵⁴ Under those provisions, victims can claim compensation from the enterprises in charge of the administration of the public utilities according to the CPL. They are therefore classified as civil disputes. However, many public utilities are managed by state organs and the damages caused thereby are sometimes enormous. The other one is that damages caused by public utilities should be covered by the SCL, as long as they are still under the management of the state government. But bearing in mind the SCL requirement of the existence of a special relationship between the claimant and the state organ concerned, it does not seem easy to prove the existence of a special relationship between a road user (i.e. a jogger) and the state organ administering the road. Though different opinions exist as to whether or not it is better for the road users to bring a claim by relying on section 121 of the GPCL or the SCL, it is fair to say that this theoretical argument will not cause any substantial difference in judicial practice. The reason is that if the person fails to bring a case successfully under the GPCL, it will then be possible for the applicant to bring a case under the ALL or the SCL.

In the case of *Lin v. the Highway Management Division of X City*,⁵⁵ the bridge is state-owned property for public use and the defendant is an administrative organ authorized by the government to manage the highways and bridges. Damages or injuries caused by the failure of the highway management division to maintain the bridge properly are due to the omission or failure to perform its statutory duty properly. In this sense, there seems to exist a special administrative relationship between the defendant and the plaintiff in this case and the nature of this case should be administrative tort.

13.13   The scope of application of the SCL has finally been restricted to administrative and criminal fields.⁵⁶ Administrative compensation covers infringement upon both personal and proprietary rights. The infringement upon personal rights includes illegal detention, adoption of compulsory administrative measures, illegal custody of citizen or deprivation of personal freedom by other means, infliction of physical injury or causing death by violent acts or illegal use of weapons or police gear, and so on.[57] Among them, unlawful detention and custody is the one most frequently litigated. The following case is one example in point.

Zhou v. Public Security Bureau of X City in Jiang Xi Province[58]

13.14 In this case, a contract was signed between Zhou and Lin for the purchase of baby fish on June 20, 1994. The contract stated that the payment of RMB26,900 should be made within one month and in no case should be later than the August 25, 1994. On July 15, Zhou took the delivery of baby fish without any payment. Lin approached Zhou who said that she had difficulty making the payment because of the huge amount of fish that died. Lin was turned down on two other occasions afterwards. He then sought help from the police department on November 15. Police officers were sent for, on January 5, 1995, to Zhou's home without any prior notice. Zhou was then sheltered for examination and taken into custody. A notice of sheltering for examination was announced the next day and delivered to Ma, Zhou's husband, on January 9. The notice required a payment of RMB30,000 for Zhou's release, which Ma did accordingly. The police kept RMB4,000 out of the sum to themselves and gave the rest to Lin. Zhou was released on January 11.

After his release, the doctor diagonised Zhou was suffering from dizziness and other illnesses due to the frightening effect caused by custody. The medical costs amounted to a sum of RMB1,800. On January 17, Zhou filed an action to the people's court. Her grounds for action was that the contract was made on a voluntary basis. It was legal and binding, and she had no intention to cheat Lin. She claimed that the non-payment was only due to cash flow problems. That only amounted to a breach of contract which had nothing to do with fraud. It was alleged that the sheltering for examination and custody was without any lawful basis. The police department should not have interfered with this kind of transaction and it was illegal for them to do so. Police interference amounted to an infringement of Zhou's personal rights and interests and the medical fees should be paid by the respondent.

It was held that the non-payment was a mere breach of contract and had nothing to do with fraud. The interference of the police and the sheltering for examination was also without lawful basis and sufficient evidence. It was thus decided that the custody decision should be revoked and the respondent should pay the appellant a total sum of RMB31,800 within 10 days of the decision.

STATE COMPENSATION

The first issue here is about the legality of the action of the police. As the contract is economic in nature, the use of sheltering for examination amounts to a misuse of power, which is illegal. The second issue is about the scope of application. The action of the police was illegal detention which restricts the personal freedom of Zhou and therefore falls within section 3(1) of the SCL.

The infringement upon property rights includes the illegal use of administrative penalties, the illegal imposition of compulsory administrative measures, the illegal collection of property charges or financial contributions, and "any other illegal act".[59] Sometimes several unlawful actions may be taken by the relevant administrative organs, which will infringe upon the proprietary rights of citizens, legal persons or other organizations. The affected party may rely on more than one of the above-mentioned reasons. The first case is about the unlawful imposition of administrative penalties.

Zhang v. Administration Bureau for Industry and Commerce in X County[60]

13.15 Zhang is an owner of a new restaurant in a famous food street where there are lots of restaurants and cafes. Xu is an officer with the Administration Bureau for Industry and Commerce in X county in charge of this street. He always eats without pay. One day, he brought along with him two friends to try out Zhang's restaurant. Without knowing Xu's "habits", Zhang treated Xu as an ordinary customer and asked him to pay the bill. Xu paid the bill but felt enraged about it. He returned to the restaurant half a month later with the excuse of conducting a business inspection. He asked Zhang for his account book. Having roughly checked through the book, he threw the book into the stove and claimed that the account items were unclear and the business was a mess. He verbally asked Zhang to stop carrying out the business and took away his business licence. Zhang appealed many times, arguing that he had not conducted business unlawfully and requested the administration bureau to return his business licence. But he failed because of Xu's interference. Zhang then filed an action to the court on June 20, 1993. He requested the court to annul the decision of the defendant on the detention of his business licence and its return, and also asked for compensation from the defendant for his lost income of RMB7,690 due to the forfeiture.

Section 4(1) of the SCL provides that victims are entitled to compensation if the governmental organs' decision amounts to illegal detention (forfeiture) of licence or demand for the cessation of business. Here the issue is whether the detention of Zhang's business licence by Xu is illegal, which depends on whether Xu's decision is a personal revenge or a proper exercise of his authority. The court held that the decision of Xu amounted to abuse of power as he exercised his authority for a different purpose of the legislation.[61] In this case the unlawful exercise of power (abuse of power) by Xu has caused financial loss to Zhang and therefore facts within section 4(1) of the SCL.

Due to the variety of administrative penalties and their adverse effect upon the citizens, legal persons or other organizations if unlawfully imposed, many cases have been brought to the people's courts basing on the ground of unlawful imposition of administrative penalties. The next case is another example relating to a diffeent kind of administrative penalty. It falls with section 4(1) of the SCL on the specific grounds of unlawful suspension of business.

Qing Hua Garment Factory in HuHeHaoTe City (Appellant) v. Administration Bureau for Industry and Commerce in XinCheng District of HuHeHaoTe City (Respondent)[62]

13.16 This case is one about illegal demand made by the defendant for the plaintiff to stop its business. The appellant had an argument with a customer named Li over processing problems of a dress in June 1991. Li alleged that Xin Chen Branch of the Administration Bureau of Industry and Commerce should be responsible for solving the problem relating to her ordered skirt which was not tailor-made properly by the Qing Hua Garment Factory Mediation was conducted for several times by Sin Chen Branch of the Administrative Bureau for Industry and Commerce. Xin Chen Branch issued an order of suspension of business to the appellant. After receiving the order the appellant did suspend its business. The appellant then applied to the respondent for administrative reconsideration of the order. The respondent upheld the decision of Xin Chen Branch. The appellant was not satisfied with the result and filed an action to the people's court.

It was held that the order issued by the respondent was without lawful basis and thus invalid. The order should be revoked. It was also held that no compensation could be made because the appellant was an unprofitable garment factory when the order was issued.

Dissatisfied with the judgment. The appellant appealed. The court of second instance held that the case was a case concerning civil rights and obligations. There do not exist any legal grounds for the respondent to issue the order of suspension which caused the appellant to suffer economic loss for which the respondent was directly responsible. In accordance with section 61 of the ALL, it was decided that the respondent was responsible for compensating all loss (a total of RMB4,900) during the period of suspension of business. This amount should be paid within 10 days after the judgment.

Zhao v. Tax Bureau in X County[63]

13.17 This case is an action brought to the people's court to challenge compulsory measure adopted by the relevant administrative organ.

Zhao and the township people's government concluded a contract in 1994. According to the contract Zhao will be in charge of the business management of Dong Feng Wooden Instrument Factory, a collectively owned township enterprise. Zhao was also responsible for all tax payments and should pay RMB10,000 to the township people's government. The contract lasts from July 1, 1994 to July 1, 1995 and the extension of the contract is subject to the negotiation of the two parties. Because of health problems, Zhao entered into another contract on July 21, 1994 with Ling. Under the contract Ling will be responsible for production by using all facilities and place provided by Zhao. Ling will be paid certain percentage of profit earned.

On December 20, 1994, Ling was informed by the tax bureau for tax payments. Ling refused to pay, claiming that it was stated in the contract that Zhao was responsible for tax payment. The tax bureau believed that Ling should be the person to pay tax. On January 6, 1995, representatives from the tax bureau went to the factory intending to take away certain products. Upon resistance by Ling, the tax bureau failed to take away the products. Instead, it made an announcement immediately to freeze all products until payment was made. If payment was not made within the specified period, the products would be forfeited and auctioned in order to get money for the payment of tax. On February 17, the tax bureau made a formal decision ordering Ling, as the manufacturer of the products, to pay the income tax of RMB6,000 before March 10 and imposing a fine of RMB500 on Ling for failing to follow formal tax registration procedures. Ling was not satisfied with the decision and applied for administrative reconsideration. But the original decision was upheld by the administrative reconsideration organ. Ling then brought the case to the people's court.

The main issue here is whether the administrative compulsory measures undertaken by the defendant were lawful. As the township enterprise is the legal person responsible for the payment of tax, not Ling. It was wrong and unlawful to identify Ling as the person responsible for tax payment. The economic loss caused by freezing up of products should fall within section 4(2) and be compensated by the defendant.

Lu v. Administration Bureau for Industry and Commerce[64]

13.18 This case is about unlawful suspension of Lu's business. Lu owned a booth, with the approval of the Administration Bureau of Industry and Commerce, situated near the crossroad. With the intention to get a better place for his relatives, Long approached Lu and offered him an exchange of booths on July 18. Enraged upon refusal, Long and Zhao closed down Lu's booth for the reason of excess of the scope of business. This was done without showing proper identification and documentary papers. Lu approached the bureau on several occasions for a revocation of Long and Zhao's decision, but in vain. Lu filed an action to the people's court on August 5, 1990, during which the booth was robbed twice and the loss amounted to RMB3,800.

It is an abuse of power case causing economic loss to the plaintiff. It was a case before the adoption of the SCL. It falls within section 11(2) of the ALL. If this is a case that happened after the SCL, it will again fall within under section 4(1) of the SCL.

Ding v. Land Administration Bureau in X County[65]

This case is a claim for compensation against unlawful compulsory measure. In this case, an application for house construction was made to the relevant division by Ding in October 1994. Due to lack of space within the village, it was decided that Ding would be given a piece of agricultural land situated around the village boundary. The exact location was given later together with a land-use certificate and the distance from the surrounding houses. On November 1, Ding brought with him the land-use certificate and his application form for land for the construction of personal dwelling to the township office for a construction approval.

13.19

Upon inspection, the officers found that the application did not contain the exact boundaries and asked whether he has any dispute with neighbours. Ding claimed that there were no complaints made by the surrounding house owners. It was then approved.

When the application went to the County Land Administration Bureau, the same problem was found and Ding was asked to fill in the section and certain certificates were also granted on the same day. The next day when Ding had the section filled, the officer at the County Land Administration Bureau copied the boundary figures down to the certificates without careful examination and inspection.

Construction work started to lay grounds in December and the County Construction Commission discovered the problem and ordered temporary suspension of construction because of its illegality. But Ding resumed the work after one week.

The County Construction Commission, Land Administration Bureau and the township jointly issued an order requiring Ding to stop construction. Paying no attention to the order. Ding rushed the work which finally finished on January 6, 1995. The house turned out to be 160.5 square metres in size, 4.17 metres longer and 3.25 metres wider than the plan. On February 12, Land Administration

STATE COMPENSATION

Bureau demanded Ding to pull down the house. Ding thus filed an action to the court.

It was held that Ding fraudulently altered the boundary figures that contravened the relevant provisions in the Land Administration Law of the People's Republic of China. Nevertheless, the Land Administration Bureau's negligence also played some part in the case which would reduce Ding's responsibility. According to section 45 of the Land Administration Law, it was decided that Ding need only pull down the relevant parts of the house exceeding the boundary and compensation should be made by the Land Administration Bureau to Ding with respect to the base construction costs.

The ground laid down by Ding was according to a proper land-use certificate that was obtained fraudulently. Then the issue is whether fraud may be argued to have the effect of vitiating the land-use certificate. The court held that it would only be so if it is discovered and the vitiating effect starts from the time a notice is given.

13.20 Compared with the scope of application of the ALL,[66] it is not difficult to find out the scope of application of the SCL overlaps with the former to a large extent.[67] That is logical as both the ALL and the SCL are concerned with administrative acts, and one of the considerations for the enactment of the SCL is to supplement the ALL and facilitate its implementation. The interrelationship between the ALL and SCL is further strengthened by section 9(2) of the SCL: "In demanding compensation, ... they (claimants) may also file their claims when they apply for administrative reconsideration or file administrative lawsuits". Thus the SCL and ALL can be jointly applied in a claim for compensation. They can supplement each other as the ALL is mainly concerned with procedure while the SCL is concerned with both procedural and substantive aspects of compensations. The joint application can contribute to better judicial protection of lawful interests of citizens.

However, differences do exist. Firstly, the SCL is concerned only with the illegal administrative acts. Whereas the ALL covers both illegal and other wrongful administrative acts.[68] Secondly, as far as illegal acts are concerned, the scope of application under the SCL can be argued to be broader than that under the ALL. For example, illegally inflicting physical injury and causing death by physical assault or illegal use of weapons or police gear, as provided by sections 3(3) and (4) of the SCL, are not covered by the ALL. Moreover, illegally taking citizens into custody under section 3(2) of the SCL seems to be wider than the compulsory administrative measure to restrict citizens' freedom under section 11(2) of the ALL. However, there is a catch-all paragraph under section 12 of the ALL, which provides that "... the people's courts shall accept other administrative suits which may be brought in accordance with the provisions of relevant laws and regulations".[69] That provision can further broaden the scope of application of the ALL. It is therefore difficult to say definitely that the scope of application under which legislation is wider.

As to criminal compensation, the principle for bringing a case against any of those administrative organs that are liable for compensation is also the principle of legality, exactly the same as the principle for administrative compensation. The following two cases may illustrate the application of the principle of illegality in criminal compensation.

Zhang and Sha v. Shi, Director of Public Security Bureau of X County in Henan Province[70]

This is a case where the claim for criminal compensation failed because there did not exist the element of illegality in the action taken by Shi.

13.21

In this case, Shi (the defendant) is the head of the public security station of X county in Henan Province. In late 1994, Shi received the report that jobless Zhang, after drinking, entered into factory X and caused trouble. Shi tried to stop him but he was pushed down on the floor by Zhang, and suffered injuries to his face and head. Shi then led Chen, a security guard of the factory, to the scene, then brought Zhang to the security office. At the scene, Zhang fought with Chen, and Zhang declared that he would kill Chen. Shi left earlier due to some urgent matters. Zhang escaped.

Zhang then went back to the security branch, with his cousin, Sha, to find Chen for revenge. Failing to find Chen in the security office, he beat Wang, another security guard, and caused serious injuries to Wang. Zhang went to find Shi to kill him. When Zhang and Sha left the security branch, they met Shi, then they produced the chopper and steel rod and ran toward Shi. Shi then produced his pistol to stop the two people. Zhang and Sha ran in the direction to Chen's home, when the two people were entering Chen's house, Shi shot into the sky to warn them. Sha turned back and hit Shi with his steel rod, then Shi aimed his pistol at Sha as well as walking backwards. When Shi ran out of the house, Zhang grasped him from the back. When Zhang tried to chop Shi with his chopper. Chen's mother grasped Zhang's right arm. Zhang kicked Chen's mother away and got ready to chop Shi. Shi struggled and escaped from Zhang and then ran away. Zhang chased after Shi and Sha followed behind Zhang. When Zhang was close to Shi, Shi shot at Zhang's waist once, but Zhang still chased after Shi. Shi then shot again at Zhang's chest. Shi shot twice at Sha who was running toward Shi with a steel rod.

The coroner held that Zhang and Sha died of wounds caused by the shots. The family members of the two deceased demanded the public security bureau, the defendant's representative, to pay the deceased compensation fee and the funeral fee which was, in total, about RMB80,000 in accordance with the newly enacted National Compensation Law of the PRC.

The main issue in this case is whether Shi is responsible to pay compensation to the family members of the deceased. As Shi is a policeman, he has the responsibility to protect the safety of other people. In this case, the shooting was purely in self defence, which is a lawful act. As the SCL has stated clearly that state organs or their personnel will not be responsible for damages caused by their lawful acts under the SCL.

Li v. Jie and Jin[71]

13.22 In this case the claim for compensation was successful because of the existence of an unlawful act undertaken by the officer of the public security bureau. In this case, Jie (the defendant) was a peasant in X county of Henang Province, and Jin (the defendant) was a public security officer of a police station of X county.

The antiques that Jie illegally purchased were confiscated. Jie suspected that somebody reported him to the public security bureau. Jie then talked to Jin (Jie's old friend) and asked him for advice. Jin was of the opinion that he had been reported by Li, who knew Jie very well. Jie then informed Jin that Li had once stolen a motorbike and Li was smuggling cigarettes. Jin promised to take revenge on Li for Jie. On December 13, 1994, Jie informed Jin that Li had returned to Henang Province, and Jin helped Li to identify Li and find his address.

On December 17, Li drove to the container terminal to take stock of cigarettes. Jin led a team of public security officers to stop Li and brought Li to the police station for investigation on the grounds that Li had stolen a motorbike. Then Jin took away the bill of lading and some blank recommendation letters in Li's vehicle and gave them to Jie. The next day, Jie took away 100 boxes of cigarettes from Li from the terminal and then sold them for RMB220,000: Jie received RMB120,000 and Jin received RMB100,000. The department store of X county reported to the public security bureau of X County and claimed that the 100 boxes of cigarettes were purchased by Li on his behalf, which was not Li's personal property. Moreover, the purchase by Li was lawful, not an illegal transaction. The department store demanded the public security bureau to return the 100 boxes of cigarettes.

The main issue in this case is whether the public security bureau in X County should be responsible for the action taken by Jin. The resolution to this issue depends on whether Li's action constituted an unlawful exercise of his powers and functions. In this case, Jin is a police officer, and Jin's action to take Li to the police station was an obvious exercise of his statutory function to conduct criminal investigation.

The state organs encompassed under the SCL include those performing investigative, procuratorial, adjudicative and prison management functions and powers. The illegal acts exercised by them mainly cover wrongful detention and arrest, enforcement of original penalty before the ruling is changed, use of torture, inflicting physical injuries, instigation, inflicting injury or causing death by illegal use of weapons or police gear, and so on.[72] The organs that may be challenged include the public security bureaus, the procuratorate, the people's courts and prison authorities. The following case is concerned with the decision of the people's court which falls within section 15(3) of the SCL.

Jiang v. People's Procuratorate at X City[73]

In this case, at about 3 pm on November 2, 1991, Jiang, a university student, went to a public trial at the first court of X city to listen to a fraud case in which her cousin was involved. When Jiang arrived at the court, she parked her bicycle at the entrance. Liu, the court sheriff, said to Jiang, "Get your piece of trash away, you are blocking the road". Jiang replied, "I suppose you don't even have such trash, you fool!" A quarrel then took place between the two. Later on, Jiang parked her bicycle at the designated place and wanted to get into the court. Liu did not allow her to get in. His reason was that the court was already full. Thinking that Liu did this on purpose as revenge, Jiang tried to force her way into the court. She was blocked by Liu, and the two fought. Liu suffered minor bruises on his face and Jiang's clothes were torn. The trial was, because of the fight, suspended for half an hour. Jiang and Liu were pulled apart by some members of the crowd and court officers.

13.23

The court, after hearing Jiang's case, held that Jiang, not satisfied with Liu's orders, had violently obstructed the police officer from executing his duty and interfered with court procedures. This had affected the court's normal trial activities, as well as seriously prohibiting judicial officers from carrying out their duties. The court, according to section 157 of the Criminal Law, sentenced Jiang to one year imprisonment.

Believing that his sister was innocent, Jiang's brother appealed to the intermediate people's court in X city. The intermediate court ordered for a retrial. After the retrial, the lower court, at which the first instance was held, overruled the original judgment, based on the reason that Jiang's conviction cannot stand, and held that Jiang was innocent.

The case actually happened in 1991 when no state compensation was possible. Suppose it happened after the SCL came into force, then

STATE COMPENSATION

which organ would be responsible for compensation? As Jiang had no intention of committing the crime, which is the essential component for the constitution of the crime, she did not commit the crime. Then according to the SCL, the court of the first instance should be the organ responsible for compensation.

The scope of criminal compensation is very wide, covering not only criminal proceedings in the people's courts, but also other administrative acts relating to criminal proceedings. Such compensation is essential to the effective protection of the lawful rights of the victims, as the victims usually do not have access to any alternative remedies. Several cases shall be discussed here to illustrate the variety of organs involved in criminal compensation.

Procuratorate in X County of Henan Province v. Jiang[74]

13.24 This case is concerned with a compensation claim against unlawful prosecution by the procuratorate. In this case, Jiang, the defendant, was the undertaker of the business of the Yuan Feng Restaurant of X county. In April 1991, Jiang undertook the business of the restaurant from a service company and received the residual operation capital of the restaurant for RMB15,000.

According to the undertaking contract, the said service company would provide RMB150,000 loan to the defendant. The defendant should pay the service company RMB2,300 profit each month, and repay the loan with interest and bearing the risk of loss. Up to 1992, Jiang in total received RMB135,000 loan, he spent RMB6,000 of the loan for himself and RMB59,000 on his own garment factory. Because of losses in the restaurant, Jiang still owed the service company RMB44,000 when the contract expired. When the public procuratorate filed the case, Jiang paid RMB35,000. After Jiang was arrested on November 12, 1994, his family paid RMB9,000 to Jiang. The procuratorate of X county initiated a public prosecution to the people's court of that county against Jiang for embezzlement of public funds.

Two different opinions existed among the judges on whether the acts of Jiang constituted embezzlement of public funds. The first opinion was that Jiang had taken advantage of his office, used the loan from the service for his own purpose, and, not able to pay back the loan with interest when the time limit was due, it amounted to a crime of embezzlement of public funds. The second opinion was that embezzlement of public funds is an infringement of the rights over the public fund which is protected by the Criminal Law: the possession right, the right to use and the right to income. In this case, the use of funds by Jiang was based on a contractual relationship and it was unlawful possession and use of public funds without paying any interest. Here, the procuratorate failed to meet the legal requirements for prosecution, i.e., identification of material facts and the existence of sufficient and conclusive evidence. It should be held liable for state compensation under section 15 of the SCL. The court adopted the second opinion.

Lei and Qin v. Public Security Bureau[75]

This case is concerned with the exercise of investigation power by the public security bureau. The claim by the plaintiff failed because the power was exercised lawfully. In this case, Lei was a cousin of Qin. Qin was in the business of selling garments and also operated a video studio. He had gained huge profits through the duplication and selling of obscene video tapes. On September 17, 1992, Lei went to Qin's house. Finding that Qin was playing some obscene tapes, Lei stayed over and watched the tapes with Qin. Qin was playing the obscene video tapes while he was duplicating them. He then played the duplicated copies to check the quality of the tapes. Lei watched the tapes while Qin was doing his work, without knowing the purpose for which the tapes were duplicated. Lei and Qin were later arrested by the criminal division of the public security bureau. Upon questioning, Lei alleged that he did not know Qin's purpose for duplicating the tapes, and that he went to Qin's place solely because he was a cousin of Lei. He stayed over and watched the tapes that night just because he was curious. Lei was released on September 19.

13.25

The issue here is whether Lei can apply for state compensation under the circumstances as required by the SCL. The state organ concerned is the public security bureau that can exercise the authority of criminal detention. Whether Lei is entitled to criminal compensation under section 15 of the SCL depends on the legality of the detention taken by the public security bureau. Here Lei was obviously a suspect and it was therefore lawful both in substantive and procedural law for the public security bureau to detain Lei for three days.

Wang v. Rural Branch of Public Security Bureau in X County[76]

This case is a rather complicated case and concerned several state organs. In this case, Zhang was caught by officers from the police station of X county in December 1990. Over the course of questioning, Wang, the vice head of a factory, was at the police station for some other business. Zhang indicated that Wang had raped a woman. The officers of the police station then found Li, the said victim, according to Zhang's information. Li admitted that she had been raped but she was not sure who raped her. The police station then detained Wang and he was forced to make a confession to the offence. In February 1991, the public procuratorate charged Wang for rape in violation of section 139 of the Criminal Law. The court of first instance held that facts

13.26

were clear and convicted Wang and sentenced him to a seven-year imprisonment. Zhang was mitigated for reporting the crime Wang had committed. Wang appealed.

The court of second instance found that there were a lot of suspicious circumstances in the case and ordered the court of first instance to suspend the execution of Wang's punishment. The court of first instance however, refused to accept the decision and transferred Wang to the prison for rehabilitation through labour. The court of second instance then annulled the decision of the court of first instance and ordered a retrial on the grounds that the facts were not clear.

In the retrial, the court ordered the public procuratorate to carry out a supplementary investigation to clarify the facts. The public procuratorate then discovered some suspicious circumstances. It finally found that Li was actually raped by Zhang, and Zhang identified Wang as the rapest for the purpose of mitigation of his own crime. Wang was finally released as innocent, but he had already been detained for more than 400 days.

This case is interesting as it involves three state organs, i.e. the court, procuratorate and public security bureau. Though Zhang was responsible for the false accusation, the three state organs could not deny their respective responsibilities. In this case, section 15 of the SCL is applicable.

Jin v. Procuratorate in X City[77]

13.27 This case may be an example of a successful claim for compensation against the unlawful action taken by the procuratorate. In this case, Jin, the vice head of the Art Department of X Educational Institute. In October 1990, Jin was invited by the Music Department of the Institute to do the stage design of an opera by the Music Department. An agreement was signed. Under the agreement, the Music Department should provide RMB20,000 for the purchase of instruments, materials and other expenses. The Music Department should also provide RMB2,000 to the Art Department for the use of Jin's working time. Jin used RMB13,000 out of the RMB20,000 on the purchase of a camera, typewriter and tape-recorder, which were stored in Jin's home because there was no laboratory for storage. In January 1991, Jin travelled to another place and she took RMB4,000 from the RMB20,000 for her own use. This was later discovered.

The southern people's court of X City held that Jin had taken advantage of her office to embezzle public property that was in violation of section 155 of the Criminal Law. The court was of the opinion that the minimum punishment, as stipulated in the laws, was still too heavy in relation to Jin's act. According to section 59(2) of the Criminal

Law, the judicial committee may impose a penalty lower than the minimum punishment. The Southern People's Court of X city on December 7, 1992, decided to impose a two-year imprisonment on Jin for embezzlement, to confiscate all properties obtained by Jin in accordance with Article 60 of the Criminal Law. Jim then appealed on the grounds that the identification of material facts by the court of first instance was wrong.

The Intermediate People's Court held that Jin did not have the intention to embezzle and her act did not endanger society. Moreover, the instruments Jin purchased were for the purpose of the stage design. Furthermore, the RMB4,000 she used was the money transferred to the account of the Art Department by the Music Department in accordance with the agreement and was not the Art Department's public fund. Jin undertook the stage design project, although it did relate to her position as vice head, but it did not satisfy the pre-requisite of taking advantage of the public office. Jin's act was merely a violation of financial system and should not be punished under the Criminal Law. The court held that the decision of the court of first instance should be annulled. When Jin checked the returned property, she found that a camera and a mini hi-fi set were lost, and a Hero portable manual typewriter was damaged.

The issue here is what kind of losses can Jin apply for as state compensation. As stated in the SCL, the victim may apply for compensation for infringement of both personal and proprietary interests. As she was unlawfully detained in the process, she could apply for compensation for damages due to infringement of her personal rights. Moreover, the loss of the property and the damaged property fall within the category of proprietary rights that should also be compensated under section 16 of the SCL.

In contrast, in civil and administrative proceedings, the illegal acts of the judiciary can cause harm or damages to the victim, as well as inappropriate enrichment of the other party to the same proceedings. The victim could be compensated by claiming the return of the inappropriate enrichment through another decision of the people's court.[78] The later decision can be enforced by the winning party against the other party rather than against the people's court. The wrong can therefore be rectified without holding the judiciary liable.[79] That is why the SCL only covers illegal judicial acts concerning criminal proceedings, but not civil and administrative proceedings.

However, one exception exists under Article 31 of the SCL, which provides:[80]

> Where, in the process of a civil or administrative suit, the People's Court illegally adopts compulsory or preservation measures against [the claimant for acts] that disrupt legal proceedings, or

where the People's Court wrongfully enforces a court decision, ruling or other legal documents that have taken effect and such wrongful enforcement causes damages, the procedure of criminal compensation as provided in this Law shall apply for the claimant seeking compensation.

Guang Ming Electrical Appliances Plaza in X City v. Administration Bureau of Industry and Commerce in X City[81]

13.28 In this case, Jia, a customer, bought two cassette tapes from the plaintiff that were found to be of poor quality. He made a complaint to the administration bureau that sent representatives to the plaza and forfeited unsold tapes for inspection. The two tapes produced by Jia were inspected and proved to be fake. The defendant imposed on the plaintiff a fine of RMB2,000 for the reason of selling fake products in accordance with section 37 of the Trademark Law of the People's Republic of China. Dissatisfied with the punishment, the plaintiff filed an action to the people's court.

At the court of first instance, it was held that the only evidence produced by the defendant was the quality inspection report of the two tapes from Jia. According to legal requirements, this was insufficient evidence to prove the plaintiff sold fake products. The penalty was revoked. The defendant appealed which was duly dismissed by the court of second instance on the grounds that the facts of the case were clear and thus good evidence. The defendant applied to the court for another inspection of the tapes, which was allowed and formal procedure was followed. Some samples were sent to the original producer for inspection. It was found that the tapes were of poor quality and were fake products. It was thus held that the plaintiff was liable for a fine.

This is an interesting case and lasted until the SCL comes into force. Here, the retrial held that products were fake and the defendant's decision of penalty was correct. Therefore the plaintiff will not be entitled to state compensation for wrongful judgments of the people's court at the first instance. The following three cases are concerned with challenges against the adoption of a preservation measure by the people's court.

East Wind Leather Factory v. Xiang Yiang Trading Company[82]

13.29 In this case, a contract was concluded for the supply of 200 coats in return for a payment of RMB20,580 in June 1994. Payment was to be made when the goods are received. The payment was not made even at the end of 1994 and on several occasions the plaintiff sent people to claim payments, but the defendant still failed to pay for reasons of poor yield. An action was filed to the people's court by the plaintiff and upon application by the plaintiff 30 television sets were forfeited from the defendant as a security for the payment.

Clothing Factory in X City v. Red Cotton Trading Company in X City[83]

In this case, Wang, a purchase and sales officer of defendant, obtained a stamped but blank contract and effected a business transaction with the plaintiff involving a delivery of 2,500 pairs of jeans. The contract was sent back to the defendant that did not express any objection. Six months later, the plaintiff made the delivery, but the defendant refused to accept the goods on the grounds that it did not delegate power to Wang to conclude such a contract. The plaintiff filed an action to the people's court and demanded the defendant to carry out its contractual obligation including a payment of RMB52,000.

13.30

It was held that the blank contract did amount to a delegation of power. The lack of disapproval upon receiving the contract also implies that it was properly made and thus binding. Red Cotton Trading Company was under an obligation to receive the goods and make the payment. The defendant appealed and the appeal was dismissed. Later on, the defendant received the goods but refused to pay. The plaintiff applied to the people's court for compulsory enforcement. The court then forfeited two trucks of the defendant and sold one of them to pay the plaintiff.

The issue here is whether the compulsory enforcement was unlawful. If it was, then state compensation can be applied for. As it is required under relevant legislation that preservation measures should be in proportion with the potential damage or losses suffered by the applicant. Here it seems clearly out of proportion, therefore, it can be argued to be unlawful. The next case is a similar one.

Plastic Company in X City of Shanxi Province v. Siping Plastic Shoes Company in Siping Town of X County[84]

In this case, payment was not made by the defendant as required in a sale-purchase contract made between the parties. The plaintiff filed an action to the people's court and requested an immediate payment of RMB240,000. The defendant applied to the court for permission to have the payment made from the sale of the shoes in the warehouse. The plaintiff then applied for a preservation of the assets of the defendant as security. The court then sealed up the finished shoes products, credit account and detained the truck. The defendant offered the factory and its facilities as security in return for the above to continue normal business operations of the factory,

13.31

STATE COMPENSATION

which was refused. On January 5, 1995, the judgment was decided against the defendant. Assets were sold to pay the plaintiff since the factory was not making an income during the trial and which accounted for the defendant's inability to pay. In September, the factory's operations were halted by the township people's government during the litigation. This is another case about security measures. The issue, again, is whether the security measures taken by the court was lawful.

This is because compulsory or preservation measures are sometimes closely related to the proprietary rights of the parties. Strict provisions are usually provided by law with regard to the conditions and procedures for the adoption of those measures. If those legal provisions are breached, the state should bear the responsibility for compensation. However, liability for compensation only arises if harm or damages have been caused by active adoption of those measures upon the initiative of the court, not by measures adopted upon application of one of the parties. Another point is that even if the adoption of the measures is lawful, the state still has to pay if damage to the property is due to the negligence of the courts.[85] This seems reasonable as the only remedy available to the victim will then be to seek compensation from the courts if the damages are caused under the situations mentioned in section 31.

Procedure for State Compensation

13.32 Another unique feature of the SCL is its combination of substantive and procedural provisions. Claimants, including any aggrieved citizens, legal persons and other organizations, must demand compensation according to the procedures provided in the SCL. Before the enactment of the SCL, as far as administrative compensation is concerned, lawsuits can be brought according to Chapter 9 of the ALL. This chapter, however, contains only three articles setting out the general principles. The SCL procedure of compensation (section 3 of Chapter 2) is therefore a noticeable development on the basis of the general principles of the ALL. Under the SCL, a two-step procedure is provided. Claimants must first file their claims in the form of an application with the state agencies responsible for compensation, which could be any one of the state agencies jointly responsible.[86] The agency which assumes the obligation of compensation shall accept the claim and calculate the amount of compensation according to the methods laid down in Chapter 4 of the SCL. If claimants are not satisfied with the amount of compensation, they may then file suit with the people's court within a limited period of time.

X Steel Company v. Environmental Protection Bureau and the People's Government in X City[87]

This case is concerned with administrative compensation. On January 1, 1995 at around 7 pm, chlorine gas leaked due to technical and control problems with the chlorine suction system from a chemical factory causing serious pollution to the neighbourhood. Fifty-eight workers from the transport division of an iron and steel factory, situated next to the chemical factory, were poisoned and injured, to different extents, by the gas. Twenty-one out of the 58 were seriously injured and sent to the hospital emergency unit. Two stayed behind for further medical treatment. The transport division was, thus, suspended from production, which caused a substantial financial loss to the factory. The Municipal Environmental Protection Bureau, according to section 18 of the Environmental Protection Law, decided to impose a fine of RMB150,000 on the chemical factory and ordered it to pay compensation of RMB12,382 to the steel factory.

13.33

The municipal people's government, according to sections 31, 33, 34 and 36 of the Air Pollution Law, made the decision to order the chemical factory to make relevant adjustments and repairs within one month and to suspend its business operation for one month.

Dissatisfied with the decisions, the chemical factory filed an action to the people's court on the grounds that no practical and relevant inspections were conducted and no accurate and standard calculation of loss was made. The chemical factory asked the court to repeal the sanction of fine and the suspension of business and compensation to the steel company, and also demand compensation from the Environmental Protection Bureau.

During the hearing the people's court found out that there were leakages of chlorine gas from the chemical factory on several previous occasions since 1978, which had caused serious pollution to the environment. Although certain repairs had been made on the factory, but never delved deep enough into the root of the problem and gas leaked again. The leakage caused direct physical injury to the workers as well as financial loss to the iron and steel factory. This was fact and there was sufficient evidence supporting this. The people's court maintained the decisions of the Environmental Protection Bureau and the people's government, and granted RMB29,624 compensation to the iron and steel factory upon its application for civil compensation.

This is a case for application for state compensation through a judicial review procedure under the ALL. The chemical factory used one of the methods prescribed under section 9(2) to claim for state compensation, but its application failed because the defendant did nothing unlawful. If the case happened after the SCL came into force, then the applicant needs to apply for compensation from the administrative organs, i.e. the Environmental Protection Bureau and the people's government. If not satisfied, it can then resort to the people's court. In this particular case, however, the issue of illegality needs to be determined first by the people's court through judicial review. It is therefore more appropriate to apply for compensation together with the challenge of the legality of concrete administrative act in judicial review, which is a method to claim compensation prescribed by the SCL.

However, sometimes the situation is that the compensation claim does not fall within the scope of judicial review. If that is the case, application for judicial review and application for state compensation have to be brought separately. Then the application for state compensation needs to follow the procedures as prescribed in the SCL. The next case is an example that falls in this category.

Li v. Public Security Bureau in X County[88]

13.34 Guan, brother of Li's wife, sold fruit at the front door of a theatre for Li on February 17, 1995. Three officials from the town management office, Qin and others, saw Guan and imposed a fine on him for unlawful occupation of the road. Guan refused to pay the fine on the basis that the fruit did not belong to him.

Qin then confiscated the weighing instrument. Guan tried to retrieve it, Qin threw it on the floor and it broke. Knowing what had happened, Li rushed to the scene and demanded Qin to give compensation. A dispute arose and was later stopped by some members of the public. Qin informed the county police station. Jiao and others, the county police station public security officers, brought Li back to the police station. Thinking that Li was tough upon questioning, Jiao beat him and on several occasions pushed Li to the ground. Later on, Li w as handcuffed from behind which caused serious injuries. He was then put into custody for 12 days for violating section 19 of the Regulation on Administrative Penalty for Public Security and, namely, an interference and obstruction of a state officer's work. Li, dissatisfied with the penalty, appealed to the Municipal Public Security Bureau. The decision by the county police station was upheld. Li then brought an action, on February 28, to the county people's court and applied for compensation for serious injuries caused by Qin's torture.

The people's court held that Li was wrong when he asked Qin to compensate for his weighing instrument, and pushed him. Nevertheless, throughout the event, Li, did not intend to refuse, interfere with or obstruct a state officer from executing his public duty. What he did, to be viewed objectively, did not have the effect of obstructing officers from carrying out their public duties. The penalty of 12 days in custody imposed by the county police station, was obviously unfair and inadequate. The Court repealed the penalty.

The court also held that the beating was done in the course of Qin's duty and was thus not within the scope of administrative litigation. Nevertheless, a judicial advice letter was sent to the county police station, after repealing the 12-day custody, suggesting that Li's injury was within the scope of state compensation and that the police station should compensate Li according to the provision of section 9 of the SCL. This is an important case to illustrate the difference in procedures as provided under the ALL and the SCL. No appeal was made.

Huang v. Forest Bureau in X District[89]

13.35 The applicant must be aware of what circumstances the SCL or the ALL are applicable and follow the due procedures to apply to compensation. The case of *Huang v. Forest Bureau in X District* shows that the failure to realize the difference may lead to the failure in the claim for compensation.

Huang, the plaintiff, contracted out a construction material company and sold wood planks. On September 10, 1992, Huang bought 183 pieces of wood planks from a wood factory situated at Ma Gang town. In November representatives from the Forest Industry Department, the defendant, went to Huang's company to inspect the source of the wood planks he had bought. Huang was requested to produce a wood plank and transportation certificate. Having examined the certificate, the defendant found out that the unit stated on the certificate, from which the wood planks were bought, was different from the name as stated on the receipt. They also found out from the certificate that the wood planks were supposed to be transported from one county to another county, whereas Huang had unloaded at X city. The certificate also stated that the number of wood planks to be transported was 200, whereas in fact only 183 were present. Based on the above information, the defendant concluded that the wood planks sold by Huang were inconsistent with the description in Huang's certificate and decided to confiscate the 183 wood planks. The plaintiff, dissatisfied with the decision, filed an action to the people's court.

The court found out the two names in the certificate and the receipt actually referred to the same factory. With advice from the provincial and city forest industry department, the certificate was valid throughout the whole journey and to unload at an intermediate station is permissible; and so long as the quality and specifications of the wood planks remained the same, it was lawful, even if the amount of wood planks was less than that stated in the certificate.

The court held that administrative sanction imposed by the defendant should be repealed on March 3, 1993 and the confiscated wood planks should be returned. After the time limit for appeal had lapsed and when the wood planks were returned, the plaintiff found out that the planks had deteriorated. The plaintiff refused to accept the planks and requested the defendant to compensate for the financial loss, which the defendant refused.

In May 1994, knowing that the SCL was then enacted, and that the court had already revoked the defendant's administrative sanction, Huang intended to request, again, the defendant to compensate for his financial loss since it was stated in the SCL that the time limit for requesting compensation was two years. On January 4, 1995, Huang delivered an application letter to the defendant requesting compensation. Huang requested for a total amount of RMB3,568.

13.36   There are two issues involved here.. One is whether the SCL is applicable. The second is whether the plaintiff is entitled to compensation. As the SCL came into effect on January 1, 1995 and did not have retrospective effect. Therefore, the plaintiff could not rely on the SCL to claim compensation. But that does not mean the plaintiff is not entitled to compensation. Instead, he may rely on section 67 of the ALL to apply for compensation.

On the other hand, section 14 of the SCL provides that state agencies may seek full or partial indemnity against its functionaries under two and only these two situations, i.e. the functionaries either intentionally committed errors or negligently committed grave errors. In other words, if no intention to commit errors can be proved, the functionaries will only be held responsible in negligence if they commit grave or serious error, not for committing ordinary errors.[90] That is to say, negligence has been divided into two categories: serious negligence and ordinary negligence. The former refers to the condition that the functionaries failed to notice the tortious behaviour that the ordinary persons would notice and are able to prevent its happening; their failure leads to the tortious consequence.[91] The main reason to hold the functionaries liable for serious negligence, as provided by the draughtsmen, is to make sure that they will do their work properly and exercise their authorities according to law. However, if the functionaries will be held liable to pay indemnity, either partial or full, for all negligent behaviour, then the efficiency of administration will be hampered as they will be over-cautious.[92] It is therefore a balancing exercise between judicial supervision of administration and administrative efficiency. Furthermore, section 14 also provides that the functionaries will face administrative penalties for intentionally committing errors or negligently committing grave errors. They may even face criminal penalties if their intentional or negligent conducts constitute a crime.[93]

The procedure concerning criminal compensation was also very controversial during the legislative process as it involved a series of issues, such as the criminal law system, legal supervision system and reform of judicial and supervision systems.[94] The focus was on whether it was necessary to have pre-trial procedure and which organ should be in charge of that procedure.[95] The procedure finally adopted by the SCL is a three-step process. The first step is the same as the procedure for claims of administrative compensation. The second step is an extra one. The claimants may apply to the next higher agency for a review if they object to the amount of compensation. The third step is also different as the claimant may apply to the compensation committee of the people's court at the corresponding level for a decision on compensation. This procedure for criminal compensation is a special one that combines administrative reconsideration[96] with administrative litigation. Whether this procedure will work remains to be seen as no cases are available at the moment to facilitate our discussion. It is at least questionable, in theory, whether this procedure is appropriate since the fundamental principle of fairness is breached by this procedure because the causes of criminal compensation are illegal acts of the bodies involved. The victim has every reason to doubt that the bodies at the next higher level of those involved can be biased if they are allowed to review the case decided at the lower level, and the unequal status between the two parties could be worsened. Moreover, as far as the judiciary is concerned, the decisions of lower judicial organs sometimes represent the opinions of those at the next higher level as it is a tradition to seek the opinions of those at the next higher level, especially in criminal cases.[97] Both review and litigation will therefore be of little value to the claimant.

Jiang v. Public Security Bureau in X County[98]

13.37 This case is one of the few cases available. In this case, on January 5, 1995, Jiang met Hong, a villager at the Jia Pi Gou village, while he was helping his friend out. Jiang was wearing a police uniform. Thinking that Jiang was a police officer, Hong invited Jiang to Jia Pi Gou village when they passed. Two days later, Jiang went to Jia Pi Gou village. While Jiang was having drinks at Hong's house, Hong's wife introduced a female friend to Jiang. This female friend thought Jiang was a police officer and Jiang did not clarify the misunderstanding. While he was drinking, Jiang was told that the village leader had been committing a substantial amount of unlawful acts and he expressed the willingness to help solve the problem by bringing the matter to the attention of relevant readers. Before leaving, Jiang said that he would have to report to his leader and would be back later on. Three days later, Jiang returned to Jia Pi Gou village for investigation. He found and collected two relevant materials about the village leader. The village security protection official was suspicious of Jiang. Jiang went home, and carved the stamp of "Police Department Materials Division" on a chess piece . He then stamped it on eight pieces of paper.

Before leaving for the village again, he wrote a letter of apology to the police department commissioner explaining that he was disguised as a police officer in order to help the village to solve problems. This letter was never sent out. Jiang was put on sheltering for investigation two days later.

It was held by the Public Security Bureau that Jiang had made the chop himself and pretended to be a police officer, which amounted to a criminal offence and requested the procuratorate to approve the arrest of Jiang.

The court held that what Jiang did was not that serious and did not have any adverse consequences, therefore did not constitute a crime and so refused to grant permission to arrest Jiang. Later on, the Public Security Bureau released Jiang and issued him a release permit.

The issue here is whether Jiang may request for compensation based on the release permit that was issued to him. In this case, it was decided by the procuratorate that the criminal charge against Jiang was unlawful, therefore, Jiang can rely on section 20(1) of the SCL to apply for compensation from the Public Security Bureau.

Partial or even full indemnity can also be claimed, under section 24 of the SCL, after the criminal compensation by the body responsible for paying compensation from the functionaries under certain circumstances, just the same as under section 14 for administrative compensation.[99] As this conduct mentioned under section 24 of the SCL is expressly prohibited by law, it is logical to hold those law enforcers who committed the illegal behaviour to pay indemnity. Moreover, in order to prevent those illegal conducts from happening, those committers will also face administrative penalties, or even criminal penalties if their conducts constitute crimes.[100]

Conclusion

13.38   The above analysis reveals that the SCL has a narrow scope of application. Theoretically, there is sufficient justification to include in the SCL at least part of the acts of some excluded state organs such as the military, public utilities and local legislature. Moreover, certain aspects of the SCL may need further improvement, such as the procedure for criminal compensation, the appropriateness of administrative reconsideration as opposed to the court as the final adjudicator for compensation. However, many factors have contributed to the formulation of the SCL, including lack of legislative experience, political considerations and existing relationship between different state organs.[101]

At the same time, the adoption of the SCL is a great achievement towards the improvement of the legal system, especially the public law system in the PRC.[102] The SCL has recognized the uniqueness of the torts committed by state organs for illegal exercise of power and subjected them to legal regulation. In so doing, not only the lawful interests of the citizens, legal persons and other organizations can be better protected, but also the accountability of those state organs regulated by the SCL can be enhanced. The enactment of the SCL has also contributed to the establishment of a comprehensive system of state responsibility. The reason to say so is because damages can be caused for different reasons. A comprehensive system of state responsibility should cover the compensation for damages or losses caused by all kinds of reasons, such as illegal and legal acts of state, or natural disasters and *force majeure*. The SCL has provided the most comprehensive state compensation legislation on illegal acts of state organs so far in the PRC.

Moreover, the enactment of the SCL has also contributed to the completion of the administrative law structure in the PRC. The ALL was enacted in 1989 with the aim to subject the administrative organs to judicial control in civil affairs. The 1990 Regulation on Administrative Reconsideration in the PRC, promulgated by the State Council, is a supplement to the ALL. In the same year, the Regulation on Administrative Supervision in the PRC was promulgated by the State Council, under which the Ministry of Supervision shall supervise the work of other administrative organs. However, the Ministry of Supervision is within the executive branch of the government. Its function is similar to that of Ombudsman in some Western countries. The focus of these legislation has been on state organs, i.e. to control the exercise of power by state organs. The protection of lawful interests of the claimants and victims and the exact remedies available to them have never been laid down in any legislation in details. The SCL has filled in that gap. In this sense, the adoption of the SCL is a great achievement in the protection of the lawful rights and interests of the citizens, legal persons and other organizations against illegal infringement of their rights or interests by state organs or their personnel.

Notes

[1] The English translation used in this paper is by Reuter Textline, BBC Monitoring Service Far East, available on Lexis/Nexis.
[2] Zhu Weijiu, "Comment on the State Compensation Law of the People's Republic of China" (1994) 7 *Zhongguo Lüshi* (Chinese Lawyer) 29.
[3] See conclusion for more detail.
[4] The earliest legal document is the Interim Provisions on the Management of

Harbours of People's Republic of China, adopted in January 1954. Art. 20 of the Interim Provisions provides that the harbour administration bureau shall be obliged to pay compensation for direct losses to ships due to the bureau's refusal to let the ships leave the harbour without any legal grounds. See Ma Huaide, *Guojia peichangfa de lilun yu shiwu* (Theory and Practice of State Compensation Law), Beijing: China Legal Press, 1994, pp. 55 and 56; and Pi Chunxie, *Guojia peichangfa shilun* (Interpretation of State Compensation Law), Beijing: China Legal Press, 1994, p. 44.

5 Xu Chongde, *Zhongguo xianfa cankao ziliao xuanbian* (Collection of Reference Material on Chinese Constitutions), Beijing: People's University of China Press, 1990, p. 36. The translation is by the author.

6 Obviously this is due to the numerous political campaigns including the Cultural Revolution from 1966 to 1976.

7 Para. 3 of Art. 41. See *Constitution of the People's Republic of China*, Beijing: Foreign Languages Press, 1987, p. 30.

8 See s. 33 of the Economic Contract Law (1981), "If, due to the fault of higher-level leading authorities or of the department in charge of specialized work, an economic contract cannot be performed or cannot be fully performed, the higher-level leading authorities or the department in charge of specialized work shall bear liability for the breach of contract"; s. 42 of the Regulations of the PRC on Administrative Penalties for Public Security (1986), "The public security organs shall admit their mistakes to those who are punished by mistake and return fines and confiscated property; in case the legal rights and interests of those who are so punished have been infringed upon, the loss shall be compensated for". The English translation is by the Legislative Affairs Commission of the NPC Standing Committee. See *The Laws of the People's Republic of China* (1979–82) and (1983–86), Beijing: Foreign Language Press, 1990.

9 The purpose of the Administrative Litigation Law as described in Art. 1 is to "... ensure the correct and prompt handling of administrative cases by the People's Court, protect the lawful rights and interests of citizens, legal persons and other organizations, and safeguard and supervise the exercise of administrative powers by administrative organs". Art. 11 lists eight categories of "concrete administrative acts" covered by the ALL, but the term "concrete administrative acts" is not defined. See *The Laws of the People's Republic of China* (1987–89), Beijing, Science Press, 1990, pp. 285 and 287.

10 Chap. 9 consists of three articles: s. 67 (rights of citizens, legal persons or other organizations to claim compensation for damages due to concrete administrative acts and the appropriate procedure including use of mediation), s. 68 (liabilities of administrative organs and personnel who committed intentional or gross mistakes to pay compensation), and s. 69 (allocation of cost of compensation).

11 "Concrete administrative act" and "abstract administrative act" are two terms used by Chinese scholars for classification and better understanding of the nature of administrative acts. The term "abstract administrative act" does not appear in the ALL. Different views exist as to the definition of these two terms. For detailed discussion, see Zhang Shuyi "On the Criteria for Distinguishing Abstract and Specific Administrative Acts" (1993), 1 *Zhongguo Faxue* (China Legal Science), 60, 64.

12 See "A Reply to Questions Raised by Journalists on State Compensation Law" (1994), 7 *Zhongguo Lüshi* (Chinese Lawyer) 31.

13 See n. 2 above, p. 29.

14 One opinion is that state compensation is the same kind of liability under s. 121 of the GPCL. Another is that state compensation arises from liability for lawful acts of state organs or their personnel, which is completely different from civil liability. A third approach holds that state compensation is a special kind of tort liability caused by illegal exercise of powers and has a lot of similarity with civil liability though they are not exactly the same. For details, see n. 2 above, p. 29.

15 See s. 2.

16 Some officials from the Legislative Affairs Commission of the NPC Standing Committee argue that civil liability has to be concerned with compensation for breaching contracts or committing torts by citizens or legal persons. N. 12 above, p. 32. However, this approach seems to be in clear contradiction with the inclusion in s. 121 of the civil liability of state organs for infringement of rights of citizens and legal persons.

17 Chinese scholars and drafters do have access to texts of foreign legislation, some of which have been translated into Chinese. See Lin Zhun et al, *Waiguo guojia peichang zhidu* (State Compensation Systems in Foreign Countries), Beijing: People's Court Press, 1992.
18 N. 12 above, p. 32.
19 In China this theory is generally attributed to Lenin. Recently, however, some Chinese scholars have maintained that Lenin's words are mistranslated. Others argue that it is essential to distinguish public law from private law for the sake of establishing a legal system for the socialist market economy. Thus the views are no longer unanimous. See Wang Chenguang and Liu Wen, "Market Economy and the Demarcation of Public Law and Private Law" (1993), 1 *Zhongguo Faxue* (China Legal Science) 28, 36.
20 N. 12 above, p. 32.
21 Para. 1 of s. 14.
22 Para. 2 of s. 14.
23 See the casebook on state compensation, pp. 159–62.
24 For detailed discussion on this point, refer to the chapter on legal control of discretionary power.
25 See n. 14 above.
26 See s. 2.
27 See "The Explanation of the State Compensation Law and the Relevant Case Analysis", pp. 81–83.
28 See "The Explanation of the State Compensation Law and the Relevant Case Analysis", pp. 93–97.
29 Many laws and administrative regulations have provided for administrative indemnity. For example, para. 2 of s. 7 of the Grass Land Law of the People's Republic of China (1985) provides that "If grasslands under ownership by the whole people that are assigned to collectives for long-term use are to be used for state construction, due compensation shall be paid to the collective concerned..."; para. 2 of s. 13 of the Fisheries Law of the People's Republic of China provides that "When state-owned water surfaces and tidal flats that have been allotted to units ... for aquaculture are requisitioned for state construction, the construction units shall give those units appropriate compensation".
30 See "The Explanation of State Compensation Law and Relevant Case Analysis" pp. 86–88.
31 See s. 51 of the PRC Civil Procedure Law provides that "the two parties may reach a compromise of their own accord". S. 85 provides further that "in the trial of civil cases, the People's Court shall ... conduct conciliation between the parties on a voluntary basis". The English translation is from *The Laws of the People's Republic of China* (1990–92), Beijing: Science Press, 1993.
32 An example of compensation only for direct loss is provided by s. 54 of the Customs Law of the People's Republic of China (1987), which provides that "If the Customs causes damage to any inward or outward goods or articles while examining them, it shall make up for the actual loss from such damage". For violation of citizens' right to life, the compensation shall cover medical expenses, loss of income, etc. under s. 27 of SCL. For violation of personal freedom of citizens, compensation will be a fixed amount calculated on the basis of the previous year's average daily wage set by the State under s. 26 of the SCL.
33 See s. 3 of Chap. 2 of the SCL.
34 For example, a special relationship is deemed to exist under s. 15 of the SCL between a policeman and a suspect of murder under investigation. If the suspect runs away, the policeman may shoot. If a third party on the street is injured by the shot fired by the policeman, the third party can only bring an action for damages under the GPCL as no special relationship exists between the policeman and the third party.
35 See "The Explanation of the Compensation Law and the Relevant Case Analysis", pp. 91–93.
36 See Shen Zonglin, *Faxue jichu lilun* (Basic Legal Theory), Beijing: Beijing University Press, 1988, p. 395; see also Qiao Wei (ed) *Xinbian faxue cidian* (New Edition of Law Dictionary), Jinan: Shandong People's Press, 1985, p. 831.
37 See Lexis-Nexis News: "China Plans to Draft Damages Law", Beijing, July 24, 1989. Item No. 0724034.

38 Pi Chunxie (n. 4 above), p. 65.
39 Pi Chunxie (n. 4 above), p. 65.
40 Zhou Hanhua and He Jun, *Wuaiguo guojia peichang zhidu bijiao yianjiu* (Comparative Study of Foreign State Compensation Systems), Beijing: Police Officers Education Press, 1992, p. 14. As far as Commonwealth countries are concerned, subsidiary legislation is subject to judicial review and claims for damages may arise if the subsidiary legislation is held to be invalid and the claimant's rights have been infringed.
41 Exceptions do exist with regard to economic legislations. For example, the Law on the Protection of Consumers' Rights of the PRC has incorporated some provisions on some matters which the PRC does not have much experience about. That is called legislation in advance of practice. According to officials from the Legislative Affairs Commission, that approach is strongly advocated by Qiao Shi, the Chairman of the Standing Committee of the National People's Congress.
42 See n. 2 above, p. 30.
43 That is very unlikely to happen at national level as the NPC and its Standing Committee do not enjoy supreme authority in reality. The guidelines on important legislation are laid down by Political Bureau of the Central Committee of Communist Party of China. However, local legislatures at provincial level do enact legislations, some of which have been found to be contradictory to national legislation.
44 Jin Liqi et al, *Guojia peichangfa yuanli* (Principles of State Compensation Law), Beijing: China Television Broadcasting Press, 1990, pp. 92 and 95.
45 In the United Kingdom, subsidiary legislation are subject to judicial supervision by the High Court. Action for damages would lie. One example given by Professor Wade is that damages could be claimed if a local authority demolished the claimant's house by relying on subsidiary legislation which was held by the court to be invalid. For detailed discussion, see H.W.R. Wade, *Administrative Law*, Oxford: Clarendon Press, 1989, 6th edn., chap. 22.
46 Pi Chunxie (n. 4 above), p. 66.
47 See n. 2 above, p. 36.
48 See n. 2 above, p. 30.
49 According to one source, the Military Law of the PRC is being drafted by the Bureau of Legislative Affairs of the Central Military Commission. See also n. 2 above, p. 30.
50 See s. 12(1) of the Administrative Litigation Law.
51 Pi Chunxie (n. 4 above), p. 66.
52 S. 4 of Chap. 3 (State Organs) of the Constitution of the PRC is on military organs.
53 See n. 2 above, p. 30.
54 Ss. 123–27.
55 See "The Explanation of the State Compensation Law and the Relevant Case Analysis", pp. 91–93.
56 See Chaps. 2 and 3 of the State Compensation Law.
57 See s. 3 of the State Compensation Law.
58 See of "The Explanation of the State Compensation Law and the Relevant Case Analysis", pp. 115–16.
59 See s. 4 of the State Compensation Law.
60 See "The Explanation of the State Compensation Law and the Relevant Case Analysis", pp. 98–100.
61 For detailed discussion of the abuse of power, refer to the s. on legal control of discretionary power under judicial review.
62 See "The Explanation of the State Compensation Law and the Relevant Case Analysis", pp. 108–11.
63 See "The Explanation of the State Compensation Law and the Relevant Case Analysis", pp. 123–24.
64 See "The Explanation of the State Compensation Law and the Relevant Case Analysis", pp. 133–34.
65 See "The Explanation of the State Compensation Law and the Relevant Case Analysis", pp. 141–46.
66 S. 11 of the Administrative Litigation Law provides that the people's courts shall

accept suits brought by citizens, legal persons or other organizations against any of the following concrete administrative acts:

(1) An administrative sanction, such as detention, fine, rescission of a licence or permit, order to suspend production or business or confiscation of property, which one refuses to accept.
(2) A compulsory administrative measure, such as restricting freedom of the person or the sealing up, seizing or freezing of property, which one refuses to accept.
(3) Infringement upon one's managerial decision-making powers, which is considered to have been perpetrated by an administrative organ.
(4) Refusal by an administrative organ to issue a permit or license, which one considers oneself legally qualified to apply for, or its failure to respond to the application.
(5) Refusal by an administrative organ to perform its statutory duty of protecting one's rights of the person and of property, as one has applied for, or its failure to respond to the application.
(6) Cases where an administrative organ is considered to have failed to issue a pension according to law.
(7) Cases where an administrative organ is considered to have illegally demanded the performance of duties.
(8) Cases where an administrative organ is considered to have infringed upon other rights of the person and of property.

Apart from the provisions set forth in the preceding paragraphs, the people's courts shall accept other administrative suits which may be brought in accordance with the provisions of relevant laws and regulations.

[67] Refer to the discussion on the scope of application of the ALL in the chapter on judicial review in China in this book.
[68] It mainly refers to the fact the judiciary also has the authority to review the reasonableness under limited circumstances when a judicial review case is brought under the ALL.
[69] See n. 59 above.
[70] See "The Explanation of the State Compensation Law and the Relevant Case Analysis", pp. 241–44.
[71] See "The Explanation of the State Compensation Law and Relevant Case Analysis", pp. 254–55.
[72] See s. 15 of the State Compensation Law.
[73] See n. 71 above, pp. 292–97.
[74] See "The Explanation of the State Compensation Law and the Relevant Case Analysis", pp. 257–60.
[75] See n. 71 above, pp. 261–62.
[76] See "The Explanation of the State Compensation Law and the Relevant Case Analysis", pp. 263–66.
[77] See "The Explanation of the State Compensation Law and the Relevant Case Analysis", pp. 280–82.
[78] Pi Chunxie, see n. 4 above, p. 212.
[79] See n. 12 above, p. 36.
[80] See s. 31 of the State Compensation Law.
[81] See "The Explanation of the State Compensation Law and the Relevant Case Analysis", pp. 336–70.
[82] See "The Explanation of the State Compensation Law and the Relevant Case Analysis", pp. 343–47.
[83] See "The Explanation of the State Compensation Law and the Relevant Case Analysis", pp. 347–52.
[84] See "The Explanation of the State Compensation Law and the Relevant Case Analysis", pp. 355–58.
[85] Pi Chunxie, n. 4 above, pp. 213–14.
[86] See ss. 9, 10 and 12 of the State Compensation Law.
[87] See "The Explanation of the State Compensation Law and the Relevant Case Analysis", pp. 180–83.

88 See "The Explanation of the State Compensation Law and the Relevant Case Analysis", pp. 183–86.
89 See "The Explanation of the State Compensation Law and the Relevant Case Analysis", pp. 191–94.
90 Hu Kangsheng (ed), Zhonghua renming gongheguo guojia geichangfa sheyi (Interpretation of the State Compensation Law of the People's Republic of China), Beijing: Law Press, 1994, 36.
91 N. 90 above, p. 36.
92 N. 90 above, p. 37.
93 Para. 2 of s. 14 of State Compensation Law.
94 See n. 2 above, p. 31.
95 Pi Chunxie, n. 4 above, p. 72.
96 It is the supervision by the administrative organ at the next higher level over the decisions made by the administrative organ immediately below it. It is governed by the Regulation on Administrative Reconsideration, which was promulgated by the State Council on December 24, 1990, effective January 1, 1991.
97 Pi Chunxie, n. 4 above, pp. 232 and 233.
98 See "The Explanation of the State Compensation Law and the Relevant Case Analysis", pp. 301–03.
99 According to s. 24 of the State Compensation Law, there are three circumstances under which indemnity can be claimed:

    i. Using torture to coerce statements, inflicting physical injuries on or causing the deaths of citizens through such violent acts as physical assault, or instigating other people to cause physical injuries or deaths through similar acts.
    ii. Inflicting physical injuries on or causing the deaths of citizens through the illegal use of weapons or police gear.
    iii. Corruption, taking bribes, fraudulent practices out of personal considerations and perverting the law when acting as a judge during the handling of cases

100 Para. 2 of s. 24 of the State Compensation Law.
101 This has been argued by Professor Pi Chunxie, another authority on Chinese administrative law. See Pi Chunxie, n. 4 above, p. 69.
102 See n. 19 above.

APPENDICES

REGULATIONS ON ADMINISTRATIVE RECONSIDERATION OF THE PEOPLE'S REPUBLIC OF CHINA

(Adopted at the 71st Meeting of the State Council on 9 November 1990 and effective on 1 January 1991, Amended on 9 October 1994)

CHAPTER ONE: GENERAL PROVISIONS

1. This Regulation is enacted, in accordance with the Constitution and other relevant laws, for the purpose of safeguarding and guaranteeing the administrative organs in exercising their authorities and performing their duties properly, preventing and rectifying any unlawful or improper concrete administrative acts, and protecting the legitimate rights and interests of citizens, legal persons and other organizations.
2. Citizens, legal persons and other organizations may apply to the competent administrative organ for administrative reconsideration, where they believe that their legitimate rights and interests are infringed by the concrete administrative act of an administrative organ.
3. The administrative reconsideration organ shall exercise its power and perform its duty in accordance with legislation. The administrative reconsideration organ shall not be subject to any unlawful interference from individuals, public organizations or other organs.
4. The "reconsideration organs", as mentioned in this Regulation, refers to those administrative organs which accept applications for reconsideration, conduct reviews over the concrete administrative acts and make decisions in accordance with the legislation.
   The "reconsideration offices", as mentioned in this Regulation, refers those offices which are established within the administrative organs, and are responsible to handle the matters relating to reconsideration.
5. The administrative reconsideration applies a single-level system of reconsideration unless it is stipulated otherwise by the laws and administrative regulations.
6. The principles of legality, punctuality, accuracy and convenience for the citizens shall be followed when the administrative reconsideration is conducted.
7. The reconsideration organs shall, in accordance with legislation, conduct review of the lawfulness and appropriateness of the concrete administrative acts.
8. Conciliation shall not be applied when the reconsideration organs handle reconsideration cases.

CHAPTER TWO: THE SCOPE OF RECONSIDERATION

9. Citizens, legal persons and other organizations may apply to the reconsideration organs for administrative reconsideration if they regard any of the following concrete administrative acts as unacceptable:

(1) an administrative sanction, such as detention, fine, cancellation of a permit or licence, order of suspension of production or business operations, or confiscation of property;
(2) a compulsory administrative measure, such as restriction of personal liberty, sealing up, distraint, or freezing of property;
(3) infringement upon one's managerial decision-making autonomy, as provided under legislation, by an administrative organ;
(4) any refusal or failure to respond by an administrative organ to the application to issue a permit or licence, which one regards oneself qualified to apply for under relevant legislation;
(5) any refusal or failure to respond by an administrative organ to the application for the performance of statutory duty to protect one's personal or property rights;
(6) failure by an administrative organ to pay the pensions for the disabled or for the family of the deceased in accordance to relevant legislation;
(7) unlawful request by an administrative organ for the performance of duty by the citizens, legal persons and other organizations;
(8) infringement by an administrative organ upon other personal or property rights;
(9) other concrete administrative acts which, as provided by legislation, may be brought for judicial review or administrative reconsideration;
(10) Citizens, legal persons and other organizations can not apply for administrative reconsideration in accordance with this Regulation if they are not satisfied with the following matters:
 (a) Administrative regulations, regulations or other decisions and orders which have general binding effects;
 (b) Decision on awards and penalties, or on appointment or dismissal of any personnel in administrative organs;
 (c) Arbitration, conciliation or other disposition of civil disputes; but disposition, by administrative organs, of the ownership or right to use relating to land, mineral resources, forests and so on will be excluded from this category;
 (d) Acts of state, such as national defence and diplomatic affairs and so on.

CHAPTER THREE: JURISDICTION OF RECONSIDERATION

11. If a concrete administrative act, against which an application for reconsideration is filed, is undertaken by a working department of the local people's government at county level or above, the case shall be under the jurisdiction of the people's government at the same level or the competent department in charge at the next higher level. However, if the laws or administrative regulations provide that the case shall be under the jurisdiction of the people's government at the same level, such provisions should be followed; if laws provide that the case is under the jurisdiction of the competent department at the next higher level, such provisions should be followed.

If the concrete administrative act, against which an application for administrative reconsideration is lodged, is undertaken by any departments under the State Council, the case shall be under the jurisdiction of the department which undertakes the aforesaid concrete administrative act.

12. If a concrete administrative act, against which an application for reconsideration is lodged, is undertaken by the local people's government at any level, the case shall be under the jurisdiction of the people's government at the next higher level.

If a concrete administrative act, against which an application for reconsideration is lodged, is undertaken by any people's government of a province, an autonomous region or a municipality directly under the Central People's Government, the case shall be under the jurisdiction of the people's government which has undertaken the aforesaid concrete administrative act.

13. If a concrete administrative act, against which an application for reconsideration is lodged is jointly undertaken in the name of two or more administrative organs, the case shall be under the jurisdiction of the administrative organ at the next higher level over the aforesaid administrative organs.

14. If a concrete administrative act, against which an application for reconsideration is lodged, is undertaken by the agency which is set up by any people's government at county level or above, the case shall be under the jurisdiction of the people's government which set up the aforesaid agency.

If the concrete administrative act, against which an application for reconsideration is lodged, is undertaken by the agency which is set up by a working department of any people's government, and the agency acts in its own name in accordance with laws, administrative regulations and departmental regulations, the case shall be under the jurisdiction of the working department which sets up the aforesaid agency.

15. If a concrete administrative act, against which an application for reconsideration is lodged, is undertaken by an organization authorized by the laws, administrative regulations and departmental regulations, the case shall be under the jurisdiction of the competent administrative organ just above the aforesaid organization. If a concrete administrative act, against which an application for reconsideration is lodged, is undertaken by an organization entrusted, the case shall be under the jurisdiction of the administrative organ at the next higher level over the entrusting administrative organ.

16. If a concrete administrative act, against which an application for reconsideration is lodged, is in accordance with laws and regulations, is subject to the approval of the administrative organ at the next higher level, the case shall be, except the laws and regulations stipulate otherwise, under the jurisdiction of the administrative organ which finally approves the aforesaid concrete administrative act.

17. If a concrete administrative act, against which an application for reconsideration is lodged, is undertaken by an administrative organ, which is abolished, prior to its abolition, the case shall be under the jurisdiction of the administrative organ at the next higher level over the administrative organ which resumes the powers the aforesaid abolished administrative organ.

18. If an administrative reconsideration organ discovers that the case it has accepted is not under its jurisdiction, the aforesaid administrative organ shall transfer the case to the administrative organ which has jurisdiction over the case. The administrative organ, to which case is transferred, shall not, on its own initiative transfer the case to any other administrative organ.

19. If a dispute arises between two administrative organs over the jurisdiction of a case, the dispute shall be resolved by the two organs through negotiation. If negotiation fails, the jurisdiction shall be designated by the administrative organ at the next higher level above the two organs.

20. If an applicant files is an application for reconsideration to two or more administrative organs, the administrative organ which firstly receives the application shall have jurisdiction over the case.

21. If citizens, legal persons or other organizations make a complaint to the correspondence and reception bureau within the time limit of application for reconsideration stipulated in the laws or regulations, the correspondence and reception bureau shall, without delay, notify the aforesaid complainant to apply for administrative reconsideration to the administrative organ which has jurisdiction over the case.

22. Other cases concerning jurisdiction for reconsideration shall be handled in accordance with the stipulations of the laws, administrative regulations and departmental regulations.

CHAPTER FOUR: OFFICE FOR RECONSIDERATION

23. An administrative reconsideration organ shall, according to the need of its work, set up a reconsideration office or appoint specific personnel to handle reconsideration cases.

24. Reconsideration office which is in the local people's government at county level or above, shall be set up within the government's legal affairs office or the reconsideration cases shall be handled by the government's legal affairs office.

25. Reconsideration office or specific personnel for reconsideration shall, under the instructions of the administrative reconsideration organs, perform the following duties:

(1) To conduct a review of whether or not the legal requirements of application for reconsideration are fulfilled;
(2) To conduct investigations among, and collect evidence from both parties to a dispute and relevant units and personnel, and to check relevant documents and materials;
(3) To review reconsideration cases;
(4) To draft reconsideration verdict;
(5) To respond to court hearing, as entrusted by the legal representative of the administrative reconsideration organ;
(6) To perform any other duties as provided by laws and regulations.

CHAPTER FIVE: PARTICIPANTS IN RECONSIDERATION

26. Citizens, legal persons and any other organizations who apply for reconsideration in accordance with this Regulation are applicants.

The close relatives of the citizens who are qualified to apply for reconsideration may apply for reconsideration when the said citizen is dead. The legal representatives of citizens who are qualified to apply for reconsideration but are incompetent or with limited capacity, may apply for reconsideration on behalf of the said citizen.

If legal persons or any other organizations which are qualified to apply for reconsideration terminate, the legal persons or organizations which inherit the rights of the aforesaid legal persons or organizations may apply for reconsideration.

27. If any other citizens, legal persons or other organizations which have any interest in the concrete administrative act which an application for reconsideration is lodged, they may apply, with the approval of the administrative reconsideration organ, for participation in the reconsideration as third parties.

28. If citizens, legal persons or organizations apply for reconsideration against a concrete administrative act undertaken by an administrative organ, the said administrative organ is the defending party.

If a concrete administrative act is undertaken jointly in the name of two or more administrative organs, the said administrative organs are joint defending parties.

If a concrete administrative act is undertaken by an organization authorized by the laws, administrative regulations and departmental regulations, the organization is the defending party.

If a concrete administrative action is undertaken by an organization entrusted by an administrative organ, the said administrative organ is the defending party.

If a concrete administrative act is undertaken by an administrative organ which is abolished, the administrative organ which inherits the powers of the abolished administrative organ is the defending party.

CHAPTER SIX: APPLICATION AND ACCEPTANCE

29. If citizens, legal persons or organizations apply to an administrative organ for reconsideration which has jurisdiction they should do so within 15 days since they become aware of the concrete administrative act, except the laws or regulations stipulate otherwise.

If citizens, legal persons or organizations fail to apply for reconsideration within the aforesaid time limit, due to force majeure or other special reasons, they may apply for an extension of time limit within 10 days since the said obstacle is removed, the administrative reconsideration organ shall decide whether or not to approve the application for extension of time limit.

30. If citizens, legal persons or organizations have brought a lawsuit to the people's court and the people's court accepts the case, the aforesaid citizens, legal persons or organizations cannot apply for reconsideration.

If citizens, legal persons or organizations apply to the administrative organ for reconsideration, and the said organ accepts the case, the aforesaid citizens, legal persons or organizations cannot bring a lawsuit to the people's court within the time limit for reconsideration as stipulated in laws and regulations.

31. Where an application for reconsideration is filed, the following requirements shall be fulfilled:

(1) The applicant believes the concrete administrative act has directly infringed the legitimate rights and interests of citizens, legal persons or others organizations;
(2) The defending party is specific;
(3) The request and factual basis for reconsideration are specific;
(4) The concrete administrative act falls within the scope of reconsideration;
(5) The concrete administrative act is under the jurisdiction of the administrative reconsideration organ accepting the case;
(6) Other requirements as stipulated in the laws and regulations.

32. An applicant, when applying to administrative organ for reconsideration, shall submit a written application.

33. The following contents shall be contained in the written application:

(1) The name, gender, age, occupation, address, so on of the applicant (the title and address of legal persons or other organizations and the name of their legal representative);

(2) The title and address of the defending party;
(3) The request and reasons for the application;
(4) The date of filing the application.

34. The reconsideration organ shall within 10 days from the date the organ receives the written application for reconsideration, handle the case in one of the following manners:

(1) To accept the application for reconsideration if the application complies with the stipulations in this regulation;
(2) To make a decision rejecting the application for reconsideration and to state the reasons of refusal, if the application does not comply with one of the stipulations in section 31;
(3) To return the written application for reconsideration to the applicant, if one of the contents in section 33 is not stated, and order the applicant to make up the contents within the time limit. If the applicant fails to make up the contents within the time limit, it shall be deemed that the application is not lodged.

35. If citizens, legal persons or organizations apply for reconsideration, the reconsideration organ refuses to accept or does not respond to the application without proper reasons, the administrative organ at the next higher level or the administrative organ as stipulated by laws and regulations shall order the aforesaid administrative organ to accept or to respond to the said application.

36. Except the relevant laws and regulations stipulate otherwise, an applicant shall first apply to the administrative reconsideration organ in accordance with the laws and regulations, then bring a law suit to the people's court if the said applicant does not accept the decision. If the said applicant does not accept the decision of the reconsideration organ to reject its application, the said applicant may bring a lawsuit to the people's court within 15 days since he receives the written decision on the rejection of the application.

CHAPTER SEVEN: HEARING AND DECISION

37. Administrative reconsideration shall adopt the system of reconsideration of written submissions. However, other methods of hearing may be adopted by the reconsideration organ if the said organ believes it necessary.

38. Reconsideration organ shall deliver a copy of the written application for reconsideration to the defending party within 7 days since the said organ accepts the application. The defending party submit relevant materials or evidences of the administrative act as well as a written defense within 10 days since the said defending party receives the copy of the written application for reconsideration. The reconsideration shall not be affected if no written defense is submitted.

39. The execution of a concrete administrative act shall not be suspended in the course of reconsideration, unless one of the following circumstances occurs:

(1) The defending party believes the suspension of execution necessary;
(2) The reconsideration organ believes the suspension of execution necessary;
(3) The applicant applies for the suspension for execution, and reconsideration organ, believes the request is a reasonable one and makes a decision for the suspension of execution;

(4) The suspension of execution is stipulated in the relevant laws, administrative regulations or departmental regulations.

40. The applicant may withdraw the application for reconsideration, or the defending may vary its concrete administrative act prior to a decision is made by the reconsideration organ. Where the applicant agrees to and applies for withdrawal of the application for reconsideration, subject to the approval and recording by the reconsideration organ, the application may be withdrawn.

41. Once an application is withdrawn, the applicant cannot lodge an application for reconsideration basing on the same facts and reasons. The reconsideration organ shall handle reconsideration cases in accordance with relevant laws, administrative regulations, local regulations, rules, and other decisions and orders, which have general binding effect, enacted and promulgated by administrative organs at the higher level in accordance with the laws.

Where the reconsideration organ handles reconsideration cases in the nationality autonomous region, the autonomous regulations and individual regulations of the nationality autonomous region shall also be applied.

42. The reconsideration organ shall, after hearing the case, make one of the following reconsideration decisions:

(1) If the application of laws, administrative regulations, departmental regulations and other decisions and orders which have general binding effect is correct, the facts of the case are clear, the legal limit of authority and procedure are compiled with, the concrete administrative act shall be sustained by the decision;
(2) If there are any inadequacies in the procedure for the undertaking of the concrete administrative act, the defending party shall be ordered by the decision to make rectification;
(3) If the defending party fails to perform its duties as stipulated in laws, administrative regulations and departmental regulations, it shall be ordered by the decision to perform the duties within a specified time limit;
(4) The concrete administrative act may be annulled, amended, and the defending party may be ordered to undertake a new concrete administrative act, if it falls into one of the following circumstances:
   (a) The essential facts are not clear;
   (b) The application of relevant laws, administrative regulations, departmental regulations and other decisions and orders which have general binding effect is incorrect;
   (c) The concrete administrative act is obviously inappropriate.

43. When the reconsideration organ reviews a concrete administrative act, if the reconsideration organ finds that there is any contradiction between the departmental regulations and decisions and orders which have general binding effects on which the concrete administrative act is based, and the laws, administrative regulations and decisions and orders which have general binding effects, the reconsideration organ shall annul or amend the administrative act within its scope of authority.

When the reconsideration organ reviews the concrete administrative act, if the reconsideration organ finds that there is any contradiction between the departmental regulations, and decisions and orders which have general binding effects on which the concrete administrative act is based, and the laws, administrative regulations and decisions and orders which have general binding effects, and the aforesaid organ does not have the authority to handle it, the said organ shall report to the administrative organ at the next higher level. If the said administrative organ at the next higher level has the authority to handle the case, it shall handle it in accordance with the relevant laws and administrative regulations. If the said administrative organ at the higher level does not have any authority to handle the case, the case shall be transferred and handled, in accordance with the relevant laws and regulations, by the competent organ which has the authority to handle the case. In the course of such handling, the hearing of the case by the reconsideration organ shall be suspended.

44. If the concrete administrative act undertaken by the defending party infringes the applicant's legitimate rights and interests and causes any loss to the applicant, the applicant may claim for compensation, the reconsideration organ may order the defending party to compensate the applicant in accordance with relevant laws and regulations.

After the defending party has compensated the applicant, it shall order the personnel within the administrative organ who acted intentionally or negligently in the undertaking of the concrete administrative act to bear part of or the whole amount of compensation.

45. The reconsideration organ shall prepare a written reconsideration decision, when it makes the reconsideration decision. The written reconsideration decision shall specifically states the following items:

(1) The name, gender, age, occupation and address of the applicant (the title and address of the legal person or organisation and the name of its legal representative);
(2) The title and address of the defending party, and the name and responsibility of its legal representative;
(3) The main requests and reasons of the application for reconsideration;
(4) The facts, the reasons, applicable laws, regulations, rules and other decisions and orders which have general binding effects which are applied by the reconsideration organ;
(5) The conclusion of reconsideration;
(6) The time limit for the applicant to bring a lawsuit to the people's court if the applicant is not satisfied with the reconsideration decision, or the time limit for the parties to execute the decision if it is a final one;
(7) The exact date (day, month, year) when the reconsideration decision is made.

The written reconsideration decision shall be signed by the legal representative of the reconsideration organ and bear the seal of the reconsideration organ.

46. The reconsideration organ should make reconsideration decision within 2 months since it receives the application for reconsideration unless the laws and regulations provide otherwise.

The reconsideration decision will have legal effect immediately after it is delivered.

47. Except that the reconsideration decision is stipulated as final in the laws and regulations, if the applicant is not satisfied with the reconsideration decision, he may bring a lawsuit to the people's court within 15 days after he receives the written reconsideration decision, or within other time limit as stipulated in relevant laws and regulations.

If the applicant has neither brought a lawsuit to the people's court and nor executed the reconsideration decision, the matter shall be dealt with respectively according to the following conditions:

(1) If the reconsideration decision sustains the original concrete administrative act, the reconsideration decision shall be compulsorily executed by the people's court on the request of the administrative organ undertaking the original concrete administrative act, or the reconsid-

eration decision ma be compulsorily executed by the said administrative organ in accordance with the laws and regulations;
(2) If the reconsideration decision amends the original concrete administrative act, and the reconsideration decision shall be compulsorily executed by the people's court on the request of the reconsideration organ, or the reconsideration decision may be compulsorily executed by the reconsideration organ in accordance with relevant laws and regulations.

CHAPTER EIGHT: THE PERIODS AND DELIVERY

48. The duration shall be counted in term of hour, day and month. The hour and day when the duration starts shall not be counted into the duration. In case the expiration date of the duration is a holiday, the date immediately after the last day of the holiday shall be the expiration date of the duration. The time of traveling shall not be counted into the duration.
49. The delivery of the written reconsideration decision shall be certified by a receipt of delivery, and the receipt of delivery shall clearly state the date of reception and be signed or sealed by the recipient.
The date signed on the receipt of delivery by the recipient shall be the date of delivery.
If the decision is delivered by post, the date on the receipt of the mail shall be the date of delivery.
50. The written reconsideration decision delivered by the reconsideration organ shall be received directly by the recipient. If the recipient is not available, the written decision shall be received by an adult family member of the recipient or by the unit in which the recipient works and the receipt of delivery shall be signed by the family member or the unit which receives the written decision. If the recipient has entrusted an agent to receive the written decision and notified the reconsideration organ, the written decision shall be received by the agent so entrusted and the receipt of delivery shall also be signed by the agent. If the recipient is a legal person or an organization, the written decision shall be delivered to the reception department of the legal person or the organization and the receipt of delivery shall also be sealed by the said department.
If the recipient refuses to receive the written decision, the person of delivery shall call upon the relevant person to be present at the scene, explain the situation to the said person, write the reason and the date of refusal on the receipt, and the receipt shall be signed or sealed by the recipient and a witness, then the written decision shall be left at the home or the reception department of the recipient, the delivery then is deemed to be completed.
51. The reconsideration organ may commission another administrative organ to deliver the written decision or have the written decision delivered by post.

CHAPTER NINE: LEGAL RESPONSIBILITIES

52. Where the applicant refuses to execute the reconsideration decision, the reconsideration organ may directly impose or suggest other relevant administrative organ to impose administrative sanction upon the legal representative of the defending party.
53. Where the reconsideration personnel have been derelict or acted for their owned benefit, they should be criticized or be imposed administrative

penalties by the reconsideration organ or other relevant administrative organs. If the case is serious and constitutes a crime, the criminal responsibilities shall be imposed in accordance with the laws.

54. Any participants of reconsideration or other people refuse or obstruct the reconsideration personnel from performing their duties in accordance with the laws, without resorting to force or threat shall be penalized by the Public Security Bureau under section 19 of the Regulation on Administrative Penalties for Public Security of the People's Republic of China. The person shall be detained for not more than 15 days. A fine of no more than RMB200. In case force or threat is used, the criminal responsibilities shall be imposed in accordance with the laws.

CHAPTER TEN: SUPPLEMENTARY PROVISIONS

55. Except the laws and regulations stipulate otherwise, this Regulation shall be applicable to the reconsideration submitted by foreign people, people without nationality or foreign organizations.

56. The power of interpretation of this Regulation shall be vested to the Legislative Affairs Bureau of the State Council.

57. This Regulation shall come into force from 1 January 1991.

ADMINISTRATIVE LITIGATION LAW OF THE PEOPLE'S REPUBLIC OF CHINA

(Adopted by the Seventh National People's Congress on 4 April 1989 and Effective from 1 October 1990)

CHAPTER ONE: GENERAL PROVISIONS

1. This Law is enacted, in accordance with the Constitution, for ensuring that the people's courts may handle administrative cases correctly and timely, protecting the legitimate rights and interests of the citizens, legal persons and other organizations, safeguarding and supervising the administrative organs in the exercise of their authorities and performance of their duties in accordance with the laws.

2. Where citizens, legal persons or other organizations believe that their legitimate rights and interests are infringed by a concrete administrative act of an administrative organ and its personnel, they shall have the right to bring a lawsuit to a people's court, in accordance with this Law.

3. The people's courts shall exercise their judicial powers independently in accordance with the laws which shall not be subject to the interference of any administrative organs, social organizations and individuals. The people's courts shall set up administrative law divisions to handle administrative cases.

4. When people's courts handles administrative cases, they shall base on the facts, and take the laws as criteria.

5. When people's courts handle administrative cases, they shall examine the legality of concrete administrative acts.

6. When people's courts handle administrative cases, they shall apply the systems of collegial panel, withdrawal of related personnel, open trial and the second instance as final adjudication, which are provided by laws.

7. Parties to administrative litigation shall have equal legal status.

8. Citizens of different nationalities shall have the right to use their own spoken and written languages in administrative litigation.

In regions where minority nationalities live or many nationalities live together, the people's courts shall handle administrative cases and issue legal documents in the most commonly used spoken and written language of the nationalities there.

People's courts shall provide interpretation service to the participants who are not familiar with the commonly used spoken and written language of the nationalities there in administrative litigation.

9. Parties to administrative litigation shall have the right to debate.

10. The people's procuratorate shall have the right to exercise legal supervision over administrative litigation.

CHAPTER TWO: SCOPE OF CASES CAN BE ACCEPTED

11. People's courts may accept lawsuits brought by citizens, legal persons and other organizations for dissatisfaction with the following concrete administrative acts:

(1) administrative penalties such as detention, fine, cancellation of permit and licence, order for suspension of production or business operation, confiscation of properties etc.;
(2) administrative compulsory measures such as restraint of personal liberty, sealing up, seizure or freezing of properties etc.;
(3) where it is believed that administrative organs have infringed the autonomous rights in business operation as provided by the laws;
(4) where it is believed that an applicant is qualified to apply to administrative organs for permit or licence, but the administrative organs refuse to grant or fail to respond to the application;
(5) where administrative organs are requested to perform their statutory duties of protecting personal or proprietary rights, but the administrative organs refuse to perform or fail to respond;
(6) where administrative organs fail to grant pensions to the disabled or family members of the deceased in accordance with the laws;
(7) where administrative organs unlawfully demand the performance of obligations;
(8) where administrative organs have infringed the other kinds of personal or proprietary rights.

Apart from what is mentioned above, people's courts may accept other cases that the laws and regulations stipulate that administrative litigation may be brought.

12. People's courts shall not accept any lawsuits brought by citizens, legal persons or other organizations against the following matters:

(1) acts of state such as national defense, diplomatic affairs etc.;
(2) administrative regulations, regulations and other decisions and orders which are formulated and promulgated by administrative organs; and have general binding effects;
(3) decisions of administrative organs on appointment and dismissal, award and punishment of their personnel;
(4) concrete administrative acts which will, as stipulated by the laws, be finally decided by administrative organs.

CHAPTER THREE: JURISDICTION

13. The basic people's courts shall have jurisdiction over administrative cases as courts of first instance.

14. The intermediate people's courts shall have jurisdiction over the following administrative cases as courts of first instance:

(1) cases relating to ascertaining of patent right of invention, and cases handled by the Customs;
(2) cases brought against concrete administrative acts undertaken by any departments of the State Council, People's Governments at the level of province, autonomous region or municipality directly under the Central People's Government;
(3) serious and complicated cases within its jurisdiction.

15. The higher people's courts shall have jurisdiction as courts of first instance over serious and complicated cases within its jurisdiction.

16. The Supreme People's Court shall have jurisdiction as court of first instance over serious and complicated administrative cases in the whole country.

17. Administrative cases shall be under the jurisdiction of the people's courts in the region where the administrative organ, which initially undertook the concrete administrative act, is located. If a case has been through administrative reconsideration, and the reconsideration organ has amended the original concrete administrative act, the case may also be under the jurisdiction of the people's court in the region where the reconsideration organ is located.

18. If the lawsuit is brought against administrative compulsory measures restricting personal freedom, the case shall be under the jurisdiction of the people's courts in the region where the plaintiff or the defendant is located.

19. If the administrative litigation is brought concerning real property, the case shall be under the jurisdiction of the people's court in the region where the real property is located.

20. If two or more people's courts have jurisdiction over the same case, the plaintiff may choose one of them to lodge an application. If the plaintiff lodges application to two or more people's courts, the people's court which accepts the case first shall have jurisdiction over the case.

21. If a people's court discovers that the case it has accepted is not under its jurisdiction, it shall transfer the case to the people's court which has jurisdiction over the case. The people's court, to which the case is transferred, shall not transfer the case to other courts upon its own initiative.

22. If the people's court which has jurisdiction over the case is not able to exercise its judicial power, the people's court at the next higher level shall designate the jurisdiction to another people's court.

If there is any dispute over the jurisdiction among the people's courts, the dispute shall be resolved through consultation. If the consultation fails, the dispute shall be reported to the people's court at higher level above them for its designate of jurisdiction.

23. The people's courts at higher level have the power to hear as courts of first instance the cases over which the people's courts at lower level have jurisdiction. The people's court at higher level may also transfer the cases which they may hear as courts to the people's courts at lower level.

In case a people's court at lower level believes that an administrative case, which it hears as court of first instance, should be handled by the people's court at the next higher level, it may report to the people's court at the next higher level for its decision.

CHAPTER FOUR: PARTICIPANTS IN LITIGATION

24. Citizens, legal persons and other organizations who lodge a lawsuit in accordance with this Law is the plaintiff.

If the citizen who has the right to lodge a lawsuit is dead, the close relatives of the deceased may lodge a lawsuit.

If the legal person or organization which has the right to lodge a lawsuit has terminated, the legal person or organization which inherits the rights and interests of the terminated legal person or organization may lodge a lawsuit.

25. Citizens, legal persons or organizations may directly lodge a lawsuit to the people's court, the administrative organ which undertakes the concrete administrative act in question is the defendant.

Where a case has been through administrative reconsideration, and the reconsideration organ sustains the original concrete administrative act, the administrative organ which undertakes the original concrete administrative act is the defendant.

Where the concrete administrative act has been jointly undertaken by two or more administrative organs, the administrative organs which jointly undertook the concrete administrative act are joint defendants in the litigation.

Where the concrete administrative act has been undertaken by an organization which is authorized by the laws and regulations, the said organization is the defendant. Where the concrete administrative act has been undertaken by an organization which is entrusted by an administrative organ, the administrative organ which entrusts the organization is the defendant in the litigation.

Where the administrative organ which has undertaken the concrete administrative act is abolished, the administrative organ resumes the authorities and performs the duties of the abolished administrative organ is the defendant.

26. In case one or both parties are of two or more persons, and the administrative cases arise out of the same concrete administrative act or are against concrete administrative acts of the same nature, the people's court may combine the cases together as a joint lawsuit if it considers that the cases can be handled together.

27. Other citizens, legal persons, or organizations who have interests in the concrete administrative act, may participate in the litigation as third parties, or be notified by the people's court to participate in the litigation.

28. Citizens with no capacity to participate in a litigation may get his representative to participate in the litigation. If the legal representatives give away the responsibility to another, the people's court shall designate one of them to participate in the litigation on behalf of the citizen.

29. Parties to litigation and their legal representatives may entrust one or two persons to participate in the litigation on behalf of them.

Lawyers, social organizations, close relatives of the citizen who lodges the lawsuit or persons who are recommended by the working unit where the citizen works, and citizens who are permitted by the people's courts, may be entrusted as agents.

30. Lawyers who represent the parties, may review the relevant materials of the case they handle in accordance with relevant provisions, they may conduct investigations of or collect evidences from the relevant organizations and citizens. They shall keep the confidentiality, in accordance with the stipulations in the laws, of the materials relating to national secrets and privacy of persons.

Subject to the approval of the people's court, parties to litigation and their agents may review the materials relating to the court proceedings of the case, except those materials relating to national secrets and privacy of persons.

CHAPTER FIVE: EVIDENCES

31. Evidences may be classified as follows:
(1) written evidence;
(2) exhibits;
(3) visual and audio materials;
(4) statements of the witnesses;
(5) representations of the parties;
(6) conclusions of expert evaluations; and
(7) records of questioning, records made on the scene.

Any of the above evidences may only be used as the basis to ascertain the facts of the case after their verification by the courts.

32. The burden of proof for the concrete administrative act undertaken by the defendant is on the defendant. The defendant has the duty to provide the evidences, and the normative documents upon which the concrete administrative act is undertaken.

33. In the course of litigation, the defendant shall not collect evidence from the plaintiff(s) and witness(es) by himself.

34. The people's court shall have the authority to require the parties to provide or supplement evidence.

The people's court shall have the authority to collect evidences from the relevant administrative organs, other organizations and citizens.

35. In the course of litigation, if the people's court considers expert verification of some specialized problems as necessary, the expert verification shall be conducted by the legally recognized verification authority as stipulated by the laws. In case no legally stipulated verification authority is available, the people's court may designate a verification authority for the expert verification.

36. Under the circumstances where it is likely that the evidence will be destroyed or lost or difficult to be obtained in the future, the participants in the litigation may apply to the people's courts for the preservation of the evidence. The people's courts may also on its own initiative adopt measures to preserve the evidence.

CHAPTER SIX: LODGING AND ACCEPTING A CASE

37. For the administrative cases within the scope of jurisdiction of the people's court, citizens, legal persons, or other organizations shall firstly apply to the administrative organ at the next higher level or the administrative organ as stipulated by the laws and regulations for administrative reconsideration. If not satisfied with the reconsideration decision, they can then lodge a lawsuit to the people's court. They may also lodge a lawsuit to the people's court directly without going through the administrative reconsideration.

Where the laws and regulations stipulate that a case shall first go through administrative reconsideration, and if the applicant is not satisfied with the reconsideration decision, he can lodge a lawsuit to the people's court.

38. Except the laws and regulations stipulate otherwise, if citizens, legal persons, or other organizations apply to administrative organs for reconsideration, the reconsideration organ shall make a decision within 2 months from the date it receives the written application.

Except the laws stipulate otherwise, if the applicant is not satisfied with the reconsideration decision, he may lodge lawsuit to the people's court with 15 days from the date he receives the written reconsideration decision. If the reconsideration organ fails to make a decision within the time limit, the applicant may lodge a lawsuit to the people's court within 15 days from the date the time limit for reconsideration expires.

39. Except the laws stipulate otherwise, if citizens, legal persons or other organizations lodge a lawsuit to the people's court directly, they shall lodge the lawsuit within three months from the date the concrete administrative act is known to them.

40. If citizens, legal persons or other organizations, due to force majeure or other special reasons, fail to lodge a lawsuit within the time limit as stipulated, they may apply for an extension of the time limit within ten days after the obstacle is removed, to the people's court for its decision.

41. The following requirements shall be fulfilled for lodging a lawsuit:

(1) the plaintiffs shall be citizens, legal persons, or other organizations whose legitimate rights and interests are infringed by the concrete administrative act;
(2) there must be specific defendant;
(3) there must be specific claim(s) and factual basis;
(4) the case must be within the scope of acceptable cases and under the jurisdiction of the people's court to which the lawsuit is lodged.

42. When a people's court receives written application for litigation, it shall, after examination, accept the case or make a decision to reject the application within seven days. If the plaintiff does not accept the decision, he may appeal.

CHAPTER SEVEN: TRIAL AND JUDGMENT

43. The people's court shall, within 5 days from the date it accepts a case, deliver a copy of the written application for litigation to the defendant. The defendant shall submit the relevant information on which the concrete administrative act is based and a written defense to the people's court within ten days from the date the copy of the written application for litigation is received. The people's court shall deliver a copy of the written defense to the plaintiff within five days from the date the written defense is received.

The trial of the case by the people's court shall not be affected by the failure of submission of written defense by the defendant.

44. In the duration of litigation, the execution of the concrete administrative act shall not be suspended. The execution of the concrete administrative act shall cease if one of the following circumstances appears:

(1) the defendant considers the suspension of execution as necessary;
(2) the plaintiff applies for the suspension of execution, and the people's court considers the execution of the concrete administrative act may cause irremediable damage, and the suspension of execution may not infringe the social interests, and the people's court so decides to suspend the execution;
(3) the laws and regulations stipulate the suspension of execution.

45. The people's courts shall hear administrative cases publicly, except national secrets or privacy of persons are involved and the laws stipulate otherwise.

46. The people's courts shall hear administrative cases by a collegial panel consisting of judges or of judges and assessor. The number of members in the collegial panel shall be odd number of at least three.

47. If the parties consider any judicial personnel has an interest in, or is related to, the case, which will affect the fair trial of the case, they shall have the right to apply for the withdrawal of the personnel.

If any judicial personnel considers himself has an interest in or is related to, the case, he shall apply for withdrawal.

The above two provisions shall be applicable to court clerks, interpreters, expert witnesses and inquesters.

The withdrawal of the president of a court as the chief judge of a case shall be decided by the judicial committee. The withdrawal of any other judicial personnel shall be decided by the president of the court. The withdrawal of any other personnel shall be decided by the chief judge of the case. If a party to the litigation refuses to accept the decision, he may apply for reconsideration.

48. If the plaintiff refuses to appear in court without legitimate reasons after the people's court has summoned him twice, it shall be regarded as an application for withdrawal of the lawsuit. If the defendant refuses to appear in court without legitimate reasons, the people's court may make a decision in the absence of the defendant.

49. If a party to the litigation or other persons commit one of the following offences, the people's court may, in the light of the seriousness of the acts, reprimand him, order him to sign a statement of regret, or impose on him a fine of no more than RMB1,000 or detain him for not more than 15 days; if a crime is constituted, criminal liability shall be imposed in accordance with the laws:

(1) a person who has the responsibility to assist the execution, delays, refuses or obstructs the execution without proper reasons after receiving the people's court's notice for assistance in the execution;
(2) to forge, conceal or destroy evidences;
(3) to instigate, bribe or threaten other people to make false witness's statements, to threaten the witnesses to give false evidence or prevent the witnesses from giving evidence;
(4) to conceal, transfer, transform or destroy any property which is sealed up, retained or frozen;
(5) to use force, duress or other means to hinder the personnel of the people's court from performing their duties or disturb the order of work of the people's court;
(6) to insult, slander, defame, assault or retaliate against the personnel of the people's court, participants to the litigation, or persons assisting the execution.

If a fine or detention is imposed, the approval of the president of the people's court must be obtained. If a party refuses to accept the penalties, he may apply for reconsideration.

50. Conciliation shall not be applicable to the adjudication of administrative cases by the people's courts.

51. If the plaintiff applies to withdraw the lawsuit or the defendant amends the concrete administrative act before a judgment or an order is given by the people's court, whether or not the application of withdrawal of the lawsuit shall be approved shall be decided by the people's court.

52. The people's courts shall rely on the laws, administrative regulations and local regulations in the trial of administrative cases. Local regulations shall be applicable to administrative cases happened within the relevant administrative region.

The people's courts shall also rely on the autonomous regulations and the separate regulations of the minority autonomous region, at the trial of administrative cases happened in the minority autonomous region.

53. The people's court shall make reference to the rules and regulations enacted, promulgated pursuant to the laws and administrative regulations, decisions, orders of the State Council, by various ministries and commissions of the State Council, and rules and regulations enacted and promulgated, pursuant to the laws and administrative regulations of the State Council, by various provinces, autonomous regions, municipalities directly under the Central People's Government and cities where the people's governments of the province or autonomous region are located and people's governments of other larger cities with the approval of the State Council.

If a people's court considers there is an inconsistency between the rules and regulations enacted and promulgated by the local people's governments and those by the ministries and commissions of the State Council, or inconsistency between the rules and regulations enacted and promulgated by the ministries and commissions of the State Council, the inconsistency shall be submitted by the Supreme People's Court to the State Council for its interpretation or decision.

54. The people's court shall, after the trial, reach the following judgments respectively according to different circumstances:

(1) If the evidence on which the concrete administrative act is based is adequate, and the application of the laws and regulations is correct, the legal procedures are complied with, the original decision shall be sustained;

(2) If the concrete administrative act falls within one of the following circumstances, the original decision shall be wholly or partially annulled, or the defendant shall be ordered to undertake a new concrete administrative act:
  (a) lack of essential evidence;
  (b) erroneous application of the laws and regulations;
  (c) violation of legal procedures;
  (d) ultra vires;
  (e) abuse of power.

(3) If the defendant fails to or delays the performance of its legal duty, he shall be ordered to perform within a specific time limit;

(4) If the administrative penalty is obviously unfair, it shall be amended.

55. In case the people's court orders the defendant to undertake a new concrete administrative act, the defendant shall not undertake a concrete administrative act which is the same as the original one, basing on the identical facts and for the identical reasons.

56. In the trial of an administrative case, if the people's court considers the administrative organ or the person directly responsible is in violation of governmental discipline, it shall transfer the relevant materials to the said administrative organ or the administrative organ at the next higher level or supervisory, personnel organs. If the people's court considers that a crime is constituted, it shall transfer the relevant materials to the public security bureau or public procuratorate.

57. The people's court shall deliver a judgment as court of first instance within three months after accepting the case. If an extension of time limit is necessary for special reasons, it needs the approval of a higher people's court. If an extension of time limit is necessary for a case tried by a higher people's court as court of first instance, it needs the approval of the Supreme People's Court.

58. If a party to litigation refuses to accept the judgment of the court of first instance, he shall have the right to appeal to the people's court at the next higher level within 15 days from the date of the written judgment is delivered. If a party refuses to accept an order of the court of first instance, he shall have the right to appeal to the people's court at the next higher level within 10 days from the date the written order is delivered. If no appeal is made within the time limit, the judgment or order of the court of first instance shall take legal effect.

59. If a people's court considers the facts of an appeal case are clear, it may deal with the case, basing on written submission.

60. A people's court, in trying an appeal case, shall deliver a final judgment within two months from the date the pleadings of appeal is received. If an extension of time limit is necessary for special reasons, it needs the approval of a higher people's court. If the appeal case is tried by a higher people's court, the extension of time limit needs the approval of the Supreme People's Court.

61. A people's court may, under one of the following circumstances, make a decision respectively:

(1) If the facts on which the original judgment is based are clear, the application of laws and regulations is correct, the appeal shall be dismissed, and the original judgment shall be sustained;
(2) If the facts on which the original judgment is based are clear, but the application of the laws and regulations is erroneous, the original judgment shall be amended in accordance with the laws;
(3) If the facts on which the original judgment is based are ambiguous, lack of sufficient evidence, or there is a violation of legal procedures which may affect the accuracy of the judgment, then the original judgment shall be annulled, and the people's court delivering the original judgment shall be ordered to hold a retrial, or the original judgment may be amended after the facts have been ascertained. If a party is not satisfied with the judgment or order of the retrial, he may appeal.

62. If a party considers that there is indeed an error in the judgment or order which has already taken legal effect, he may make a complaint to the people's court which tried the case or the people's court at the next higher level, however, the execution of the judgment or order shall not be suspended.

63. If the president of a people's court discovers that there is a violation of stipulations of the laws or regulations in the judgment or order of the court which has already taken effect, and considers that a retrial is necessary, he/she shall refer the matter to the judicial committee for its decision on whether or not a retrial shall be held.

If a people's court at the next higher level discovers that there is a violation of stipulations of the laws or regulations in the judgment or order of a people's court at the lower level, which has already taken legal effect, the people's court at the next higher level shall have the right to try the case again or order the people's court at the lower level to hold a retrial of the case.

64. If a people's procuratorate discovers that there is a violation of stipulations of the laws or regulations in the judgment or order of the people's court, which has already taken legal effect, the people's procuratorate shall have the right to lodge a protest in accordance with the procedures of judicial supervision.

CHAPTER EIGHT: EXECUTION

65. Parties to the litigation shall execute the judgment or order of the people's court, which has already taken legal effect.

If a citizen, legal person or another organization refuses to execute a judgment or an order, the administrative organ shall have the right to apply to the people's court of first instance for a compulsory execution, or executes the judgment or order compulsorily in accordance with the laws. If an administrative organ refuses to execute the judgment or order, the people's court of first instance shall have the right to adopt the following measures:

(1) to notify the bank to transfer from the bank account of the administrative organ the amount of fines which should be returned and the amount of damages which should be paid;
(2) to impose on the administrative organ a fine of RMB50 to RMB100 per day from the date when the time limit of execution is due, provided that the administrative organ did not execute the judgment or order within the time limit;

(3) to submit a judicial suggestion to the administrative organ at the next higher level of the administrative organ in question, or to supervisory, and personnel organs. The organ receiving the judicial suggestion shall handle the case in accordance with relevant stipulations, and notify the people's court of the result of handling;

(4) criminal responsibilities shall be imposed in accordance with the laws on the person in charge or directly responsible in accordance with the laws, if the refusal of execution of the judgment or order is serious and a crime is constituted.

66. If citizens, legal persons or other organizations neither lodge lawsuits against nor execute the concrete administrative act within the time limit as stipulated in the laws, the administrative organ which undertakes the concrete administrative act may apply to a people's court for compulsory execution or execute it compulsorily itself according to the laws.

CHAPTER NINE: COMPENSATION LIABILITY FOR INFRINGEMENT OF RIGHTS

67. If the legitimate rights and interests of citizens, legal persons or other organizations are infringed by the concrete administrative acts of administrative organs or their personnel and damage is therefore caused, they shall have the right to apply for compensation.

An application for compensation made by citizens, legal persons or other organizations shall be firstly handled by the administrative organ. If citizens, legal persons or other organizations are not satisfied with the decision of the administrative organ, they may lodge lawsuits to people's courts.

Mediation may be applied in compensation litigation.

68. If the concrete administrative act undertaken by an administrative organ or its personnel has infringed the legitimate rights and interests of a citizen, legal person or other organization and damage is caused, the said administrative organ or the administrative organ, to which the personnel undertaking the concrete administrative act belongs, shall be liable to compensate.

After the administrative organ pays the compensation, it shall order its personnel who intentionally or negligently made the mistake in the case to bear part or whole of the compensation cost.

69. The cost of compensation shall be included as expenditure in the financial budget of the people's government at various levels. The people's governments at various levels may order the responsible administrative organ to bear part or whole of the compensation cost. The detailed measures shall be formulated by the State Council.

CHAPTER TEN: ADMINISTRATIVE LITIGATION INVOLVING FOREIGN INTERESTS

70. Except the laws stipulate otherwise, this Law shall be applicable to the administrative litigation lodged by foreign people, people without nationality or foreign organizations.

71. Foreign people, people without nationality and foreign organizations who lodges an administrative litigation in the People's Republic of China, shall enjoy the equal rights and bear the equal responsibilities in litigation with the citizens and organizations of the People's Republic of China.

72. If there is any difference between the stipulations in this Law and the international treaties which the People's Republic of China has concluded or acceded to the stipulations in the international treaties shall prevail, except those provisions which the People's Republic of China has made preservations.

73. If a foreign person, person without nationality or a foreign organization lodges an administrative litigation, and he appoints a lawyer to act as his agent, he shall appoint lawyers of the lawyers associations in the People's Republic of China.

CHAPTER ELEVEN: SUPPLEMENTARY PROVISIONS

74. The people's courts shall charge litigation fees for handling administrative litigation. The litigation fee shall be borne by the party which loses, or shared by both parties if both parties are responsible. The detailed measures for litigation fee charges shall be formulated separately.

75. This Law shall come into force on 1 October 1990.

OPINIONS OF THE SUPREME PEOPLE'S COURT ON SOME ISSUES RELATING TO THE IMPLEMENTATION OF THE ADMINISTRATIVE LITIGATION LAW (FOR TRIAL IMPLEMENTATION)

(Adopted by the 499th Meeting of the Judicial Committee of the Supreme People's Court on 29 May 1991)

A. SCOPE OF ACCEPTABLE CASES

1. "Concrete administrative act" refers to unilateral acts or conducts, relating to specific matters and the rights and interests of specific citizens, legal persons or other organizations, which are made by the country's administrative organs and their officials, organizations authorized by laws, organizations authorized or entrusted by the administrative organs, and individuals exercising their powers or duties during the performance of their administrative functions.

2. According to the scope of acceptable cases as provided by s. 11 of Administrative Litigation Law of the PRC, citizens can bring a case for judicial review to the people's court when they are not satisfied with decision on education through labour made by the Education through Labour Management Committee.

Citizens may bring a case for judicial review to the people's court if they are not satisfied with the compulsory custody decision made by the public security bureaux.

Citizens may also bring a case for judicial review to the people's court if they are not satisfied with administrative penalties such as the imposition of a fee or fine for giving birth to more than one child made by the Birth Control Management Departments.

3. The word "law" in the sentence "concrete administrative acts decided by administrative organs as stipulated by the laws as final " in s. 12(4) of PRC Administrative Litigation Law means the normative documents enacted by the National People's Congress and its Standing Committee.

Administrative regulations or regulations may provide that administrative organs may make "final decisions" on certain matters. Citizens, legal persons or other organizations can, if unsatisfied with the decisions made according to those provisions, bring an action to the people's court for judicial review, and the people's courts are bound to accept such cases.

4. Citizens, legal persons or other organizations shall be able to bring an administrative action to the people's court if they are not satisfied with the compensation decisions made by the administrative organs.

5. Citizens, legal persons or other organizations shall be able to bring an administrative action to the people's court if they are not satisfied with compulsory indemnity.

6. Any action brought by a party who is not satisfied with any mediation or arbitration decision made by administrative organs in accordance with the laws or other relevant rules and provisions, in order to settle disputes concerning civil rights and interests among or between individuals, legal persons, or other organizations, shall not be dealt with by the people's court as administrative cases.

7. Citizens, legal persons or other organizations shall be able to bring an action to the people's court in accordance with the laws, and the courts are bound to deal with such cases, if they are not satisfied with decisions of the people's governments or relevant administrative organs concerning the ownerships or land-use rights of lands, mineral resources, forests or other resources.

8. Any actions, brought by citizens, legal persons or other organizations, against conducts or behaviors made by administrative officials acting outside their scope of authority should not be accepted and dealt with by the people's court's as administrative cases.

B. JURISDICTION

9. Specialized courts do not establish administrative law divisions, and, will not deal with administrative cases.

10. The following three situations would fall within the category as stated in section 17 of the ALL that "the original concrete administrative act is amended by the reconsideration organ:

(a) The reconsideration organs change the facts ascertained by the original concrete administrative acts;
(b) The reconsideration organs change the applicable laws, administrative regulations or regulations applied for the undertaking of original concrete administrative acts;
(c) The reconsideration organs change the decision of the original concrete administrative acts by way of repeal, partial repeal or amendment of the original concrete administrative acts.

11. The "place where the plaintiff is located" in section 18 of the ALL includes the plaintiff's domicile, the place he often stays in, and where his personal freedom is restricted.

C. PARTICIPATING PARTIES

12. If the citizen, who has the right to bring an administrative action, has died, his close relatives shall become the plaintiff of the case. Close relatives include spouses, parents, children, brothers and sisters, grand parents, and grand children.

13. If two or more parties are involved, and they bring an action to the people's court because of their dissatisfaction with the same administrative act, they will be joint plaintiffs.

14. Other organizations which do not meet the requirements of legal persons shall be legally represented by the heads in charge of those organizations in judicial review cases brought by them to the people's courts. If no such heads exist, then any persons actually in charge will be the legal representatives.

15. In the course of litigation, if the heads of the legal persons or other organizations, as the plaintiff of the case, and administrative organs, as the

defendant of the case, are replaced, and which causes the replacement of the legal representatives in the litigation, identification documents of the new legal representatives should be submitted to the court in order for them to continue participation in the litigation. The litigation activities already conducted shall be binding on the new legal representatives.

16. If the reconsideration organ fails to make a reconsideration decision within the specified time limit, the administrative organ, which made the original concrete administrative acts shall be the defendant when the affected party brings an action to the court.

17. The people's court may order, within its power and after obtaining the plaintiff's approval, a change or an addition of defendant(s) in the trial as court of first instance. The plaintiff's application for judicial review shall be dismissed if he does not agree to such changes.

18. If citizens, legal persons or other organizations are dissatisfied with any decisions made by organs further established by the administrative organ, an administrative action may be brought to the people's court with the administrative organ as the defendant except the laws and administrative regulations provide otherwise.

19. If citizens, legal persons, or other organizations are dissatisfied with the decision jointly made by an administrative organ and a non-administrative organ, and bring an administrative case to the people's court, the administrative organ shall be the defendant. The non-administrative organ cannot be the defendant. But if the non-administrative organ has infringed or violated the rights and interests of citizens, legal persons or other organizations, and should pay compensation, then the people's court may notify the non-administrative organ to participate in the litigation as a third party.

20. Summons for appearance in the court shall be used whenever the people's court calls the affected party to the court.

21. The phrase of "have interests in the concrete administrative acts under litigation" in s. 27 of the ALL refers to the legal relationship of rights and obligations with the concrete administrative acts to be litigated.

22. If two or more parties are punished by the administrative organ for the same unlawful acts committed, and one of the parties, not satisfied with the punishment, brings an action to the court, the other parties, who are found by the court to have legal interests in the concrete administrative acts under litigation, shall be informed by the court to participate as third parties.

23. The third party shall have the right to make requests during a litigation. If he is not satisfied with the judgment made by the court of first instance, he shall have the right to appeal.

24. If a party entrusts an agent for litigation , a notice of entrustment shall be sent to, and approved by, upon inspection, the people's court. The notice of entrustment shall include the details of the matters under entrustment and the scope of authority. A written notice should be sent to the court if the entrustment is dissolved.

25. If a social organization is entrusted, its legal representative shall be the agent for litigation. The legal representative, with approval of the entrusting party, may appoint a particular member of the social organization, or a lawyer to be the agent for litigation.

26. The affected party and the agent for litigation shall be able to make notes of court materials which are allowed to be reviewed. But they are not allowed to make copies of the materials on their own.

27. The reconsideration organ, which alters or amends the original concrete administrative act, shall be the defendant. The reconsideration organ may entrust 1 or 2 members of the original decision making organ as agents for litigation, they shall also be able to entrust its other members or lawyer to be the agent for litigation according to the law.

D. EVIDENCE

28. According to the provision of section 33 of the ALL, the defendant, in the course of litigation, should not collect evidence from the plaintiff or the witnesses. The lawyer entrusted by the defendant as agent for litigation should not be allowed to collect evidence from the plaintiff or the witnesses, either.

29. The burden of proof shall lie on the defendant if there is a dispute concerning whether the action, brought by the plaintiff, has exceeded the specified time limit.

30. If the defendant cannot provide the material evidence and the normative documents it relied on to undertake the concrete administrative act before the completion of the trial at the court of first instance, the people's court may repeal the concrete administrative act under litigation according to s. 33 and s. 54(2) of the ALL.

E. LODGING A CASE AND ITS ACCEPTANCE

31. If the law provides that the affected party, who is not satisfied with a concrete administrative act undertaken by an administrative organ, may either file an action to the people's court or apply for administrative reconsideration of which the decision shall be final, and the affected party has applied for administrative reconsideration, he shall not be able to bring an action to the people's court subsequently. If the affected party has both brought an action to the people's court and applied for administrative reconsideration, the one which receives the application first shall have jurisdiction. If both receive the application at the same time, it is up to the affected party to choose.

32. If the law provides that the affected party should apply for administrative reconsideration first according to law when he is not satisfied with a concrete administrative act undertaken by an administrative organ, but he brings a case for judicial review directly to the people's court without going through reconsideration, the people's court shall not accept the case.

33. The court shall not accept and deal with any action brought by the affected party, who is not satisfied with a concrete administrative act undertaken by an administrative organ before the ALL comes into force, if the laws and administrative regulations do not provide that the affected party may bring a case for judicial review if he is not satisfied with the concrete administrative act of an administrative organ. But, the people's court shall accept and deal with an action brought by the affected party if the affected party only realizes that the administrative organ has undertaken the concrete administrative act after the ALL has come into force.

34. If there is no notice of decision being made and delivered by the administrative organ in undertaking the concrete administrative act, the affected party may bring an action to the people's court and the people's court shall accept and deal with such action if the plaintiff can prove the existence of the concrete administrative act and that the requirements for litigation are satisfied.

35. If the affected party is not informed of his right to sue and the time limit within which an action should be lodged by the administrative organ in its undertaking of the concrete administrative act so that the affected party fails to bring an action to the court within the time limit, the time limit for lodging a case shall be calculated from the date when the affected party actually knows the right to sue or the time limit. But the duration exceeding the time limit should be no more than one year.

36. If an administrative organ undertakes another concrete administrative act after the original administrative act has been repealed by the court, the affected party may bring a new action to the people's court provided that he is still not satisfied with the second act. If the administrative organ has undertaken another concrete administrative act which is basically the same as the original one, it shall be repealed by the people's court in accordance with s. 54(2) and s. 55 of the ALL and the case shall be dealt with in accordance with s. 65(3) of the ALL.

37. If the reconsideration organ repeals the original penalty decision in administrative cases relating to public security and the victim brings an action to the people's court according to the laws, the people's court shall accept and deal with such action if the victim is not satisfied with the reconsideration decision.

38. The victim or the person being sanctioned may bring a case directly to the people's court if he is not satisfied with a reconsideration decision amending the original decision and imposing a fine of more than RMB50 or penalty of custody, made by the public security organ after they bring a case for reconsideration to the public security organ against the penalty of a warning or a fine less than RMB50 imposed by the further established public security branch in accordance with s. 33(2) of the Regulation on Administrative Penalty for Public Security.

39. It the victim believes that the person being sanctioned committed two acts in violation of public security regulation, but the public security bureau only ascertained one and imposed relevant penalty accordingly, and the victim brings another case to the people's court requesting the imposition of sanction on the other act, such a case shall not be accepted by the people's court.

40. After the people's court receives the application for judicial review, the administrative law division shall carry out examination. For those cases satisfying the requirements of litigation, the people's court should file a case within 7 days. If such an action does not satisfy litigation requirements, a decision of non-acceptance shall be given within 7 days.

41. The affected party should be notified to apply for administrative reconsideration to administrative organ when he brings a case to the people's court if the ALL provides that such case can be brought to the people's court but the other laws and administrative regulations only provides that administrative reconsideration may be applied for when the affected party is not satisfied with a kind of concrete administrative acts without mentioning the right to bring a case to the people's court.

42. If the administrative organ commits a concrete administrative act by relying on different laws and administrative regulations, the time limits should be calculated differently according to the respective provisions of the relevant laws and administrative regulations. The court shall accept and deal with the relevant part which is brought within the time limit, and shall not accept the other part which is brought in excess of time limit.

43. If the administrative organ commits a concrete administrative act in accordance with two or more laws or administrative regulations and there is only one decision, and the laws and administrative regulations provide for different time limits for bringing a case, the people's court should accept the case if the longer time limit is not exceeded.

44. Administrative organ may commit concrete administrative acts against many persons by relying on the same facts. The law may provide that the affected party, if not satisfied with such concrete administrative acts, may either apply for reconsideration to the administrative organ at the next higher level of which the decision shall be final or bring a case to the people's court. If some persons choose reconsideration, they can no longer bring a case to the people's court. The other persons may still bring a case to the people's court.

45. The laws and regulations may state that the affected party shall apply for reconsideration first, in case of dissatisfaction with concrete administrative acts undertaken by the administrative organ, before bringing an action to the people's court. Other persons, who are brought into the reconsideration as parties by the reconsideration organ, may bring a case directly to the people's court.

F. ADJUDICATION AND JUDGMENT

46. If different penalties are imposed by different administrative organs, according to two or more laws and administrative regulations, on a party of whom the same act is in violation of two or more laws and administrative regulations, and the affected party is not satisfied with the penalties and brings an action to the court, the people's court may hear the case jointly.

47. If several persons, not satisfied with an administrative act undertaken by the administrative organ against them, bring actions to the people's court separately, the people's court shall have the right either to deal with the actions jointly at one instance or deal with them separately.

48. If, during litigation, the party, who brought an action to the people's court, is found to have committed new unlawful act by the defendant who has made a decision on the new unlawful act with which the affected party is not satisfied and brings a case to the people's court, the people's court may either deal with the subsequent action jointly with the previous one in litigation or to deal with it as a separate action.

49. A withdrawal should be applied for by the affected party when the adjudication starts. If the reasons are only known after the adjudication has already started, withdrawal may also be applied when the cross-examination completes. The application for withdrawal may either be made orally or in written form.

Except the case requires the adoption of emergent measures, the party who has been requested to be withdrawn shall be suspended temporarily from participating in the work on the case before a decision is made by the people's court.

50. A reply to the application for withdrawal shall be made by the people's court either orally or in written form within 3 days since the application is lodged. The party applying for withdrawal may seek reconsideration for one time if he is not satisfied with the decision. The person concerned shall continue to participate in the adjudication work of the case during the reconsideration period. The people's court should handle reconsideration application and make a reconsideration decision within 3 days and notify the applicant for reconsideration.

51. For those cases of which judgment may not or will be difficult to be enforced due to the acts of the parties or other reasons, the court may, on application by the affected party, issue an order for reservation of assets. If no such application has been made, the people's court may also issue an order, if necessary, for reservation of assets.

The people's court may order the party to provide guarantee if it has issued an order for reservation of assets. If no such guarantee is provided, the court may revoke such application.

The people's court shall make a decision within 48 hours upon receiving the application under emergent circumstances. If an order for reservation is issued, it shall be immediately executed .

52. Reservation of assets shall be limited to the scope covered by the pleadings of the application, or to the properties relating to the case.

Reservation of assets shall be executed by way of sealing up, detainment, freezing or other measures as prescribed by the law.

53. The people's court shall remove the reservation if the affected party provides guarantee.

54. If there is any mistake as to the application for reservation of assets, the applicant should compensate for all the losses suffered by the other party as a result of the reservation.

55. Upon application, the people's court may order the payment of pension through a written decision prior to the trial for those cases where it is alleged that pension was not paid.

56. If the party is not satisfied with the reservation of assets or payment of pension in advance, he may have one chance to apply for reconsideration. During the reconsideration process, the execution of the reservation order and the decision on pension payment shall not be suspended.

57. The people's court shall refuse to enforce the concrete administrative act under litigation when the administrative organ applies, in the course of litigation, to the people's court for compulsory enforcement. The people's court may order a reservation of assets whenever it is necessary.

58. If the administrative organ involved in the litigation is situated at a place different from where the people's court is situated. The people's court, when considering the issue of applicable legislation in its adjudication, shall apply relevant local regulations of the place where the administrative organ is situated.

59. The application shall be deemed to be withdrawn if the plaintiff is absent, without appropriate reasons, after being summoned twice. The people's court may allow or disallow a withdrawal depending on the circumstances.

60. If the plaintiff is still absent from the court after the people's court disapproved of his application of withdrawal, the people's court shall decide the case in the absence of the plaintiff, in accordance with s. 48 of the ALL.

61. Once the people's court has approved the application of withdrawal, it shall not accept and deal with the case when the applicant brings it again.

If no litigation fee is paid by the plaintiff during the time limit, and no application for the postponement of payment is made, the case shall be treated as voluntary withdrawal. If the plaintiff brings an action again within the time limit, the people's court shall accept and deal with the case.

62. If the administrative organ, the defendant, has changed its concrete administrative act during the trial of the case at the court of first instance, and the plaintiff's application for withdrawal is not approved, or the plaintiff does not apply for withdrawal, the people's court shall continue the proceedings on the original concrete administrative act.

63. In the course of administrative litigation, if the people's court discovers that the act of the person being sanctioned has constituted a crime, a criminal liability should be imposed. The litigation shall continue and the relevant criminal materials shall be immediately transferred to the relevant organs if the imposition of criminal liability shall not affect the adjudication of the case in trial. The litigation should be suspended if the imposition of criminal liability affects the adjudication of the case. The litigation shall resume after such organs have made final judgments.

64. The litigation shall be suspended if one of the following situations occurs in the process of litigation:

- (a) where the plaintiff is dead and it is necessary to wait for the plaintiff's close relatives to decide whether or not to participate in the litigation;
- (b) where the plaintiff has lost its capacity to participate in the litigation, and his legal representative has not yet been determined;
- (c) where the legal person or other organizations as plaintiff terminates, and its successor of the related rights and duties has not been determined;
- (d) where one of the parties is absent due to force majeure;
- (e) other situations where it is deemed necessary to suspend the litigation.

The litigation shall be resumed once the causes of suspension disappear.

The litigation shall be terminated if nobody continues the litigation three months after the litigation is suspended due to the reasons stated in (a), (b), and (c) of this section.

65. The reconsideration decision shall be void if the original concrete administrative act is revoked by the people's court.

66. In the trial of administrative cases, the people's court shall not directly impose any administrative penalty on the person, on whom the administrative organ should have imposed, but did not impose, administrative penalty.

67. When it is decided by the people's court that the defendant should undertake a new concrete administrative act, if the facts and reasons for the new concrete administrative act has been changed a bit, no matter how trivial the change may be, it shall not belong to "the same facts and reasons" as provided by s. 55 of the ALL.

68. If the people's court has revoked the original concrete administrative act of an administrative organ by reason of abuse of legal procedures, the administrative organ, in undertaking a new concrete administrative act, shall not be restricted by s. 55 of the ALL.

69. The titles for all legal documents issued by the people's court in the trial of administrative cases stall be administrative judgment, administrative decision, administrative compensation mediation decision and so on.

70. When the people's court, in reaching its judgment or decision, needs to refer to regulations, it shall be expressly written as, "according to Section 53 of the Administrative Litigation Law of the PRC, reference is made to the provisions of . . . regulation".

71. Decisions may be made in the following situations:

- (a) the non-acceptance of an application;
- (b) dismissal of an application;
- (c) cessation of the execution of a concrete administrative act during litigation or refusal of the application for the cessation of a concrete administrative act;
- (d) reservation of assets or advance execution;
- (e) approval or disapproval of the withdrawal of a case;
- (f) suspension or termination of litigation;
- (g) rectification of writing errors in the judgments;
- (h) suspension or termination of execution;
- (i) other matters where decisions are required.

The plaintiff shall be able to appeal against decisions made under (a) and (b).

Written decisions shall be signed by the Collegial panel and the court recorder, and sealed with the people's court's chop. If the decision is made orally, it should be recorded.

72. If there is an appeal, after the judgment of the court of first instance, by one or some of the parties, and the appeal is a separable one, the names of those who have not appealed can be excluded from the legal documents. If the appeal is not separable, the names of those who have not appealed can be listed as respondents.

73. The number of copies of appeal pleadings, if made through the original court, shall be made in accordance with the number of respondents.

If the appeal is lodged directly by the party to the court of second instance, the court of second instance should deliver the appeal pleadings to the original court within five days.

The respondent should be informed immediately once the original court or the court of second instance receives the appeal pleadings.

74. When the original court receives the appeal pleadings, a copy of it shall be delivered to the respondent within 5 days. The respondent shall file a defense within 10 days on receiving the appeal pleadings. If no defense is made, the trial of the people's court shall not be affected.

On receiving the appeal pleadings and the defense, the original court shall deliver them, together with all the files and evidences, to the court of second instance as soon as possible.

75. On appeal, the court of second instance shall conduct comprehensive examination, without restriction to the scope of appeal, to determine whether the lower court has identified and understood the facts clearly, applied the relevant laws and administrative regulations accurately, violated certain legal procedures.

76. The administrative organ shall not be allowed to alter its concrete administrative act during the process of adjudication at the court of second instance. If the appellant applies for withdrawal of the case because the administrative organ has changed its original concrete administrative act, the people's court shall not grant approval.

77. If the court of second instance, in hearing an appeal case concerning a decision of the court of first instance of non-acceptance, believes the case should be accepted, it may make a decision to repeal the decision of the court of first instance and order the original people's court to file a case and deal with it.

If the court of second instance, in hearing an appeal case concerning a decision of the court of first instance of dismissal of application, believes that there is something wrong with the decision of the court of first instance, it should make a decision to repeal the decision of the court of first instance and send the case to the original people's court for retrial.

78. If the court of second instance decides to send a case back to the court of first instance for retrial of an administrative case, the original people's court should organize a new collegial panel to try the case.

79. If the court of second instance, in hearing appeal case, needs to change the original judgment, it should repeal, or partially repeal the judgment of the lower court, and decides according to law, to sustain, repeal or alter the concrete administrative act under litigation.

80. When a case is decided to be retried according to the adjudication supervision procedures, a decision should be made to suspend the execution of original judgment. The decision should be signed by the president of the court and sealed with the stamp of the people's court.

G. ENFORCEMENT

81. Any administrative judgment, decision and compensation mediation decision having legal effects shall be enforced by the people's court of first instance.

82. An application for compulsory enforcement of a concrete administrative act by the people's court in accordance with s. 66 of the ALL shall be dealt with and enforced by the lowest people's court situated at the place where the party to be enforced against is located. The lowest court may report to the intermediate people's court for its decision if it believes necessary for the latter to take enforcement measures.

83. If the law states that the decision of the administrative organ shall be final and the administrative organ applies to the people's court for compulsory enforcement, the people's court shall not accept the application.

84. If citizens, legal persons or other organizations neither bring an action to the people's court within the time limit nor carry out the concrete administrative act, and the laws and administrative regulations state that the administrative organ shall be the organ to take compulsory enforcement measure, the court shall not accept the application for compulsory enforcement if the administrative organ applies to the people's court for it.

If the citizens, legal persons or other organizations neither bring an action to the people's court within the time limit, nor carry out concrete administrative act, and the laws and administrative regulations state that the administrative organ may either take the enforcement measure itself or apply to the people's court for compulsory enforcement, the people's court shall accept the application for compulsory enforcement.

If the citizens, legal persons or other organizations neither bring an action to the people's court within the time limit nor carry out the concrete administrative act, and the administrative organ does not have the authority to take compulsory enforcement measures according to law and applies to the people's court for enforcement, the people's court shall accept the application.

85. When the administrative organ files an application for compulsory enforcement, formal application, the legal documents to be enforced and other necessary materials shall be delivered to the people's court. If the people's court finds that there is mistake in the legal documents to be enforced, it shall not accept the application, upon approval by the president of the court, and return all application materials to the administrative organ.

86. If a party refuses to carry out any administrative judgment, decision and administrative compensation mediation decision which already have legal effects, the other party may apply to the people's court for compulsory enforcement in accordance with s. 65 of the ALL.

When the enforcement officers receive the application or the transferred application, they shall find out the situation within 10 days and inform the affected party to carry out the implementation. otherwise, compulsory enforcement measures will be taken.

87. The time limit for the party to apply to the people's court of first instance for compulsory enforcement of judgment and decision is 3 months. The calculation of the time limit shall start from the last day specified in the legal documents. If the legal documents do not specify the time limit, it should be calculated from the day the legal documents take effect. Any late application shall not be dealt with by the court unless appropriate reasons are given.

88. Any application by the administrative organ for compulsory enforcement of concrete administrative act to the people's court shall be examined and enforced by the enforcement division. The time limit for the application of enforcement is 3 months starting from the day when the time limit for bringing a judicial review case expires. Any late application shall not be dealt with by the court.

Any money and property against which enforcement measure has been taken shall be given to the administrative organ, and the people's court shall charge fees for enforcement in accordance with the law.

89. When the people's court takes compulsory enforcement measures, it can make a decision to freeze, transfer money from the bank account of the party against whom enforcement is taken, or to detain or withdraw their income from work. It can also make a decision to seal off, detain, freeze, auction, and sell the assets of the party against whom enforcement is taken.

The court, when applying the above measures, shall not exceed the scope of liability which the party is supposed to bear. If affected party is a citizen, he shall be allowed to retain living expenses and property necessary to support himself and his family.

90. The people's court shall issue and deliver a notice of assistance for enforcement when it makes a decision to freeze, transfer money or detain and withdraw income. The working unit where the party against whom enforcement is taken works, bank and cooperative credit company and other deposit-taking companies should comply with the decision.

91. The people's court shall inform the affected party and his mature family members to be present, if the affected party is a citizen, when the people's court decides to seal off, detain property. If the affected party is a legal person or an organization, then its legal representative or the person in charge should be present. The enforcement shall not be affected if they refuse to turn up. If the affected party is a citizen, representatives should be sent from the working unit where the citizen works or from basic level administrative organization where the property is located.

92. A clearing list shall be made by the enforcement officers concerning the assets which are to be sealed off and detained. The list shall be signed or stamped by the people present at the scene and a copy shall be delivered to the affected party. If the affected party is a citizen, the copy of the clearing list can be delivered to the party's mature family members.

93. After the assets are sealed off or confined, the enforcement officers shall demand the affected party to carry out his duties according to the legal documents within the time limit. If the affected party fails to do so, the people's court shall, according to the relevant provisions, transfer the sealed off or detained assets to the relevant organs to auction or sell the assets. If the assets are prohibited from sale freely, they should be transferred to the relevant organ for its purchase according to the price prescribed by the state government.

94. Notice should be issued by the president of the court for compulsory evacuation, demolition of unlawful construction, compulsory giving-up of land, and the affected party shall be ordered to comply with within the time limit. Compulsory enforcement will be undertaken by the enforcement officers if the affected party fails to comply with the order.

If the affected party is a citizen, in the course of compulsory enforcement, he or his mature family members should be informed to be present at the scene. If the affected party is a legal person or organization, then their legal representatives or the person in charge shall be informed to be present at the scene. The compulsory enforcement shall not be affected if they refuse to turn up. If the affected party is a citizen, representatives from his working unit or the basic level organizations where the house or land is located. The enforcement officers shall make a written record of the compulsory enforcement which shall be signed or stamped by the people present at the scene of event.

All property removed through compulsory evacuation from the house shall be delivered to a specified place by representatives from the people's court and then to the affected party. If the party is a citizen, the property may also be delivered to his mature family members. The affected party shall be responsible for all the losses due to his refusal to accept the property.

95. The people's court shall make a decision to suspend the enforcement temporarily if one of the following situations occurs:

(a) the applicant expresses that enforcement can be delayed;
(b) there are reasonable objections raised by third parties against the assets against which enforcement will be taken;
(c) the citizen as one of the parties is dead, and it is necessary for a successor to succeed to the rights and liabilities;
(d) the legal person or organization as one of the parties terminates, and it is not decided who shall be responsible for all the rights and duties;
(e) any other situations where the people's court deems that it is necessary to temporarily suspend the execution.

If the reasons causing the temporary termination cease to exist, the enforcement shall be resumed.

96. The people's court shall terminate the enforcement in the following situations:

(a) the applicant withdraws his application;
(b) the revocation of the legal documents on which the enforcement relies;
(c) the citizen to be enforced against is dead and he has neither left any assets nor got any successor to his liabilities;
(d) the party seeking the payment of pension is dead;
(e) any other situations where the people's court determines that it is necessary to terminate the enforcement.

97. Any decision of temporary suspension or termination of the enforcement made by the people's court shall take effect immediately upon deliver to the affecting parties.

H. LIABILITY OF COMPENSATION FOR TORTS

98. Any citizens, legal persons or other organizations shall be able to apply for administrative compensation together with or in the course of administrative litigation.

99. Except the laws and administrative regulations provide otherwise, citizens, legal persons or other organizations may bring a case to the people's court within 30 days after receiving the written administrative compensation decision with which they are not satisfied.

100. Mediation may be applied in administrative compensation litigation. Decisions on administrative compensation may be sustained or changed through judgment directly.

I. DURATION

101. The duration of administrative litigation should be calculated from the second day after it starts. If the calculation does not start from the first day of the month, then one month shall be deemed to have 30 days.

102. If the last day of the duration is a Sunday or other public holidays, it shall not be included within the duration and the litigation shall be delayed accordingly. The duration does not include the time period spent on the way.

103. If the lowest people's court applies for an extension of duration for litigation, it shall seek approval directly from the Supreme People's Court, and report to the intermediate people's court for record.

J. LITIGATION FEE

104. If the same case has two or more plaintiffs, the litigation fee shall be borne by the one who brought the action first. If the action has been brought at the same time by the plaintiffs, the fees shall be decided by the plaintiffs through negotiation. If negotiation fails, the people's court shall make the decision for them.

105. The administrative organ shall be responsible for all the litigation fees, including those at the first instance and the second instance, if the court of second instance repeals altogether the decision made at the first instance as well as the concrete administrative act.

106. The litigation fee shall be divided according to the respective liabilities of the parties if the people's court partially sustains and partially repeals the concrete administrative act.

107. If the administrative organ changes its concrete administrative act in the course of litigation and the plaintiff withdraws his application, which is approved by the people's court through a decision, the litigation fee shall be reduced to half of the original amount and be paid solely by the defendant. Other expenses shall be collected according to the actual expenditure. If the plaintiff does not withdraw, or the people's court does not approve the withdrawal, the litigation fee shall be paid by the losing party.

108. If the plaintiff or the appellant neither pays in advance the relevant litigation fee within the time limit nor applies for a postponement in payment, the case shall be treated as a voluntary withdrawal of application.

109. Litigation fee will be paid in advance according to the standard for cases relating to assets if dispute exists over the amount of money involved in the concrete administrative act under litigation in administrative litigation.

110. No litigation fee shall be paid if an action is not accepted by the people's court.

K. ADMINISTRATIVE LITIGATIONS INVOLVING FOREIGN PARTIES

111. Any letters of authorizations delivered from foreign countries to entrust PRC lawyers or other persons by foreign individuals, or those who does not have a nationality, or foreign companies or organizations, should be notarized by public notary of their own country and be certified by Chinese Embassy or consulate in that country, or will have legal effect after compliance with the certification procedures as prescribed by the relevant treaties concluded between China and that country.

112. Litigation documents can be delivered to parties not situated within the PRC boundaries in the following ways:

 (a) to deliver in the methods as prescribed by international treaties made between China and that country or to which both China and that country have acceded;

(b) to deliver through diplomatic channel;
(c) to deliver through Chinese Embassy or consulate in that country if the recipient has Chinese nationality;
(d) to deliver to the litigation agent who has been authorized by the recipient to accept the delivery:
(e) to deliver to the representative organizations established in China, or its branches or business representatives within the PRC boundary;
(f) to deliver by mail if that is permitted by the laws of the recipient's country, and the mail is deemed to be received if there is no return within six months since the day the litigation documents are sent and under circumstances where it is reasonable to come to such a conclusion and the date on which duration expires shall be deemed to be the day of delivery.
(g) If the litigation documents cannot be delivered by the above methods, it shall be delivered by public notice. It shall be deemed to be received six months after public notice is served.

113. The party, who does not live within the PRC boundary, may appeal to the people's court within 30 days upon receiving the litigation documents if he is not satisfied with the judgment or decision of the court of first instance. If he cannot appeal or submit defense with the time limit, he may apply for extension. It is up to the people's court to decide whether or not to approve.

L. OTHERS

114. Apart from compliance with the provisions of the ALL, the people's court shall refer to the Civil Litigation Law for matters on which there are no provisions in the ALL in the adjudication of administrative cases.

115. These opinions shall be on trial implementation since 11 July 1991. All parties shall refer to these opinions if there is any conflict between previous judicial interpretations made by the Supreme People's Court and these opinions.

ADMINISTRATIVE PENALTY LAW OF THE PEOPLE'S REPUBLIC OF CHINA

(Adopted by the Eighth National People's Congress on 17 March 1996 and Effective from 1 October 1996)

CHAPTER ONE: GENERAL PROVISIONS

1. This Law is enacted, according to the Constitution, to regulate the setting-up and implementation of administrative penalties and to ensure and monitor effective administrative management by the administrative organs, so as to protect public interests and social orders, and to protect the legitimate rights and interests of citizens, legal persons and other organizations.
2. This Law is applicable to the setting-up and implementation of administrative penalties.
3. If the acts of citizens, legal persons or other organizations violate administrative orders, penalties should be imposed. According to this Law, the imposition of penalties should be provided for by the laws administrative regulations or regulations and executed by administrative organ by complying with the procedures as stated in this Law.

The administrative penalties shall be void if its imposition does not have legal basis or comply with the legal procedures.

4. The imposition of administrative penalties shall follow the principles of fairness and openness.

The setting-up and implementation of administrative penalties must rely on facts and be commensurate with the facts, nature, and the degree of endangering effect on the society of the unlawful acts.

The provisions imposing administrative penalties on unlawful acts shall be made public. Otherwise, they shall not be relied on as basis to impose administrative penalties.

5. The implementation of administrative penalties and the rectification of unlawful acts should be based on the combination of punishment and education for the purpose of educating the citizens, legal persons or other organizations to comply with the laws voluntarily.
6. Citizens, legal persons or other organizations shall have the rights to explain and defend against administrative penalties imposed on them by administrative organs. If they are not satisfied with the administrative penalties, they shall have the right, according to law, to apply for administrative reconsideration or to bring a case for judicial review.

Citizens, legal persons or other organizations shall have the right to apply for compensation according to law if they have suffered damage due to the unlawful imposition of administrative penalties.

7. Citizens, legal persons or other organizations, on whom administrative penalties are imposed because of their unlawful acts, shall be responsible for all civil liability according to laws if their unlawful acts cause damage to other persons.

If such unlawful acts constitute crime, then criminal liability shall be imposed according to law. Criminal punishment can not be substituted with administrative penalties.

CHAPTER TWO: VARIETY AND SETTING-UP OF ADMINISTRATIVE PENALTIES

8. Administrative penalties include :

(a) warning;
(b) fines;
(c) confiscation of unlawful acquisition of property, or other pecuniary interests;
(d) an order for the cessation of production and business operation;
(e) temporary detention or revocation of licences or permits;
(f) administrative custody;
(g) other administrative penalties as provided for by the laws and administrative regulations.

9. Laws may set up all kinds of administrative penalties.

Administrative penalties restricting personal freedom can only be set up by the laws.

10. Administrative regulations may set up other administrative penalties than those restricting personal freedom.

If administrative regulations want to provide for detailed provisions of administrative penalties concerning unlawful acts, against which the laws have already provided for administrative penalties, detailed provisions shall only be made within the acts, types and scope of administrative penalties as stated in the laws.

11. Local regulations may set up other administrative sanctions than those restricting personae freedom and revoking business licences of enterprises.

If local regulations want to provide for detailed provisions of administrative penalties concerning unlawful acts, against which the laws and administrative regulations have already provided for administrative penalties, detailed provisions shall only be made within the acts, types and scope of administrative penalties as stated in the laws and regulations.

12. Regulations made by the Ministries and Commissions under the State Council may promulgate more detailed provisions of administrative penalties within the acts, types and scope of the administrative penalties to be imposed as stated in the laws and administrative regulations.

Administrative penalties such as warning and fines up to a certain amount may be set up against the acts in violation of administrative orders by the regulations as mentioned in the proceeding paragraph, provided that such administrative penalties have not been set up by the laws or administrative regulations. The amount of fine shall be determined by the State Council.

The State Council may delegate its power to the departments under its direct control, which enjoy the right to impose administrative penalties, to set up administrative penalties in accordance with paragraphs 1 and 2 of this section.

13. Regulations made by the people's governments of a province, autonomous region, municipality directly under the State Council, cities where provincial, and autonomous regional people's governments are located and those relevantly large cities with the approval of the State Council may provide for detailed provisions of administrative penalties within the acts, types and scope of administrative penalties as stated in the laws and administrative regulations.

Administrative penalties such as warning and fines up to a certain amount may be set up against the acts in violation of administrative orders by the regulations as mentioned in the proceeding paragraph, provided that such administrative penalties have not been set up by the laws or administrative regulations. The amount of fine shall be determined by the Standing Committee of People's Congresses of provinces, autonomous regions, and municipalities under direct control of the State Council.

14. Other normative documents shall not be able to set up administrative penalties apart from what are provided under sections 9, 10, 11, 12 and 13 of this Law.

CHAPTER THREE: IMPLEMENTATION ORGANS OF ADMINISTRATIVE PENALTIES

15. Administrative penalties shall be implemented by administrative organs having the power to impose administrative penalties within their statutory authority.

16. The State Council, or the people's governments of provinces, autonomic regions, and municipalities under direct control of the State Council shall be able to determine one administrative organ to exercise the power of relevant administrative organs to impose administrative penalties. The power to impose administrative penalties restricting personal freedom can only be exercised by the public security bureau.

17. Organizations authorized by laws and administrative regulations to manage public affairs shall be able to impose administrative penalties within the scope of its legally authorized power.

18. Organizations, which meet the requirements stated in section 19, shall be able to, upon entrustment by the administrative organs within its legal authority in accordance with the laws, and administrative regulations, impose administrative penalties. No other organizations shall be entrusted, by the administrative organs, to impose administrative penalties.

The entrusting administrative organ shall supervise the acts of the imposition of administrative penalties by the entrusted organization, and shall be responsible for the consequences of such acts.

The entrusted organization shall impose administrative penalties within the scope of entrustment in the name of the entrusting administrative organ. No other organizations or individuals shall be entrusted by the entrusted organization to impose administrative penalties.

19. The entrusted organization shall meet the following requirements:

(a) Institutions established according to law to be in charge of public affairs;
(b) Persons familiar with relevant laws, administrative regulations, regulations, and the business;
(c) Qualified to carry out technical inspection or confirmation whenever such inspection or confirmation is required to be carried out for unlawful acts.

CHAPTER FOUR: THE JURISDICTION AND APPLICATION OF ADMINISTRATIVE PENALTIES

20. Except the laws and administrative regulations provide otherwise, administrative penalties shall be under the jurisdiction of the administrative organs, which enjoy the power to impose administrative penalties, of the local people's government at the county level or above where the unlawful acts occur.

21. If any dispute arises over the jurisdiction, it should be submitted to the administrative organ at the next higher level for its designation of jurisdiction.

22. If the unlawful act constitutes a crime, the administrative organ shall transfer the case to the judicial organ, and criminal liability shall be imposed according to law.

23. When an administrative organ imposes an administrative penalty, it shall demand the relevant party to rectify the unlawful act or to rectify the unlawful act within a specified time limit.

24. Administrative penalty such as fine should not be imposed twice for the same unlawful act committed by the relevant party.

25. No administrative penalties shall be imposed on a person of less than 14 years old, who undertakes unlawful acts; instead his guardian shall be demanded to tighten the control of the person. The imposition of administrative penalties shall be lenient or mitigated if a person who is above 14 but less than 18 years of age undertakes an unlawful act.

26. No administrative penalties shall be imposed on a mentally disabled person who undertakes unlawful acts when he cannot recognize or control himself. His guardian shall be demanded to take good care of him as well as to provide relevant medical treatment. Administrative penalties may be imposed on those, who suffer from intermittent mental disorders, commit unlawful acts while they are normal.

27. The imposition of administrative penalty should be lenient or be mitigated if the parties fall into one of the following circumstances:

(a) if a person voluntarily eliminates or alleviates the endangering consequences of the unlawful acts;
(b) if the unlawful act is done under duress of other persons;
(c) if a person performs good in his cooperation with the administrative organ in its investigation and punishment of unlawful acts;
(d) other situations as provided by law that the imposition of administrative penalties should be lenient or be mitigated.

No administrative penalty shall be imposed if the unlawful act is trivial and rectified immediately without causing any endangering consequences.

28. If an unlawful act constitutes a crime, and the people's court imposes a custody, or a fixed term of imprisonment, the term of imprisonment shall be reduced accordingly by the duration of administrative custody imposed by the administrative organ and already served by the person concerned.

If an unlawful act constitutes a crime, and the people's court imposes a fine on the party, the amount of fine shall be reduced by the amount previously imposed by the administrative organ.

29. Except the laws provide otherwise, no administrative penalties shall be imposed if the unlawful act is not discovered within 2 years.

The time limit provided by the above paragraph shall be calculated from the day when the unlawful act is committed. If the unlawful act is a continuous one, then the time limit shall be calculated from the day the unlawful act is completed.

CHAPTER FIVE: THE DETERMINATION OF ADMINISTRATIVE PENALTIES

30. Administrative organs shall investigate and ascertain the facts of those acts which, committed by citizens, legal persons, or other organizations in violation of administrative orders, administrative penalties should be imposed on. No administrative penalties shall be imposed if the facts of unlawfulness are unclear.

31. Before it makes a decision on administrative penalty, the administrative organ shall inform the affected party of the facts, reasons and grounds on which the decision of the imposition of administrative penalty shall be made, and inform the affected party of the rights it enjoys.

32. The affected party shall have the right to explain and defend. The administrative organ shall listen carefully to the party's opinions, and review the facts, reasons, and evidences put forward by the affected party. The administrative organ shall adopt the facts, reasons or evidences put forward by the affected party if they are established.

The administrative organ shall not increase the administrative penalty simply because the affected party defends.

Section One: Summary Procedures

33. The administrative penalties such as warning or a fine of less than RMB50 on the individual, or a fine of less RMB1,000 or a warning on the legal person or other organizations shall be determined on the spot if the facts of the unlawful act are clear and there are legal grounds. The affected party shall be obliged to bear the administrative penalty in accordance with sections 46, 47 and 48 of this Law.

34. If the law enforcement officers impose an administrative penalty on the spot, they shall disclose, to the affected party, their identifications, and fill in prepared forms and issue a written administrative penalty decision duly numbered. The written administrative penalty decision shall be handed over to the affected party on the spot.

The written administrative penalty decision mentioned in the above paragraph shall contain the unlawful act committed by the affected party, the grounds for the imposition of administrative penalty, amount of fine imposed, time, venue and the name of the administrative organ. The decision shall be signed or stamped by the law enforcement officers.

The law enforcement officers shall report the decision for record to the administrative organ they belong to.

35. If the affected party is not satisfied with the administrative penalty imposed on the spot, he shall be able to apply for administrative reconsideration or bring a case for judicial review.

Section Two: Ordinary Procedures

36. Except as provided by section 33 where administrative penalty can be imposed at the spot, the administrative organ shall have to conduct investigation comprehensively, objectively and fairly and collect relevant evidence if it discovers that citizens, legal persons or other organizations have committed unlawful acts on which administrative penalties should be imposed, according to the laws. The administrative organ may conduct inspection according to the laws and administrative regulations if necessary.

37. There shall be at least 2 law enforcement officers and their identification should be disclosed to the affected parties or relevant persons when the

administrative organ conducts investigation or inspection. The affected party or relevant persons should answer all questions in truth, and assist, not hinder, the investigation or inspection. The enquiries and inspection should be recorded in writing.

The administrative organ may, in collecting evidence, adopt the method of taking samples. If the evidence may be damaged or may be difficult to be obtained in the future, it can be first registered and preserved upon the approval of the person in charge in the administrative organ. A decision as to how to deal with the evidence shall be made within 7 days during which the affected party or other officers are not allowed to destroy or transfer the evidence.

The law enforcement officers should withdraw if they have direct interest (in the case).

38. The person in charge in the administrative organ shall examine the result once the investigation concludes, and make the following decisions respectively according to different situations :

  (a) If there are indeed unlawful acts on which administrative penalties should be imposed, a decision to impose administrative penalties shall be made according to the seriousness and specific circumstances;
  (b) If the unlawful acts are trivial and administrative penalties may not be imposed according to law, then no administrative penalties shall be imposed.
  (c) If the facts of unlawful acts cannot be established, no administrative penalties shall be imposed;
  (d) If the unlawful act constitutes a crime, it shall be transferred to judicial organ.

The persons in charge in the administrative organ shall make a collective decision through discussion if the unlawful act is serious and heavier administrative penalty may be imposed.

39. A written administrative penalty decision shall be prepared when the administrative organ imposes an administrative penalty in accordance with section 38 of this Law. The written administrative penalty decision shall contain the following items:

  (a) the affected party's name and address;
  (b) the facts and evidence to prove the violation of the laws, administrative regulations or regulations;
  (c) the type and ground of the administrative penalty;
  (d) the time limit and the way to perform administrative penalty;
  (e) the time limit and the way administrative reconsideration or judicial review may be lodged if the affected party is not satisfied with the decision of administrative penalty;
  (f) the name of the administrative organ which makes the administrative penalty decision and the date on which it is made.

The written administrative penalty decision should be stamped by the administrative organ which has made the administrative penalty decision.

40. The written administrative penalty decision shall be announced and handed over on the spot to the affected party. If the affected party is not present at the scene, then the administrative organ shall deliver the written administrative penalty decision to the affected party within 7 days according to the relevant provisions of the Civil Litigation Law.

41. Except the affected party voluntarily gives up his right to state and defend, the administrative penalty decision shall not stand if the administrative organ or its law enforcement officers, before making administrative penalty decision, did not disclose, according to sections 31 and 32 of this Law, to the affected party the facts, reasons and grounds on which the administrative sanction is decided, or refused to listen to the statements or defense raised by the affected party.

Section Three: The Hearing Procedures

42. The administrative organ shall inform the affected party of his right to request a hearing before it imposes administrative penalties such as the cessation of production or business operation, revocation of licence or permit, or a fine involving large sum of money. The administrative organ shall be obliged to organize the hearing if it is requested by the affected party. The affected party shall not be responsible for the costs for the organization of the hearing. The hearing should be organized according to the following procedures:

(a) a request for hearing should be submitted by the affected party within 3 days upon the notification of the administrative organ;
(b) the administrative organ shall inform the affected party of the time and venue 7 days before the hearing is conducted;
(c) The hearing should be public except State's secrets, business secrets or personal privacy is involved;
(d) The hearing shall be chaired by officers designated by administrative organ, who are not the investigating officers; the affected party shall have the right to request the withdrawal of the officer chairing the hearing if he considers that the officer has direct interest in the case;
(e) The affected party may participate in the hearing by himself, or he may entrust one or two individuals to participate;
(f) In the course of hearing, the investigating officers shall put forward the facts, evidence and the suggested administrative penalty while the affected party may question the facts and evidences and raise his defense;
(g) The hearing should be recorded in writing. The record shall be signed or stamped by the affected party upon examination and confirmation of no mistakes.

If the affected party is not satisfied with the administrative penalties restricting his personal freedom, the case should be dealt with according to the relevant provisions of the Regulation on Administrative Penalties for Public Security

43. A decision shall be made in accordance with section 38 of this Law after the hearing ends.

CHAPTER SIX: THE IMPLEMENTATION OF ADMINISTRATIVE PENALTIES

44. The affected party should comply with the administrative penalties decision within the time limit after it is made according to law.

45. Except the laws provide otherwise, the execution of the administrative penalty shall not stop when the affected party, dissatisfied with the administrative penalty decision, applies for administrative reconsideration or judicial review.

46. The administrative organ which makes the decision to impose fines should be a separate one from that which collects the fine.

Except as provided under sections 47 and 48 that fines shall be collected on the spot, the administrative organ or its law enforcement officers, after imposing fines as an administrative penalty, shall not collect the fines themselves.

The affected party shall make payment at the specified bank stated in the administrative penalty decision within 15 days upon receiving the decision. The bank shall directly transfer the fines to the State's treasury upon receiving the fines.

47. The law enforcement officers shall be able to collect the fines on the spot in the following situations if the administrative penalty is imposed in accordance with section 33 of this Law:

(a) A fine of RMB20 or less;
(b) A fine which may be difficult to collect in the future if it is not collected on the spot;

48. In remote areas, or on the waterway, or in areas where transportation is very inconvenient, the administrative organ and its law enforcement officers shall be able to collect fines imposed in accordance with sections 33 and 38 of this Law on the spot if the affected party does have difficulty to make payment to the designated bank and the affected party raises the concern.

49. The administrative organ and its law enforcement officers should produce to the affected party a receipt uniformly issued by the finance department of provinces, autonomous regions, and the municipalities under direct control of the State Council. The affected party shall be able to refuse to pay the fine if such a receipt cannot be produced.

50. The law enforcement officers shall deliver the collected fines to the administrative organ within 2 days since the collection of fines on the spot. If the fines are paid on the water, the fines shall be delivered to the administrative organ within 2 days since the officer reaches the land. The administrative organ shall deliver the fines to the designated bank within 2 days.

51. The administrative organ imposing the administrative penalty may take the following measures if the affected party does not perform the administrative penalty decision after the expiration of the time limit:

(a) a 3 per cent extra fine per day shall be added onto the fine if the fine is paid within the time limit;
(b) To auction the sealed off or detained property or to transfer the frozen deposit from the bank account of the affected party to pay the fine according to laws;
(c) To apply to the people's court for compulsory enforcement.

52. If the affected party is in financial difficulty and needs extension for the payment of fines or payment of fines by installment, he shall be able to apply to the administrative organ and may, upon approval, delay the payment or pay by installment.

53. Apart from those goods which must be destroyed according to law, other unlawful property, confiscated according to the law, shall be auctioned publicly according to State provisions or dealt with in accordance with relevant state provisions.

All fines and confiscation of unlawful pecuniary interests, and money obtained from the auction of the confiscated unlawful property shall be delivered to the state's treasury. No administrative organ or individuals shall be allowed to retain, or unlawfully divide up in a disguised manner the pecuniary interests obtained. The finance department shall not be allowed to return in any form to the administrative organ fines, unlawful pecuniary interests, and money obtained from the auction of unlawfully obtained property.

54. The administrative organ shall develop a comprehensive supervisory system over administrative penalties. The people's governments at county level or above should strengthen their supervision and examination of the administrative penalties.

Citizens, legal persons or other organizations shall have the right to defend or report against administrative penalties imposed by administrative organs. The administrative organ should review carefully and make rectification voluntarily if it discovers mistakes in the imposition of administrative penalties.

CHAPTER SEVEN: LEGAL LIABILITIES

55. The administrative organ at the next higher level or other relevant departments may order the administrative organ to make rectification or impose according to law administrative disciplinary sanction on the person directly in charge or other persons directly responsible if any of the following circumstances occur when the administrative organ imposes administrative penalties:

(a) no legal grounds for the administrative penalty;
(b) unauthorized alteration of the type and scope of administrative penalty;
(c) violation of legal procedures for the imposition of administrative penalty;
(d) violation on section 18 of this Law concerning the entrustment of the imposition of administrative penalties.

56. If no receipt of fine or forfeiture of property is used by the administrative organ while it imposes administrative penalty on the affected party, or if receipt of fine or forfeiture of property, which is not from the legally designated department, is used in the imposition of administrative penalty by the administrative organ, the affected party shall have the right to refuse the administrative penalty and report the case. The administrative organ at the next higher level or other relevant departments shall confiscate and destroy such receipts and impose administrative disciplinary action on the person in charge or other persons directly responsible according to law.

57. If the administrative organ makes an unlawful collection of fines in violation of section 46 of this Law, or if the finance department unlawfully returns to the administrative organ fine or money obtained from auction in violation of section 53 of this Law, the administrative organ at the next higher level or the relevant department shall request the administrative organ to make rectification and impose administrative disciplinary action according to law on the person in charge or other persons directly responsible.

58. If the administrative organ retains, unlawfully divides up or unlawfully divides up in disguise the fine or confiscated unlawful pecuniary interests, or forfeited property, the finance department or other relevant departments shall be responsible for their recovery and impose administrative disciplinary sanction on the person in charge or other person responsible. If the situation is serious so as to constitute a crime, then criminal liability will be imposed according to law.

Any law enforcement officer who, taking advantage of his authority, demands or receives property from others, or collect fines and keep them for himself, which constitutes a crime, criminal liability shall be imposed. If the situation is trivial and does not constitute a crime, administrative disciplinary action shall be imposed according to the law.

59. The administrative organ shall compensate for all the loss suffered by the affected party and disciplinary sanction shall be imposed on the person in

charge and other persons directly responsible according to law if the administrative organ utilizes or damages the forfeited property and causes damage to the affected party.

60. If the administrative organ unlawfully conducts inspection measures or enforcement measures, which cause personal or proprietary damage to the citizens, and cause losses to the legal persons or other organizations, the administrative organ shall make compensation according to law. Administrative disciplinary actions shall be imposed on the person in charge or other persons directly responsible. If the situation is serious and constitute a crime, criminal liability shall be imposed according to law.

61. If the administrative organ, for the sake of gaining interests for itself, fails to transfer, in accordance with the law, to the judicial organ those cases, on which criminal liability should be imposed, replaces the criminal punishment with administrative penalties, the administrative organ at the next higher level or other relevant department shall be responsible for requesting rectification. If the administrative organ refuses to make rectification, administrative disciplinary actions shall be imposed on the person in charge or other person directly responsible. Criminal liability shall be imposed in accordance with section 188 of Criminal Law on unlawful acts of malpractice for the benefit of one's friends and subjects and intentional protection from prosecution of a person who is clearly guilty.

62. The law enforcement officers, because of negligence or an omission of duty, fail to stop or punish unlawful acts which should be stopped or punished, so as to cause damage to the rights and interests of citizens, legal persons or other organizations, public interests and social orders, administrative disciplinary actions shall be imposed on the person in charge or other persons directly responsible. If the situation is serious enough to constitute a crime, criminal liability shall be imposed according to law.

CHAPTER EIGHT: SUPPLEMENTARY PROVISIONS

63. The detailed rules for implementation concerning the separation of decisions of fines or the collection of fines as provided in section 46 of this Law shall be promulgated by the State Council.

64. This Law shall come into force on 1 October 1996.

If any provisions on administrative penalties provided by administrative regulations and regulations, which are enacted before this Law, are inconsistent with this Law, they should be amended according to the provisions in this Law since it is promulgated. All amendments should be completed before 31 December 1997.

REGULATION ON ADMINISTRATIVE SUPERVISION OF THE PEOPLE'S REPUBLIC OF CHINA

(Adopted by the 72nd Meeting of the State Council on 23 November 1990)

CHAPTER ONE: GENERAL PROVISIONS

1. This Regulation is enacted in accordance with the Constitution, for strengthening the administrative supervision, improving the administrative management, enhancing the efficiency of administration, promoting the honest behaviors and compliance of laws and governmental discipline by the state's administrative organs and their personnel.
2. Supervisory organs are special organs of the people's governments to exercise supervisory function. The supervisory organs shall supervise the execution of state's laws, administrative regulations, policies and decisions, and order, and the acts in violation of the laws by the administrative organs and their personnel and other personnel appointed by the administrative organs.
3. The supervisory organs shall be responsible to the people's government at the same level and the supervisory organ at the next higher level to report its work. Their supervisory work shall be subject to the leadership of the supervisory organ at the higher level.
4. The supervisory organs shall exercise their power and function independently in accordance with the state's laws, administrative regulations and policies. They shall not be subject to any interference of other administrative organs, social organizations and individuals.
5. The supervisory work shall be based on the facts, rely on the evidences, and investigation and research, apply the laws and governmental discipline equally to the people.
6. Administrative supervision in executing the supervisory work shall apply the principles of combination of administrative supervision and ordinary citizens supervision, combination of supervisory investigation and work improvement, and combination of punishment and education.
7. Supervisory organs shall set up the systems of reporting and appealing.

CHAPTER TWO: SUPERVISORY ORGANS AND SUPERVISORY PERSONNEL

8. The Ministry of Supervision shall, under the leadership of the State Council, be in change of national administrative supervision work.
   The supervisory organs in the people's governments at the county level and above shall, under the leadership, respectively, of the governor of a province, autonomous region, city, autonomous prefecture, county, district and the

supervisory organs at the next higher level, be responsible for the administrative supervision work in its administrative area.

9. The supervisory organs may, according to the need of work, set up supervisory office or employ supervisory personnel, in a specific region, government organ and working units.

The delegated supervisory offices and personnel shall, in accordance with the requirement of the supervisory organs which set up them, to perform their supervisory functions.

10. The appointment, dismissal or transfer of any head or vice head of the supervisory organs at the county level or above, shall be first of all approved by the supervisory organ at the next higher level, before their submission to the people's congress and the people's government at the same level for their decision.

The supervisory organs shall be responsible for the appointment, dismissal and transfer of the person in charge of their delegated supervisory offices or delegated supervisory personnel. Before any appointment, dismissal and transfer, opinions should be sought from the district, organs or working units where the supervisory office or supervisory personnel will be.

11. The supervisory organs may set up the posts such as supervisory commissioner, in accordance with relevant stipulations.

12. The supervisory organ may, according to the need of work, employ part-time supervisor. Part-time supervisor shall work according to the entrustment of the supervisory organ.

13. The supervisory personnel must get themselves familiar with their work, be loyal to their duties, enforce the laws without prejudice, be honest and keep the confidentiality.

CHAPTER THREE: THE JURISDICTION OF THE SUPERVISORY ORGAN

14. The Ministry of Supervision shall conduct supervision of any Departments of the State Council and their personnel, any personnel appointed by the State Council and its various Departments, and any people's government of a province, an autonomous region, or a municipality directly under the Central People's Government, and their heads and vice heads.

15. Supervisory bureaus at the level of province, autonomous region and municipality directly under the Central People's Government shall have jurisdiction over various bureaus of the people's governments at the aforesaid level and their personnel, other personnel appointed by the people's governments and their various bureaus at the aforesaid level, people's governments at the level of autonomous prefecture, city which establishes districts, districts or counties in the municipality directly under the Central People's Government and their heads and vice heads.

16. Supervisory Bureau at the level of autonomous prefecture, city which establishes districts shall have jurisdiction over various bureaus of the people's governments at the aforesaid level and their personnel, other personnel appointed by the people's governments and their various bureaus at the aforesaid levels, people's governments at the level of county, autonomous county, city which does not establish districts, districts in the city and their heads and vice heads.

17. Supervisory Bureau at the levels of county, autonomous county, city which does not establish districts shall have jurisdiction over various bureaus of the people's governments at the aforesaid level and their personnel, other personnel appointed by the people's governments and their various bureaus at the aforesaid level, people's governments at the level of township, minority township village, and their personnel, other personnel appointed by the people's governments at the aforesaid levels.

18. Supervisory organs at higher levels may handle the supervision cases which are under the jurisdictions of the supervisory organs at lower levels. Supervisory organs at higher levels may also handle the supervision cases which under the jurisdictions of supervisory organs at various lower levels when they deem it as necessary.

In case two or more supervisory organs have jurisdiction over the same case, the said organs shall ascertain the jurisdiction over the case through consultation, or the jurisdiction shall be designated by the supervisory organ at the next higher level above the aforesaid organs.

CHAPTER FOUR: FUNCTIONS AND POWER OF SUPERVISORY ORGANS

19. The followings are the main functions of supervisory organs:

(a) to supervise and examine the implementation and enforcement of national laws, administrative regulations policies, decisions and orders by the state's administrative organs and their personnel and other personnel appointed by the state's administrative organs;
(b) to accept and handle complaints and reports against the acts in violation of national laws, administrative regulations and governmental disciplines by the state's administrative organs and their personnel and other personnel appointed by the administrative organs;
(c) to investigate the acts in violation of national laws, regulations and governmental disciplines by the state's administrative organs and their personnel and other personnel appointed by the administrative organs;
(d) to accept and handle the appeals by the personnel of and other personnel appointed by the administrative organs, who are not satisfied with the disciplinary sanctions imposed on them, and other appeals which are subject to the jurisdiction of the supervisory organs as stipulated by the relevant laws and administrative regulations.

20. Supervisory organs shall perform their functions through the following methods:

(a) to hold regular or irregular examinations on the implementation and enforcement of national laws, administrative regulations, policies and decisions by the administrative organs and their personnel under supervision, in accordance with the supervisory plans;
(b) to hold specific examinations on the work of the administrative organs under supervision, in accordance with the decisions of people's governments at the same level or supervisory organs at higher level, or according to the need of work of administrative area and the supervisory organ itself;
(c) to file a case and carry out investigation of the acts in violation of the laws and administrative regulations.

21. Supervisory organs shall adopt the following measures in the course of examination or investigation:

(a) to review and duplicate the documents and information which relate to the items under supervision; to understand other relevant circumstances;
(b) to seize temporality and seal up the documents, information, goods and other things unlawfully obtained which can prove the acts in violation of the laws and regulations, and governmental discipline.
(c) to investigate according to prescribed procedures the accounts of the personnel, who are directly related to the case under investigation, in banks or other financial organizations and inform the banks and other financial organizations to suspend any payments temporality when the supervisory organ deems it as necessary.
(d) to request the administrative organs under supervision and relevant personnel to report and submit documents, information and other necessary information which are related to the case under supervision;
(e) to order relevant personnel to answer and explain the questions relating to the case under supervision during the time limit and at the place as stipulated;
(f) to order the administrative organ and personnel under supervision to stop the acts which infringe or may infringe the interests of the state and the legitimate rights and interests of citizens;
(g) to suggest the relevant administrative organs to suspend the performance of public functions and duties by the personnel who is suspected of serious violation of the laws and regulations, and governmental discipline.

22. Supervisory organs shall have authority to carry out inquiry and investigation of the administrative organs and personnel outside the jurisdiction as stipulated in Chapter 3 of this Regulation, the said administrative organ and their personnel shall give assistance to the supervisory organs.

23. Supervisory organs may make supervisory suggestions, in accordance with the results of examination and investigation, for the following circumstances:

(a) where non-enforcement, improper enforcement or delay of enforcement of national laws, regulations, policies and decisions should be rectified;
(b) where the decision, order or instruction issued is inappropriate and should be amended or annulled;
(c) where appointment, dismissal, award or penalty is obviously inappropriate;
(d) where administrative disciplinary sanction shall be imposed on the acts which are in violation of governmental disciplines;
(e) where administrative penalty is deemed necessary according to relevant laws and administrative regulations;
(f) where supervisory suggestion is necessary in other circumstances than the above mentioned.

24. Supervisory organs may make a supervisory decision, in accordance with the results of examination and investigation, in the following circumstances:

(a) where disciplinary sanctions such as warning, recording of a demerit, recording of a serious demerit, demotion in administrative rank, demotion of post, dismissal from post, shall be imposed on the acts in violation of governmental discipline, in accordance with the scope of jurisdiction;

(b) where the income obtained in violation of relevant national laws and administrative regulations, shall be confiscated, recovered, or ordered to be returned, by the supervisory organ in accordance with the laws;
(c) where national interests and the legitimate rights and interests of citizens are infringed, and remedial measures should be adopted;
(d) where the personnel who is loyal to his duties, honest, and whose performance is outstanding or who reported the acts which are seriously in violation of the laws and regulations, should be awarded;

Supervisory organs may also make supervisory suggestions in the above circumstances.

25. Where the supervisory organs accept and handle appeals according to their jurisdiction against administrative disciplinary sanctions, and hold that, after review the original decision is inappropriate, the supervisory organs may suggest the administrative organ which made the original decision to amend or annul the original decision, or the supervisory organs may also amend or annul the original decision directly.

Other appeals which shall be accepted and handled by supervisory organs as stipulated in the laws and regulations, shall be handled according to the authorization of the relevant laws and administrative regulations.

26. Supervisory decisions made by the supervisory organs, shall be complied with by the administrative organs under supervision and their personnel. Supervisory suggestions made by the supervisory organs, shall be adopted by the relevant administrative organs and their personnel without appropriate reason to refuse.

27. The person in charge of the supervisory organ may attend the relevant standing committee meetings of the people's government at the same level, supervisory personnel may attend the relevant meetings of the administrative organs under supervision.

28. In the course of investigation, the supervisory organ may seek the assistance of the public security bureau.

CHAPTER FIVE: PROCEDURES OF SUPERVISION

29. Supervisory organs at various levels shall, in accordance with the national laws, administrative regulations and policies and the requests of the people's government at the same level and the supervisory organ at the next higher level, formulate supervisory plans and implementation proposals.

30. Where the supervisory organ carries out an examination, it shall notify the administrative organs and relevant personnel under examination by sending them a written notice prior to the examination. Where the supervisory organ files a case and carries out an investigation, it shall notify the administrative organ at the next higher level of the one under investigation or the working unit where the personnel under investigation belongs to.

The relevant administrative organ and personnel shall provide the necessary working conditions for the examination and investigation.

31. Supervisory organs shall, within their scope of jurisdiction, conduct a preliminary review of the case to be handled. When the supervisory organs hold that administrative disciplinary sanction should be imposed on the acts in violation of the laws, regulations and governmental disciplines it shall file a case. Where the case is important and complicated, the supervisory organ may, together with relevant governmental organs, file a case.

The filing of important cases shall be reported for record to the people's government at the same level and the supervisory organ at the next higher level.

32. Supervisory organs shall, in the course of investigation, collect evidences from all aspects, listen to the explanation and defense of the people under investigation.

33. In case the supervisory personnel have to exercise the authorities as stipulated in sections 21 (2), (3), (6) & (7) of 21 of this Regulation, the approval by the person in charge of the supervisory organ at the county level or above must be obtained.

In case the exercise of authorities stipulated in 21 of this Regulation involves national secrets, it shall be handled in accordance with the relevant stipulations.

34. Supervisory organs may, according to the need of work, appoint personnel from relevant departments and personnel with special knowledge and technology to participate in the examination and investigation.

35. Where a case handled by a supervisory personnel concerns the interests of that personnel or his close relatives or the fair handling of the case may be affected due to other relations, the said personnel shall withdraw from the handling of the case.

36. Where a case is filed and investigated by the supervisory organ, the investigation of the case shall be completed within 6 months after the filing. In case the extension of time limit is necessary due to special reasons, it shall be reported to the supervisory organ at the next higher level for record, and the investigation shall be completed within 1 year. Where the case is transferred to the supervisory organ by the people's government at the same level or the supervisory organ at the next higher level, and the investigation cannot be completed within the time limit, the supervisory organ shall explain the reason to the organ which transferred the case.

37. Where the supervisory organ, after the investigation of the case filed, holds that there are not any acts in violation of the laws, regulations, and governmental disciplines, or the administrative liabilities need not be imposed, the case should be withdrawn, and the organ at the next higher level of the one under investigation or the working unit which the personnel under investigation belongs to, shall be notified.

Withdrawal of important cases shall be reported to the people's government at the same level and supervisory organ at the next higher level for record.

38. Important supervisory decisions and suggestions shall be reported for the approval of the people's government at the same level and supervisory organ at the next higher level. Important supervisory decisions and suggestions by the Ministry of Supervision should be reported to the State Council for its approval.

39. Supervisory decisions and suggestions by the supervisory organs shall be delivered to the relevant department or personnel in written form.

40. The relevant department and personnel shall, within 15 days from the day of receiving the supervisory decision or suggestion, report the circumstances of execution or adoption of the said decision or suggestion to the supervisory organ.

In case the relevant department or personnel is not satisfied with supervisory decision, he may within 15 days from the day of receiving the supervisory decision, apply to the supervisory organ which made the said decision for re-examination, the decision of re-examination shall be made within 1 month. If the relevant department or personnel is still not satisfied with the decision of re-examination, he may apply to the supervisory organ at the next higher level for review, the supervisory organ at the next higher level shall make a decision of review within 2 months.

If the relevant department or personnel is of different opinion with the supervisory suggestion, he may within 15 days from the day of receiving the supervisory suggestion apply to the supervisory organ which made the said suggestion, and the supervisory organ shall reply within 15 days. If the relevant department or personnel is still of different opinion with the reply, the supervisory organ shall invite the people's government at the same level or the supervisory organ at the next higher level to handle the case.

41. Where the personnel of or the personnel appointed by national administrative organs refuses to accept the administrative disciplinary sanctions imposed upon him by the administrative organ in charge, he may appeal to the supervisory organ at the same level. In case the applicant is still not satisfied with the decision of re-examination by the supervisory organ at the same level, he may apply for review to the supervisory organ at the next higher level.

42. Other appeals, which are provided by laws and administrative regulations to be handled by the supervisory organs, shall be handled in accordance with the stipulation of section 41 of this Regulation.

43. In case an appeal is made to the supervisory organ against the supervisory decision or decision of administrative disciplinary sanction by the administrative organ, the execution of the decision should not be suspended in the course of re-examination or review.

44. The decision of review by the supervisory organ at the next higher level or by the Ministry of Supervision shall be final.

45. Supervisory organs shall establish the case transfer system. The handling of working unit and individuals outside the scope of jurisdiction as stipulated in section 3 of this Regulation shall be transferred to the working unit which has jurisdiction over the case. The working unit which the case is transferred to shall notify the supervisory organ of the result.

If a crime has been constituted in the case, it shall be transferred and be handled by the judicial organ.

CHAPTER SIX: PUNISHMENTS

46. Where any administrative organs or personnel under supervision violate this Regulation and commit one of the following acts, the department in charge or supervisory bureau shall issue a warning to the relevant administrative organs. Corresponding administrative disciplinary sanction shall be imposed upon the person in charge and the person directly responsible:

(a) concealing the facts, producing false evidence, or hiding, destroying evidence;
(b) protecting acts in violation of the laws and regulations by using authority;
(c) refusing to provide the relevant documents, information and evidence materials;
(d) refusing to answer and give explanation to the questions by the supervisory organ within the time limit and at the place as stipulated;
(e) refusing to execute the supervisory decision, or refusing to adopt supervisory suggestion without appropriate reasons;
(f) obstructing or resisting the supervisory personnel from exercise of authorities and functions in accordance with the laws;
(g) taking revenge on the person reporting the case and the supervisory personnel.

In case the above acts have constituted any crime, the case shall be transferred to and handled by the judicial organ.

47. In case the supervisory personnel has committed one of the following acts, the supervisory organ shall, in the light of the seriousness, impose corresponding administrative disciplinary sanction upon him:

- (a) neglecting his duties, and causing serious damage;
- (b) gaining interests by using delegated authorities;
- (c) sheltering others or making other suffered by using delegated authorities;
- (d) abusing powers to infringe the democratic rights, personal rights and proprietary rights of the others;
- (e) leaking of national secrets.

In case the above acts have constituted any crime, the case shall be transferred to and be handled by the judicial organ.

CHAPTER SEVEN: SUPPLEMENTARY PROVISIONS

48. "Various departments of the State Council and their personnel" mentioned in section 14 of this Regulation refers to various Ministries and Commissions of the State Council, various institutes directly under the State Council, various working organizations and national economic organizations which exercise administrative functions and their personnel.

49. The state-owned enterprises, institutions may make reference to this Regulation, to carry out supervision over personnel appointed by other organs than state administrative organs.

Supervisory organs shall provide instructions and support to the supervisory work of the state-owned enterprises and institutions.

50. The Ministry of Supervision of the State Council shall be responsible for the interpretation and the formulation of implementation methods of this Regulation.

51. This Regulation shall be implemented from the date of its promulgation.

STATE COMPENSATION LAW OF THE PEOPLE'S REPUBLIC OF CHINA

(Adopted at the 7th Meeting of the Standing Committee of the 8th National People's Congress on 12 May 1994)

CHAPTER I: GENERAL PROVISIONS

1. This law has been formulated in accordance with the Constitution to guarantee the right of citizens, legal persons and other organizations to obtain state compensation in accordance with the laws, and to encourage state organizations to exercise their powers and functions in accordance with the laws.

2. Where state organizations or state functionaries cause harm by infringing upon the legitimate rights and interests of citizens, legal persons and other organizations through their illegal exercise of powers and functions, the victims are entitled to state compensation in accordance with this Law.

Organs responsible for paying compensation as perscribed by this Law shall bear the liability for making state compensation.

CHAPTER II: ADMINISTRATIVE COMPENSATION

Section I: Scope of compensation

3. Where administrative organs or their personnel infringe upon personal rights while exercising their administrative powers and functions in any of the following circumstances, the victims are entitled to compensation:

(1) illegally detaining citizens or adopting compulsory administrative measures that restrict their personal freedom;
(2) illegally taking citizens into custody or depriving them of their personal freedom through other means;
(3) inflicting physical injuries on or causing the deaths of citizens through such violent acts as physical assault or instigating other people to cause physical injuries or deaths through similar acts;
(4) inflicting physical injuries on or causing the deaths of citizens through the illegal use of weapons and police gear; and
(5) other illegal acts that inflict physical injuries on or cause the deaths of citizens.

4. Where administrative organs or their personnel infringe upon property rights while exercising their powers and functions in any of the following circumstances, the victims are entitled to compensation:

(1) illegally imposing administrative penalties such as fines, revocation of permits and licenses, cessation of production and business, and confiscation property;

(2) illegally instituting compulsory administrative measures such as confiscating, seizing and freezing property;
(3) collecting property charges or financial contributions in violation of state provisions; and
(4) other illegal acts that cause property damage.

5. The state shall not be responsible for paying compensation in any of the following circumstances:

(1) where personnel of administrative organs commit individual acts that have no relation to their exercise of powers and functions;
(2) where citizens, legal persons, and other organizations cause harm through their own acts; and
(3) other circumstances prescribed by law.

Section II: Claimants for compensation and organs responsible for paying compensation

6. Aggrieved citizens, legal persons and other organizations have the right to demand compensation.
If an aggrieved citizen is dead, his heir and other relatives whom he has fostered a relationship with have the right to demand compensation.
If an aggrieved legal person or organization no longer exists, the legal person or organization that inherits its rights has the right to demand compensation.
7. Where administrative organs or their personnel cause damage through their infringement of the legitimate rights and interests of citizens, legal persons and other organizations while exercising their powers and functions, the administrative organs in question shall be responsible for paying compensation.
Where two or more administrative organs cause damage through their infringement of the legitimate rights and interests of citizens, legal persons and other organizations while jointly exercising their powers and functions, they shall be jointly responsible for paying compensation.
Where organizations empowered by laws and regulations cause harm through their infringement of the legitimate rights and interests of citizens, legal persons and other organizations while exercising the administrative powers granted them, they shall be responsible for paying compensation.
Where organizations or individuals entrusted by administrative organs cause harm through their infringement of the legitimate rights and interests of citizens, legal persons and other organizations while exercising the administrative powers entrusted to them, the administrative organs that entrust the organizations or individuals shall be responsible for paying compensation.
Where the organs responsible for paying compensation have been abolished, the administrative organs that continue their powers and functions shall be responsible for paying compensation; in the absence of such successor organs, the administrative organs that abolished the organs in question shall be responsible for paying compensation.
8. Where a claim is reconsidered by a reconsideration organ, the administrative organ that committed the tort in the first place shall be responsible for paying compensation; however, if the reconsideration organ decides to increase damages, it shall be responsible for paying compensation for the additional portion.

Section III: Compensation procedures

9. Organs responsible for paying compensation shall do so under any of the circumstances listed in sections 3 and 4 of this Law whose occurrence has been legally confirmed.

In demanding compensation, claimants shall first file their claims with the organs responsible for paying compensation; they may also file their claims when they apply for administrative reconsideration or file administrative lawsuits.

10. Claimants may demand compensation from any of the organs jointly responsible for paying compensation, and the organ in question shall first pay the compensation.

11. Claimants may file several claims simultaneously in light of the different types of harm they have endured.

12. To demand compensation, an application shall be filed. The application so filed shall contain the following information:

(1) the name, gender, age, work unit and residence of the aggrieved party, or the name and residence of the aggrieved legal entity or organization, as well as the name and position of its legal representative or principal responsible person;
(2) specific claims, facts and reasons; and
(3) the date, month and year on which the application is filed.

Where a claimant really has trouble filling in an application, he or she may entrust another person to do so; alternatively, he or she may apply orally and the organ responsible for paying compensation shall record the information.

13. An organ responsible for paying compensation shall do so within two months of receiving an application in accordance with the provisions in Chapter IV of this Law; where compensation is not paid beyond the deadline or the claimant objects to the amount of compensation, the claimant may file suit with a people's court within three months after the deadline.

14. After compensating for losses, an organ responsible for paying compensation shall demand its personnel who intentionally committed errors or who committed grave errors, or the entrusted organ or individual, to pay for part or all of the compensation.

Relevant organs shall impose disciplinary sanctions on, in accordance with the Law, responsible people who intentionally committed errors or who committed grave errors; where the errors constitute crimes, the criminal responsibility shall be pursued in accordance with the Law.

CHAPTER III: CRIMINAL COMPENSATION

Section I: Scope of compensation

15. Where organs that perform investigative, procuratorial, adjudicative and prison management functions and powers infringe upon personal rights while exercising their powers and functions in any of the following circumstances, the victims are entitled to compensation:

(1) wrongfully detaining people in the absence of corpora delicti (the body of facts that constitute an offence) or people who are not proven by facts to be suspects of major crimes;
(2) wrongfully arresting people in the absence of corpora delicti;
(3) enforcing the original penalty before the ruling is changed to not

guilty during retrials held in accordance with judicial supervisory procedures;

(4) using torture to coerce statements, inflicting physical injuries on or causing the deaths of citizens through such violent acts as physical assault, or instigating other people to cause physical injuries or deaths through similar acts; and

(5) inflicting physical injuries on or causing the deaths of citizens through the illegal use of weapons or police gear.

16. Where bodies that perform investigative, procuratorial, adjudicative and prison management functions and powers, or their personnel, infringe upon property rights while performing their functions and powers in any of the following circumstances, the victims are entitled to compensation:

(1) illegally instituting such measures as confiscating, seizing, freezing and retrieving property; and

(2) collecting fines or confiscating property as originally sentenced before the verdict is changed to not guilty during retrials held in accordance with judicial supervisory procedures.

17. The state shall not be responsible for paying compensation in any of the following circumstances:

(1) taking into custody or sentencing to criminal punishment citizens who intentionally fabricated confessions or falsified other evidence of guilt;

(2) taking into custody people who are not criminally responsible pursuant to the provisions in sections 14 and 15 of the Criminal Law;

(3) taking into custody people whose criminal responsibility is not to be investigated pursuant to the provisions in section 11 of the Criminal Procedure Law;

(4) where organs that perform investigative, procuratorial, adjudicative and prison management functions and powers, or their personnel, carry out individual acts that have no relation to the exercise of their functions and powers;

(5) where harm arises from intentional acts by citizens to injure or maim themselves; and

(6) other circumstances prescribed by law.

Section II: Claimants for compensation and bodies responsible for paying compensation

18. Claimants for compensation shall be defined according to the provisions in section 6 of this Law.

19. Where organs that perform investigative, procuratorial, adjudicative and prison management functions and powers, or their personnel, cause harm through the infringement of the legitimate rights and interests of citizens, legal persons and other organizations while exercising their functions and powers, the organs in question shall be responsible for paying compensation.

Where people are wrongfully detained in the absence of corpora delicti or people who are not proven by facts to be suspects of major crimes are wrongfully detained, the organs that decided on the detention shall be responsible for paying compensation.

Where people are wrongfully arrested in the absence of corpora delicti, the organs that decided on the arrests shall be responsible for paying compensation.

Where a verdict is changed to not guilty after a retrial, the people's court that rendered the original, binding verdict shall be responsible for paying compensation. Where a court of second instance changes a verdict to not guilty, the people's court that rendered the original verdict, as well as the organ that decided on the arrest, shall be jointly responsible for paying compensation.

Section III: Compensation procedures

20. Organs responsible for paying compensation shall do so in any of the circumstances outlined in sections 15 and 16 of this Law whose occurrence has been legally confirmed.

Where an organ requested by a claimant to confirm the occurrence of any of the circumstances spelled out in sections 15 and 16 of this Law refuses to do so, the claimant has the right to file a petition.

In demanding compensation, claimants shall first file their claims with the organs responsible for paying compensation.

Sections 10 through 12 of this Law shall apply to compensation procedures in this respect.

21. An organ responsible for paying compensation shall do so in accordance with the provisions in Chapter IV of this Law within two months of receiving an application for compensation; where compensation is not paid beyond the deadline or the claimant objects to the amount of compensation, the claimant may apply for reconsideration to the next higher body within 30 days after the deadline.

Where the organ responsible for paying compensation is a people's court, the claimant may apply to the compensation committee of the next higher people's court for a decision on compensation in accordance with the provisions in the preceding paragraph.

22. An organ reconsidering a claim shall make a decision within two months of receiving an application.

In the event the claimant does not agree with the reconsideration decision, he or she may apply for a decision on compensation within 30 days of receiving the decision to the compensation committee of the people's court at the corresponding level in the place where the organ that reconsidered the claim is located. If the organ reconsidering the claim does not make a decision beyond the deadline, the claimant may apply for a decision on compensation within 30 days after the deadline to the compensation committee of the people's court at the corresponding level in the place where the organ reconsidering the claim is located.

23. The compensation committee is to be set up by the people's court at and above the intermediate level, and is to be formed by three to seven judicial officers of the people's court.

The compensation committee makes decision on compensation and implements the principle that the minority is subordinate to the majority.

The decision on compensation made by the compensation committee has a legal effect and must be enforced.

24. After having compensated victims for their losses, organ responsible for paying compensation should demand a refund from the working personnel found guilty of either one of the following two categories of irregularities for part or all of the expenses incurred in making payment for compensation:
   (1) provisions (4) and (5) under section 15; and
   (2) corruption, taking bribes, fraudulent practices out of personal considerations and perverting the law when acting as a judge during the handling of cases.

Relevant organs shall impose disciplinary sanctions on, in accordance with the law, those personnel held accountable for having committed such irregularities as described in the aforesaid provisions (1) and (2); where the irregularities constitute crime, the criminal responsibility shall be pursued in accordance with the law.

CHAPTER IV: COMPENSATION METHODS AND CALCULATION STANDARDS

25. Compensation by the state shall adopt the payment of indemnities as its main method of compensation. If property can be returned to the victims or restored to its original condition, it shall be so handled.

26. Daily indemnities to be paid for violating the personal freedom of citizens shall be calculated on the basis of the previous year's average daily wage set by the state for workers.

27. Indemnities for violating citizens' right to life and health shall be calculated on the basis of the following provisions:

   (1) Medical expenses plus indemnities for the loss of income due to the inability to work shall be paid to victims sustaining physical injuries. Daily indemnities for the loss of income shall be calculated on the basis of the previous year's average daily wage set by the state for workers; the maximum amount of such indemnities is five times the previous year's average annual wage set by the state for workers.
   (2) Medical expenses plus indemnities for causing disability shall be paid to victims who have lost part or all of their ability to work. The amount of indemnities for disability caused shall be determined by the extent of victims' loss of their ability to work. The maximum amount of indemnities for causing partial disability is 10 times the previous year's average annual wage set by the state for workers. The maximum amount of indemnities for causing the complete loss of victims' ability to work is 20 times the previous year's average annual wage set by the state for workers. In addition, living expenses should be paid to those who are unable to work and are supported by the victims who have sustained the complete loss of their ability to work.
   (3) Indemnities for causing deaths plus funeral expenses should be paid to families of victims who have died. Their total amount is 20 times the previous year's average annual wage set by the state for workers. In addition, living expenses should be paid to those who are unable to work and were supported by the deceased when they were still alive.

The determination of standard for the payment of living expenses stipulated in the aforesaid provisions (2) and (3) shall take reference to local civil affairs departments' regulation on relief for those who cannot support themselves. In case those who depend on the support of others are youngsters who are juvenile, living expenses shall be paid to them until they are 18 years old. As for those who are unable to work, living expenses shall be paid to them until they die.

28. Infringement of the property rights of citizens, legal persons, and other organizations that causes them to sustain losses shall be handled according to the following provisions:

   (1) infringers shall be fined, penalized, ordered to hand over their illegal gains to the authorities and have their property confiscated, or they shall be ordered to return property to victims if they collect

property and belongings and apportion expenses in violation of state provisions;
(2) the illegal sealing up and confiscation, seizure, and freezing of property shall be lifted; in case such violations cause damage to or the loss of property, victims shall be compensated according to provisions (3) and
(3) if damage is done to property that should be returned to victims, such property should be restored to its original conditions wherever possible; in case restoration is impossible, appropriate indemnities should be paid to victims in proportion to the extent of damage;
(4) if victims sustain the loss of their property which should be returned to them, appropriate indemnities should be paid to them;
(5) if property is auctioned, the proceeds from the auction shall be handed over to victims;
(6) if victims' permits and licenses are illegally revoked and they are illegally mandated to stop production and business operations, they are entitled to compensation for necessary daily expenses during the cessation of production and business operations; and
(7) if other damage is done to property, compensation shall be given to victims on the basis of their direct losses.

29. Compensation expenses shall be included in the budget for governments at all levels. Specific measures shall be provided by the State Council.

CHAPTER V: OTHER PROVISIONS

30. After having ascertained, in accordance with the Law, that any of the violations as described in provisions (1) and (2) of section 3 and provisions (1), (2), and (3) of section 15 of this Law did occur and damaged victims' rights to their reputation and honour, the organs responsible for paying compensation should eliminate the impact on victims, restore their reputation, and apologize to them insofar as they are affected by the violation of their rights.

31. The provisions on the procedures for criminal compensation contained in this Law apply to the procedures for victims requesting compensation for their losses caused by the people's court illegally adopting compulsory measures and security measures that disrupt legal proceedings or by the people's court making a mistake in enforcing a court decision, ruling and other legal documents that have taken effect in the process of a civil or administrative lawsuit.

32. The valid time limit for victims' request for state compensation is two years, starting from the date that the exercise of functions and powers by state organs and their working personnel is determined as illegal in accordance with the law. However, the period of detention shall not be counted.

33. This Law applies to requests made by foreign nationals, enterprises and organizations within the territory of the PRC for state compensation by the PRC. If the countries to which foreign nationals, enterprises and organizations belong restrict or do not protect the rights of PRC citizens, legal persons and other organizations to request state compensation from them, the PRC will act on reciprocal basis.

CHAPTER VI: SUPPLEMENTARY ARTICLES

34. Organs responsible for paying compensation, reconsideration organs, and the people's courts are prohibited from collecting any fees from those who request state compensation. Indemnities obtained by those who request compensation are exempt from taxes.

35. This Law will go into effect on 1st January 1995.

ARTICLES FROM RELEVANT LAWS

1. Criminal Law

14. If those who are 16 years old commit crimes, they should take responsibility for their crimes. If those who are 14 years old but not yet 16 cause serious injury to others or commit homicide, robbery, arson, habitual theft or other crimes that seriously disrupt public order, they should take responsibility for their crimes. Either lenient punishment should be handed down on criminals who are 14 years old but not yet 18, or their punishment should be reduced. If those who are not yet 16 years old are exempt from punishment for their crimes, their parents or guardians shall be instructed to subject them to discipline. In case of necessity, they may also be accepted by governments for re-education.

15. If mental patients cause harm when they are unable to recognize or cannot control their own behaviour, they shall not be held responsible for their crimes; however, their families or guardians should be ordered to keep them under strict surveillance and to arrange for their medical treatment. If mental patients suffering from intermittent attacks of their disease commit crimes when they are in a normal mental state, they should take responsibility for their crimes. If those who are drunk commit crimes, they should take responsibility for their crimes.

2. Criminal procedural law

11. Those who fall under any of the following categories shall be exempt from the investigation of their criminal responsibility. If their criminal responsibility has already been investigated, either the case should be withdrawn or they should be exempt from prosecution or pronounced not guilty:

(1) the seriousness of their offences is obviously minor, does not cause much harm, and is not considered a crime;
(2) the time when their offences were committed has already exceeded the valid period of time for prosecution;
(3) those who are exempt from punishment by a decree of a special pardon;
(4) either no lawsuit has been brought against a criminal who a court will not handle until a lawsuit is brought against him or her, or the lawsuit has been withdrawn;
(5) the accused is dead; and
(6) those who are exempt from the investigation of their criminal responsibility for offences according to the provisions of other laws and decrees.

INDEX

Acts of state, 2.27, 2.28, 8.18
  definition, 8.19
  exclusion from judicial review, 8.20
  scope, 8.19
Adjudication, 7.06, 9.02, 9.05, 12.11, 12.12
  acts, 2.16, 2.22
  administrative, 2.22
Administrative acts
  abstract
    description, 2.17, 8.21
    review of, 12.09
  characteristics, 2.12
  classification, 2.13, 2.16
    Concrete and Abstract, 2.14
    Internal and External, 2.15
  concrete
    as abuse of power, 11.12
    final, 8.24
    joint, 6.09
    suspension of, 6.03
    void, 6.11
  definition, 2.11
  illegal or inappropriate, 3.06, 6.04
  internal, 8.23
  judicial review of, 9.03
    not subject to judicial review, 8.18, 12.09
    reviewable under other legislation, 8.16
  legal control of, 8.22
  see also Acts of State, Adjudication, Compensation, Licensing Acts
Administrative compensation, 13.11
Administrative law
  concept, 1.01
  contents, 1.07
  definitions, 1.01, 1.02
  functions and status, 1.08
  history, 1.04, 1.05, 2.22
  implementation and enforcement, 2.20
  meaning and contents, 1.01
  principles, 2.07
    emergency (force majeure), 2.09
  recording system, 2.19
  structure, 1.09
  see also Procedural law

Administrative Litigation Law (ALL), 3.02, 13.03
  development, 7.05
  drafting, 1986, 7.05
  objectives, 7.06, 7.09, 8.17, 11.06
  promulgation, 1989, 1.06
  provisions for
    judicial review, 13.11
    people's courts, 9.01, 10.37
    procedural legislation, 8.02
    reconsideration, 3.02, 4.16, 6.06
    state compensation, 13.06
  scope, 13.03
  relationship with State Compensation Law, 13.11
Administrative organs
  compensation for illegal acts by *see* Compensation
  control of, 2.19
  derelict or abolished, 5.10, 10.3
  power of, 4.11
  representatives, 2.02
  rights and obligations, 2.02
  superior, 2.27
  ultra vires, 10.03
Administrative Penalty Law, 1996, 1.06, 8.04, 8.07, 10.03, 10.37
Administrative relations and administrative legal relationships, 2.01
Anti-rightist movement 1957, 1.04
Appeal, right of, 10.04
Arbitration, 2.22, 2.23
Assembly, right of, 2.03, 3.02, 3.11, 8.16
Association, right of, 8.16
Authorized organizations, authority of, 5.08
Autonomous regions, authority of, 5.05, 6.05, 9.03
Autonomous regions, ethnic regulations of, 12.06

Banks, authority of professional, 3.08
Beliefs, right to, 2.03, 8.16
Burden of proof, 10.06, 11.11

INDEX

Business
  autonomy of management, 4.08, 8.10
  suspension of, 4.04, 8.07

Civil affairs, 3.08, 4.06
Civil compensation, 13.04, 13.06, 13.09, 13.10
Civil disputes, 2.22, 2.23
Civil law, 7.04
Civil rights, 4.16, 13.02
Civil servants, 1.06, 2.07, 8.23
  liability for compensation *see* Liability
Communist party
  11th Meeting, 1978, 3rd plenary, 1.04, 7.02
  14th Plenary, 7.09
  Central committee 12th, 1984, 1.05
  Central committee 13th, 1987, 1.05
  legal system under the, 7.02
  policy making role, 11.01
Compensation, state, 3.05, 13.01
  administrative, 13.13
  abstract administrative acts, 13.03
  acts by non-administrative organs, 13.03
  acts by public utilities, 13.12
  claim, 13.34
    filing of, 13.09, 13.20, 13.32
    where filed, 13.09
  claimant
    relationship between the state organ and the, 13.09
  compared to civil, 13.04, 13.06, 13.10
  entitlement, 13.36
  grounds, 3.08, 13.04, 13.06, 13.13, 13.22
    breach of duty, 13.04
    compulsory measures, illegal imposition of, 13.13, 13.15, 13.17
    deprivation or personal freedom, 13.13
    forfeiture of licence, 13.15
    illegal acts by the judiciary, 13.27
    illegal exercise of authority, 13.08
    infringement of personal rights, 13.13
    injury or death, 13.13
    intentionally committed errors, 13.04
    mismanagement of public utilities, 13.12
    negligence, 13.36
    unlawful exercise of administrative power, 13.06
  infringers, 13.04, 13.06
  nature of, 13.04
  payment of
    amount, 13.09
    liability for, 13.04
    time limit for, 13.09

  procedure, 8.02, 13.03
  proof of damages or losses necessary, 13.04
  scope, 13.04, 13.08
  tortious actions, 13.04
  types of, 13.11, 13, 17, 13.28, 13.29, 13.30, 13.31
  unforeseeable events, 13.08
  see also Damages, Indemnity, Liability, State compensation system
Complaints, 5.14, 8.02, 10.02
  see also Compensation
Compulsory enforcement, administrative, 2.24, 4.07
Compulsory measures, 4.02
  compensation for illegal imposition of, 13.13, 13.15, 13.17
  concerning licences, 4.09
  enforcement, 4.07
  failure to pay subsidies or pensions, 4.10
  failure to perform statutory duty, 4.10
  implementary, 8.09
  infringement upon managerial decision-making power, 4.08
  preventive, 8.09
  prohibitive, 8.09
  protective, 8.09
  restricting the moving of property, 4.05, 4.07
  restriction of personal freedoms, 4.05, 4.06, 5.06
  unlawful request for performance of obligation, 4.11, 4.12
Constitution
  Constitution 1954, 1.04, 13.02
  Constitution 1975, 13.02
  Constitution 1978, 13.02
  Constitution 1982 (4th), 1.05, 2.27, 3.02, 13.02
  Constitutional Reason, 7.08
  contents, 3.05
  development, 11.01
  highest law, 12.03
  judicial control under the, 8.19
  provisions, 2.14, 6.07, 12.06, 12.12
  repeal of legislation under the, 13.11
  unconstitutionality, 12.03
Contracts, 2.06, .22
Correspondence and Reception Department,
  and Reconsideration, 5.14
County authorities, powers of, 3.10, 4.03, 5.02
Courts
  compensation for courts' acts, 13.22, 13.29, 13.30, 13.31
  County, 9.01, 9.02
  District, 9.01
  Economic Adjudication panel, 7.04
  functions, 7.06
  High court, 10.04

374

INDEX

higher, 9.01, 9.02, 9.04
Intermediate, 9.01, 9.02, 9.03, 10.46
jurisdiction of, 2.20, 7.06, 10.37, 12.10, 12.12
powers, 7.12
Procuratorate, 3.02, 8.02, 10.46, 11.18
Supreme, 7.04, 9.01, 9.05
powers, 11.18, 12.11
Criminal compensation, 13.20, 13.21, 13.22
procedure, 13.36
scope, 13.23, 13.24, 13.25, 13.26, 13.27
Cultural administration, 6.16
Customs office, 6.16, 9.03

Damages
mismanagement of public utilities, by, 13.12
state compensation, amount of, 13.09, 13.12
tortious acts, 13.08
see also Compensation, Military compensation
Defence, national, 2.28, 8.19
compensation for acts of, 13.12
see also Military acts
Demonstrations see Assembly, right of
Detention
administrative, 4.04, 8.04, 8.05, 11.04
criminal, 4.06
illegal, 13.03, 13.13
shelter for examination, 4.05, 11.18
Diplomatic relations see Foreign Affairs
Discretion, 8.02
determining the essential legal elements of, 11.05
procedural, 11.06
statutory, 11.27
Discretionary power, 3.21, 6.13, 10.02
abuse
different from obvious unfairness, 11.26, 11.27
classification, 11.02, 11.03, 11.04
definition, 11.09
development of, 11.01, 11.02
legal control, 11.01, 11.06, 11.10, 11.41
limits, 11.04
substantive, 11.04
Disputes
administrative, 3.04, 3.05
civil, 2.22, 2.23
scope, 13.12
labour, 2.22, 4.10
resolution, 3.01, 3.02, 3.17, 8.15
consultation, 5.12, 9.10
see also Adjudication, Remedies
Drinkers, compulsory restraint of, 4.06

Economic Law, 7.04
Education
as preventive compulsory measure, 4.06, 8.09
right to, 8.16
Elections
administration of, 3.02, 7.03
rights to, 4.16
Electricity administration, 6.16
Employment, right to, 8.16
Entrusted organizations, authority of, 5.08
Entry and Exit (China) administration, 3.02
Environmental administration, 6.16, 7.04, 11.03
Equality, right to, 2.03
Evidence
essential
collection of, 4.07
failure to provide, cases, 10.07, 10.08, 10.09, 10.10, 10.11, 10.12, 10.13, 10.15, 10.16
insufficiency of, 10.04, 10.05, 10.06
combined with wrongful applic of the law, 10.19
lack of, 10.14, 10.16, 10.17, 10.34, 10.45, 11.24
interpretation of, 10.18
late submission, 10.06
ordinary, 10.05
see also Burden of proof, 10.06
Expatriation, compulsory, 4.05

Fines, 4.04, 8.04, 8.05, 8.06
Food and hygiene administration, 7.04, 11.02
Foreign affairs, 2.23, 8.19
Forestry administration, 5.05, 7.04
Freedom
compensation for deprivation of personal, 13.13
protection of personal, 4.10
restriction of personal, 2.25, 4.05, 8.05
rights to enjoy personal, 2.03, 3.05, 8.12
see also Personal and Proprietory rights

General Principles of Civil Law, (1986)
provisions, 13.02, 13.09
Government organs see State Government organs
Governmental Structure, 5.02

Indemnity, administrative, 13.08, 13.09, 13.12
Industry and commerce organs
authority, 2.02, 2.16, 5.07, 7.04, 11.02
Bureau for, 2.21, 12.10
Intellectual property administration, 2.22, 7.04

Jiang Mingan, Professor, 8.19, 8.24
Judges

375

INDEX

authority and powers, 3.04, 10.04, 12.12
illegal acts by judges, 13.27
independence of, 7.08
relationship between the judiciary and the executive, 8.02, 8.24
see also Judicial functions, Judicial review, Jurisdiction
Judicial compensation, 13.11, 13.27, 13.28
Judicial functions, 9.05, 10.02, 10.03, 11.07
  conciliation, 13.09
  control, 2.19
  enforcement, 2.20
  quasi-judicial acts, 3.04
  supervision, 8.17
Judicial organs, power of, 13.11
Judicial review
  conditions for, 7.15
  courts for the hearing of, 9.02
  different from administrative reconsideration, 6.06
  finality provision, 8.25
  function, 2.11, 6.01
  grounds for, 3.23, 10.01
    arbitrariness, 11.25
    delay in performance, 11.42, 11.43, 11.44
    double penalties, 11.38, 11.39
    excess of authority, 10.47, 10.48, 10.49, 10.50, 10.52, 10.53
    failure to provide information, 10.07, 11.40
    failure to perform statutory duty, 3.23, 8.12, 10.04, 11.10, 11.41
    failure in performance, 11.45, 11.46
    failure to provide evidence, 10.07
    illegality *see also* inaccuracy, 10.04
    inappropriate consideration, 11.30, 11.31, 11.32
    inaccuracy in the application of legislation, 10.09, 10.22, 11.15
      law not yet come into effect, 10.30, 10.31
      wrong law, 10.20, 10.21, 10.22, 10.25
      wrong law, cases, 10.09, 10.27, 10.28, 10.29, 10.32, 10.33, 10.35
      wrong person, to the, 10.23, 11.18
      wrong provision of correct legislation, 10.24, 10.25
    inconsistency, 11.35, 11.36, 11.37
    insufficiency of essential evidence, 10.05
    irrelevant consideration, 11.16, 11.19
    lack of investigation, 10.41, 10.42
    obvious unfairness, 11.26, 11.27, 13.06
      improportionality, 11.28, 11.29, 11.33, 11.34
  principles
    legality, 11.07
    reasonableness, 11.08
    time limit not respected, 11.41, 11.47
  ultra vires, 10.25, 10.43, 10.46, 10.51
  unlawful intention, 11.17
  historical development, 7.02, 7.03, 7.04, 7.05
  lateness of, reasons for, 7.07, 7.08, 7.09, 7.10, 7.11,
  legislation applicable for, 6.05, 12.01, 12.08
  objectives, 10.02
  relationship with administrative reconsideration, 6.15
  scope, 3.04, 8.03, 8.04, 8.09, 8.17, 11.41, 12.03, 13.11, 13.34
    exclusions, 8.18, 8.20, 8.23
  sources of, 7.12, 7.13, 7.14
  structures, 7.01
  suspended, 12.11
  time limit for a case, 8.16, 10.16
  see also Courts, Evidence, Jurisdiction, Litigation, Power, abuse of, Reasonableness, Supervision
Jurisdiction, 5.15
  categories of, 5.02
  common, 9.08
  description, 5.01
  designation of, 5.12
  geographical *see* horizontal
  horizontal (geographical), 9.01, 9.06, 9.07, 9.10, 10.46
  over administrative acts, 5.04, 5.06, 5.08, 5.09, 5.10
  over administrative organs, 5.05
  priority of, 5.13
  reconsidered cases, 9.09
  scope, 8.01
  transfer, 5.11
  vertical, 5.02, 9.01, 9.02

Labour
  administration, 3.02, 6.16
  disputes, 2.22
  Managing Commission for Rehabilitation through Labour, 9.08
Land administration, 5.05, 5.09, 6.16, 7.04, 10.03
Legality
  and Judicial Review, 10.03
  principles of, 2.08, 10.02, 10.04, 11.07, 11.11
  relationship between Reasonableness and, 11.09
Legal relationships, 2.01, 2.02, 10.03
  administrative and, 2.01
  characteristics, 2.04
  classification, 2.05, 2.06

INDEX

contents, 2.03
rights and obligations in, 2.03
Legislation, 13.11
  administrative, 2.18
    regulations, 12.04
  scope, 2.06, 2.19
  conflict between Rules and
    Regulations and legislation, 12.11
  hierarchy of laws, 13.10
  inaccuracy in the application of, 10.20,
    10.21, 10.22
  local regulations, 12.05
  repealed, 13.11
  see also Constitution, National laws
Legislative acts, compensation for,
  13.11
Legislative Affairs Bureau of the State
  Council, 3.02
Legislative Affairs Commission
  of the National People's Congress,
    3.02, 7.05
Legislative compensation, 13.11
Liability
  civil, 13.02
  grounds for, 13.02, 13.06, 13.31
  payment, for, 13.04
  tortious liability, compared to state,
    13.04
  state organs, 13.03, 13.04, 13.22
    functionaries, 13.02, 13.36
Licences and permits
  compensation case concerning, 13.11
  description, 8.11
  failure or delay to grant, 4.02, 4.09,
    11.41
  illegal detention of, 13.15
  refusal to grant, 4.02, 4.09, 8.11
  rescission of, 4.04, 8.04, 8.07, 8.11
  revocation, 10.33, 13.08
Licensing procedures, 2.21
Litigation
  administrative, 6.01, 3.06, 8.02
    function, 7.01
  scope, 2.19
  civil, 8.02, 13.09
  criminal, 8.02
  see also Judicial review
Local authorities
  agencies, 5.07
  authority to issue regulations, 5.02,
    12.07
  jurisdiction over, 5.05
  powers of, 5.05
Local regulations, 12.05
Luo Haocai, Professor, 8.20, 10.20, 10.43,
  11.12, 11.26, 11.41
  classification of inaccuracy in the
    application of legislation, 10.22
  view on "take as reference", 12.09

March, freedom to, 8.16

Mediation, administrative, 2.23
Medical administration, 7.04
Medical compulsory treatment, 4.05
Military compensation, 13.11, 13.11
  categories, 13.12
Mineral resources, administration of,
  5.05, 8.15
Ministries, functions of, 6.05, 12.07
Ministry of Supervision, 2.27, 13.38
Municipal authorities, authority of, 3.10,
  5.05, 9.03

National economic development plan,
  1953-1957, 1.04
National laws, 12.03
  conflict with legislation, 12.11
  see also Constitution
National Legislature, 7.08
National People's Congress, 2.25, 8.19
  Legislative Affairs Commission, 7.05
  powers, 7.08, 7.13, 8.24
  Standing committee, 2.19, 8.22, 12.03
National Statistics, Bureau of, 5.09
Normative documents, 12.07, 12.08,
  12.09, 12.10
  conflict with laws and regulations,
    6.07

Opinions on the Administrative
  Litigation Law
  provisions, 8.03, 9.09

Patents applications administration, 3.02,
  9.03
Penalties
  administrative, 4.02, 4.04, 8.04
    illegal use of, 13.15, 13.15
  definition, 2.25
  principles, 2.26
  procedural requirements, 10.37
  Regulation on Administrative Penalty
    for
    Public Security, 1986
    provisions, 10.03, 10.37
  subject to judicial review, 8.04
  see also Detention
Pensions and subsidies, failure to pay,
  4.02, 4.10, 8.13
Performance of duty
  capacity of performance, restriction of,
    8.07
  duty, failure or delay to perform,
    10.04
  unlawful request for, 4.02, 8.09, 8.14
Performance of obligations
  unlawfull request for, 4.11, 6.12
Permits *see* **Licences**
Personal and Proprietary rights interests,
  2.24, 4.02, 8.12
  infringement of, 8.15, 13.13, 13.14
Pi Chunxie, Professor, 2.07, 2.12, 13.12

INDEX

Planning administration, 6.16
Political rights, 4.14
Power
  abuse of, 10.04, 11.11, 13.06
    cases, 11.15, 11.18, 11.19, 13.15
    capriciousness or unreasonableness, 11.20, 11.21, 11.22
    categories, 11.12
    definitions, 11.11
    excess of, 10.43, 10.44, 10.45
    excess *ultra vires*, 11.26
    failure to perform statutory duty, 11.41, 11.44
    improportionality of penalties, 11.28, 11.29
    irrelevant consideration, 11.18
    legal procedure, abuse of legal procedure, 11.41
    misuse of, 13.14
    unfair penalties, 11.26
    unlawful intention, 11.13, 11.13, 14, 15, 16, 17
  administrative, 7.06, 7.07, 10.46, 11.23
    administrative discretion, 8.02
    excess of, 10.44
    unlawful exercise of, 13.06
  executive, 3.01, 3.08, 8.15, 12.02, 12.12
    control of, 7.01
    relationship between judicial and, 8.02
  legislature, by, 1.311
  management decision-making, infringement on, 4.08
Private law
  public law distinguished from, 13.04
Procedural law, 2.10, 6.11, 7.06, 10.03, 10.20
Procedure, legal, 10.03
  abuse of, 11.41
    failure to act within time limit, 10.40, 10.41
    inaction, 10.42
    missing legal procedure, 10.39
    no authority, 10.44
    violation of, 3.23, 10.14, 10.36, 10.38, 10.39, 10.42
    requirements, 10.05
  rule of statutory procedure, 10.03
Processions *see* Assembly
Property, measures restricting the moving of, 4.05, 4.07
Proprietary penalty, 8.06
Provinces, authority of, 3.10, 4.12, 5.05, 6.05, 9.03
Public administration, 1.01, 1.04, 3.01, 7.14
  scope, 8.17
Public gathering, right of, 3.02
Public Law
  distinguished from private law, 13.04
Public security authorities, 2.02, 6.16

Ministry of, 11.18
powers, 2.26, 4.06, 5.07, 8.05, 11.03, 11.05
reconsideration of acts by, 6.16, 7.04
Public utilities
  administration of, 6.16
  damages by mismanagement of, 13.03, 13.12
Publications, right to publish, 2.03, .16

Quasi-judicial acts, 3.04
Quasi-judicial procedure, 2.22

Real Estates administration, 6.16
Reasonableness, 1.07, 6.13, 7.06, 10.02, 11.08
  principle of, 2.10, 7.06, 11.08, 11.11
  relationship between Legality and, 11.09
Reconsideration, 2.11, 2.22, 9.03, 9.09
  acts subject to, 4.02, 4.04, 4.05, 4.14
  acts not subject to, 3.08
  aim, 6.01
  application
    abuse of the right to, 6.03
    cannot be lodged, 6.06
    capacity to lodge an, 6.09
    conditions for, 3.02, 3.08, 3.09
    late, 3.09
    refused, 3.09
    rules for, 5.03
    time for, 3.14
    withdrawal of, 6.04
    written, 3.16
  compulsory measures subject to, 4.06
  Correspondence and Reception Department
    and Administrative Reconsideration, 5.14
  definition, 3.01
  effect of the concrete administrative act under, 6.03
  format, 6.02
  grounds for, 3.23
    illegality, 3.19, 3.20, 3.23
    inappropriateness, 3.19, 3.21, 3.23
  judicial review, reconsideration and, 6.06, 6.15
  jurisdiction, 3.02
  legislation applicable, 6.05
  nature and functions, 3.04, 3.05, 3.06, 3.07
  organs and organization, 3.10, 3.11, 5.02, 6.07
  participants in, 6.09
  principles, 3.12, 3.18
    accuracy, 3.15
    convenient to the People, 3.16
    legality, 3.13
    no Conciliation, 3.17
    timeliness, 3.14

378

procedural requirements, 6.11, 6.13
procedures, 3.02
  order of rectification, 6.11
  scope, 3.02, 4.01, 4.07, 4.13, 4.15, 4.16, 6.16
  time limit for, 5.14
  see also Compulsory measures, Regulation on Administrative Reconsideration, Remedies
Regions, authority of, 3.10
Regulation on Administrative Reconsideration (RAR), 5.07
  1989 draft
  implementation, 6.16
  objectives, 3.05, 3.13
  provisions, 2.22, 3.16
  scope, 3.04
  sources, 3.02, 3.03
Regulations, 12.05, 12.06, 12.0712.08
  administrative, 12.04
  conflict with Rules, 12.11
  intra vires, 12.10
  see also Regulation on Administrative Reconsideration
Religion *see* Beliefs
Remedies, 4.01, 6.10, 8.01, 8.02, 13.31
  confiscation of property, 8.08
  nullification case, 6.13, 6.14
  order of rectification, 6.11
  specific performance, 6.12
  see also Compensation, Penalties, Reconsideration
Repatriation, compulsory, 4.06
Rest, right to, 8.16
Rights and interests, 8.16
  statutory, 10.04
  to judicial review, 7.13
  see also Personal and Proprietary

Segregation, 4.06
Separation as sanction, 8.09
Special Economic Zones
  authority to issue regulations, 11.07
Speeches, right to make, 8.16
Standing Committee of the National People's Congress
  see National People's Congress,
State Compensation Law (SCL) (1995)
  development, 13.03
  interrelationship with the ALL, 13, 12, 13.34
  no retrospective effect, 13.36
  provisions, 13.01, 13.09, 13.32
  scope, 13.11, 13.12, 13.13, 13.36
State compensation system, 13.12
  legislative development, 13.01, 13.02
  see also Compensation, Liability, State Compensation Law
State Council, 3.10, 7.08
  authority and powers, 5.04, 6.07, 8.22, 9.03, 12.04
  functions, 5.09, 6.05
State Government organs, 3.05, 8.02, 13.22
  see also Compensation, Liability
Statutory duty
  failure or delay to perform, 3.23, 4.02, 8.12, 10.04, 11.41, 11.44
Statutory interpretation, 8.24, 10.20
Subsidies, failure or delay in providing, 4.10, 11.41
Sun Yat-sen, Dr., 7.02
Supervision, administrative, 2.27, 3.13, 4.01
  Ministry of Supervision, 2.27, 13.38
  of concrete acts, 3.04, 5.04, 8.17
Suspension of production, 8.07

Taxation administration, 2.02, 3.08, 5.07, 7.04, 11.02
Telecommunications administration, 3.02
Tort, tortious activities, 3.05
  civil tort, 13.09
  compensation for, 13.04
  damages for, 13.08
Township authorities, 3.10, 3.19, 4.03, 5.08
Trade administration, 3.02
Transportation administration, 3.02, 5.03, 6.16
Treatment as sanction, 8.09
Tribunals, 2.23, 5.02

Ultra vires, 10.04
  abuse of power, 11.23
  acts, 11.21, 13.10
  activities, 10.43, 12.12
  concept of, 10.03, 10.43
  grounds for judicial review, 10.15
  horizontal, 10.43, 10.46
  illegal, 3.19
  procedural, 11.12
  vertical, 10.43, 10.52
Undue interference, 7.06

Wanderers, 4.06
Wang Hanbing, Mr., 9.02, 11.08, 11.27
Warning, 8.08, 11.04

Xu, Professor, 2.01, 2.07, 2.12

Ying Songnian, Professor, 13.11